CADOGAN   Dana Facaros & Michael Pauls

Madrid

W9-DET-835

Introduction	ix
Travel	1
Practical A–Z	9
History	21
Architecture	35
Tales of Madrid	39
The Neighbourhoods	53
Museums	173
Food and Drink	177
Where to Stay	191
Entertainment and Nightlife	199
Shopping	209
Living and Working in Madrid	215
Day Trips	219
Language	267
Chronology, Further Reading	273
Index	277

Cadogan Guides
West End House, 11 Hills Place,
London W1R 1AH, UK
becky.kendall@morrispub.co.uk

Distributed in the USA by
The Globe Pequot Press
6 Business Park Road, PO Box 833, Old Saybrook,
Connecticut 06475–0833

Copyright © Dana Facaros and Michael Pauls 1999

Book and cover design by Animage
Cover photographs (front and back) by the Travel Library/Stuart Black
Maps © Cadogan Guides, drawn by Map Creation Ltd
Chapter title pages designed by Kicca Tommasi
from photographs by Dana Facaros and Mary-Ann Gallagher

Editorial Director: Vicki Ingle
Series Editor: Linda McQueen
Editors: Mary-Ann Gallagher and Dominique Shead
Proof-reading: Mary Spicer Lambert
Indexing: Isobel McLean

ISBN 1–86011–950–6
A catalogue record for this book is available from the British Library
Printed and bound in the UK by Cromwell Press Ltd

The author and publishers have made every effort
to ensure the accuracy of the information
in the book at the time of going to press.
However, they cannot accept
any responsibility for any loss,
injury or inconvenience resulting
from the use of information
contained in this guide.

About the Authors

Dana Facaros and Michael Pauls have written over 20 books for Cadogan, including a series on Spain. They have lived all over Europe but recently hung up their castanets in a shoreside cottage in southwest Ireland.

Acknowledgements

A big, big thank you to Mary-Ann Gallagher, who made Madrid even more fun than it already is, and whose verve, doggedness and sacrifice of at least two weekends made it all possible. Thanks also to Nick Lyne for his many contributions, to Laura Toledo for telling us all about the dances of Madrid, to Dominique for her editing, to the Madrid tourist office for all their help, and to Carolyn, Chris, Robin and Audrey (and Lily too) who came and kept us from working too hard.

Please help us to keep this guide up to date

Despite the valiant efforts of the author and publishers to keep the guide up to date, standards in restaurants and practical details such as prices are liable to change. We would be delighted to receive any comments concerning existing entries or indeed any suggestions for inclusion in future editions or companion volumes. Authors of the best letters (or e-mails) will receive a copy of the Cadogan Guide of their choice.

Contents

Introduction   vii

Travel   1–8

Getting to Madrid   2   Getting Around Madrid   5
By Air   2   By Metro   6
By Train   3   By Bus   6
By Bus   3   *Cercanías* (local trains)   6
By Car   4   By Taxi   6
Border Formalities, Visas   4   Hiring a Car   7
                                    Tour Operators   7

Practical A–Z   9–20

Children's Activities   10   Media   16
Climate and When to Go   11   Money and Banks   16
Cybercafés   11   Opening Hours   17
Disabled Travellers   12   Police Business   17
Electricity   12   Post Offices   17
Embassies   12   Public Holidays   18
Festivals and Calendar   Telephones   19
of Events   13   Time   19
Health and   Tipping   20
Emergency Services   15   Toilets   20
Lost and Found   16   Tourist Information   20

History   21–34

Arab *Mayrit* becomes Madrid 22   Republic and Civil War   30
Madrid Becomes a Capital   23   Four Miserable Decades
The Horrible Habsburgs   25   with Franco   32
Bourbons and More Palaces   27   Madrid of the *Movida*   33
A Big Revolution   28

Architecture   35–38

Tales of Madrid   39–52

La Villa del Oso y Madroño	40	The Spanish Match	46
Air, Light and Litter	41	Visions in Silence	47
Getting Real: the *Castizos*	42	Bullfights	48
The *Ciudad Lineal*	44	*No Pasarán*	50
La Movida; Swinging Madrid	45		

The Neighbourhoods   53–172

Introduction to Madrid's Neighbourhoods   **53**

The Vortex: The Plaza del Puerta del Sol   **55–60**
                                                          map   57

Old Madrid   **61–70**
Plaza Mayor–Around the Plaza Mayor–Place de la Villa–Plaza de la Paja
                                                          map   62–3

La Latina, Embajadores, and Lavapiés   **71–80**
La Latina–Puerta de Toledo and Beyond–The *Rastro*–Embajadores–
La Corrala–Plaza de Lavapiés   *map*   72–3

Around Plaza Santa Ana: Literature and Bars   **81–90**
Carrera de San Jerónimo and the Cortes–Plaza Santa Ana–Casa Museo
Lope de Vega to the Church of San Sebastián–Calle de Atocha
                                                          map   83

La Paseo del Arte and the Retiro Gardens   **91–120**
The Paseo del Prado–Museo del Prado–Casón del Buen Retiro–
Plaza de la Lealtad–Museo Colección Thyssen-Bornemisza–
Behind the Prado–The Retiro–Plaza Emperador Carlos V–
Museo Nacional Centre de Arte Reina Sofía–Between Atocha
Station and the Retiro   *map*   93

New Madrid: Salamanca and the Castellana   **121–136**
Plaza de la Cibeles–Paseo de Recoletos–Salamanca–Up the Paseo
del Castellana–Museo Sorolla and Museo Lázaro Galdiano–
Museo de Ciencias Naturales to Museo de la Ciudad–
Urbanización AZCA–The Periphery: Parque Juan Carlos I
and the Caprichio de Osuna   *map*   123

Royal Madrid   137–48
Convento de las Descalzas Reales–San Ginés–Convento de la
Encarnación–Plaza de Oriente and the Teatro Real–Palacio Real
(Palacio de Oriente)–South of the Palace–Ermita de la Virgen
del Puerto and the Campo del Moro   *map*   139

Madrid of the Bright Lights   149–62
The Real Academia de Bellas Artes de San Fernando–Down the Calle de
Alcalá–The Gran Vía–Malasaña–Chueca–Las Salesas   *map*   150–51

Madrid's Parklands   163–72
Plaza de España–Museo Cerralbo–Parque del Oeste–
Ermita de San Antonio de la Florida (Goya Pantheon)–Casa de Campo–
Argüelles, Moncloa and the Ciudad Universitaria   *map*   164–5

Museums   173—6

Art   174   Military   175
Archaeology and Ethnology   175   Science and Technology   176
Historical   175   One-Offs   176

Food and Drink   177–90

Eating Out   178   Open-Air Eating   187
Madrid Specialities   178   Cafés, Bars and Interesting
Tapas Bars   179   Places to Drink   185
East of the Castellana   179   Madrid Specialities   185
South of the Puerta del Sol   180   Spanish Wines   186
North of Puerta del Sol   183   Other Spanish Tipples   187
Vegetarian   185   Café Society   187

Where to Stay   191–8

North of Puerta Del Sol   192   South of the Puerta del Sol   196
East of the Castellana   194   Accommodation Agencies   198

Entertainment and Nightlife   199–208

Classical Music   Dance   200
and Zarzuela   200   Film   201

Flamenco	202	Sports and Activities	206
Nightclubs and Bars	202	Spectator Sports	206
Discos	203	Activities	207
Clubs/Bars	204	Theatre	207
Gay	205	Classical and	
Lesbian	205	Contemporary Theatre	207
Rock, Blues, Jazz	205	Alternative Theatre	208

Shopping   209–14

Fashion	210	Markets	213
Books, Records, News	211	Sweet Treats	123
Specialities	211	Oddments	214
Sweet Nuns	212		

Living and Working in Madrid   215–18

Long Term Residence		Finding Somewhere to Stay	217
and Finding a Job	216	Help and Services	217

Day Trips from Madrid   219–66

El Escorial	224	Alcala de Henares, Guadalajara	
Valle de los Caídos	228	and Sigüenza	224
Segovia	229	Aranjuez	249
Ávila	238	Toledo	251

Language (including restaurant vocabulary)   267–272

Chronology   273–274

Further Reading   275–276

Index   277–87

Maps

Madrid City Map   *inside front*
Madrid Metro   *inside back*

Neighbourhood Maps:

Puerta del Sol   57
Old Madrid   62–3
La Latina, Embajadores, Lavapiés   72–3
Aound Plaza Santa Ana   83
The Paseo del Arte and the Retiro   93
The Retiro   111
New Madrid: Salamanca and the Castellana   123
Royal Madrid   139
Madrid of the Bright Lights: Gran Vía, Malasaña and Chueca   150–51
Madrid's Parklands   164–5

Sifting through all the books that have ever been written about Spain, opinion on this unlikely capital seems evenly divided. Some are convinced that it's the heart and soul of the nation, but dissent has been coming in ever since the city has been on the map; many follow the irrepressible Richard Ford, who wrote the first guide-book to Spain back in 1855, in counselling that the less time you spend in Madrid, the more you'll like it. The city certainly defies the archetypes of Spanish romance. But a *madrileño* will tell you that Madrid is better than romantic, and that poking around

Introduction

Spanish castles (or otherwise being outside of Madrid) is dead time, because a body is only really alive while in the city. Or as one *madrileño* told us: 'Madrid is killing me, but it's a great way to die.'

This may well be true in light of Madrid's origins. Like Bonn or Washington or Brazilia or Canberra, Madrid is an artificial capital, created in the late 16th century on the whim of the early Habsburg kings. Its position—smack in the centre of Spain—apparently had nothing to do with it: Philip II chose Madrid because the hunting was good and it came ready-made with a long, straight, broad street, laid out by transhumant sheep moving between Castile and Extremadura. What the capital does *not* have is perhaps more extraordinary: a beautiful setting, a decent river or port, or a tolerable climate ('three months of winter, nine months of hell' is the old saying) or even many noteworthy churches or monuments. It's difficult to imagine a major capital more

impoverished architecturally, especially when you remember that Madrid ruled the most extensive, the most gold- and silver-rich empire of all time.

What Madrid does have, however, is off the charts. Art is one: the city of Velázquez and Goya and connoisseur Habsburg kings stores one of this planet's greatest hoards of paintings in the Prado, Thyssen and the Reina Sofía, and in a number of fine smaller museums lurking in the shadow of the Big Three. Old Madrid is another plus, evocative certainly, but not in the usual way; in Madrid it's the interiors that really stand out. Few cities have better preserved their old restaurants and bars and shops, not as historic monuments but because the *madrileños* have an instinct beyond fashion for what is right, and the sense to keep it that way.

For many, Madrid's biggest asset is its ability to show you a good time. The city of the cats (*los gatos*, an old nickname for the *madrileños*) proudly claims to stay up later than any in Europe, and there's good cause to stay up, with an infinite variety of bars, nightlife and attractions that may make you forget all about Velázquez and Goya. And this would not be the tremendous fun it is if it weren't for the *gatos* themselves, a population distilled from the rest of Spain, tried and tested over the centuries, to emerge with top honours as one of the most sane and wise people you'll ever meet. In 1886, a perceptive Frenchwoman named Juliette Lamber (writing under the pseudonym of Count Paul Vasili) got them down pat:

> *Madrid society, unconsciously perhaps, is democratic; it is frank and sincere, and you do not find there any stiffness or affectation. The Castillian arrogance is only the covering for an optimistic self-sufficiency which does not wound, does not shock, which you will grow accustomed to, and in which you will drape yourself unknowingly on your return.*

In fact, visiting Madrid, where people seem uniquely aware that life is no dress rehearsal, is a risky business. It makes the rest of the world seem neurotic.

Getting There	2
By Air	2
By Train	3
By Bus	3
By Car	4

Travel

Border Formalities and Visas	4
Getting Around	5
By Metro	6
By Bus	6
Cercanías (local trains)	6
By Taxi	6
Hiring a Car	7
Tour Operators	7

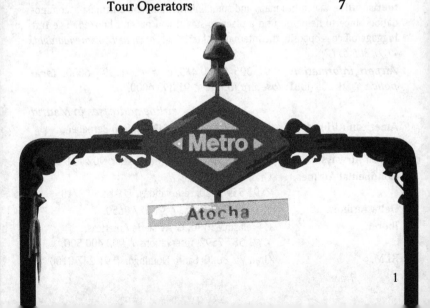

Madrid is smaller than most great European capitals, and getting into and out of the centre is surprisingly easy and convenient.

By Air

The Aeropuerto de Barajas, Madrid, is 13km northeast of the city centre, off the N11 highway, and is currently being expanded, so expect a bit of confusion and delay. There are three terminals; most international flights arrive and depart from T1, most domestic flights from T2, and Iberia Air Shuttle and other regional flights from T3.

Fast, air-conditioned **buses** (white with yellow and green stripes) run between Barajas's national and international terminals and the underground bus terminal at Plaza de Colón, 500m north of Retiro Park, every 12 minutes except between 1.50 and 4.45 in the morning, taking around 25mins when the traffic is reasonable, and about an hour if not. The fare is 380 pts one way. **Airport bus information:** ℡ 91 431 6192. A **taxi** from the airport to the centre will be about 2,500 pts, including various supplements. A **metro** line is planned for Barajas by the end of 1999.

The airport has two **banks** where you can change foreign currency (BEX and Caja de Madrid), and a Visa/Mastercard cashpoint. Avis, Hertz, Europcar and Atesa all have car hire offices here. There's also a **post office** (*open Mon–Fri 8–8, Sat 8–1*), a **RENFE office** (*open 8am–9pm, ℡ 91 305 8544*), a small **tourist office** which has maps and some information, and a Brújula accommodation office to help you find a place to stay if you haven't booked. The **left luggage** office is opposite the international terminal (*open daily, 7am–midnight, ℡ 91 305 6112*).

Airport information: ℡ 91 305 8343/4/5/6 or ℡ 91 393 6000; *local police:* ℡ 91 305 4381; *lost and found:* ℡ 91 393 6000.

airline addresses in Madrid

American Airlines:	C/Pedro Teixeira 8, 5°, Ⓜ Santiago Bernabéu, ℡ 91 597 2068 or ℡ 900 1005 56
British Airways:	C/Pinar 7, Ⓜ Gregorio Marañón, ℡ 902 111 333
Continental Airlines:	Gran Vía, Ⓜ Callao, ℡ 91 559 2520; reservations, ℡ 91 559 2710
Delta Airlines:	C/Goya 8, Ⓜ Goya, ℡ 91 577 0650
Iberia:	C/Velázquez 130, Ⓜ Avda. de Américas, ℡ 91 587 7592, reservations ℡ 902 400 500.
KLM:	Gran Vía 88, Ⓜ Santo Domingo, ℡ 91 247 8100

Spanair:	Barajas Airport, Sala 4, ✆ 902 131 415
TWA:	Plaza de Colón 2, 2°, Ⓜ Colón, ✆ 91 310 3094
US Airways:	C/Alberto Aguilera 38, Ⓜ Bilbao, ✆ 91 444 4700
Virgin Express:	C/Emiliano Barral 18, Ⓜ Arturo Soria, ✆ 900 467 612

By Train

All long distance trains now leave from just two stations: Estación de Atocha and Estación de Chamartín. **Atocha**, newly refurbished and quite close to the city centre at the southern end of the Paseo del Prado, handles AVE trains to and from Córdoba and Sevilla, *Largo Recorrido* (long distance) trains to and from Lisbon, Valencia, Andalucía and all points south, plus trains on the *Regionales* (short distance), and *Cercanías* (local) rail networks (*see* p.6). **Chamartín**, just past Plaza Castilla at the northern end of the Paseo de la Castellana, is also fairly new and has the air of a shopping mall. It takes most of the trains to and from France, and those serving northern and central Spain, plus some local trains. There's a metro stop at both Atocha and Chamartín, but the quickest way to travel between the two stations is via the underground section of the main rail line, with stops at Recoletos (just northwest of the Retiro park) and Nuevos Ministerios (on the Paseo de la Castellana, 2.5km north of the Plaza de Cibeles). Many trains to and from distant places use it to hit both Atocha and Chamartín, and you may jump on any train that does to get from one to the other.

Tickets can be bought at the main RENFE office at C/Alcalá 44 (*open Mon–Fri, 9.30–8*). For all RENFE enquiries, call ✆ 91 328 9020. RENFE offers telephone reservations: for an extra 500 pts, they will messenger the ticket to you, as long as it's within the capital. AVE information: ✆ 91 534 0505.

By Bus

Most, but not all, inter-urban and international buses use the big new **Estación Sur de Autobuses**, at C/Méndez Alvaro (Ⓜ Méndez Alvaro). A big exception is the Auto-Res company, which has its own terminal at Pza. de Conde de Casal 6 (Ⓜ Conde de Casal, southeast of Retiro Park, ✆ 91 551 7200) with services to Cuenca, Valencia, Extremadura, and parts of Castile. Continental Auto, C/Alenza 20 (head north from Ⓜ Ríos Rosas) takes you up to Burgos and the Basque country; they also have a terminal at Avda. de América 34 for buses to Alcalá de Henares, Guadalajara and Sigüenza. For other destinations close to Madrid, check the 'Getting There' sections for those towns (*see* pp.219–66, **Day Trips**).

Information: Estación Sur, ✆ 91 468 4200; Auto-Res, ✆ 91 551 7200; Continental Auto, ✆ 91 533 0400 (C/Alenza 20) or ✆ 91 356 2307 (Avda. de América 34). Or the Tourist Office can always help you (*see* p.20).

left luggage

As well as at Barajas airport (*see* p.2), there are public *consignas* at Estación Sur (*open Mon–Fri, 6.35am–11.45pm*), Atocha (*open daily, 7am–11pm*) and Chamartín (*open daily, 6.30am–12.30am*).

By Car

If you bring your car to Madrid, note that you'll need a pink EU driving licence or an International Driver's Licence. Although it's not compulsory, you may want to consider extending your motor insurance to include a bail bond. Should you have an accident without a bail bond, your car will be be impounded and you may find yourself in jail for the night. Carry your Green Card and other vehicle documents with you at all times. Wearing seat belts is mandatory.

Once you get your car to Madrid, you will be confronted either by traffic tie-ups or the fact that once they get into third gear, *madrileños* don't like to stop; a yellow light means accelerate, not slow down. Parking is a nightmare. While your car is certainly a nice thing to have to get around on day trips out of the city, it is fairly useless for getting around most places in Madrid because of the rarity of parking places. Some hotels have car parks; otherwise you may as well put your car in the nearest 24-hour underground car park (rates are 2,250 pts for 24 hours, or 150 pts an hour). Cars with foreign plates are especially vulnerable to thieves.

If it's not banned, you can park for up to two hours on the street, as long as you pick up a permit from an *estanco* (tobacco shop) and display it on your windscreen. Parking is regulated by ORA (Operación de Regulación del Aparcamiento) and rules are in force from Monday to Friday, 9am–8pm and Saturday 9–2. Illegally parked cars may well be towed; © 91 345 0050 to find out if they've nabbed yours.

Border Formalities and Visas

Visitors from the UK or other EU countries must present a valid passport; holders of US, Canadian, or New Zealand passports can enter Spain for up to 90 days without a visa; holders of Australian, South African or other passports will need a visa, available from any Spanish consulate, either at home or in Europe.

If you intend to stay for more than three months, you must apply for a community resident's card (*permiso de residencia*) at the Foreign Nationals Office (Comisarias de Extranjería); *see* p.214.

Getting Around

Madrid goes on and on—today it is home to 4 or 5 million people, depending how you add them up, but almost everything of major interest will be found within one mile of the **Puerta del Sol** between the Retiro park in the east and Plaza de Oriente in the west, home of the newly opened opera house and the Royal Palace. Nearby is the **Plaza de España**, a modern square laid out during the Franco regime. Back over on the east, near the Retiro and the broad boulevard called the **Paseo del Prado**, you'll find the '*triángulo del arte*', Madrid's triple crown of art museums, the Prado, Thyssen, and Reina Sofia. The Puerta del Sol sits squarely in the centre, and the oldest quarter of the city, around the **Plaza Mayor**, is just to the east of it.

Keep these landmarks in mind, and learn a few of the main streets, and you'll not get too lost—Madrid isn't nearly as complicated as it looks on the map.

Because it's so compact, Madrid is easy to get about on foot, and if you've got sore feet, taxis are relatively cheap. That said, Madrid's buses and metro do come in handy to reach some of the more outlying sights. They operate on the same ticket, with a single price for all journeys, costing 130 pts. A '*bono*', for ten trips, costs 680 pts and can be a good investment if you're going to be in the city for a few days.

By Metro

Opened in 1919, Madrid's metro is the third oldest system in Europe (after London and Paris) and is safe, clean and well used, even late at night: trains run from 6am to 1.30am. The metro's main faults are that its connections are often inconvenient and that in the summer it can be more than a bit stuffy and hot, although air conditioning is in the works.

Study the metro map carefully before setting out. There are so many stops and lines in the centre of the city, it's easy to be tricked into taking a half-hour ride (with a change or two) for a distance that easily could be covered in 10 minutes on foot.

For navigation, you have to know your line number, and the name of the terminus in the direction you want to travel. Stations are distinguished by a red diamond over the entrance. For information, call © 91 522 5909.

The metro has been undergoing a massive expansion plan in recent years. By the end of 1999, not only will Barajas Airport have a metro station, but a cross-town line will extend from Fuencarral in the north to Aluche in the far south.

Only a few EMT bus lines will be of use to the visitor—but buses can be prefer-able to the metro if you want to see Madrid (remember, they both take the same tickets). Many buses go through the Plaza de Cibeles, Puerta del Sol and Plaza del Callao, where there are information kiosks which sell *bonobus* tickets. *Estancos* (tobacconists) and news-stands also sell them. You enter the bus at the front, pay the driver or validate your ticket, and leave by the doors in the middle. Some dri-vers may object if you try to bring large suitcases on board. The sequence of places served from each stop is usually clearly marked. Buses run from 6am to midnight, after which there is a skeleton night service through the city, leaving from Plaza de Cibeles and Puerta del Sol every half hour until 3am, and every hour from 3–6am. For EMT information, call ✆ 91 401 9900.

Useful lines:

Line 1:	Moncloa–Pza. de España–Gran Vía–Pza. de Cibeles–Puerta de Alcalá–C/Velázquez or C/Serrano–C/Ortega y Gasset (Salamanca district).
Line 3:	Pza. de Alonso Martínez–C/Fuencarral or C/Hortaleza–Puerta del Sol–C/Arenal or C/Mayor–Pza. de San Francisco–Puerta de Toledo.
Line 14:	Pza. de Conde de Casal–Atocha–Pso. del Prado–Pso. de Recoletos– Pso. de la Castellana—Chamartín.
Line 19:	C/Velázquez or C/Serrano–C/Alfonso XII (Retiro Park)–Atocha– Palos de la Frontera (Estación Sur bus terminus).
Line 33:	Pza. de Isabel II–Casa de Campo: Parque de Atracciones, Parque Zoológico (funfair and zoo).

Cercanías (Local Trains)

Run by RENFE, Spain's national railroad, this network is primarily useful for commuters, but also comes in handy for daytrips to El Escorial, Guadalajara, Aranjuez, or Alcalá de Henares. All trains pass through the main stations of Atocha, Recoletos, Nuevos Ministerios and Chamartín.

By Taxi

Madrid has 15,500 taxis, more than any city in the world except Cairo, so finding one is rarely a problem. Local government-regulated taxis are white with a red diagonal stripe on each front door, and a sign saying 'Libre' if they're free. Any city taxi that has a meter (some don't—they're best avoided) is expected to use it, but don't be surprised if the fare comes out a little higher: there are surcharges for luggage, for the airports and bus and railway stations, for journeys at night (11pm–6am), and for leaving the city limits. As elsewhere in Spain, taxis are cheap enough; the average ride across the city centre costs well under 500 pts. If you call a radio taxi, the meter will be set from the spot where the driver receives the call.

Radio taxi: ✆ 91 447 5180.
Tele-Taxi ✆ 91 445 9008
Radio Taxi Independiente ✆ 91 405 1213

Hiring a Car

This is moderately cheaper than elsewhere in Europe, especially if you hire from a local Spanish-owned company. You may find some interesting discounts with the big international firms if you book a car along with your flight: it's worth asking. You need to be at least 21 and have held a licence for at least a year; you'll also need a credit card or be prepared to pay an enormous cash advance. You can save on parking fees by having the car delivered to your hotel when you're ready to go.

Besides the usual branches at the airport, you can hire a car from:

Atesa (Eurodollar):	Pso. de la Castellana 130, Ⓜ Santiago Bernabéu, ✆ 91 561 4800
Europcar:	C/San Leonardo 8, Ⓜ Plaza de España, ✆ 91 541 8892. Other branches at Avda. del Partenón 16–18, Ⓜ Campo de las Naciones, ✆ 91 722 6226; Atocha Station, ✆ 91 530 0194; and Chamartín Station, ✆ 91 323 1721
Avis:	Gran Vía 60, Ⓜ Plaza de España, ✆ 91 547 2048
Hertz:	Atocha Station, Ⓜ Atocha, ✆ 91 468 1318
Rent Me:	Plaza de Herradores 6, Ⓜ Sol, ✆ 91 559 0822

Tour Operators

The following offer city breaks to Madrid, some catering to a special interest:

Abercrombie & Kent, Sloane Square House, Holbein Place, London SW1W 8NS, ✆ (020) 7730 9600. ✉ (020) 7730 9376.

Kirker Travel, 3 New Concordia Wharf, Mill Street, London SE1 2BB, ✆ (020) 7231 3333, ✉ (020) 7231 4771.

Magic of Spain, 227 Shepherds Bush Road, London W6 7AS, ✆ (020) 7533 8888, ✉ (020) 7533 8830.

Martin Randall Travel, 10 Barley Mow Passage, Chiswick, London W4 4PH, ✆ (020) 8742 3355, ✉ (020) 8742 7766. Cultural tours accompanied by a lecturer.

Mundi Color Holidays, 276 Vauxhall Bridge Road, London SW1V 1BE, ✆ (020) 7242 5044, @ (020) 7242 5070.

Page & Moy, 135–140 London Road, Leicester LE2 1EN, ✆ (01162) 507000, @ (01162) 507123.

Prospect Music and Art Tours, 454–458 Chiswick High Road, London W4 5TT, ✆ (020) 8995 2151, @ (020) 8742 1969. Tours of the big museums.

Solos Holidays, 54–58 High Street, Edgware, Middx HA8 7ED, ✆ (020) 8951 2800, @ (020) 8951 2848.

Spanish Study Holidays, 35 Woodbrook Road, Loughborough, Leics LE11 3QB, ✆ (01509) 211612, @ (01509) 260037. Language courses in Madrid, with local accommodation arranged.

Time Off, 1 Elmfield Park, Bromley, Kent BR1 1LU, ✆ (020) 8218 3537, @ (020) 8218 6363.

Unicorn Holidays, 2 Place Farm, Wheathampstead, Herts AL4 8SB, ✆ (01582) 834400, @ (01582) 831133. Also arranges stays in *paradores*.

Children   10
Climate and When to Go   11
Cybercafés   11

Practical A–Z

Disabled Travellers   12
Electricity   12
Embassies   12
Festivals and Calendar of Events   13
Health and Emergency Services   15
Lost and Found   16
Media   16
Money and Banks   16
Opening Hours   17
Police Business   17
Post Offices   18
Public Holidys   18
Telephones   19
Time   19
Tipping   20
Tourist Information   20
Toilets   20

Children

Spain has the lowest birthrate in Europe, but children are omnipresent in Madrid. This is not so much to do with some demographic quirk as the fact that children aren't regarded as a race apart: if the *madrileños* are cats, they are kittens, and you'll find them up until the wee hours in bars and restaurants, having a good time as their parents blithely sit and chat away into the night with a group of friends.

If you've kids in tow, soaring summer temperatures make one of the waterparks on the outskirts a good bet: **Aquasur**, in Aranjuez (℗ 91 673 1013; open from 10.30am–9pm, *cercanía* trains from Atocha) includes minigolf, a wild west fort, mini zoo and even karaoke as well as a pools and slides, and makes a good trade-off after visiting the Aranjuez's royal palace.

Madrid's **zoo** (and new aquarium), amusement park and largest outdoor **swimming pools** are all in the Casa de Campo (*see* pp.169–70). Take the metro to Lago or Batan, or float over via the *teleferico* cable car from Paseo del Pintor Rosales and walk from there. The **Parque de Atracciones** (*open daily Oct–June, noon– 11pm, till 1am on Sat; July–Sept open till 1am during the week, and 2am on Sat*) has some of Europe's scariest rides and noisiest music. The Casa de Campo prostitutes are kept at bay until it closes.

Close to its Puerta de Alcalá entrance, the **Parque del Retiro** features open-air puppet shows weekends at 6pm. During August, an international puppet festival attracts companies from around the world (performances at 7.30pm, 9pm and 10.30pm every day). For kids aged 6 and up, the **IMAX cinema** in Parque Tierno Galván, ℗ 91 467 4800, puts on big wildlife documentaries where language won't pose much of a problem.

Museums that children tend to tolerate include the Museo de la América, Museo de la Cera (totally tacky waxworks, complete with a terror train and Virtual Reality Stimulator), Museo de las Ciencias Naturales (Natural History) and Museo Ferrocarril (trains). Then there's the **Acciona-Museo Interactivo de la Ciencia**, Pintor Murillo, Parque de Atracciones, Alcobendas, ℗ 91 661 3909, a hands-on science museum in the northern dormitory town of Alcobendas (about 20 minutes away by bus: take Interbus 151, 152, 153, 154, all of which leave from Plaza Castilla). For kids under 12, Madrid has several *centros de ocio* (pay by the hour play centres); check the *Guía del Ocío* listings magazine under 'Niños'.

For a **night out** minus the crumb-snatchers, drop them off at El Descanso de Mama at Condes de Torreanaz 4, ℗ 91 574 3994, where they will be looked after by trained staff, overnight if necessary.

Climate and When to Go

Located on the plateau of Castile, Madrid at 2,135ft is the highest capital in Europe, which contributes to its famous rarefied air. It also has one of the most godawful climates of any European capital—blistering in the summer and freezing in the winter. It builds character. Spring and autumn are the most comfortable times to visit but, like any great capital city, you can have a good time in Madrid year round. Even summer, traditionally touted as the season to avoid, isn't all that infernal especially if you can manage to keep *madrileño* hours: do the cultural sights in the morning, have a long boozy lunch, and sleep from 4pm to 10pm. Although the city is at its emptiest in August, various organizations put on plenty of events to keep it from being dull.

average daily temperatures in °C/°F

Jan	Feb	Mar	April	May	June
max min	max min	max min	max min	max min	max min
9/47 2/34	12/54 2/35	15/60 5/42	18/66 7/44	22/71 10/50	27/79 5/58
July	August	Sept	Oct	Nov	Dec
max min	max min	max min	max min	max min	max min
32/88 17/63	31/87 17/63	25/77 14/57	19/66 10/48	13/54 5/42	9/49 2/36

average monthly rainfall in mm/in.

Jan	Feb	Mar	April	May	June	July	Aug	Sept	Oct	Nov	Dec
45/1.6	36/1.3	46/1.7	48/2	46/1.9	28/1	7/0.3	11/0.4	30/1.2	50/2	48/2	49/2

Cybercafés

Cybermad: C/Laurel 6, Ⓜ Acacias y Embajadores (*open Sun–Mon 10am–midnight, closed Sat; English spoken*).

Cestein: C/Leganitos 9 y 11, Ⓜ Plaza de España, ✆ 91 548 2775

El Escribidor: C/Ponzano 93, Ⓜ Cuatro Caminos, ✆ 91 553 5637

La Casa de Internet: C/Luchana 20, first floor, Ⓜ Bilbao, ✆ 91 446 5541

Internet access and e-mail also available from the offices of **Sol Telecom**:

Puerta del Sol 6, Ⓜ Sol, ✆ 91 531 0382

Gran Via 84, Ⓜ Plaza de España, ✆ 91 559 7977

Plaza del Callao, Ⓜ Callao, ✆ 91 532 7977

Disabled Travellers

Although many of the larger hotels as well as the big museums (especially the Prado, Reina Sofía and Thyssen) are wheelchair friendly, facilities for disabled travellers are limited in Madrid. Public transport can be difficult. Some buses on the major lines have been adapted, with accessible low entry and seating behind the drivers for the less mobile. Although the new metro stations are being built with lifts, most of the old ones have lots of stairs. The Atocha train station has lifts, while the others are less user-friendly. One radio taxi company has vehicles adapted for wheelchairs that you can book, © 91 547 8600 or © 91 547 8200. Thanks to the ONCE, the blind organization financed by its own lottery, pedestrian crosswalks in Madrid are specially textured and crossing lights are accompanied by a chirping bird sound that slows down as time runs out.

For more information on accessibility and facilities in Madrid, contact:

ONCE, C/de Prado 24, © 91 589 4600.

COMFM (Coordinadora de Minusválidos Físicos de Madrid), C/Ríos Rosas 54, © 91 535 06 19 (*open Mon–Fri, 8–3*).

RADAR (The Royal Association for Disability and Rehabilitation), Unit 12, City Forum, 250 City Road, London EC1V 8AF, © (020) 7250 3222.

Mobility International USA, PO Box 3551, Eugene, OR 97403, © (503) 343 1248.

SATD (Society for the Advancement of Travel for the Disabled), Suite 610, 347 5th Avenue, New York, NY 10016, © (212) 447 7284, offers advice on all aspects of travel for the disabled.

Electricity

Current is 225 AC or 220 V, the same as most of Europe. Americans will need converters, and the British will need two-pin adapters for the different plugs. If you plan to stay in the less expensive *hostales*, where the current is often 125v, it may be better to leave your gadgets at home.

Embassies

Great Britain: C/Fernando el Santo 16, © 91 319 0200, Ⓜ Alonso Martínez.

USA: C/Serrano 75, © 91 577 4000, Ⓜ Rubén Darío or Serrano.

Canada: C/Núñez de Balboa 35, © 91 431 4 00, Ⓜ Núñez de Balboa.

Australia: Pso. de la Castellana 143, © 91 579 0428, Ⓜ Pza. de Castilla/Cuzco.

New Zealand: Pza. de la Lealtad 2, © 91 523 02 26, Ⓜ Banco de España.

Ireland: C/Claudio Coello 73, © 91 576 35 00, Ⓜ Serrano.

Festivals and Calendar of Events

For a city that embraces the old and the new with gusto, Madrid puts on some excellent fiestas, ranging from new artsy events to the most traditional. Among the most fun are the old-fashioned neighbourhood *verbenas*, or street festivals, the occasion for women to haul out their long flouncy dresses and put a carnation in their hair, while men don their flat caps and jackets.

1 Jan   *Noche Vieja.* Communal gathering in the Puerta del Sol to see the old year out, with the Latin custom of eating a grape with each of the twelve chimes. It brings good luck.

5–6 Jan   *Los Reyes* (Epiphany). The end of the holiday season is marked by a big parade celebrating the arrival of the Magi in Bethlehem on the 5th, and a big feast; children open their presents on the 6th.

Early Feb   ARCO, huge international contemporary art fair, at the Feria de Madrid.

Carnival   The week leading up to Lent (mid–late Feb) is occasion for a parade, a certain amount of dressing up, gigs in the bars and parties. Uniquely *madrileño*, however, is the wacky Burial of the Sardine (*Entierro de la Sardina*), an old tradition in which the sardine coffin is paraded around the city with a jazz band and laid to rest in the Paseo de la Florida.

8 Mar   *Día de la Mujer.* International Woman's Day, celebrated with a march down Calle Atocha and festivities in the evening across town, especially in the various bars.

Holy Week   There are enough citizens with Andalucian roots in Madrid to make sure *Semana Santa* doesn't pass by unnoticed. Processions of various weighty religious floats showing scenes of the Passion by various brotherhoods of *Penitentes* in their hoods (copied by the Ku Klux Klan) take place in most of Madrid's old neighbourhoods; the tourist information office has details.

1 May   *Fiesta del Trabajo.* Still the occasion for a Communist-Socialist-Anarchist march through the city centre, and a party in the Casa de Campo, with music, beer and food from all the regions of Spain.

2 May   *Dos de Mayo.* An official holiday celebrating Madrid's rising against Napoleon's forces in 1808, so memorably depicted by

Goya. The main events take place around the Plaza Dos de Mayo in Malasaña, including live bands; the *Comunidad de Madrid* stages other events, especially in the Parque de las Vistillas by the Palacio Real.

Early May   *Festimad.* A festival of alternative music, film, and goods by the new and young in Spain. Main musicals take place in the Circulo de Bellas Artes, in the suburb of Móstoles.

Early May–early June   *Madrid en Danza.* International dance festival in various venues across the city.

8–15 May   *San Isidro.* Madrid's patron saint has his feast day on the 15th, but merits a whole week of festivities leading up to the big day. The bullfights at La Venta last an entire month, and with typical *madrileño* modesty are claimed to be the most important in the world. Traditional events take place in the Plaza Mayor, rock and pop concerts at Casa de Campo.

late May–early June   *Feria del Libro.* The biggest book fair in the Spanish-speaking world in the Parque del Retiro.

early June   International Dance Festival in various venues.

12 June   *San Antonio de la Florida.* A *verbena* honouring Madrid's celestial match-maker.

mid-June–mid-July   *PhotoEspaña.* A new and very popular expo and workshops featuring photographers from around the world in venues across the city

July   *World Music Getafe* and the *Fiesta Africana,* both in the industrial suburb of Getafe. A short walk from one another, the first concentrates on music and the second on culture, crafts, food and more music.

July–mid-Sept   *Veranos de la Villa,* 'Summers in the City', features a wide range of music and dance, in the Centro Cultural Conde-Duque, La Venta arena and elsewhere.

6–7 Aug   *Verbena de San Cayetano* (Lavapiés). Neighbourhood festival, with lots of costumes and prettily decorated streets.

9–10 Aug   *Verbena de San Lorenzo.* Nearby and similar to the above.

14–15 Aug   *Verbena de La Paloma.* Nearby and the biggest of the lot, celebrating the Assumption of the Virgin.

mid-Sept	*Fiestas del Partido Comunista*. A three-day (Fri–Sun) fun-fest of music, food and theatre in the Casa de Campo.
late Oct–Dec	*Festival de Otoño*. The autumn festival has grown to become one of the biggest music and theatre events in Madrid, with a huge variety for all tastes.
6 Dec–6 Jan	*Feria de Artesanía*. A crafts fair in Paseo de Recoletos.

Health and Emergency Services

Madrid has a single number for all emergency services (fire, police, ambulance): ✆ 112.

There is a standard agreement for citizens of EU countries, entitling you to a certain amount of free medical care, but it's not straightforward. You must complete all the necessary paperwork before you go to Spain, and allow a couple of months to make sure it comes through in time. Ask for a leaflet called *Before You Go* from the Department of Health and fill out form E111. Non-EU travellers should check with their policies at home to see if they are covered in Spain, and judge whether it's advisable to take out additional insurance.

English-speaking doctors are on duty at the privately run **Unidad Médica Anglo-Americana**, C/Conde de Aranda 1, Ⓜ Retiro, ✆ 91 435 18 23, open Mon–Fri 9am–8pm, Sat 10am–3pm. They will also make house or hotel calls. Before resorting to a *médico* (doctor) and his £20 ($34) fee, go to a pharmacy and tell them your woes. Spanish *farmacéuticos* are highly skilled and if there's a prescription medicine that you know will cure you, they'll often supply it without a doctor's note. *El País* and the other national newspapers list *farmacías* that stay open all night; alternatively, outside the door of most pharmacies you'll find the rota listing the nearest ones on duty.

In an **emergency**, ask to be taken to the nearest *hospital de la seguridad social*, all of which have 24-hour casualty (Urgencias) departments. Closest to the centre are: **Hospital Gregorio Marañón**, C/Dr Esquerdo 46, Ⓜ O'Donnell, ✆ 91 586 8000; **El Clínico San Carlos**, Plaza de Cristo Rey, Ⓜ Moncloa, ✆ 91 330 3747; **Ciudad Santiaria La Paz**, Pso. de la Castellana 261, Ⓜ Begoña, ✆ 91 358 2831.

Insurance

You may want to consider travel insurance, available through most travel agents. For a small monthly charge, not only is your health insured, but your bags and money as well, and some will even refund a missed charter flight if you're too ill to catch it. Be sure to save all doctors' receipts (you'll have to pay cash on the spot), pharmacy receipts, and police documents (if you're reporting a theft).

Lost and Found

Objetos Perdidos, Pza. de Legazpi 7, Ⓜ Legazpi. ℰ 91 588 4400. This is primarily for objects found on the metro or in taxis, or even on the street. If you've lost something on an EMT bus, go to C/Alcántara 24, Ⓜ Lista, ℰ 91 406 8810.

Media

The Socialist *El País* is Spain's biggest and best national newspaper, though circulation is painfully low. Most Spaniards just don't read newspapers (the little magazine *Teleprograma* with television listings and scandals is by far and away the best-selling periodical). The other big papers are *El Mundo* (the middle of the road challenger that revealed many of the Socialist scandals that *El País* daintily overlooked), *Diario 16* (centrist and good for coverage of the *toros*), and *ABC* (conservative, in a bizarre '60s magazine format). Two free monthly magazines in English, *The Broadsheet* and the less glossy *In Madrid*, offer insights into the city, listings and ads, and are generally available in tourist offices, some kiosks, pubs and language schools. Major British newspapers are widely available, along with the American *International Herald Tribune*, the *Wall Street Journal*, and the awful *USA Today*. As for Spanish TV, the soaps and dopes and adverts that challenge the US for sheer excess are great for honing your Spanish if nothing else.

Money and Banks

Spanish **currency** comes in notes of 1,000, 2,000, 5,000 and 10,000 *pesetas* (pts), all in different colours, and coins of 1, 5, 10, 25, 50, 100, 200, and 500 pts. At street markets, and in out-of-the-way places, you may hear prices given in *duros* or *notas*. A *duro* is a 5 pts piece, and a *nota* is a 100 pts piece. On 1 January 1999, the euro became the official currency of Spain, although Spanish peseta notes and coins will continue to be used during the three-year transitional period. The introduction of euro bank notes is slated to start on 1 January 2002. Exchange rates vary of course, but unless any drastic changes occur, £1 is 250 pts, and $1 equivalent to 150 pts. Think of 100 pts as about 40p or 75 cents—so those green 1000 pts notes, the most common, are worth about £4 or $7.50.

Madrid seems to have a bank on every street corner, and most of them will exchange money; look for the *cambio* or *exchange* signs and the little flags. Most international banks have major branches around the Calle de Alcalá or in the Salamanca district. **Banking hours** in Madrid are Mon–Fri 8.30am–2pm, and on Sat, same hours, but only from Oct to April; from May–Sept they close on Saturdays. Most will change foreign currency and **travellers' cheques** from one of the major companies, even if they don't have a sign saying *Cambio*.

American Express is at Pza. de las Cortes 2, ℘ 91 322 55 00, Ⓜ Banco de España (*open Mon–Fri 8.30–4.30pm*); also at C/Francisco Gervás 10, ℘ 91 572 03 03. Besides traveller cheque services, post restante for card holders, and so on, American Express is a reliable way to have cash sent from home.

Change Express, Cra. de San Jerónimo 11, Ⓜ Sol, ℘ 900 633 633, is the agent for Western Union, the fastest way to have money transferred to you in Spain.

Beware of **exchange offices**, which are conveniently open when banks are not, but often charge a hefty commission on all transactions. You can sometimes change money at travel agencies, fancy hotels, restaurants and big department stores. There are 24-hour *cambios* at the big train stations. A Eurocheque card will be needed to support your Eurocheques, and even then they may not be welcome.

Credit cards will always be helpful in town, and are accepted in most hotels, shops, and restaurants (just look for the little signs in the windows). You may be asked to show some ID. Perhaps the handiest way to keep yourself in cash is by using the automatic bank tellers (*telebancos*) that have appeared on most street corners—check with your bank before leaving to ensure your card can be used in Spain. But do not rely on hole-in-the-wall machines as your only source of cash; if, for whatever reason, the machine swallows your card, it usually take 10 days to retrieve it. If this or some other mishap occurs, there are help lines: American Express: ℘ 91 572 0320 (24-hour); Diner's Club: ℘ 91 547 4000; MasterCard/Eurocard: ℘ 91 519 2100; Visa: ℘ 900 974 445.

Opening Hours

Shops in Madrid usually open from 10am. Spaniards take their main meal at 2pm and most smaller shops close for 2–3 hours in the afternoon, usually from 1 or 2pm. Most establishments re-open from 5 or 5.30 until 8 or 8.30pm. Most stay closed on Saturday afternoons, while some, like book and record shops, may open on Sundays.

The larger **churches** roughly keep shop hours, while the smaller ones are often only open for an hour or two a day. Some may close down altogether in August.

Museums and historical sites tend to follow shop opening hours too, though abbreviated in the winter months; nearly all close on Mondays. Seldom-visited ones have a raffish disregard for their official hours, or open only when the mood strikes them. Don't be discouraged: bang on doors and ask around.

Police Business

Crime is not a big problem in Spain. In Madrid, pickpocketing and robbing parked cars are the specialities in crowded areas, and most notoriously at the

Rastro, but violent crime is rare. Walking around at night is safe—primarily because everybody does it, although you may want to avoid Calle de la Montera, the base for central Madrid's prostitutes.

There are several species of **police**. Franco's old goon squads, the Policía Armada, have been reformed and relatively demilitarized into the *Policía Nacional,* dressed in black and white uniforms; their duties largely consist of driving around in cars and drinking coffee, although they are also chiefly responsible for crime control in the city. If you have to report a crime in Madrid, you'll have to make a statement (*denuncia*) at their headquarters for your insurance claim if nothing else (Jefatura Superior de Policia, C/Fomento 24, Ⓜ Plaza de España, Ⓒ 91 541 7160).

In Madrid, the *Policía Municipal* (in blue) are in charge of traffic, parking, and local regulations. Then there's the *Guardia Civil*, with green uniforms and their distinctive black patent-leather tricorn hats. The 'poison dwarfs of Spain', as Laurie Lee called them, may well be one of the most efficient police forces in the world, but after a century and a half of upholding a sick social order in the volatile countryside, they have few friends. They too are being reformed; now they're most conspicuous in Madrid guarding government buildings and outside the city as a highway patrol, assisting motorists and handing out tickets (ignoring 'no passing' zones is the best way to get one). Most traffic violations are payable on the spot; the traffic cops have a reputation for upright honesty.

Post Offices

The main post office is the Palacio de Comunicaciones on the Plaza de la Cibeles (*open Mon–Fri 8–10, Sat 8.30–10*). In central Madrid there are also post offices at: El Corte Inglés, C/Preciados, Ⓜ Sol; C/Hermosilla 103, Ⓜ Goya; C/Mejí Lequerica 7, Ⓜ Alonso Martínez, *all open weekday mornings*. Postboxes, marked *Correos y Telégrafos*, are yellow; collections are generally Monday to Friday only. Most tobacconists sell stamps (*sellos*) and they'll usually know the correct postage for whatever you're sending. The standard charge for sending a letter is 70 pts (European Union) and 115 pts (North America).

Public Holidays

The Spanish, like the Italians, try to have as many as possible. Everything closes on:

1 January:	Año Nuevo (New Year's Day)
6 January:	Epifanía (Epiphany)
March:	Viernes Santo (Good Friday)

1 May:	Día del Trabajo (Labour Day)
2 May:	Día de la Comunidad de Madrid (Madrid Day)
May/June:	Corpus Christi
25 July:	Santiago Apóstol (St James' Day)
15 August:	Asunción (Assumption)
12 October:	Día de la Hispanidad (Columbus Day)
1 November:	Todos los Santos (All Saints' Day)
6 December:	Día de la Constitución (Constitution Day)
8 December:	Inmaculada Concepción (Immaculate Conception)
25 December:	Navidad (Christmas Day)

Telephones

Spain has long had one of the best telephone systems in Europe. Local calls are relatively cheap (25 pts), and it's easy to place international calls from any booth. These accept coins, credit cards or phone cards (sold in *estancos* and post offices). You can also call from metered booths at the Telefónica offices at Gran Vía 28 *(open Mon–Sat 9am–midnight, Sun noon–midnight)* or at the Palacio de Comunicaciones, Plaza de Cibeles, during regular post office hours; they are indispensable for reversed charge or collect calls (*cobro revertido*).

That said, overseas calls from Spain are expensive: calls to the UK cost about 250–350 pts a minute, to the US substantially more. Expect to pay a big surcharge if you do any telephoning from your hotel. Cheap rate is from 10pm–8am Monday–Saturday and all day Sunday and public holidays.

For calls to Spain from the UK, dial 00 followed by the country code (34), the area code (remember that if you are calling from outside Spain you drop the '9' in the area code) and the number. For international calls from Spain, dial ℗ 00, wait for the higher tone and then dial the country code, etc. All local calls in Madrid now require the 91 before them, which may not appear on lists prior to April 1998. Free phone numbers begin wtih 900. For national directory enquiries, call ℗ 025; international directory enquiries, ℗ 1003.

Stationery shops are the best places from which to send faxes; Telefónica offices also offer a fax service, but it's expensive. Faxes and phones are also available in the offices of Telefónica's rival, Sol Telecom (*see* Cybercafés, p.11).

Time

Spain is an hour ahead of Greenwich Mean Time, and generally six hours ahead of Eastern Standard Time in the US.

Tipping

Tips in Madrid are welcome but not really expected. For taxis it's common to tip 5 per cent, or ten per cent if the driver's friendly and helpful; in bars and restaurants leave 10 per cent, and 300 pts a night for the chamber maid.

Toilets

Apart from in bus and train stations, public facilities are rare in Madrid. A few pay ones (25 pts) are tucked in the Columnas Informativas—those brown plastic imitation Morriss Columns covered with advertising. On the other hand, every bar on every corner has a toilet; don't feel uncomfortable using it without purchasing something—the Spaniards do it all the time. Just ask for *los servicios.*

Tourist Information

Before you go, pick up more information from a Spanish National Tourist Office:

Australia: 203 Castlereagh Street, Suite 21a, PO Box A-685, Sydney South NSW 2000, ✆ (2) 264 7966, ✉ (2) 267 5111.

Canada: 102 Bloor Street West, Toronto, Ontario, M5S 1M8, ✆ (416) 961 3131, ✉ (416) 961 1992.

UK: 22–23 Manchester Square, London, W1M 5AP, ✆ (0171) 486 8077, ✉ (0171) 486 8034.

USA: 8383 Wilshire Boulevard, Suite 960, Beverly Hills, California, 90211, ✆ (213) 658 7188, ✉ (213) 658 1061; 665 Fifth Avenue, New York, NY 10022, ✆ (212) 759 8822, ✉ (212) 980 1053; Water Tower Place, Suite 915 East, 845 N. Michigan Ave, Chicago, Illinois 60611, ✆ (312) 642 1992, ✉ (312) 642 9817; 1221 Brickell Ave, Miami, Florida, 33131, ✆ (305) 358 1992, ✉ (305) 358 8223.

In **Madrid**, the main tourist office is at C/Duque de Medinaceli 2, close to the Prado, ✆ 91 429 4951 (*open Mon–Fri 9–7, Sat 9–3*). There are branch offices (but don't count on their being open) at Barajas airport (✆ 91 305 8656) and Chamartín station, gate 16 (✆ 91 315 9976) both supposedly *open Mon–Fri 8–8, Sat 8–1.* A third office is in the Puerta de Toledo Market, Stand 3134 (let us know if you find it!), ✆ 91 364 1876 (*open Mon–Fri 9am–9pm, Sat 9.30–1.30*).

The city of Madrid has an office right at Plaza Mayor 3, opposite the Casa de la Panadería, ✆ 91 366 5477 or 91 588 1636 (*open Mon–Fri 10–8, Sat 10–2*). They also run an **information phoneline**: dial ✆ 91 010 in Madrid, or ✆ 91 366 6606 from outside the city (*Mon–Fri 8.30–9.30*).

There is a **tourist telephone line**, ✆ 902 202 202, and a **helpline for information in English**, ✆ 91 559 1393.

Arab *Mayrit* becmes Madrid   22

Madrid Becomes a Capital   23

The Horrible Habsburgs   25

Bourbons and More Palaces   27

A Big Revolution   28

Republic and Civil War   30

Four Miserable Decades with Franco   32

Madrid of the *Movida*   33

History

860–1308: Arab *Mayrit* becomes Madrid

Fui sobre agua edificada
mis muros de fuego son
esta es mi alcurnia y blasón

(I was built on water, my walls are of fire; this is my lineage and emblem).

Madrid's motto

Settlements along the Manzanares have come and gone since the Palaeolithic era, but the first permanent town on its banks was built by the Arabs. After conquering most of Spain in the early 8th century, Córdoba's Emir **Mohammed I** constructed a fortress or Alcázar here sometime around 860. It stood on the clifftop site of today's Palacio Real, along with a circuit of walls that extended only as far as the Plaza Mayor and the Plaza Isabel II. The Arabic name for the little settlement, *Mayrit*, 'place of many springs', describes one of the site's chief attractions. Another, and more important one, was Mayrit's wide ranging views over the Sierra Guadarrama, which enabled it to guard the lines of communication between the important city of Toledo and Aragón from the increasing attacks by the Christian armies of the Reconquista.

Mayrit stood up to one of these attacks in 932, then, during the 970s it was used as the base for the campaigns of **Al-Mansur**, the chamberlain of the Caliph Hisham II, who reconquered many of the territories gained by the Christians. It was a time when the Moors were strong enough to erase the puny Christian kingdoms in the north had they cared to. But upon Al-Mansur's death in 1002, the Caliphate entered a fatal period of factional struggles and civil war. The Christians regrouped and tried again in 1047, and won Mayrit in 1083, two years before Toledo; according to legend, El Cid may have been around to assist King **Alfonso VI** of Castile in its capture. The king's first task, at least according to the city's legends, was to recover a statue of the Virgin of the Almudena, restoring the city's Christian credentials.

As elsewhere in Castile, the Reconquista brought in new Christian settlers from the north, who enclosed themselves in a new set of walls, made of adobe and flint ('*mis mueros de fuego son*'). But for two centuries Mayrit would remain a little frontier outpost while the locals decided on a name (Maiorito, Magerito, Mayoritum, Majaeritum, Magerit, Madritum, Maidrit were among the score that were felicitiously rejected). Many of the Moors remained, many now Christianized as *Mudéjars*, living side by side with Christians and a small Jewish community. The *Mudéjars* were responsible for channeling the many springs into kitchen gardens (some 60km of their irrigation tunnels are said to remain under the city). They were also in charge of much of the early building, although only a pair of minaret-like church towers survive, at San Pedro el Viejo and San Nicolás. The Arabs tried once more to take Madrid back in 1109, pitching their tents in the Campo del Moro, but failed. In 1202, this mostly agricultural settlement or *villa* of 3000 was given its *Fueros*, the statutes and rights of a free city, from Alfonso VIII.

1309–1561: Much to its Surprise, Madrid Becomes a Capital

The young and aggressive Christian kingdom of Castile managed for a long time without a capital. The Cortes (Parliament) traditionally alternated its meetings so that none of its cities would be offended, and the necessity of an occasional royal presence in all of Spain's diverse regions made vagabonds of all the earlier kings. In 1309 Madrid was chosen for the honour for the first time. If it made an impression, no one bothered to mention it. But like the rest of Castile the town was doing all right for itself: the kingdom's crown-chartered cooperative of sheep farmers, the Mesta, supplied much of Europe's wool. Also, because of the experience of the Reconquista, when new hands were always needed to settle the newly conquered lands, economic feudalism ended in Castile long before anywhere else in western Europe. Still, the nobility flourished, exempt from tax and loaded with privilege.

Madrid first attracted serious royal notice in the 1360s, when **Pedro the Cruel** spent money turning the Alcázar into a residence, attracted by the good hunting in the surrounding forests. The next thing we hear is that the town managed to become something no one could have predicted: Armenian. In a strange interlude in the city's history, King Juan I gave Madrid in fief to the exiled last king of Little Armenia, **Leon VI**, in 1383, as a gesture of Christian solidarity and a consolation prize for losing his kingdom to the Turks. When Leon died four years later, Madrid returned to the Castilian fold. On a less generous note, the negative effects of the Reconquista were beginning to kick in: the bigotry that had been growing like a vicious weed saw the first pogrom of the Jews in 1391, instigated by the Church. Around the same time, **Henry III** gave Madrid its first Crown-appointed mayor, or *corregidor*, to preside over the local council.

Madrid was doing well enough to require a new wall in the 1430s, which incorporated a marketplace that would one day became the Plaza Mayor. More royal patronage came with **Henry IV** (1454–74), who gave the town the status of *muy noble y muy leal*. Henry tacked a Renaissance façade onto the Alcázar to make it a proper palace, and he married Juana of Portugal there in 1463. A dynastic dispute followed Henry's death, and the victor was the king's sister **Isabel I**, whose marriage to Ferdinand of Aragon united Spain. In the unforgettable year of 1492 the pair, known as *los Reyes Católicos* for their religious fervour, completed the Reconquista in Granada, sent Columbus to discover the

Americas, and expelled the Jews who refused to convert. Not long after, they applied the same terms to the Moorish *Mudéjars*, and revitalized the Inquisition to terrorize them. Then, with the army they had amassed in Granada, they began to meddle in European affairs, seizing Naples and marrying their daughter, known as Juana the Mad, to Philip of Burgundy, the son of Habsburg Holy Roman Emperor Maximilian.

Isabel and Ferdinand's role in Europe was trivial compared to that of their Habsburg grandson, Charles, whose first act as the ruler of Spain was to bring in a whole troop of Flemish and French outsiders to hold the important offices, and bleed Castile white with taxes so he could bribe the German Electors to give him another title: Holy Roman Emperor, as **Charles V**. These and other outrages occasioned the Comunero Revolt of 1520–21, in which the cities of Old Castile rose to defend their liberties—and their purses—only to be crushed by Charles's foreign troops. Once they were bullied into submissive loyalty, and could be counted on to supply the treasure from the Americas to finance decades of futile wars, Charles became fond of Castile and especially of Madrid, giving the town the fancy sobriquet of *Imperial y Coronada*. He liked the climate because it eased his gout, and went hunting at El Pardo; when he captured his rival, King Francis I of France, at the Battle of Pavia, he imprisoned him in Madrid.

It was his son, **Philip II**, King of Spain and Burgundy, who made the decision in 1561 that changed the town's history. His travels in Europe and especially his long residency with his court in Flanders had convinced him that Spain needed to compete with other states, which had permanent courts and palaces that encouraged the arts and humanities. The fact that Spain was deeply in debt never stopped him for a second; the Habsburg monarchy needed a strong, central, specifically Castilian capital, and Madrid fitted the bill.

Still, the choice of a minor town without a navigable river seemed highly eccentric, even if it was smack in the centre of Spain; until the invention of rail, most of Madrid was doomed to penury, owing to the high cost of transport. His choice may have been influenced by the fact that the previous royal favourite, Valladolid, had an outbreak of heresy in 1559, followed by a devastating fire, and that the other leading contender, Toledo, the old capital of Spain, lacked the necessary space to house Philip's 4,000 courtiers and bureaucrats, much less their carriages. Madrid had room to expand. But apparently the overwhelming factor in Philip's decision to make this town of 9,000 Spain's permanent capital was the fact that it was in easy distance of woodlands full of rabbits, boar, and deer for the king to kill (he was pretty good, by all accounts, with the bow). Palatial hunting lodges went up around Madrid, at El Pardo, Aranjuez, Aceca, Vacia-madrid and elsewhere, all dwarfed by the massive monastery cum royal pantheon extravaganza at El Escorial. While running Spain into the ground, the 'royal bureaucrat' spent a great deal of his time following every detail of their construction and landscaping.

1561–1700: Splendour and Dirt with the Horrible Habsburgs

Unfortunately, outside of refurbishing and enlarging the Alcázar, Philip didn't have any attention or money left over to lavish on his new capital. His star architect, Juan de Herrera, designed the great Plaza Mayor, although he didn't get around to actually building it. Nevertheless, thanks to the permanent presence of the court, Madrid's population boomed; by 1562, it had already risen to 16,000. A new wall went up in 1566; by 1600 the population was up to 84,000. Like other 'artificial' capitals, such as Washington DC, Madrid from the beginning was a city of people from other parts of Spain, giving rise to the paradox that survives to this day: it is the most Spanish city, although it is (by appearance) the least Spanish city. Nearly all who flocked here—from ambitious second sons of noble families to broke *hidalgos*—sought employment or patronage of some kind with the court, and from the start Madrid fitted directly into the hallowed European role-model of the parasitic capital, sucking in every luxury, talent and skill from the rest of the country to make the city the centre stage for Spain's Golden Age.

The neglect and overburdening of the *Mudéjars'* waterworks also made it 'the dirtiest and filthiest city in Spain' according to a Flemish visitor in 1570. Philip II tried, briefly, to clean it up, and admitted defeat; whenever an important visitor arrived in the medieval squalor of Madrid, the king would whisk them away at once to his pristine El Escorial. It was the beginning of a long and distinguished saga of dirt; until the 18th century, Madrid would lag far behind other European capitals of the day in sanitation and other urban amenities.

But sanitation is far too much a thing of this world for kings who were placing their bets on the next; Philips II, III and IV founded a total of 48 monasteries and convents in Madrid, which took up much of the space in a town growing at breakneck speed; they also acted as a magnet for the very poor, who could rely on their charity to eat. The pressure for lodging was so acute that a law decreed that any house of more than one floor could be requisitioned for courtiers; the *madrileños* responded by building houses of only one floor, on streets of mud so thick even horsemen floundered. The law stayed on the books so long that a new kind of architecture developed, the *casas a la malicia* ('cunning houses'), that from the front appeared to have only one floor, but squeezed two storeys around the back; you can still spot them in the older parts of town. Another law, promulgated by Philip II in 1585, banned profanity and gambling and other aspects of riotous living that took hold in Madrid from the start. The first purpose-built theatre, the Corral del Principe, was built in 1583, and it and others were packed every day.

Philip III (1598–1621), the product of an incestuous marriage (a Habsburg family tradition) was a shadow of his intelligent, duty-bound and wrong-headed father, and left most of the governing of Spain to his favourite, the **Duke of Lerma**. In 1601, Lerma shocked Madrid by declaring it a mess and moving the Corte to Valladolid. It just wasn't right; in forty years Madrid, with its majority of people living off the Crown or Church, had already acquired the sparkle of a capital city that made workaday Valladolid seem provincial and backward, and back to Madrid the king and some 40,000 others traipsed after five years in exile. The fact that Madrid offered the king and Lerma 250,000 gold ducats and a percentage of the rents on all houses for a decade may have had something to do with changing their minds. 'Sólo Madrid es Corte,' declared Philip, and that was that.

Once it had been shown that the capital was indeed fixed and permanent, real efforts began to make it look like one. The superb Plaza Mayor, completed in 1619, gave Madrid a much needed focal point and central stage, as well as its first buildings of more than one storey. **Philip IV**, product of another cousinly marriage (1621–65), was little better than his father but a gallant with the ladies, happy to leave the running of the state to the energetic **Conde-Duque de Olivares**, who in 1632 gave the king a proper home in Madrid: the magnificent Buen Retiro palace and park, on the eastern edge of the city. Other aristocrats (like the Church, the nobility was completely exempt from taxes) began to build palaces. The city's population reached 170,000, and was enclosed in a new, rather shoddy wall in 1656, not to protect the population but to ensure that the proper taxes and tolls were paid on goods coming in.

Most of all, the reign of Philip IV marked the Golden Age—the time of Velázquez, Cervantes, Calderón de la Barca, Tirso de Molino, Quevado and Lope de Vega, of legendary pageants and fiestas, whose dazzle hid the rot within. The Empire was collapsing. Spain's defeat at the hands of the Dutch, English, and French in the Thirty Years' War, especially at Rocroy (1643), meant that Spain was no longer a respected power, and revolts in Catalunya and in Portugal (annexed by Philip II) brought the trouble closer to home. The Conde Duque, who had spent his career hiding unpleasant truths from the king, went mad and died shortly after.

In this twilight Philip IV managed at last to produce a living male heir, out of 13 legitmate ones and countless illegitimate ones. This was the staring, drooling **Charles II** (1665–1700), whose mother was also his first cousin, and whose famous Habsburg jaw was so pronounced he couldn't eat solid food, part of the cause of his perpetual diarrhoea. With his mother as regent, he spent his reign playing in the crypt of El Escorial, while the police futilely searched the streets of

Madrid for the sorceress whom the priests said had put a curse on him. Although married off twice, producing an heir was quite beyond him. Meanwhile, the royal families of Europe circled Spain like vultures, waiting for him to die. Madrid, a *muy leal* reflection of its monarch, seemed to be dying as well, dropping nearly half its population by the time of the War of the Spanish Succession.

1700–1808: Bourbons, and More Palaces

The winner of the war, of course, was the grandson of Philip IV of Spain and Louis XIV of France, **Philip V** (1700–46), although it took twelve years to knock out the contenders, especially the Archduke Charles of Habsburg. A great centralizer like Louis XIV, Philip V also shared his grandfather's need for more palaces. He started with La Granja, but this was only the warm-up for the 3,000-plus room Palacio Real that replaced the Alcázar when it burned down in 1734. The other accomplishment of the reign was also inspired by his grandfather: he founded academies of language and history, while his son, **Ferdinand VI** (1746–59) founded the Real Academia de Bellas Artes de San Fernando.

The one Bourbon who made a difference, especially in Madrid, was his brother the 'Mayor-King', **Charles III** (1759–88), a son of the Enlightenment who, with his ministers Floridablanca and Jovellanos, tried to reform everything. He expelled the dreadful Jesuits and cut the privileges of the other religious orders down to size; he commissioned sewers and streetlighting in Madrid, laid out the Paseo del Prado, founded worthy scientific bodies, built Madrid's first post office and, at the instigation of the dapper Italian minster the Marqués de Squillace, even tried to regulate fashion to put the *madrileños* in step with the rest of Europe, banning their long capes and wide brimmed hats on the basis that the disguise made it easier to conceal weapons and go about incognito. This was going one step too far: the *madrileños* rioted and forced the government to back down.

Apart from the war over fashion, the mid to late 18th century was a happy time for Madrid; the population rose to 180,000 in 1800 and, unlike the previous century, its citizens weren't entirely living off the court, but worked in various small manufactures—one that was just taking off, and would soon employ an entire quarter of the city's workforce, was the tobacco factory.

Unfortunately for Madrid and Spain, the son of Charles III, **Charles IV**, was as useless and stupid as any Habsburg, and perhaps best remembered for the indignities he and his horrible wife, Maria Luisa, suffered at the hand of their court painter, Goya. Their rococo daydream was disrupted by the French Revolution. Napoleon first threatened Spain, then enticed Charles IV's corrupt minister (and Maria Luisa's lover) **Manuel Godoy** into cooperating in his campaigns, leading to the destruction of the Spanish fleet at Trafalgar.

Support of the godless French didn't sit well with the majority of the Spaniards, however, and in 1808 an anti-French riot shook Madrid; Godoy's house was attacked and the people proclaimed Ferdinand, son of Charles IV, the new king of Spain. Emboldened by the confusion, Napoleon sent down an army to take Madrid in March 1808, while the whole Spanish royal family fled into exile in France.

1808–1900: A Big Revolution, and its Disappointing Results

Politically the city learned to speak for itself on 2 May 1808, in the famous revolt of the *Dos de Mayo*. Although the government was ready to cave in at once before the troops of General Murat, a spontaneous patriotic uprising occurred among the *madrileños*, who fought the French and their Egyptian Mamaluke mercenaries hand to hand in the streets; although soon brutally suppressed by the French (as immortalized by Goya) it has been a golden memory for Madrid ever since.

The new king, **Joseph Bonaparte**, had no illusions about his popularity and the durability of his reign over what he himself described to his brother Napoleon as a 'nation of twelve million souls, exasperated beyond endurance'. In his six years in power, however, he did Madrid two big favours: he suppressed both the liquor tax and the city's excess convents and monasteries, demolishing them and turning them into squares—his nicknames were 'Joe Bottles' and *El rey de plazuelas*, the King of Squares.

Meanwhile, the Peninsular War, led by the Duke of Wellington, led to privations that became extreme in 1812, when he took Madrid from the French, gravely damaging the Palacio del Buen Retiro. In the subsequent famine some 30,000 died in the city alone. Politically, however, there was a ray of hope in the Consti-tution, Spain's first, written by the Cortes while in exile in Cádiz. The ink was barely dry before it was declared invalid by the new Bourbon king from France, Charles IV's son **Ferdinand VII** (1808–33), as backward and absolutist as his ancestors; he not only invited back the Jesuits, but the Inquisition as well, begin-ning the *desfrase* (out-of-synchness) that would characterize Spain's politics and its social realities for the next 150 years. With the reactionary Ferdinand at the helm there was no hope for change, but plenty for more humiliation as nearly all of Spain's colonies in Latin America rebelled and won their wars of indepen-dence. A successful revolt in 1820 led by General Rafael Riego forced him to re-instate the Constitution for three years. This breath of fresh air, known as the *Trienio Liberal*, saw the founding of Madrid's first real newspapers and the set-ting up of its first *tertulias* (cultural-political coffeehouse discussions), before it was suppressed by a French army in 1823.

Ferdinand's death in 1833 occasioned the **First Carlist War**, pitting the Liberal supporters of Ferdinand's daughter, the Infanta **Isabel II,** against Ferdinand's reactionary brother Don Carlos. The Liberals won, and under their first minister, **Mendizábel**, accomplished more than all the succeeding dictatorships of Isabel's generals and lovers, when in the *desamortización* of 1836 he expropriated the monasteries of Spain—in Madrid they had owned half of the town. The new secularized space offered the capital an unparalelled chance to put some order into its medieval warren of lanes, but Madrid declined, and used the land to throw up jerry-built housing for its growing population. Thanks to Mendizábel, there was a new intellectual element in the mix: that same year he moved the university from Alcalá de Henares to Madrid.

Even more important for Madrid was the completion of the first railroads in the 1850s. The new communications finally made up for the lack of a navigable river and offered the city its first real chance to become more than a parasite and make its own way in the world. The opening of a new water supply from the Sierra de Guadarrama, the Canal Isabel II in 1858, was another major step for Madrid, which had been muddling through and was increasingly thirsty.

By this time Madrid was bursting at the seams, with a population of over 300,000 inside its 200-year-old walls. In 1860, the city was given its first planned expansion or *ensanche*. This, designed by Carlos Maria de Castro, was laid out in a waffle iron grid of streets, but it tempted few developers and for the next couple of decades it was all but politely ignored. Meanwhile dissatisfaction with the corrupt court of Isabel II led to Spain becoming a sort of banana-monarchy, in which any ambitious general could deliver a *pronunciamiento* and strive for power. The First Republic was declared in 1868 but it soon succumbed to a Second Carlist War as futile as the first. A *pronunciamiento* by General Campos in 1876 restored the Bourbons in the form of Isabel's son **Alfonso XII**, who presided over a government kept stable only through a cynical deal under which the Liberals and Conservatives would alternate in power.

The average *madrileño* was fairly uneffected by all the *pronunciamientos*. In fact the city boomed in the 1880s. Country folk were pouring in at the rate of 10,000 a year, some finding jobs in the expanding number of workshops and small factories, others just getting by in the shanty towns that encircled the city. No longer able to squeeze into her girdle, Madrid decided to let herself spread with abandon in an orgy of new building in the *ensanche*, especially in the upper-class Salamanca district, named after the most flamboyant of Madrid's speculators. In the 1890s, in response to the city's rapid growth, an engineer named Arturo Soria came up with one of the most innovative designs for new housing, the Ciudad Lineal.

The century ended on a sour note, in the embarrassing defeat in the 1898 Spanish-American War that resulted in the loss of Spain's fleet as well as Cuba and the Philippines, her last important colonies. The country became introspective, and in Madrid's *tertulias*—frequented by leading figures of the 'Generation of '98' such Antonio Machado, Miguel de Unamuno and José Ortego y Gasset—the main subject was Spain's curious destiny and how the country seemed incapable of modernity. People grew disenchanted with the inane political arrangement, and with the unpopular king, **Alfonso XIII** (1885–1931), who just barely missed being blown to smithereens on Calle Mayor in a bomb attempt on his wedding day.

1900–39: Republic and Civil War

The new century found Madrid with a population of half a million, and things not quite as gloomy as they might have seemed at the time. New factories and working-class districts were filling up the planned streets of the *ensanche*, and the loss of the colonies was actually good for the economy, as the money once sent abroad was reinvested at home. Banks and other financial institutions spread east along the Calle de Alcalá, and mansions to house their bosses went up along the Paseos de Recoletos and Castellana. In 1910 the Gran Vía, a cross between a French boulevard and New York's Broadway, was bulldozed through the medieval centre as a showcase for the city's new love affair with modernity. In 1919 the metro made its inaugural run.

Spain's neutrality in the First World War made Madrid a nest of spies and intrigue, but was a boon to her farmers and manufacturers, who sold goods to the Allies, and positioned the country to reap a whirlwind of investment in the 1920s. Much of the action was in Madrid; the city's population doubled in 30 years. It was a time of cultural ferment, especially in the Residencia de Estudiantes, founded in 1910 as an open university of the liberal arts by Albero Jiménez Fraud, where leading writer and thinkers from around the world lectured and classes were attended by Unamuno, Alberti, the Machados, Buñuel, Dalí and Lorca.

Meanwhile, the rise of Anarchism in more industrialized Barcelona led to a new general taking power, **Miguel Primo de Rivera**, who declared himself dictator under the king. Primo de Rivera was repressive and closed a number of Liberal establishments in Madrid, but he was rather genial and well-meaning as dictators go, and during his brief regime it began to occur to people that they didn't really need a shabby monarchy. The Depression brought about the resignation of Primo de Rivera and the decision by the government in 1931 to hold local elections. The results were a unexpected victory for Republican candidates all across Spain. In Madrid the exuberant population gathered at the Puerta del Sol to celebrate, and danced in the streets when it was announced that the king had abdicated.

The **Second Republic** saw the new moderate-left government of Manuel Azaña try to make the reforms the country's rural and industrial regions were crying out for. With the Depression and spiralling unemployment, the cards were stacked against any government, but in Spain, where desperation had led people to take extreme positions, the situation was impossible: any change was regarded as 'Bolshevik' by the reactionary upper classes and Church, while the Marxists and Anarchists saw the new government only as a prelude to revolution. Their abstention from the elections in 1933 brought the radical right to power under Gil Robles and Lerroux, which was sufficiently alarming for the left to regroup as a Popular Front and win the election in 1936.

The situation immediately deteriorated. Street fighting and assassinations became an almost daily occurrence, much of it caused by extreme right-wing provocateurs, most notably by a violent new fascist party, the Falange Español, founded and led by José Antonio Primo de Rivera, son of the old dictator. The Left responded in kind, expropriating the property of aristocrats, burning churches, and forming militias. On 13 July 1936 tension reached its height with the assassination of right-wing politican José Calvo Sotelo by revenge-seeking Republicans. At this point the army stepped in.

Spain's creaking military, with one officer for every six soldiers, had a long tradition of meddling in politics. Orchestrated by Generals **Francisco Franco** and **Emiliano Mola**, simultaneous uprisings took place across Spain on 17 July. The government was panicked into inaction, but the workers' militias took control of the situation in many areas, and a substantial part of the army remained loyal to the Republic. Instead of the quick coup they had planned, the Generals got a Spain divided into two armed camps, and the **Civil War** was underway. Almost at once it became an international affair. Fascist Italy and Germany sent hundreds of aeroplanes and some 200,000 troops. The only government that helped the Republic were the Russians (all arms to be paid in gold); the Communists organized the famous International Brigades, but they were only a handful. The overwhelming imbalance of foreign help aiding Franco decided the war.

In the early days of the conflict, in November 1936, four Nationalist columns, including most of Franco's Army of Africa, advanced to positions within sight of the Palacio Real. The Republican government, certain that the capital would fall in a week, fled to Valencia—an act seen as abandonment in Madrid—leaving the defence of the city almost entirely in the hands of the newly formed Socialist, Communist and Anarchist militias. In the nick of time, morale was given an enormous boost with the arrival of the International Brigades and the first squadrons of Soviet aeroplanes and, as the world watched in suspense, Madrid held. '*No pasarán*'—'they shall not pass'—was the famous slogan coined by La Pasionara, and the city became a symbol that caught the imagination of Europe, the first community in that dark time to make a successful stand against Fascism. Madrid spent the rest of the war under siege, bombarded from the Casa de Campo and undergoing terrible privations. After Catalunya fell in January 1939 it was the sole holdout and, completely isolated, was forced to surrender in March 1939.

1939–75: Four Miserable Decades with Francisco Franco

Before the Civil War, Madrid had grown into a bright and cosmopolitan cultural capital; most of the glitter, as well as the substance, disappeared under 40 years of Franco. Badly damaged, both physically and spiritually, by the war, the first decade was especially dire. Franco's main concern was for revenge rather than any kind of reconciliation: there were massive reprisals against any and all Leftists or their sympathizers—some 200 to 250 people a day were shot in Madrid alone; two million Republicans altogether were sent to prison or labour camps, forced to build, among other things, Franco's chief monument, the Valle de los Caídos (see p.224). Any Republicans who escaped death or prison were just as likely to find their name on a blacklist, limiting their possibilities of travel or finding a decent job. The economy was in shambles, and while the rest of Europe was engaged in the Second World War, Spain suffered the 'years of hunger'.

Franco considered punishing Madrid even further by moving the capital to Seville, only to be foiled by the huge expense. Plans were then made to convert the city into an Imperial Fascist capital in the Hitlerian kitsch mode, but luckily there was no money in the pot for that either. Instead, the defeat of Franco's old allies in the Second World War saw the Caudillo scrambling to present Spain afresh as a bulwark against Communism and a safe haven for international capital. His efforts paid off in 1953, when Spain signed a treaty with the United States, exchanging military base sites for international respectability and a huge infusion of cash. To please his new friends, Franco dismantled the cumbersome Fascist economy and left the economy in the hands of a new generation of technocrats (many of them members of the secret Catholic society Opus Dei). Their reforms and the American loans began to pay off in the 1960s, when Spain experienced an industrial take-off that gave it the highest economic growth in the world—really just making up for lost time.

The Franco government, determined to see their Castilian capital outstrip Catalan, radical Barcelona, encouraged new industry and migration from other corners of Spain. Madrid's population in the 1960s rocketed to three million. But the environmental cost was high; once-lovely tree-lined boulevards were flattened into urban motorways, and the outskirts of the city were disfigured by wastelands of industry and shantytowns. Strikes and protests by students and faculty in the University led to frequent closings.

Confronted with inevitable social change, Franco remained stubbornly entrenched. A monarchist at heart, he declared in 1969 that his successor would be **Juan Carlos I**, grandson of Alfonso XIII and an unknown quantity, skipping over Juan Carlos' democratically minded father Don Juan. Meanwhile, clandestine political groups began to emerge, most of them just waiting for the old Caudillo to die. An exception was the Basques, who evolved the terrorist ETA. They first rose to prominence in 1973, when their master blasters assassinated Admiral Carrero Blanco, sending his limousine over the roof of a Madrid church. Carrero Blanco had been the ageing dictator's strong man and his best hope for the continuity of the regime. Franco found no one hard enough to replace him.

1975–: Madrid of the *Movida*

After Franco's death in 1975, however, Madrid's civic pride was allowed to resurface. King Juan Carlos surprised everyone by adroitly moving Spain back to a democracy. His choice for Prime Minister, Adolfo Suárez, an ex-Falange bureaucrat, proved to be another surpise when he set about reforming the government and preparing it for elections. The transition, though it had its hiccups, was smoother than anyone could have imagined; Suárez's centre-right UCD party won the first general election in 1977, with the recently legalized Socialist Workers' Party coming in as the main opposition. Spain was given one of the most liberal constitutions in Europe in 1978, and the long heritage of Castilian centralism was undone, making Spain a federal state of 17 autonomous communities, like Germany and the United States (Madrid is the centre of the Comunidad de Madrid). The new democracy easily survived the old guards' last hurrah, when the Guardia Civil under Colonel Tejero attempted a coup by occupying the Cortes in February 1981. Elements in the army were behind it, but they backed down when ordered to do so by the king.

In 1982 the real transition came, when general elections were won overwhelmingly by the Socialists under the suave Sevillian with the chipmunk cheeks, **Felipe González,** under whom Spain joined the European Union. As the Eighties progressed, the traditionally puritanical and austere Spaniards woke up to the attractions and pleasures of economic success, and Madrid found itself at the cutting edge of a social revolution. Earning (or otherwise acquiring) vast sums became a fashionable compulsion, and the popular press hispanicized the term '*los beautiful people*' for the new, money-flaunting jetset that filled Madrid's restaurants and *terrazas*. The 1980s was the decade of the *movida Madrileña*, when bars sprang up throughout the city, legalized drug consumption flourished, and under a Socialist government's patronage the arts underwent not so much a renaissance, as a resurrection.

Former university professor **Enrique Tierno Galván**, who was elected Socialist mayor of Madrid in 1979, was seen by many as the sponsor and orchestrator of the city's great cultural revival. A remarkable mayor, he dedicated himself to improving the city's quality of life; he planted thousands of trees, created new parks in the outlying districts, poured money into the arts, repaired some of the damage done by the traffic planners, and even found some water to direct through the dusty stream bed of the city's oldest joke, the so-called river Manzanares. *Madrileños* nicknamed Tierno 'The Old Professor' for his habit of lecturing them on the importance of trees and greenery, and all of them, regardless of politics, mourned his death in 1986.

In the first five years after Spain joined the European Union, its economy grew faster than that of any other member country and, as property prices soared, Madrid benefitted from much needed investment. Art fever gripped the city with the success of ARCO, Madrid's annual contemporary art fair, the opening of the Reina Sofía modern art museum and the acquisition of the famous Thyssen-Bornemisza collection. In 1991, the right-wing Partido Popular gained control of Madrid's regional parliament, and, under Mayor **José María Alvarez del Manzano**, one of their first priorities was to set about making final preparations for Spain's golden year of celebrations, 1992. Barcelona had won the Olympics, Seville was hosting the World Fair, and Madrid came in a rather poor third as European Cultural Capital.

As it turned out, Madrid's contribution to the 1992 celebrations was not particularly remarkable; many of the projects planned to mark the event, such as the re-opening of the Opera, were still unfinished. But it was at the end of the year that the real blow came. For three years Felipe González's government had been artificially warding off an economic slump by pouring money into construction projects to furnish the nation for the celebrations. Even before the year-long fiesta was over, recession hit hard, with all the usual trappings—high unemployment, high interest rates, and currency devaluation. Nobody appreciated this sudden downturn, and, in the 1993 general election, the Socialist party PSOE, its name already blackened by corruption scandals, lost control of the greater Madrid area to the new conservative Partida Popular. In 1996, the PP's **José Maria Aznar** won the general elections. For the future, the right's hold on the capital looks assured.

Madrid has now come to terms with the fact that the boom years are over; although city life has lost the hedonistic, opportunistic sparkle and easy glamour that distinguished it in the swinging Eighties, the *madrileñan* spirit is not dampened easily, and there's as much optimism as caution built into their image of the future. Meanwhile, restoration of the old neighbourhoods continues (at the time of writing, half of the city seems to be swathed in scaffolding) and the metro and airport are expanding, as if preparing the stage for the next act.

Architecture

Madrid may have some of the most fabulous art collections of any city in the world, but most cities in Spain have grander, older and more beautiful buildings. Even after Madrid was made the capital, the Habsburg and Bourbon obsession with constructing palaces was inflicted on suburban locations, leaving the city (with a few notable exceptions) to its own devices. Until the late 18th century, most of what was built was of cheap brick or rubble and mortar; with the high transport costs in a city without a seaport or proper river it could hardly be otherwise. Secondly, like Dublin, Madrid is a city of theatre and literature rather than architecture, and like Dubliners the *madrileños* in the past two centuries have knocked down rather a lot of historic buildings. The surrounding cities of Castile have been less hasty, however; if you need a fix of Old Spain, Toledo and Segovia are among its most beautiful examplars, both easy day trips from the capital.

Very little survives of Madrid prior to 1561, when Philip II made it the capital. The oldest buildings are a pair of simple brick towers (San Nicolás de las Servitas and San Pedro el Viejo) built by the **Mudéjars**, or Christianized Moors after the Reconquista; to see their masterpieces of decorative, geometric brickwork and *azulejo* tiles, you only have to go to Toledo. Toledo, in its cathedral, also has the best example of the succeeding **Gothic** style, inspired by the French; in Madrid there's the Lunares tower, but nearly everything else from the era was destroyed.

By the late 15th century, Castilian Gothic evolved into a style similar to English Perpendicular known as **Isabelline Gothic** (San Juan de los Reyes, in Toledo). This in turn led to the uniquely Spanish Renaissance style called the **Plateresque** (from the *plateros* or 'silversmiths') characterized by lavish sculptural decoration and façades, providing a striking contrast with the simpler lines of the rest of the building. Madrid has examples, in the Capilla del Obispo and the façade of the Casa de Cisernos, but again, some of the best in Spain is just outside Madrid: Alcalá de Henares university and the sculptural decoration of Sigüenza cathedral.

Philip II's obsession with the construction of El Escorial may have spared his capital some frigid symmetry of its own; as it is, the death palace was far enough away to avoid infecting Madrid's organic squalor. The king did, however, begin the custom of appointing municipal architects to develop Madrid, beginning with **Juan Gómez de Mora**. Mora was a follower of El Escorial's chief architect, **Juan de Herrera**, whose austere *estilo desornamentado*, with its characteristic Flemish slate-topped towers and decorative motif of obelisks and balls (a favourite conceit of Philip's, derived from his days in Flanders), may be seen in the Habsburg-era buildings in Madrid proper—the Plaza Mayor, the Casa de la Villa (city hall) and the Palacio de Santa Cruz; Herrera himself designed the stately Puente de Segovia over the Manzanares to provide Philip II with a quick escape from Madrid to the surrounding hunting grounds.

All of these are marked by an understated reserve, almost as if there was a tacit agreement to keep the canvas blank for the actors—the citizens—to write their own stories. This restraint also characterizes the surviving convents and churches from the reigns of Philips III and IV. Unfortunately the one Habsburg building that might have balanced the record, Philip IV's lavish Palacio del Buen Retiro, was damaged in the Peninsular War and later demolished.

The Bourbons of the early 18th century desired to make Madrid look more like a proper European capital, and brought in Italians to do the job, beginning with Philip V's Palacio Real, designed by Filippo Juvarra and Saccheti. These were only the first of the late Baroque Italian architects and artists who would wash up in Madrid—Giambattista Tiepolo, Luca Cambiaso, and Luca Giordano were others.

Meanwhile, Madrid was blessed with a *corregidor*, the Marqués de Vadillo, who made the homegrown **Pedro de Ribera** municipal architect. Pedro di Ribera introduced **Baroque** to Madrid, Spanish-style, combining austere Herreran symmetry with lavish, oozing surface decoration known as **Churrigueresque** after the Churriguera family that made it famous, and with whom Ribera sometime worked. Ribera left Madrid a number of fine buildings—the Puente de Toledo, the Cuartel Conde Duque barracks (now a cultural centre), the delightful Ermita de la Virgen del Puerto, and the Hospicio de San Fernando (now the Museo Municipal).

Charles III and his Enlightenment philosophy put him firmly into the **neo-classical** camp of the late 18th century, and his favourite architect-engineer was another Italian, **Francesco Sabatini**, author of the Puerta de Alcalá and hospital that now holds the Reina Sofia museum. Towards the end of his reign, in Charles III's pet Paseo del Prado project, two Spanish architects left a greater imprint on Madrid: **Juan de Villanueva**, who built the Observatory and the Prado, an exceptionally elegant neo-classical palace and one of the first in Europe especially designed to hold a museum (of natural history), and the more decorative and fanciful **Ventura Rodríguez**, who became the city's master fountain builder.

The reign of Isabel II saw the height of Madrid's characteristically eclectic 19th-century architecture dominated by a taste for the French Second Empire, especially in the fancy houses of the Salamanca district and the big banks that sprouted up along Calle de Alcalá. A late 19th-century reaction to this foreign fashion was the fancy brickwork and playful geometry of **Neo-mudéjar**, a revival of 'Spain's national style' led by Rodríguez Ayuso. It found its greatest expression in Madrid over the next few decades, in the Ministry of Agriculture, in the church of the Virgen de La Paloma, and especially in Las Ventas bullring.

A cosmopolitan eclecticism with references to Spain's past would continue to dominate well into the 20th century, most strikingly along the Gran Vía, a street opened up in 1910 to provide a setting for Madrid's first skyscrapers. The magnificent Art Nouveau style or *modernismo* of Barcelona never caught on in Madrid (although it has one celebrated example, the Sociedad de los Autores), but Art Deco fared better. One of Madrid's chief architects into the 1920s was **Antonio Palacio**, capable of such varied buildings as the Hollywoodesque Palacio de Communicacions and the cooler Círculo de Bellas Artes. On the domestic side, the El Viso residential area north of Salamanca is one of the most interesting Art Deco projects in Europe. The dictatorship of Primo de Rivera in the '20s initiated some of Madrid's biggest and heaviest projects: the Nuevos Ministerios and the University City, both of which would be completed under Franco. Perhaps Primo's most appreciated legacy was the founding of the *parador* hotels in historic buildings.

Franco's ingrained atavism and imperial pretentions are reflected in the grandiose and flaccid architecture he gave Madrid—modernist plainness embellished with Herreran doodads, in the Edicifico España (1953), or the nearby Ministerio del Aire, a Disney-like replica of El Escorial. Like Philip II, however, Franco concentrated his attention on constructing an extraordinary Pantheon for his dead—in this case for the Nationalists of the Civil War, in the Valle de Caídos.

The desperate state of Spain's economy constricted building until the take-off in the 1960s, although much of this was in the form of anonymous *urbanizaciónes* in the dreary outskirts, thrown up to house the swelling population drawn by Franco's industrialization of Madrid. As Spain opened up to the West, so Madrid's architects opened up to the rationalism, functionalism, and modernism of the International style, beginning with **Luis Gutíerez Soto**, who introduced all of the above to Madrid in the 1950s, after a trip to the USA. His more imaginative colleagues, **Alejandro de la Sota** and **Francisco Saénz de Oíza**, are considered the 'fathers' of Madrid's current crop of architects; they have filled the Paseo de la Castellana with enormous bank, insurance and corporate headquarter towers, gleaming like trophies over the busy street. Among the most audacious are Europe's first leaning towers since the Middle Ages—the Puerta de Europa, completed in 1996.

Under the previous Socialist administration, Madrid also became the theatre for a slew of new schools, community and neighbourhood cultural centres, and public housing. The conservative Partido Popular has since put the brakes on, and focuses its attention on restoration of old Madrid and more commerical enterprises. Many of the recent media-grabbing projects in Madid since the 1990s have been conversions of historic buildings, in which Saénz de Oíza's student, **Rafael Moneo**, has proved himself to be the master (the Thyssen Museum and Atocha Station). In the next millennium, look forward to the long deferred expansion of the Prado, but at the time of writing exactly how, who, what, where and why has yet to be decided.

La Villa del Oso y Madroño   40

Air, Light and Litter   41

Getting Real: the *Castizos*   42

The *Ciudad Lineal*   44

La Movida: Swinging Madrid   45

The Spanish Match   46

Visions in Silence   47

Bullfights   48

No Pasarán   50

Tales of Madrid

La Villa del Oso y Madroño

In spite of its relative youth, the capital of Spain has a strong character all of its own. First of all, it may have 4 million inhabitants, but Madrid is not even a city or *ciudad*—it's still a *villa*, or town, just as it was in 1202 when it had all of 3,000 souls and received its first statutes from the crown. When it became the capital, it became the *Villa y Corte*. And so it remains to this day.

In particular, Madrid is the *villa* of the bear and strawberry tree. You'll see this totem everywhere, from weathervanes down to the old sewer lids. Where the city found such a peculiar emblem, however, is a rather sticky subject. Most sources explain the bear, the older symbol (it appeared on a wax seal for the first time in 1381, although with a tower instead of a tree) by saying there were once plenty of them around Madrid. One bear in particular, an enormous specimen killed by King Alfonso XI in the late 13th century, made such an impression that it is recorded in his biography or *Crónica*. There is some doubt, however, that the king's bear is precisely *the* bear, which, according to a petition from the city to Emperor Charles V in 1548, is not an *oso* but an *osa*, a she bear, a heraldic symbol of fertility—in particular ursine fertility, meaning more big game, which was Madrid's big attraction to the kings of Castile in the first place.

As for the strawberry tree or *Arbutus unedo*, according to some, the fact that *madroño* (its name in Spanish) has the same first syllable as Madrid explains it all; all the other cities of Castile had castles or towers on their arms, so Madrid adopted a tree just to be different. This is a pretty boring story so over the years better ones have arisen. Some say that Madrid once had forests of these little evergreens (it now has two, to be precise, both in front of the building at Calle del Madroño 4, near the bullring), and that bears, when their eyes hurt, seek out strawberry trees to rub their eyes against the prickly exterior of the tree's fruit. Others say that in the Middle Ages the leaves of the strawberry tree were considered a remedy for the plague, which is why the bear seems to be licking the tree as if it were a giant lollipop. Or that in the 13th century, when Madrid was divided into parishes, the town and the clergy went to court over ownership of some land, and it was divided in a curious fashion: the Church got the meadows and the town got all the land under the trees. The Madrid clergy, they say, had a bear grazing in a field for its emblem, while the city bear loves its trees.

The seven stars from the constellation of the Big Dipper or Plough or Big Bear, Ursus Major, were added much later, under Charles V in 1544. According to the document that made the symbol official, the stars merely symbolized the beautiful clear sky over the city, but others will have it that the stars of the constellation were rearranged to form a crown, hence the city's fancy title *Coronado Villa de Madrid*.

Even with a million cars in the metropolitan area, the skies of Madrid are still clear and startlingly blue. Height has something to do with it. On the lofty central plateau of Castile, where the air is thin, the sun becomes a manifest power; at noon, even on a cool day, it can seem like some diabolical ray, probing deep inside your brain. Always, it illuminates with a merciless brilliance; Spanish writers evoke it when trying to explain their country's literature and history. 'Spain,' according to one, 'is a country where things can be seen all too clearly.' Spanish art could not be what it is without this light. In the Prado, you'll look at Goya paintings set under an impossibly lovely pale blue sky with clouds like the breath of angels. You'll probably blame the arist for picturesque excess—and then walk outside to find that same Castilian sky, and those same clouds, reproduced over your head. There is a famous saying in the city, '*De Madrid al Cielo*': from Madrid the next stop is heaven itself.

Madrid's air is equally renowned, though with somewhat less lyricism. The winds off the Sierra sweep away the pollution caused by a million cars, but according to a famous proverb it 'will not extinguish a candle, but will put out a man's life'. One 18th-century traveller noted: 'it is like quick lime, drying and consuming a corpse in a trice'. Doctors believed the air was so potent that it would be toxic unless humans were there to dilute it with fetid exhalations. One worried doctor did a census and estimated that 10,000 turds a day (there was no sanitation) hit the streets of Madrid, much to everyone's relief. 'That which one shits in the winter, one drinks in the summer,' they used to say. One reason why a transhumance trail passed through the centre of Madrid for centuries was the notion that hundreds of thousands of sheep with their dirty fleece running through the city somehow kept the plague at bay.

Madrid has reformed somewhat since then, and now has excellent drinking water and sewers (to the extent that one of the Nationalist commanders, an aristocratic caricature named Captain Aguilera, blamed the creation of the Republic on good sewers, which allowed too much riffraff to survive). Still, the city hardly aspires to anything as anally retentive as tidy streets. The streets after all are merely an extension of Madrid's bars, which are often ankle deep in paper napkins, toothpicks, olive pits, and shrimp heads. In the late 1980s, in the heyday of the *movida*, statistics showed that every single morning the street cleaners in the city centre were amassing, among other items such as beds and tables, nearly a million and a half cigarette butts, 2,280kg of paper, 7,400 syringes, and 120,000 sanitary towels. The late mayor Tierno Galván, gamely struggling to get the *madrileños* to clean up their act, declared that: 'a growing number of our citizens throw paper and litter on the ground which the city pays more and more citizens to go around and pick up. If we continue in this manner, soon we will reach the stage where half the population litters the streets with garbage while the other half gathers it up.'

Getting Real: the *Castizos*

Although Madrid is both the microcosm of Spain and its greatest melting pot, where the majority of inhabitants have parents or grandparents from somewhere else, there has always been an attachment to authenticity. In the bad old days of the 17th century, this translated into a neurotic obsession with *limpieza de sangre*, or purity of blood: the discovery by the Inquisition of a Jewish or Moorish great grandparent in a man's family tree was enough to get him sacked from a high position in the Church or Court.

The wealthy, as usual, found ways to take care of themselves, while in the 19th century the people in the working class *barrios*—La Latina, Lavapiés, and Chamberí, developed their own brand of authenticity. Their denizens are the real McCoy, the *castizos*, 'true born' children of the city, not unlike the Cockneys in London. The word, which originally applied to anything distinctly Spanish, has since been taken over for whatever is genuinely Madrid, from stew to a painting by Goya to the ultimate *castizo* art form, the *zarzuela*.

The *castizo* neighbourhoods come into their own during the fiestas, or *verbenas*—beginning with San Isidro in May, and reaching a climax with the Virgen de la Paloma in August, when everyone in Madrid can dress the part: the men as *chulos* (from *chaul*, the Arabic for lad) in flat caps, tight black trousers, neck scarves and waistcoats, their female counterparts as *chulapas* in full flounced skirts, flowery shawls with fringes and head scarves, set back to reveal the de rigueur carnation in the hair. They dance a quick-stepping dance called the *chotis*, derived they say from the Scottish jigs danced in Madrid by British troops in the Peninsular War, with a bit of the Wild West saloon stomp thrown in.

But *castizos* have never been anyone's fashion's slave, not since the days of their dandified ancestors, known either as *manolos* (*see* p.79) or *majos*, a word derived from the old May Day festivities, when everyone dressed in their best. While other European men duly conformed to the late 18th-century style of skirted frock coat, wig and tricorn hat, the *majos* pulled their long hair back in hair nets, wore short jackets with many buttons over embroidered shirts, wrapped themselves in long cloaks, and wore large brimmed hats. Their female equivalent, the *majas*, dressed in full mid-calf skirts, embroidered bodices, white stockings with a dagger in the garter, and a black lace mantilla over their complicated hair. Goya's depictions of Madrid's *majos* were so popular that even the nobility liked to pose for him in the costume. One of his favourite subjects was the festive pilgrimage or *romeria* of St Isidro, Madrid's patron saint, showing the *majos* and *majas* dancing Madrid's beautiful native dance, the *bolero*; performed with castanets, with intricate ballet-like toe work and a good deal of flexible upper body work, its very difficulty condemned it to fall from popularity. You'd have to be very lucky to see it on Madrid's dance floors today, among the more popular *sevillanas* and *pasodobles*.

As the song goes, 'It ain't what you do, it's the way that you do it.' From the days of the *majos*, *castizo* has also been about attitude, a swaggering easygoing jauntiness, a streetwise cockiness and quick sharp wit. Thanks to Franco and modern mass culture, this saucy attitude has been somewhat diluted, although not lost altogether; if your Spanish is up to scratch, you can hear the verbal rapiers of the descendants of the *majos* and *majas* in any neighbourhood bar in La Latina and Lavapiés.

Castizo wit and repartee inspired the composers of the *zarzuela*, Madrid's own contribution to Spanish popular culture. The name derives from the operatic entertainments written by Calderón de la Barca and performed for Philip IV in the Palacio de la Zarzuela (now the main residence of King Juan Carlos I). Popularized in the 18th century, these developed into light, sentimental operatic comedies, a cross between Gilbert and Sullivan and soap opera, many of which are set in Madrid's intimate 19th-century tenements, the *corralas*. The subjects are usually everyday subjects, or topical ones—one of the biggest *zarzuela* hits of 1910 was about the opening of the Gran Vía. All are performed with a mix of witty dialogue, song and dance. The parents of Placido Domingo were singers in the *zarzuela*; Charlie Chaplin borrowed the story of one, *La Violetera*, for his *City Lights*.

Zarzuela hit its peak at the end of the 19th century, but was still going strong until the Civil War and the utterly humourless dictatorship that followed it. Since then, however, it has enjoyed something of a revival, and while not many new productions are hitting the boards, there are revivals of the classics in the summer. The *zarzuela* performed *in situ*, at La Corrala in Lavapiés (*see* p.78) is the best way to see one; the favourite is the classic *La Revoltosa* by Rupero Chapí, where all the action takes place in a similar tenement house.

The *Ciudad Lineal*

Arturo Soria y Mata was a *madrileño* who got his fingers into everything that moved in his native town. Born in 1844, he made a career as a journalist and a pro-Republican politician, while finding time to invent an improved telegraph, and working unsuccessfully to bring telephones and subways to the city when such things were still new toys. In the 1880s he helped build Madrid's first streetcar line, and it was this interest in transportation that led Soria to become interested in the design of cities.

Madrid, booming, dirty and overcrowded like all the capitals of Europe a century ago, was full of discontents, and Soria, writing in the newspaper *El Progreso*, came up with a startlingly original remedy—the *Ciudad Lineal*, the Linear City.

It was a truly remarkable concept, and a simple one: a broad central street with separate tracks for long-distance trains and local trolleys in the middle, along with a single tunnel for telephone and electric cables and gas mains. On either side of this, a block or two of houses, and no more. Everyone who lived in the Ciudad Lineal would be a minute's walk from shops and efficient public transport, and a minute's walk from open countryside. Soria promoted his idea as the perfect form for the adaptation of the city to modern technology, and he imagined his linear cities one day running from Cadiz to St Petersburg, and from Peking to Brussels.

Madrid is one of the few places in the world where a utopian plan like this could not only be imagined, but actually attempted. Even then, however, the project didn't turn out to be exactly what Soria had in mind. He started a development firm, the Compañía Madrileña de Urbanización, but the only land he was able to acquire for a linear city was not between two existing towns, but on the periphery of the Madrid suburbs between Chamartín station and the eastern reaches of Calle de Alcalá. The plan is still visible on any city map—two neatly parallel rows of blocks on either side of a broad boulevard, still just as Soria designed them. Only instead of passing through open country, the Ciudad Lineal now is part of one of the busiest neighbourhoods of Madrid—unfortunately, Soria was not able to stop other developers from building up all the land on either side. Visiting the site today, you will hardly see a hint of the original intention. But the world's planners still honour Soria as one of the most original urban designers ever, and the city of Madrid has commemorated him with the Ciudad Lineal metro stop, and with the central street of the original development, now named Calle Arturo Soria.

La Movida: Swinging Madrid

As novel as it seemed almost two decades ago, historians tell us that the *movida* was nothing new: in the time of Philip III, when Madrid was the capital of an empire, it was considered the second best party city after Paris. If not sex, drugs and rock'n'roll, there was plenty of sex, wine and *boleros* to draw in pleasure-seekers from across Europe. It was the start of a distinguished tradition. Sometime between then and now the *madrileños* acquired their nickname, *los gatos*, the 'cats', for their nocturnal habits.

Although you may well think Madrid still burns the candle at both ends, *madrileños* wax nostalgic about the boom years of the 1980s, when four decades of creativity and energy pent-up under Franco suddenly exploded on the scene, and Madrid swung like a pendulum on speed and declared itself the capital of the world. The Socialists' hearty support of the arts and culture, the rise of a vibrant counterculture, the general prosperity and good times, liberal drug laws, and the *madrileños'* own appetite for fun combined to make a heady decade of white nights. Their feet never seemed to touch the ground, as *la marcha* swept them from bar to bar in a frenetic cacophany of laughter, smoke and high spirits, recorded in the films of Pedro Almodóvar, the Pied Piper of the *movida*, and one of the very few figures to come out of the whirlwind with an international reputation. Some find fault there, but that seems unfair: the *movida* was essentially a Madrid thing that defied translation, or translocation. You had to be there.

The inevitable hangover began when the bills came due, even before Spain's great year of 1992 had ended. The Socialists were slowly washed away in a tide of scandal and corruption, the wilder clubs and bars were forced to close, and funding for the arts and festivals got slashed. The huge energy of the *movida* has split into various scenes or *ambientes*, including a very lively gay scene that attracts trendy straights. The current right-wing administration, representing a Silent Majority who like to retire early, has been agitating furiously to squeeze Madrid into the mould of a respectable northern European-style capital, to the point of writing laws that would fine people for waiting for a bus outside a bus shelter, and closing down the bars at 3am. Fortunately no one pays much attention; the *gatos* are still prowling most nights until dawn, or well into the morning, only now they do it mostly on weekends (which usually start on Thursday).

The Spanish Match

Spain in the 17th century made itself the true homeland of the picaresque, the inspiration for the first novels, and Spaniards set the fashions and the manners for all Europe in the age of Baroque. Life was a stage, and a man wasn't a man until he'd gone out and had an adventure—even if he was the son of a king. In Calle de las Infantas, just north of the Gran Vía, there stands an old residence called the 'Casa de las Siete Chimeneas', the house of seven chimneys. In 1623, this house belonged to John Digby, Earl of Bristol, in Spain on government business, and in March of that year it received a very unusual lodger—none other than the 21-year-old Prince of Wales, the future Charles I. Charles had travelled to Spain incognito, with his friend the Duke of Buckingham, using the names of 'John Brown and Tom Smith'. The Earl, who was keeping an eye on Charles for his father, James I, wrote home that the pair were 'sweet boys and dear virtuous knights, worthy to be put in a new *romanso*'.

The visit had a purpose; Spain and England were enjoying a rare period of peace, and there was talk of marrying Charles to the Infanta Doña Maria. Naturally, he wanted to have a look at her first. Riding to Spain was the easy part; getting into the court of Philip IV, who didn't much care for Protestant heretics, proved much harder. Charles first saw his Infanta when their coaches passed in a Madrid street; later, go-betweens managed to contrive a meeting during the *paseo* on the Prado—Charles would know her by the blue ribbon in her hair. When word of this got out, Charles' presence could no longer be kept a secret; more and more English were arriving all the time to see the show, including King James's celebrated fool, Archie Armstrong. Finally the king consented to a state entrance for Charles in the biggest spectacle Madrid had to offer, a gala bullfight in the Plaza Mayor with all the court in attendance, watching from the balconies.

Charles apparently liked what he saw (according to Olivares, he devoured the Infanta with his eyes 'like a cat does a mouse'), for he tried without success to surprise her in the Casa del Campo, where she and her friends were out at dawn gathering May dew. But this is history, not a romanso, and politics and religion made it a match never to be. Charles stayed in Madrid for six months; he met Velázquez and Van Dyck, and went back home with presents from the royal family that included paintings by Titian and Correggio, an elephant, an ostrich and five camels. This began Charles's own career as an art collector, and he amassed quite a remarkable collection before he lost his head. His philistine Roundhead successors had no use for such trumperies and sold them off at a ridiculous price—to the king of Spain.

Every century and a half, it seems, an artist is born in Spain who is destined to reinvent painting. Between Velázquez (1599) and Picasso (1881) there was Francisco de Goya y Lucientes, born in an Aragonese village in 1746. Goya's life came in the form of two distinct stages, so wildly different as to seem like two different artists, and separated by a strange interlude. In 1775, he came to Madrid, and spent the next seventeen years doing little but cartoons for the Real Fábrica de Tapices. Cartoons seems a misleading word; they had to be complete paintings, perfect in line and colour, each the full size of the tapestry that would be copied from it. Some of these were over 20ft wide, and the indefatigable Goya managed 63 of them in those 17 years. Most are now in the Prado, and their sweetly colourful, dreamlike scenes are as much of a revelation to many visitors as the more famous paintings that came later.

The strange interlude's name was Maria Cayetana, Duchess of Alba. Goya met this beautiful and alarming widow at the court around 1786, and rumours of their affair scandalized Madrid. Goya may have used her as the model for the naked and clothed Majas (some art historians, incidentally, guess that the two paintings were designed to be exchanged behind a panel by a hidden mechanism). Partly due to the Duchess's influence, Goya became court painter in 1786, with a salary of 15,000 reales. For a few years the artist was at the top of the world; friends found him 'intoxicated by fame'. In 1792, he picked up a serious disease, probably syphilis, that left him stone deaf.

During his convalescence, Goya began to sketch small fantasy scenes to take his mind off his sufferings, probably unaware that he was beginning one of the strangest voyages ever taken through the Western mind. For the rest of his life, the fantastical world would be his stock in trade; the first work of the new Goya was the incredible series of engravings called *Los Caprichos* (also in the Prado). Done in the shadow of the French Revolution and Napoleon, they evoke a world strangely akin to that of Goya's contemporary William Blake. The inscription for one of these engravings could serve as a motto for the rest of Goya's work: *the sleep of reason produces monsters*. Next came his grotesque portraits of the royal family, the *Disasters of War*, and finally the apocalyptic vortex of the *Black Paintings*, painted on the walls of his country house outside Madrid, the Quinto del Sordo (house of the deaf man), and now too in the Prado.

Rulers from Charles IV (who thought the portraits were all too true) to Joseph Bonaparte to the horrible Ferdinand VII all recognized Goya's talent and let him do as he liked, even though Ferdinand once told him. 'If we did not admire you so much, you would deserve garotting.' In 1824, the king allowed his painter to move to Bordeaux for health reasons; perhaps he had suffered too much Spain and needed someplace foggy and drear. Goya worked right until the end, always innovating and perfecting his technique, and died in Bordeaux in 1828 at the age of 82; if his last works are any indication, if he lasted any longer he might have invented Impressionism.

Bullfights

In the newspapers, don't look for accounts of the bullfights (*corridas*) on the sports pages; look in the 'arts and culture' section, for that is how Spain has always thought of this singular spectacle. Bullfighting combines elements of ballet with the primal finality of Greek tragedy. To Spaniards it is a ritual sacrifice without a religion, and it divides the nation irreconcilably between those who find it brutal and demeaning, an echo of the old Spain best forgotten, and those who couldn't live without it. Its origins are obscure. Some claim it comes ultimately from the bull games of Minoan Crete, or from Roman circus games, others say it started with the Moors, or in the Middle Ages, when the bull faced a mounted knight with a lance, a practice called *rejoneo*; the first recorded one in Madrid took place in 1474.

Modern bullfighting, like that other ultra-Spanish art form, flamenco, is quintessentially Andalucian. The present form had its beginnings around the year 1800 in Ronda, when Francisco Romero developed the basic pattern of the modern *corrida*; some of his moves and passes, and those of his celebrated successor, Pedro Romero, are still in use today. The first royal *aficionado* was Ferdinand VII, who promoted the spectacle across the land as a circus for the discontented populace.

In keeping with its ritualistic aura, the *corrida* is one of the few things in Spain that begins strictly on time. The show commences with the colourful entry of the *cuadrillas* (teams of bullfighters or *toreros*) and the *alguaciles*, officials dressed in 17th-century costume, who salute the 'president' of the fight. Usually three teams fight two bulls each, the whole show taking only about two hours. Each of the six fights, however, is a self-contained drama performed in four acts. First, upon the entry of the bull, the members of the *cuadrilla* tease him a bit, and the *matador*, the team leader, plays him with the cape to test his qualities. Next comes the turn of the *picadores*, on padded horses, whose task is to slightly wound the bull in the neck with a short lance or *pica*, and the *banderilleros*, who agilely plant sharp darts in the bull's back while avoiding the sweep of its horns. The effect of these wounds is to weaken the bull physically without diminishing any of its fighting spirit, and to force it to keep its head lower for the third and most artistic stage of the fight, when the lone *matador* conducts his pas de deux with the deadly, if doomed, animal. Ideally, this is the transcendent moment, the *matador* leading the bull in deft passes and finally crushing its spirit with a tiny cape called a *muleta*. Now the defeated bull is ready for 'the moment of truth' and dedicated to a member of the audience. Silence falls. The kill must be clean and quick, a sword thrust to the heart; ideally the bull dies in seconds. The corpse is dragged out to the waiting butchers.

More often than not the job is botched, and the always vociferous crowd is merciless in its criticism. Most bullfights, in fact, are a disappointment, especially if the *matadores* are beginners, or *novios*, but to the *aficionado* the chance to see one or all of the stages performed to perfection makes it all worthwhile. When a *matador* is good, the band plays and the hats and handkerchiefs fly to the shouts of *olé, olé!* (from the Moorish *Allah! Allah!*). A truly excellent, spine-tingling performance earns as a reward from the president one, or both, of the bull's ears; or rarely, for an exceptionally brilliant performance, both ears and the tail. A spirited bull who puts on a good show can get the thumbs up from the crowd, and get a return ticket to the ranch.

Since the Civil War, bullfighting has gone through a period of troubles similar to those of boxing in the USA. Scandals of weak bulls, doped-up bulls and bulls with the points of their horns shaved have been frequent. Attempts at reform have been made, and while it was commonly thought it would all lead to a decline in bullfighting's popularity, the opposite has occurred. More people than ever, from all walks of society, flock to the bulls, and some of the young star *toreros* have attained the celebrity status that pop singers have elsewhere: José Tomás, the heart-throb Jesulín de Ubrique, Enrique Ponce, El de Galapagar, and Cristina Sánchez, the best of the few women who have taken up the cape. Major fights are nationally televised.

There are bullrings all over Spain, and as far afield as Arles in France and Guadalajara, Mexico, but Madrid's striking neo-Mudéjar arena, Las Ventas, is the high shrine of the art, the Carnegie Hall for *toreros*. The season runs from March to October, but the best time to come for the bulls is May, during the month-long Fiesta of St Isidro, when there are fights nearly every day. Note that tickets (no credit cards) are sold only two days in advance at the ring and range from 1000 pts for a cheap seat in the full sun (*sol*) to 12,000 pts or more for the best seat in the shade (*sombra*); buy directly from the office at Las Ventas to avoid the hefty commission charges. No matter where you sit, rent a cushion, and buy a sandwich wrapped in foil from one of the nearby bars, where, not surprisingly, the speciality on the menu is *rabo de toro*—stewed bull's tail.

Madrid is fond of remembering 2 May 1808, when its citizens spontaneously rose up against the Napoleonic invader, but you won't find any monuments to its equally heroic stand in the Civil War. A dispassionate observer might say that on both occasions, Madrid's spirited citizen defence was in fact counterproductive, and that if they had just given in to the superior force, the *madrileños* would have been much better off at the end of the day. But the fact that on two occasions Madrid proved 'to have more balls than the horse of Espartero', as they say in the capital (referring to the well-endowed horse on the monument to General Baldomero Espartero, on Calle de Alcalá), has given this city, the creation of kings and their court, a distinction and pride independent of its government. Franco did all he could to crush it for four decades, but didn't succeed. Madrid has a soul of its own, and it's very much alive, even after the frenetic race to make up for lost time in the 1980s' *movida*.

The 1936 coup led by Generals Franco and Mola had thrown Madrid into revolutionary high gear. Everyone was addressed informally as *tú*, the grand hotels were commandeered by trade unionists, the schools were radicalized, and as the four Nationalist columns massed in the Casa del Campo and besieged the city, the cars of the wealthy were taken over to transport troops to the front. It was a time of extremes: members of the armed forces and the police either supported the Nationalists or were suspected of doing so, and order and discipline went by the wayside. Churches were burned and priests and nuns killed, as the Church openly supported the rebels.

The situation worsened when the Republican government, giving up the capital for lost, fled to Valencia (6 November 1936), leaving panic and disarray behind, increased by tales of atrocities committed by Franco's Moorish troops and General Mola's boasting of a 'Fifth Column' of sympathizers supposedly hidden within the city. It was just propaganda, but a new phrase was born, and the city's prisons were evacuated of potentially dangerous right-wing sympathizers, some 2000 of whom were shot. Even the man left behind by the government to defend Madrid, General José Miaja, was certain that he had been chosen as a sacrificial lamb in a hopeless cause.

Franco's relief of the defenders of the Alcázar in Toledo, while a bonanza for Nationalist propaganda (another word that became known worldwide in the Civil War), allowed Madrid to prepare its defence. Most importantly, it allowed time for the arrival of arms from the Soviet Union (paid for with half of Spain's gold reserves) and the first units of the International Brigades, many of them German and Italian exiles who knew Fascism only too well. They would comprise about a fifth of Madrid's defenders, and their presence was a tremendous morale booster for the besieged city. They also gave the citizen militias quick lessons in the street tactics they had learned battling the Fascists back home.

The Republican government's absence allowed the Communists to play a leading role in the capital's defence, and eventually in the entire war. The most flamboyant of them all, Dolores Ibárruri, better known as 'La Pasionara', rallied the *madrileños* with her speeches: 'Madrid will be the tomb of Fascism!' and 'They shall not pass!' and 'It is better to die on your feet than live on your knees.' Their untrained fighters, many women among them, wore street clothes, held meetings to discuss tactics with the officers, and some actually commuted daily to the front on the metro. By mid-November, Madrid's southern suburbs and the University City were the scenes of savage hand-to-hand fighting. Bombardments from the Nationalists hit the poorer *barrios* hard but avoided the wealthy homes of the Salamanca neighbourhood, where Mola's 'Fifth Columnists' presumably lived.

Franco's Moorish army came very close to capturing the centre of Madrid in late November 1936, only to be repulsed by the people in a stirring defence. Franco ordered an end to the attack, and General Miaja was declared a popular hero. But the result was a stalemate. In the Casa del Campo, Franco's army settled in for an intermittent siege; signs of the trenches remain, as well as the occasional unexploded shell (one was found during the recent expansion of the zoo). Republican attempts to push them back failed.

As the siege dragged on for three years, the lawlessness in Madrid that had prevailed over the previous months was replaced with an almost surreal normality; the papers went back to reporting social occasions and theatre reviews, while Franco's artillery aimed its fusillades along the Gran Vía, otherwise known 'Avenida de los Obuses' (Howitzer Avenue). Despite the danger, nearly all the Gran Vía's shops remained open behind walls of bricks and sandbags. The *madrileños* became used to living in metro stations, just as Londoners would a few years later during the Blitz. Food and fuel were difficult to find; thousands of trees were chopped down in the severe winter of 1937–38, and furniture and even doors were burned for heat. Most people survived on a daily ration of lentils, 'Dr Negrin's victory pills'. By late 1938, when the Republic's money was almost worthless, a barter economy took over. One telling story of the time concerns a gentleman going up to a market stall with a painting by Velázquez under his arm, which he offered to exchange for two tins of condensed milk. 'Is it a real Velázquez?' asked the seller. 'Yes indeed, signed and catalogued,' replied the gentleman. The seller was convinced. 'Then it's a deal,' he said. 'But you'll have to make up the difference in price with cash.'

As everyone knows, it ended badly. When the rest of Spain fell, fighting broke out between Madrid's defenders in a civil war within a Civil War—the Communists, wanting to fight to the bitter end against the commander of the Army of the Centre and others who wanted to stop the killing and negotiate a settlement with Franco. But Franco was in no mood to compromise and, seeing resistance was at an end, his army entered the eerily silent streets of Madrid on 28 March 1939. Reprisals were at the top of his agenda, and stayed there.

After Franco died, the vast majority of Spaniards felt that enough blood had been shed and enough vengeance had been wrecked over the past 40 years to want to do anything that might conceivably restart the cycles of violence. They call it the *pacto del olvido*, the pact of forgetfulness. As time goes on, however, Francoism is increasingly becoming more of a bad memory than a threat. Streets honouring Nationalist heroes have mostly been changed back to their original names. A statue to Largo Caballero, who served as Prime Minister and Minister of War in the Republic, has recently gone up in front of the Nuevos Ministeros. In 1995, 60 years after the outbreak of the Civil War, the Cortes voted to make all surviving members of the International Brigades citizens of Spain, a belated gesture, perhaps, but one that hadn't been possible a decade earlier.

Introduction   54

The Vortex: Plaza de Puerta del Sol   55

Old Madrid   61

Around Plaza Santa Ana:
    Literature and Bars   81

The Paseo del Arte and the Retiro   91

New Madrid:
    Salamanca and the Castellana   121

Royal Madrid   137

Madrid of the Bright Lights   149

Madrid's Parklands   163

Madrid's Neighbourhoods

Madrid is divided into distinct neighbourhoods, which we've followed (more or less) in arranging this book, beginning with the **Puerta del Sol**, that solar point of reference around which Madrid radiates and orbits. The first section, **Old Madrid**, is just to the west of this, and includes the Plaza Mayor, the heart of the city under the Habsburgs. This seamlessly flows into the lively old *castizo* neighbourhoods to the south, **La Latina, Embajadores and Lavapiés** and the third section, **Around Plaza Santa Ana**, the artsy-low life theatre district of the Golden Age, where Cervantes and Lope de Vega used to live. It was full of bars then, as now, and triumphs as the heart of tourist Madrid.

Santa Ana is adjacent to the **'Paseo del Arte' and the Retiro**, a neighbourhood best done in small doses to avoid keeling over in a surfeit of culture: this is where you'll find the bulk of Madrid's art treasures, headlined by the Prado, and its most beloved city park. The affluent area north of the Retiro, **New Madrid: Salamanca and the Castellana.** is as much a showcase as the Paseo del Arte, but here the emphasis is on bourgeois chic (Salamanca) and the New Spain, or at least the New Spain as expressed in some very surprising contemporary architecture; there are also some excellent museums tucked in here and there—the National Archaeology Museum, the Sorolla and Lázaro Galdiano will not disappoint.

The next section, **Royal Madrid: The West End** is just that; what isn't occupied by one of the biggest palaces on the planet is taken up with two wealthy convents and an opera house founded by the royal family. North and east of this lies the old business district and still thriving shopping ground, **Madrid of the Bright Lights: Gran Vía, Malasaña and Chueca.** This includes such delights as the paintings in the Academia de San Fernando and some genuinely palatial cinemas, while Chueca and Malasaña, the two *barrios* north of the Gran Vía, are undergoing a new lease on life as gay and trendy nightspots—especially Chueca. Last of all, the big section we've lumped together as **Madrid's Parklands** begins at the west end of the Gran Vía, and includes Franco's dubious legacies to the city, as well as the university, an excellent American museum, the large parks of the Parque del Ouest and Casa de Campo, and a lovely jewel: the Goya Pantheon, in the Ermita de San Antonio de la Florida.

The Vortex: Plaza Puerta del Sol

...if a wedding or a baptismal procession fails to pass through the Puerta del Sol, neither is the wedding a proper wedding in the eyes of God, nor the baptised properly baptised.

Gómez de la Serna

Unlike many European cities, old Madrid isn't easily shoehorned. Boundaries merge, distinctions blend, and interesting architecture is sowed with abandon; a beautiful palace will stand a stone's throw from a run-down sex shop. But everyone agrees that Sol remains the centre of all things in Madrid, if now in the slightly obsolete manner that the sun used to be the centre of the universe.

cafés, bars and restaurants

La Marrorquina, Puerta del Sol on the corner of C/Mayor, ✆ 91 521 1201. The island of Mallorca is famous for its puffy sugar-dusted spirals called *ensaimadas*, and you can find them here along with a vast choice of other heavenly pastries to accompany your midmorning *café con leche* pick-me-up, either at the bustling counter or serene upstairs with a view. Loiter in the great early 1950s atmosphere.

El Riojano, C/Mayor 10, ✆ 91 366 4482. Just a few steps from Sol, this charming shrine to cream puffery is nothing less than the purveyor of fine traditional pastries to Spain's senators since 1885.

Casa Labra, just north of the square at C/Tetuán 12, ✆ 91 531 0081. One of the oldest surviving bar-*tabernas* in this area, founded in 1860, Casa Labra gets a mention in Spanish history books as the spot where the Spanish Socialist Party was founded in 1879. Good tapas, especially salt cod *croquetas*, served on the original zinc counter, are another plus. However, if you are likely to burst into song after a couple of beers, this isn't the place for you—a brusque sign reads *Prohibido cantar*. The restaurant closes on Sun, but the bar stays open.

As de los Vinos, C/de la Paz 4, ✆ 91 532 1473. Just south of Sol, another atmospheric blast from the past, serving a fine selection of wines and a rarity—*torrijas*, sweet bread fritters, a bit like French toast but soaked in wine and spices and dipped in sugar before they're fried. Savoury tapas, too. *Closed Sun, Aug.*

Ten streets radiate from here, as well as three metro lines and dozens of buses; however you're travelling in Madrid, you're soon likely to cross the 'Gate of the Sun', the very centre of Spain. To the uninitiated the name conjures up a memory of the Great Inca or at least a clever ploy of the Spanish Tourist Office, but no: in the walls of 1430 there was a tower gate decorated with a relief of the sun. Both gate and walls are long gone, and the great elliptical plaza is chaotic and crowded as it always has been, but it endears itself to the *madrileños* in a way no formal plaza with a postcard view ever could.

Puerta del Sol

When the gate and walls went down in the 1520s, new streets uncoiled like springs to the east, making Sol the centre of an intricate cats' cradle—old Madrid was never blessed nor cursed by planning, and its webs are organic and on a very human scale. You can walk to any of the old city gates, perhaps Puerta del Toledo or Puerta de Alcalá, in ten to fifteen minutes. And, until 1860, all of Madrid fit inside.

When the medieval gate was demolished, the new space was soon filled up with monasteries, market stalls, and taverns. None of these have survived, beyond the memory of a monastery terrace that became known in the 17th century as the *Mentidero*, or 'Gossip shop', a well-patronized forum of scuttlebutt that featured in the writings of Lope de Vega, Quevedo and Cervantes. The plaza began to take on its current appearance in 1810 under Joseph Bonaparte, who demolished the monasteries, and began the plans that doubled the size of the square, now minus the market stalls.

Most of the new buildings featured large fashionable cafés, which made the Puerta del Sol the liveliest place in Madrid in the 19th century, a centre not only for gossip but for the revolts and demonstrations that convulsed the city. The most famous (thanks to Goya), took place on 2 May 1808, when Napoleon's Egyptian Mameluke cavalry brutally attacked the rioting mob that had gravitated here. A happier impromptu gathering occurred when the municipal elections of 14 April 1931 swept in Republican candidates across Spain, and the expectant crowds that massed here were enough to make Alfonso XIII abdicate. When the Republic was announced from the balcony of the Casa de Correos, the cheering rocked the city.

As the showcase of the nation, the Puerta del Sol saw Spain's first gas lights (1830), the first tramline (1870, pulled by mules), its first electric street lights (1906), and its most famous **Tio Pepe sign**, still *in situ* on top of the city's first luxury hotel, the Paris, which still manages to keep two stars in its constellation. A plaque commmorates La Nueva Montaña, a famous literary café that once occupied the hotel's ground floor, and the ludicous where Galician author Valle-Inclan lost his arm. Sol saw the first line of the city's metro in 1919, and the addition of two others have made Sol something of an *al fresco* Grand Central Station where many pass but few loiter.

The **Casa de Correos** fills up the south end of the big square. It is the oldest surviving building in Sol, Madrid's first post office, built in 1766 by the 'Mayor king' Charles III. Like the Golden Milestone in ancient Rome, all distances in the nation are measured from the **Kilometro Cero** in front of the door, a custom established by Philip V (although the current marker dates from 1950); plaques on the Casa de Correos itself commemorate the victims of the Mameluke sabres, and the fact that you are 650.7m above sea level.

Just don't try to buy a stamp here: the building lost its postal purpose in 1847, when it became the Ministry of the Interior; under Franco, its shadowy presence led to the eclipse of Sol's cafés. Much of what occurred inside its walls under the dictatorship will remain unknown until Judgement Day, although the whole world knew of an event that happened just outside the walls in 1963, when Communist-agitator Julián Grimau was tossed from an upper window. He survived, only to be kept alive to meet a firing squad, in spite of international protests. The building now houses the Comunidad de Madrid, Madrid's regional government.

The **clock** on top of the Casa de Correos was added as an afterthought in 1866 and has come to be regarded as Spain's official timepiece. Apparently too many *madrileños* were failing to say their *Ave Marías* at twelve, with the excuse that they didn't know the time. For emphasis, a metal sphere was placed under the clock, that slowly descends at noon, although this proved too much of a distraction; everyone stood about with their mouths open, watching the ball drop.

These days the only crowds who regularly linger in Sol watching the clock are there on New Year's Eve for the countdown to midnight. They come bearing fireworks and grapes; one grape to be gobbled per stroke of the bell, to ensure luck throughout the year. Although architectural purists have always found fault with the little tower, it was rebuilt from scratch just as it was when it was at the point of collapse in 1996.

The most recent modifications of Sol, in 1986, saw a new pedestrian area in the centre illuminated by the 'suppositories'—the nickname the *madrileños* bestowed on the new lighting fixtures, until the city cracked under the weight of mockery and reinstalled some of the originals—and the placement of an equestrian **statue of Charles III**. Madrid's greatest royal benefactor is set up on a plinth between two fountains, smiling benignly at his Casa de Correos with his hand outstreched, as if to feed the pigeons. His presence dwarfs the sculpture at the mouth of Calle de Carmen, of the **Oso y Madroño** (bear and strawberry tree, *see* p.40), a small, unshowy bronze, a low-key symbol of community identity and now a favourite spot for petition signings and buskers and a few prostitutes, spilling over from the red light district along Calle Montera.

Nothing that is *auténtico* in Madrid ever strays far from Sol; jammed into this tight-knit district of narrow streets are scores of curious shops and family businesses that have been running for generations. From Sol, it's only a few minutes' walk to the Palacio Real (*see* pp.145–7), to the Retiro and the museums (*see* pp.91–120), to the city's main shopping district along the Gran Vía (*see* pp.149–62) or only a step into old Madrid (*see* pp.61–70).

I have visited most of the principal capitals of the world, but upon the whole none has ever so interested me as this city of Madrid, in which I now found myself. I will not dwell upon its streets, it edifices, its public squares, its fountains, though some of these are remarkable enough; but Petersburg has finer streets, Paris and Edinburgh more stately edifices, London far nobler squares, while Shiraz can boast of more costly fountains, though not cooler waters. But the population! Within a mud wall scarcely one league and a half in circuit, are continued two hundred thousand human beings, certainly forming the most extraordinary vital mass to be found in the entire world; and be it always remembered that this mass is strictly Spanish... Hail to you, valets from the mountains, *mayordomos* and secretaries from Biscay and Guipúzcoa, *toreros* from Andalusia, *reposteros* from Galicia, shopkeepers from Catalonia! Hail to ye, Castilians, Estremenians, and Aragonese, of whatever calling! And lastly, geniune sons of the capital, rabble of Madrid, ye twenty thousand *manolos*, whose terrible knives, on the second morning of May worked such grim havoc amongst the legions of Murat!

George Borrow, *The Bible in Spain* (1843)

Old Madrid

Plaza Mayor	65
Around the Plaza Mayor	66
Plaza de la Villa	67
Plaza de la Paja	69

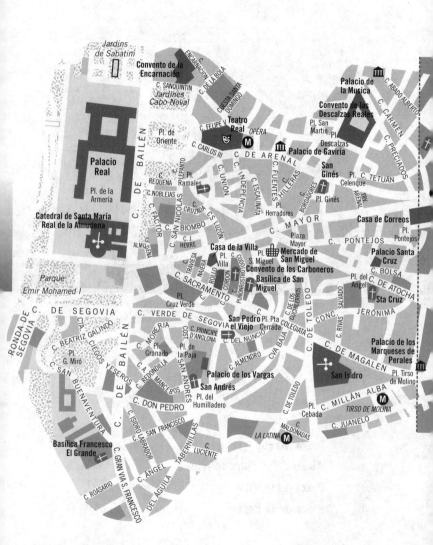

Jardins de Sabatini

Convento de la Encarnación

C. ENCARNACIÓN

C. DE LA BOLA

C. SANQUINTIN
Jardines Cabo Noval

C. SANTA DOMINGO

Palacio de la Musica

C. ABADO ALBERTO

Convento de las Descalzas Reales

C. CARMEN

Pl. San Martin

Descalzas

C. PRECIADOS

C. FELIPE V

Teatro Real

OPERA

Pl. de Oriente

C. CARLOS III

C. DE ARENAL

Palacio de Gaviria

San Ginés

Pl. C. TETUAN

C. DE BAILÉN

Pl. Ginés

Celenque

C. DE REQUENA

Pl. Ramales

C.NOBLEJAS

C. LEPANTO

C. UNION

C. INDEPENCIA

C. ESCALINATA

HILLERAS

C. BORDADORES

Palacio Real

Pl. de la Armería

C. FACTOR

C. SAN NICOLAS

CRUZADA

C.S. LUZON

Pl. Herradores

C. MAYOR

Casa de Correos

Pl. Pontejos

Catedral de Santa María Real de la Almudena

ALMUDENA

C. BIOMBO

C.J. HERRE

Plaza Mayor

C. PONTEJOS

Palacio Santa Cruz

Casa de la Villa

Pl. Villa

Mercado de San Miguel

S. Miguel

Convento de los Carboneros

C. BOLSA

Parque Emir Mohamed I

C. TRAVESIA MAJERA

ROLLO

C. SACRAMENTO

CORDON

PUNONROSTRO

Basílica de San Miguel

C. DE LOS CUCHILLEROS

Pl. del Angel C. DE ATOCHA

Sta Cruz

RONDA DE SEGOVIA

Pl. Cruz Verde

C. VERDE DE SEGOVIA

C. DE TOLEDO

SALVADO

C. CONC.

JERÓNIMA

C. DE SEGOVIA

CTA. CIEGOS YESEROS

San Pedro el Viejo

Pl. Pta Cerrada

COLEGIATA

C. RIVAS

C. BEATRIZ GALINDO

MORERIA

C. PRINCIPE D'ANGLONA

C. DEL NUNCIO

CVA BAJA

Palacio de los Marqueses de Perales

Pl. G. Miró

Pl. Granado

Pl. de la Paja

C. ALMENDRO

C. DE MAGALEN

Pl. Tirso de Molino

C. SAN BUENAVENTURA

C. DE BAILÉN

C.A. REDONDILLA

MANCEBOS

Palacio de los Vargas

San Isidro

C. MILLÁN ALBA

TIRSO DE MOLINA

San Andrés

Pl. del Humilladero

C. DON PEDRO

Pl. Cebada

C. JUANELO

C. ISIDRO LABRADOR

C. SAN FRANCISCO

TABERNILLAS

C. DE TOLEDO

MALDONADAS

LA LATINA

Basílica Francesco El Grande

C. ROASARIO

C. ÁNGEL

DEL AGUILA

GRAN VIA S. FRANCISCO

C. LUCIENTE

200 metres
200 yards

N

Pl. Carmen
C. ABADO ALBERTO
C. MONTERA
C. DE LA ADUANA
Casino de Madrid
Real Academia Belles Artes
C. DE ALCALÁ
Banco Bilbao-Viscaya
PUERTO DEL SOL
C. CARMEN
Banco Español de Crédito
LA SEVILLA
C. ARLABÁN
Pl. Puerta del Sol
CARRERA DE SAN
C. POZO
Pl JERÓNIMO
Canalejas
C. VICTORIA
PRINCIPE
C. CADIZ
C. ESPOZ Y MINA
DE LA CRUZ
NUÑEZ ARCE
C. BARCELONA
C. CARRETAS
Pl. Jacinto Benavente
Hotel Reina Victoria
C. DE ATOCHA
Palacio de los Marqueses de Perales
Pl. Tirso de Molino

Squeezed into a tight half kilometre between the Puerta del Sol and the Palacio Real is a solid, enduring Castilian town known as 'El Madrid de las Austrias' because most of it was built under the reign of the Habsburgs, those most prodigious of Austrian experts. It's as evocative in its own way as Segovia or Toledo. Many of the streets and squares follow the town plan of the original Moorish settlement, and the buildings have changed little since Goya painted the city's delicate skyline of cupolas and spires.

Neither menaced by modern office blocks nor done up picture-pretty for the tourists, the quarter has enjoyed the best of possible fates—to remain as it was. Its residents are perhaps poorer than the city average but their presence keeps the place a living neighbourhood, loud, busy and a bit unkempt, but still Madrid's best and cosiest refuge from the cosmopolitan noise of the rest of the city. As you wander, don't miss the ceramic street signs, many of which illustrate the often quaint names of the streets.

Il Pulpito, Plaza Mayor 10, ✆ 91 366 2188. The least touristy bar on the plaza, named not for its octopus *tapas* but for the little 'pulpit' tucked in over the Arco de Cuchilleros, from where a friar harangued the *madrileños* to rise up on 2 May 1808. Try the little meatballs.

Casa Paco, Plaza de Puetra Cerrada 11, ✆ 91 366 3166. One of Madrid's classic *tabernas*, intimate and covered with colourful tiles, a good stop for just a tapa or a dinner built around excellent grilled meats. Around *4,500 pts* for the full whack.

Botîn, C/de Cuchilleros 17, ✆ 91 366 4217. Hemingway called it 'the best restaurant in the world' no less. Justly renowned for its beautiful original interior and roasts, it is one of the priciest in the area, but there's a three course set menu for *4,265 pts*. The no-frills **Bodegas Riela** just opposite must be nearly as old, serving its *vermut de la casa* on an old zinc bar.

Vinoteca Maestro Villa, C/Cava Baja 8, ✆ 91 564 2036. A new wine bar in a handsome old building, named after an old band leader; a wide selection of Spain's best vintages, by the glass or bottle, with tapas and *raciones*.

Posada de la Villa, C/Cava Baja 9, ✆ 91 366 1860. *Muy auténtico*, both in the décor and in the kitchen, where a wood-fired oven produces succulent suckling pig. *Around 6,000 pts. Closed Sun eve, Aug.*

Casa Lucio, C/Cava Baja 35, ✆ 91 365 3252. Historic *mesón* serving up hearty traditional *madrileño* faves, from *cocidos* to roasts. Often packed, so it's best to book, especially for dinner. *Around 6,000 pts. Closed Sat lunch, Aug.*

Casa Ciriaco, C/Mayor 84, ✆ 91 548 0620. Founded in 1917, with a beautiful old tiled bar for tapas grazing, and a tasty paella in the restaurant on Sundays. *Around 2,800 pts. Closed Aug and Wed eve.*

Palacio de Anglona, C/Segovia 13, ✆ 91 366 3753. Popular, multi-level restaurant serving a wide choice of international salads, pizzas and other dishes. *Around 3,500 pts. Open late—till 2am Fri and Sat, till 1am other nights.*

El Estragón, Costanilla de San Andrés 10, (Plaza de la Paja) ✆ 91 365 8982. A vegetarian oasis, with light, tasty dishes at light friendly prices; set menus from around *1,500 pts.*

Plaza Mayor

This was a scruffy market square in the time of Philip II, who was apparently the first to come up with the idea that it might be something more dignified. He got his favourite architect, Juan de Herrera, to make a few sketches, but nothing really happened until the present buildings were completed in 1619 for Philip III by Juan Gómez de Mora. After several fires, the Plaza achieved its present form in 1811 under the hand of Herrera's disciple, Juan de Villanueva.

It would be the great prototype for many *plaza mayores* across Spain: an enclosed, rectangular space surrounded by arcaded walks under buildings, all more or less the same height, that resemble walls of a single structure, giving the impression of a building turned inside out. Such a square counts for much more than just a knot in a tangle of streets: it is like a stage in the theatre, where public life can be acted out with proper Spanish dignity. The analogy to a stage is no accident, for theatres of the Golden Age were perfect little Plaza Mayors, with balconies all around and the proscenium at the narrow end.

The equestrian king in the centre is Philip III, a statue designed by Giambologna. Much of the time he looks at sea amid the white plastic market stalls selling stamps and coins that sabotage the Plaza's *raison d'être* as theatre. Philip III officially inaugurated the square in 1620 with a ceremony celebrating the canonization of St Isidro, Madrid's patron. Later kings of Spain were crowned here, before a capacity audience of 50,000, and they would often return to preside over fiestas, bullfights, carnivals, archaic knightly tournaments and the Inquisition's *autos-da-fé*, colourful public spectacles preceded by much pageantry and preaching, before the unlucky ones were led off to the stake.

In 1690, the last and biggest *auto-da-fé* in Spain's history was staged in the Plaza Mayor by the insane Charles II, a 14-hour affair that tried 120 backsliders and fried 21 alive. The bullfights that took place here lasted nearly as long and were almost as dangerous; one that took place here in 1619 resulted in five fatalities, which evoked the comment in the chronicles that the bulls that day were very well behaved.

During events, the city council would rent the balconies from their owners to seat the distinguished visitors. Kings traditionally took their places in the elegant building with twin spires on the north side, the **Casa Panadería**, so called after the bakery that preceded it on the site. Its façade was decorated with murals in the late 17th century, and was decorated again in 1992 by Carlos Franco in a colourful baroque groovy neo-hippie celebration of Madrid, leaving the city's few historic preservationists gnashing their teeth in impotent rage.

Around the Plaza Mayor

Like many a front parlour, the Plaza Mayor these days is mainly used for receiving guests, while the family prefers the more lived-in streets around. These are full of shops that leave you wondering just how many Spaniards could possibly collect miniature soldiers.

If you leave the Plaza to the southeast (Calle Gerona to Plaza de la Provinicia) you will soon encounter another major Habsburg monument: commissioned by Philip IV, the **Palacio de Santa Cruz** (1639) was designed by Juan Gómez de Mora in the El Escorial mode, with the *de rigueur* Herrera slate towers and pinnacles, although with a decorative frontispiece that lends it a gentler appearance. Now the Foreign Ministry, it comes as a surprise to realize that it was built originally as a prison; noble inmates were treated to cells with gilded bars, while those without a pedigree rotted in its lightless dungeons.

From here, Calle Lechuga ('Lettuce Street') leads to the **Calle de Toledo**. This offers up several old shops—one, the always crowded Casa Hernanz, selling every conceivable kind of rope and espadrilles, another selling teeny tiny gold flamenco shoes for babies, while on the opposite end of the scale, the Corsetería (No.49) claims to sell the largest underwear in Spain, and occasionally puts on window displays that could be your most memorable vision in Madrid. Then there's Caramelos Paco (No.55) with a window display that is nothing less than the Sistine Chapel of boiled sweets.

The biggest building on this stretch of Calle de Toledo is the twin-towered church of **San Isidro**, which served as the city's stand-in cathedral until 1992 © 91 369 2310, Ⓜ La Latina (*open Mon–Sat 8.30–12.30 and 6.30–8.30, Sun and hols, 9–2 and 5.30–8.30*). Founded by a special bequest from Philip IV's wife, Mariana of Austria, this gloomy pile was begun in 1620 as the church of the Colegio Imperial, Jesuit central headquarters in Spain, where the subtle doctors schooled Calderón de la Barca, Lope de Vega and Quevedo. The elaborate Churrigueresque façade was added later. When Charles III sent the Jesuits packing, the church was re-dedicated to Madrid's humble but beloved patron-saint, Isidro, a 12th-century ploughman of exceptional piety, who was famous for his ability to find water, but who is usually depicted in art lost in prayer, while two angels pop down from heaven to do the ploughing for him. His wife, María de la Cabeza and their son, the hermit Millán (or Illán) have also been canonized, a record matched only by the original Holy Family. Isidro and María's remains are still over the high altar, imprisoned in the basilican gloom, although they are allowed out whenever Madrid is suffering a severe drought.

The Plaza Nueva crossroads just up from San Isidro merge to the west into **Plaza de la Puerta Cerrada**, 'the closed gate'. The dragon gate in the old walls stood here although it was rarely open because its design allowed robbers to easily ambush passers-by. The cross in the plaza is one of the last of hundreds that once stood in the streets of Madrid. They were removed in the last century because of the profane things people did to them; this one survived because it stops up a water pipe, even though many tourists think it's a monument to the Civil War.

Most importantly, this is the crossroads for traditional *mesóns* serving up hearty Castilian fare, especially down along picturesque **Calle de La Cava Baja** (originally an underground passage under the walls, used by the Moors and later the Christians, for sneak attacks) and up **Calle de los Cuchilleros** ('of the knife-makers'). The latter follows the impressive foundations of the Plaza Mayor—you can see it was no easy task creating such a large level space in the sloping heart of Madrid. Calle de los Cuchilleros is also the address of **Botín** which, according to the Guinness Book of Records, is the oldest restaurant in the world, founded in 1725; 19-year-old Goya worked in the evening washing dishes here, and it even features, as the plaque reads, in a scene in the classic 19th-century novel about Madrid, *Fortunata y Jacinta*, by Benito Pérez Galdós. Just up the street from this serious Madrid institution is El Cuchi, at the sign of the broken fork (in Spain, restaurants are awarded forks instead of stars): 'Hemingway never ate here' it boasts on the door lintel, also 'We don't speak English but we promise not to laugh at your Spanish.'

El Cuchi sits at the bottom of the picturesque **Arco de los Cuchilleros**, with its great stone staircase cascading operatically down into the Plaza Mayor. The rest of the street is lined with beautifully restored flats from the 19th century. Just up, at the top of the street on the corner of Calle Mayor stands the charmingly rickety glass-and-ironwork **Mercado de San Miguel**, painted a pretty acqua. All of the city's markets originally looked like this one, built in 1916, have since been replaced by more solid, if less aesthetically pleasing, structures.

Plaza de la Villa

For centuries, **Calle Mayor** was the main street of Madrid, linking the Puerta del Sol to the original fortress or Alcázar. At No.59, there's a rare Art Nouveau building dating back to 1914. It houses the much older **Farmacia de La Reina Madre**, founded as an alchemist's in 1574 and filled with blue and white apothecary jars from the 16th century and later. The story goes that highstrung Isabella Farnese, the second queen of Philip V, always obtained her potions here rather than in the royal pharmacies from fear of being poisoned by her stepson. Now open 24 hours a day, the pharmacy has useful machines where you can check your weight, blood pressure and vision. To the right, the very narrow house at No.61 has a plaque commemorating the playwright Pedro Calderón de la Barca, who died here in 1681, while the modern building opposite replaces the house that was the first home of his rival, Lope de Vega, who was born there in 1562, after his mother tracked down his scalliwag father all the way from Vallodolid.

Just beyond, Calle Mayor passes through the **Plaza de la Villa**, the former Moorish *souk* and first main square of Madrid. This is dignified by some of the city's oldest buildings as well as a statue of Philip II's most successful admiral, Alvaro de Bazán, who helped to win Spain glory at the Battle of Lepanto against the Turks in 1571, and who was spared going down with the Invincible Armada by dying before his fleet left Portugal.

Now that the cars have been given the boot, you can fearlessly enjoy Madrid's distinguished city hall, the **Casa de la Villa**, designed by Gomez de Mora in his old age, although his original design of Herreran simplicity was corrupted by baroque flourishes over the doors and on the tower by the architects who completed it in 1693. There are guided tours (in Spanish only) at 5pm on Mondays, your one chance to visit the **Sala de Actos** (council chambers), where the elected officials of Madrid deliberate in a setting of unmatched parlimentary splendour, under a *trompe l'oeil* ceiling by Antonio Palomino. Another attraction is the enormous painting of the *3rd of May* (1872) by Parmorli, a panorama of Madrid at dawn; the women lamenting in the foreground hint that all is not well. There's also a copy of Goya's famous *Allegory of Madrid*, the original now in the Museo Municipal (*see* p.159). A carillon plays at 10am, noon, and 7pm.

Opposite, the **Torre de los Lujanes** with its tri-lobed Gothic portal, *Mudéjar* arch and neighbouring palace is the only secular complex to survive from 15th century Madrid, although one that was very, very restored in 1910. Its plaque tells us that it was the birthplace of Federico Chueca, the '*castizo* prodigy of Madrid music' and, according to legend, it once served as a prison for no less a personage than King François I of France. This monarch, bitterest enemy of Charles V and Habsburg ambition, was captured at the Battle of Pavia in Italy in 1525. He spent a few months as Charles' unwilling guest in Madrid, and won his release by signing a treaty and agreeing to marry Charles' sister; once safely over the border, he said it was all a joke, and he and Charles were at war for most of the next 20 years.

The **Casa Cisernos** (1537) occupies the south end of the plaza, and is linked by a gallery to the Casa de la Villa. It was built for the nephew of the famous Cardinal and now houses José Maria Alvarez di Manzano, the Partido Popular mayor of Madrid, who boasts that he keeps a crucifix in his office and spends much of his time worrying that his fellow citizens might be having too much fun. Casa Cisernos is a fine example of yet another Spanish national style, the Plateresque, remarkable for its filigree detail. Much of what you now see is the result of the 1909 Neo-Plateresque restoration; only the façades on Calle Cordon and Calle Sacramento are original, and the latter has a splendid doorway.

Just around the corner from this doorway, on Calle Puñonrostro, stands the late 17th-century **Basilica de San Miguel**, a baroque jewel by Italian Santiago Bonavía, designed for the Archbishop of Toledo, Don Luis, then aged 5. While most Spanish churches of the period are only cosmetically baroque, this basilica has baroque bones, with its convex façade and undulating interior. The most popular chapel is dedicated to Josemaria Escrivá de Balaguer, the founder of Opus Dei in 1928 who, amid some controversy, was beatified by John Paul II.

From here Calle Codo ('Elbow Street') leads past the nondescript brick façade of the early 17th-century **Convento de Las Carboneras** ('the Convent of the coal bins', so called for a painting of the Virgin discovered in one, *open daily 9.30–1 and 4–6.30*), where the cloistered nuns sell their biscuits and sweets on a revolving drum that preserves their privacy . This is one of only two convents in Madrid that still support themselves in this centuries-old fashion; the cloistered nuns at the Monasterio de la Natividad, for instance, have traded in their rolling pins for computers, and do the accounts for the Corte Inglés department stores.

Calle del Codo returns to Plaza de la Villa, from where you can head east along Calle Mayor to the atmospheric tiled bar and restaurant **Casa Ciriaco**, founded in 1916. Ten years previously, an upper balcony of the building witnessed one of Madrid's most famous assassination attempts, when a certain Mateo Morral tossed a bouquet down on the wedding procession of King Alfonso XIII and his bride Victoria Eugenia. The flowers hid a bomb, which killed some 26 bystanders but left its royal targets unscathed. Eye witness accounts give the blood spattered king credit for taking control of the situation and calming spirits. A bronze angel by the church of the Sacramento opposite commemorates the victims.

Further up Calle Mayor, Calle San Nicolás leads shortly to **San Nicolás de los Servitas** (*open Mon only 8.30–1.30 and 5.30–8.30pm*), the oldest surviving church in Madrid with its minaret-like *Mudéjar* tower, from the 12th century; if you come when it's open, take in the little display about its Moorish builders.

Plaza de la Paja

Returning once more to the Plaza de la Villa, Calle Cordon will take you south across busy Calle de Segovia to Costanilla de San Pedro and Madrid's other *Mudéjar* tower, this one from the 14th century and attached to the little church of **San Pedro el Viejo**, built on the site of a mosque. The dirty beige interior, jammed with a hodge-podge of shrines, electric candles, and a few old inscriptions embedded in its pillars, is one of the busiest in Madrid. A statue of Jesus wearing the crown of thorns, with a wooden toe protruding through the glass case for kissing, is the big draw, but don't miss the processional float in the chapel on the left, with its tractor steering wheel peeking out from under the drapery.

From here Calle Principe d'Anglona leads across to the leafy and sloping **Plaza de la Paja**, 'Straw Square'. In spite of its name this was once the most aristocratic square of medieval Madrid. Today only the large **Palacio de los Vargas** survives, but in spite of its façade it dates only from the 1920s and is now home to a school rather than to the powerful family who once hosted Isabel la Católica. The seated bronze man in front reads the slogan that you may have already noticed elsewhere, *Entre Todos Rehabiltamos Madrid*; the city's rehabilitation squads have already led to a rebirth of interest in this quiet, genteel corner of town.

The plaza's church **San Andrés** (*open Mon–Sat 8–9.30 and 6–7.30, Sun 9–2*) typical of the blank, severe style of Madrid's older parishes, was burned during the Civil War, and recently restored. Behind it, on Costanilla San Andrés, restoration continues on the façade of the lavish baroque **Capilla de San Isidro**, with its heavy ornate cornice; originally it held the relics of San Isidro which were long privately owned by the Vargas family. Next door to this, the **Capilla del Osbispo** (the entrance is at the back) luckily escaped the flames. Designed in the 1540s as a pantheon for the family of Don Francisco de Vargas, Councillor to Ferdinand and Isabella and their grandson Charles V, it is the finest Renaissance era church in Madrid, although even at that late date the vaulting is Flamboyant Gothic. The intricate Platesrsque carvings, the family tombs, and the stupendous gilded high altar soaring to the ceiling are the finest in Madrid. The baroque dome, visible from the back, was added after Isidro's canonization in 1620 and, although it went up in flames in 1936, both the exterior and sumptuous interior have been recently restored.

The refinement of the Capilla del Osbispo stands in marked contrast to Madrid's largest church, the **Basílica de San Francisco el Grande** (1785, restored 1890, restored again in 1999), down at the foot of the Carretera de San Francisco (© 91 365 3800, Ⓜ Puerto de Toledo; *open summer, Tues–Sat 11–1 and 5–8; winter, 11–1 and 4–7, adm*). With a dome measuring 108ft in diameter and radiating chapels similar to the Pantheon, it lives up to its big name. Originally a modest hermitage founded in the late 1200s, perhaps by St Francis himself, it became wealthy enough in the 18th century to build this oppressive gloomy pile, but there's little more to say for it, except that it has an early Goya, *San Bernardino of Siena* in one of the chapels. A separate entrance to the right leads into the **Capilla del Cristo de los Dolores**, a fine work of the 1660s, while a plaque on the left is one of the last in Madrid referring to Franco, who inaugurated the ungracious busy street in front. Note the handsome apartment building in coloured brick, opposite, at the beginning of Calle de la Calatrava. La Latina (*see* pp.75–77) begins here.

La Latina	75
Puerta de Toledo and Beyond	75
The Rastro	
Embajadores	78
La Corrala and Around	78
Plaza de Lavapiés	79

La Latina, Embajadores and Lavapiés

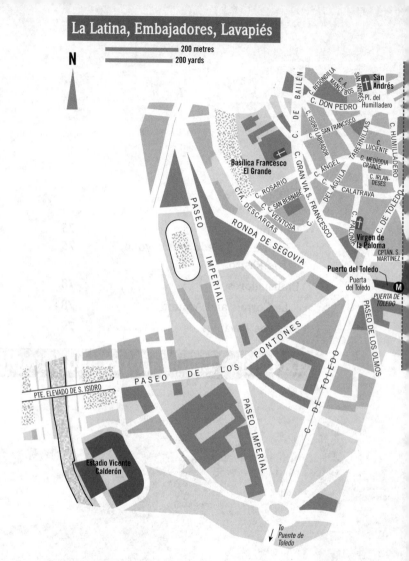

La Latina, Embajadores, Lavapiés

200 metres
200 yards

N

San Andrés

C. REDONDILLA
C.A. MANCEBOS
C. SAN ANDRÉS
Pl. del Humilladero
C. DE BAILÉN
C. DON PEDRO
C. ISIDRO LABRADOR
C. SAN FRANCISCO
C. HUMILLADERO
C. LUCIENTE
C. TABERNILLAS
C. MEDIODIA GRANDE
C. IRLAN-DESES
Basílica Francesco El Grande
C. ROSARIO
CTA. DESCARGAS
C. SAN BERNABÉ
C. VENTOSA
C. GRAN VIA S. FRANCISCO
C. ANGEL
C. DEL AGUILA
C. CALATRAVA
C. PALOMA
C. DE TOLEDO
Virgen de la Paloma
CPTÁN. S. MARTINEZ
RONDA DE SEGOVIA
PASEO IMPERIAL
Puerta del Toledo
Puerta del Toledo
M
PUERTA DE TOLEDO
PASEO DE LOS OLMOS
PASEO DE LOS PONTONES
PASEO IMPERIAL
C. DE TOLEDO
PTE. ELEVADO DE S. ISIDRO
Estadio Vicente Calderón
To Puente de Toledo

Fanning south of San Isidro are Madrid's *barrios bajos* ('low neighbourhoods') , so named because they are built on the slope down to the Mazanares. They grew up quickly in the 18th and 19th centuries to house the burgeoning city population, especially the tradesmen and workers who began to make the once parasitical capital into a city that earned its own way in the world.

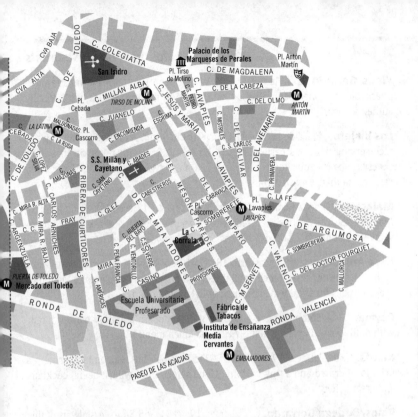

Today these *barrios* lend the city much of its distinct character; unlike most European capitals, the heart of Madrid has not yet been given over to *los yuppies*, but maintains several colourful neighbourhoods with a mix of people who have been there for generations, the 'true sons and daughters of Madrid' or *castizos* (*see* p.42) mingled with newcomers both Spanish and foreign. How long they can resist gentrification probably depends on how long *madrileños* stay in love with their cars; the city's policy of pedestrianizing the streets makes parking difficult. For the time being the trendy *madrileños* are only another element in a vibrant mix. The *barrios bajos* have only a few monuments, but really come into their own for the Sunday morning Rastro market, and for the summer festivals, the *verbenas*, and the more spontaneous neighbourhood parties that happen on weekend evenings in the bars, which include some of the most traditional in Madrid.

73

Vinos Gerardo, C/Calatrava 21, ℗ 91 365 3646. One of the most atmospheric old fashioned bars in La Latina, dressed in traditional tiles, with equally authentic tapas.

Los Viajeros, Plaza de la Cebada 11, ℗ 91 366 9064. A rare rooftop dining terrace serving delicious pasta dishes (the ravioli filled with pumpkin in a light cheesy sauce is exquisite), succulent grilled meats. *Menú del dìa 1,600 pts*, à la carte twice that. *Closed Mon.*

Malacatín, C/de la Ruda 5 (off Plaza Cascorro), ℗ 91 365 5241. For a genuine Madrid experience, book their renowned *cocido* for lunch and ask what time to show up. Set lunch *2,600 pts. Closed Sun, July and Aug.*

Casa Amadeo, Plaza de Cascorro 18, ℗ 91 365 9439. A favourite post-Rastro haunt for a drink, tapas, lunch or all three, and one of the last places in Madrid to prepare snails the local way, flavoured with spicy *chorizo*.

Peyma, C/del Sombrerete, ℗ 91 467 1369. A modern and busy bar restaurant with outdoor seating and a filling *1,800 pts* lunch menu.

Kairos, C/del Nuncio 19, ℗ 91 364 0125. A small but welcoming bar with a loyal local crowd and a tiny balcony. Good selection of wines, beers, cocktails and great coffee.

Vinos/Bodega Gerrardo, C/Calatrava 19, ℗ 91 365 3646. A stalwart of this traditional neighbourhood, serving excellent seafood and crisp, chilled *vermut*.

El Granero del Lavapiés, C/Argumosa 10, ℗ 91 467 7611. Popular vegetarian lunch choice. *Around 2,200 pts. Closed Aug*. This street, running down to the back of the Reina Sofia, has a range of outdoor bars and eateries, earning it the nickname 'Costa Argumosa'. Also try **Alchuri**, at No.21, small and friendly, with some vegetarian dishes .

La Taberna de Antonio Sánchez, C/Mesón de Paredes 13, ℗ 91 539 7826. One of the landmarks of Lavapiés, a friendly *taberna* founded by a bullfighter in 1830 and full of taurine memorabilia. Excellent tapas or full meals.

Pastelería Licorería El Madroño, C/Caravaca, ℗ 91 527 6843, birthplace of the *licore de Madroño*, distilled from the fruit of the strawberry tree as well as some unusual cakes. *Closed July and Aug.*

As far as we know, this is the only neighbourhood in Europe named after a Latin teacher, although this was no ordinary one: Beatriz Galindo taught Isabel la Católica her conjugations and became one of the queen's closest confidantes. Along the way she amassed enough money to found a charitable hospital that took her nickname, La Latina, in central **Plaza del La Cebeda** (**Ⓜ** La Latina). In 1900 the hospital was demolished and replaced by the Teatro La Latina, which specializes in musicals nowadays.

Plaza de La Cebeda was the site of the Toledo Gate until 1656, when the walls were expanded for the last time, and ever since then it has been a colourful and piquant corner of Madrid. Goya's *Madrid Fair* (in the Prado) was set here, and for centuries the square was the venue for public executions. In 1824, Liberal General Rafael de Riego, the hero of the Peninsular War was hanged for his uprising against Ferdinand VII, but put on a bad show by dying like a coward. Madrid's beloved bandit by night and dandy by day, Luis Candelas, did rather better in 1837, before one of the biggest crowds ever to witness an execution in Spain, when he spoke his last words with a smile: *'Sé feliz, patria mía'.* ('Be happy, my country'). The scaffold was eventually replaced by a lovely market, designed in the style of Les Halles in Paris, but in the 1950s it was torn down for the present lumpish yet bustling *agora* with piles of fresh meat, fish and produce, knowingly eyed and prodded by the locals. It also shelters the neighbourhood pool, and the bars and surrounding streets are hopping at night.

Puerta de Toledo, and Beyond

From Plaza del La Cebeda, Calle de Toledo descends to the neo-classical **Puerta de Toledo**, isolated in a hornets' nest of traffic buzzing around the Ronda de Toledo. This gate in the 17th-century walls was begun as a triumphal arch by Joseph Bonaparte to mark the beginning of his reign, but it was finished by Ferdinand VII to celebrate the ending of it and the start of his own calamitous rule, and is covered with much Latinizing about the excessive and tyrannical Gauls. It has recently been restored, not because anyone likes it, but as a stern history lesson.

This arch to a hated king ironically nicknamed 'the Desired One' had fishmongers for neighbours, who held court in the **Mercado Puerta de Toledo**, between the Ronda de Toledo and Plaza Campillo Mundo Nuevo. Within easy walking distance of the Rastro (*see* below), it seemed logical in the late 1980s to replace the fish with antique shops, and in its inaugural year over a million people visited the new Mercado de Anticuarios. A decade later, most of the shops are empty, a victim, they say, of mismanagement. Over-design may also have had something to do with its current desolation, an effect heightened by the piped in Musak. You could shoot a modern film version of Theseus and the Minotaur here; a tourist office is said to be lurking its depths, but take a ball of twine if you go in search of it.

Another case of design gone wrong is adjacent: the singularly uninviting **Puerta de Toledo complex** (1985–87), which incorporates a social service and cultural centre, a library, and a kindergarten made of unadorned geometrical forms in granite and Colemar limestone draped over different levels and smeared with graffiti. Juan Navarro Baldeweg is one of Spain's best-known architects internationally, but this has been his only commission in his native land. It is not hard to undersand why. The cylindrical library resembles a World War II pillbox with slightly larger windows.

You'll have to negotiate your way through this to see the spiritual focus of La Latina and the seat of Madrid's unofficial patroness, **La Virgen de la Paloma** ('of the dove'), on Calle de la Paloma. This replaces the convent of the Virgin of Las Maravillas, where a pet dove made a singular impression by piously following a religious procession. In the 18th century, a painting of the Virgin was rediscovered on the convent wall. This became such a popular focus of local devotion that a chapel was built to house it, which in 1913 was replaced by the the handsome Neo-*Mudéjar* church you see now, designed by Lorenzo Alvarez Capra. During the first church burnings in 1931, the painting was hidden away and replaced by a copy. A couple years later even the copy was stolen by a local shoemaker, who kept it safe throughout the Civil War. On 15 August the surrounding streets witness the most *castizo* of all Madrid's local festivals, the Verbena de La Paloma.

Until the 1860s Madrid ended at the Puerta de Toledo and, gazing down the Calle de Toledo past rows of apartment blocks, you may not feel tempted to continue any further, at least on foot (although if you like funny old buildings, there's a good drunken, swaying one topped by clock a few steps down Paseo de los Olmos). Down at the bottom of Paseo de los Pontones you can make out the 60,000 seat **Estadio Vicente Calderón**, headquarters of Atlético de Madrid, next to another essential part of Madrid: the Mahou Brewery.

The historical attractions are way down at the bottom of Calle de Toledo; bus nos. 81 or 23 or Ⓜ Marqués de Vadillo will take you down to the **Puente de Toledo**, a handsome nine-arched bridge over the Manzanares in the midst of a traffic cloverleaf, designed by Pedro de Ribera for Philip V and completed in 1732. A pair of ornate shrines, one dedicated to St Isidro and another to his wife,

St María de la Cabeza, recall the festive pilgrimage or *romería* that crosses this bridge on St Isidro's day on 15 May, the subject of several of Goya's finest paintings in the Prado.

The pilgrims' destination is a ten-minute walk up the Paseo Quince de Mayo, the 18th-century **Ermita de San Isidro**, marking the spot where Isidro made a well flow in a barren field. The hermitage enjoys fine views back to the Madrid's skyline, also observed by the bust of Goya in the adjacent park, although the view is decidedly less arcadian than the one depicted in his *Pradera de San Isidro*, painted around 1780. The adjacent cemetery of San Isidro has been the last resort of aristocrats in Madrid for a couple of centuries, and has its share of pantheons and impressive tombs aimed at defying the great Equalizer.

The Rastro

Madrid's legendary market begins up in **Plaza de Cascorro** (Ⓜ La Latina), a square named after a village in Cuba where, during the Spanish-American War of 1898, Eloy Gonzalo (whose statue you see) offered to go on a suicide mission to torch the fort, asking only that his comrades drag his body back. You see him standing there with his petrol can and the rope he tied about his waist. Gonzalo had volunteered because he was raised in a nearby orphanage and had no family to mourn him, and although his fellow solders did rescue him after he was shot, he died a few weeks later. According to a popular saying, if you enter the Rastro without the courtesy of greeting Eloy Gonzalo, you will leave empty handed.

Eloy, in effect, marks the beginning of **El Rastro,** Spain's best known and longest running outdoor market, which takes place on Sunday mornings from 9 to 2 along **Calle de Ribera de Curtadores**. Rastro pungently translates as 'the Stain' for the blood that trickled down the street from the slaughterhouses that once stood in Plaza de Cascorro. The skins passed directly from abbatoir to the tanners (the *curtadores*). One thing it's hard to be nostalgic about is the pong that must have once hung over this area.

Nowadays, the Rastro can provide you with everything from bargain fashions, to electric extension cables, peacock feathers, second-hand flamenco dresses and plastic flowers, while in the side streets you may find not only some genuine antiques, but reputedly stolen goods—perhaps very recent stolen goods; the Rastro is renowned for its pick-pockets. During the other days of the week, Calle de Ribera de Curtadores and its tributaries are a fertile field for poking around antique and furniture shops, including an engagingly dusty one, on the corner of Calle de Carnero; another, at Calle de Arganzuela 13, sells everything from a range of wooden pitchforks to opulently garish chandeliers.

Embajadores

Another street fanning down from Plaza de Cascorro, Calle de Embajadores, got its name in the 15th century when a plague in the centre of Madrid sent the resident ambassadors fleeing here to safety. A lively street dotted with a selection of old shops, the focus of its upper section is a twin-towered Baroque church dedic ated to **San Cayetano**, the patron saint of the *barrio*, founded by the Theatines in the 17th century. Although the interior was burnt out in the Civil War, the church has kepts its original red brick façade flush with the street, encrusted with columns and barnacle ornamentation by José de Churriguera (1761). Like the Virgen de la Paloma, the August *verbena* here is a chance for some wild footstomping.

At the foot of Calle de Embajadores are two grand buildings, a Neo-Mudéjar **Instituto de Ensañanza Media Cervantes** (1881), opposite the **Fábrica de Tabacos**, nothing less than Europe's oldest tobacco factory, founded in 1809 in what had started out as a distillery. Although Carmen, Spain's most famous cigar-roller, was a Sevilliana, Madrid's *cigarraras* were a feisty and proud lot who gave the *barrio* much of its character; in the last century, they composed a fifth of the entire working population of Madrid. They were also the most organized, and went on strike and achieved all sorts of reforms (most notably childcare and schools) from the management that few male workers ever managed to achieve.

La Corrala and Around

Calle de Mesón de Parades, the street behind the Fábrica de Tabacos, leads up shortly to Calle Tribulete and **La Corrala** (1839–80), an example of a typical 19th-century tenement block. Its companion building has been destroyed and the intimate inner courtyard which it helped create is now a wide open space. This type of housing, once dominant in Madrid and other Spanish cities, by its very nature led to a close-knit existence that had little room for privacy and 'personal space' and all our contemporary defenses. Many of Madrid's operettas or *zarzuelas* are set in these social beehives; La Corrala's empty lot provides the perfect setting for perfomances in July and August, and the chance for swanning about in full *castizo* attire.

The ruined church opposite La Corrala, San Fernando, was burned in the Civil War and left standing as a monument as well as a canvas for anarchist spraypaint. The school once connected to the church was demolished to create Plaza de La Corrala and its pleasant playground, a rare commodity in these parts. The presiding statue is of Mexican poet Augustin Lara, author of Madrid's anthem, which you'll hear over and over and over again at the summer fiestas: *Madrid, Madrid, Madrid/Pedazo de la España en que naci* ...(Madrid Madrid Madrid/Bit of Spain where I was born...)

Down from the statue of Lara, Calle de Sombrerete ('Little Hat Street') recalls the strange story of Sebastian of Portugal, the heir to that throne, who went to fight in Morocco at the age of 21 and was apparently killed in the battle of Alcazar-el-Kebir (1578) although his body was never identified. His disappearance allowed his uncle, Philip II, to claim the crown of Portugal. The Portuguese, however, refused to believe Sebastian was dead and rumours circulated that he would return to them after seven years of penance. Although some remains, reportedly his, were buried in Lisbon in 1582 in the presence of Philip II, most of the Portuguese weren't convinced, and the first 'Sebastians' began to appear in 1585. The most celebrated one was a pastry cook named Gabriel de Espinosa, who was put forward by a former confidante of the real Sebastian, the Portuguese friar Miguel dos Santos. Santos was also a confidante of the young Anna, illegitimate daughter of Philip's half-brother Don Juan of Austria, convincing her that she should marry the pastry cook Sebastian and help him regain the throne of Portugal, and liberate Jerusalem. The project had support in high places, most notably from Henry IV of France.

Philip, not surprisingly, wasn't having any of this and, after parading Santos through Madrid in a silly pointed hat, had him hanged in the Plaza Mayor, while the hat was ceremoniously taken down this street and left on a pile of dung. The false Sebastian received similar treatment, and Anna was locked up in a convent.

Plaza de Lavapiés

To the east, Calle de Sombrerete opens into busy **Plaza de Lavapiés**, a lively square with an hourglass figure. The name translates as 'wash feet', and it may have derived in some way from a fountain in the centre of the square. Some writers have spelled it El Avapiés, and find the origin in the Hebrew *aba-puest*, 'the place of Jews.' This was certainly true in the Middle Ages: the square was the centre of Madrid's ghetto until 1492, when Ferdinand and Isabel issued their order to convert or leave Spain. Those *conversos* who remained were forced to change their names as well as their religion, and as most chose Manolo (Manuel) for their firstborn sons, the neighbourhood became known as the *barrio de los Manolos*. As they were all sharp dressers, *Manolos* in the late 18th century became a specifically *madrileño* synonym for *majos* (*see* p.42).

The main synagogue stood on the site of the **Teatro Olímpia**. This, one of the theatres of the Centro Dramático Nacional, attracted a number of fringe theatre companies to the area, but the Olimpia itself is currently being rebuilt from the ground up. Around here, you may well notice that the *castizos* are something of a minority: Northern Europeans, Africans, Americans, artists and others have moved in and change is afoot. On Calle de La Fé, just off the square, you can visit the one neighbourhood constant: **Café Barbieri**, virtually unchanged since it opened its doors in 1902, and as popular as ever with both elderly *castizos* and newer arrivals.

Plaza Tirso de Molino

From the square, Calle de Lavapiés leads up to Calle de la Cabeza; the building on the corner, now housing the pleasant Bar Lavapiés, was once the dreaded prison of the Inquisition. Just up the street is the leafy triangular plaza dedicated to the playwright Fray Gabriel Téllez (1583–1648), who wrote under the name Tirso de Molino. Fray Gabriel entered the Mercedarian Order at the age of 17, and spent his last 25 years in a monastery that stood here. In 1836, Liberal Minister Mendizábal confiscated and demolished it. Mendizábal's expropriation of Church property smacked too much of Republicanism for the victors of the Civil War, and his statue in the square was replaced in 1943 with Tirso de Molino's. Not many of Tirso de Molino's plays are performed these days, but of all the Golden Age dramatists, he created the most enduring character in his play *The Trickster of Seville*: Don Juan Tenorio, the original of Mozart's *Don Giovanni*.

Calle de la Magdalena, running north of the square, has the **Palacio de los Marqueses de Perales** (1734), designed by Pedro de Ribera, with a fine Baroque door. One of the scions of the house had the misfortune to be governor of Madrid in 1808; his defenses of the city were found to be so inadequate owing to corruption and inefficiency, that the furious citizenry attacked this palace and killed him. On a more pleasant note, Plaza Tirso de Molino is a good place to find a reasonably priced meal, or a memorable one at the historic **La Taberna de Antonio Sánchez**, just south at Calle Mesón de Paredes 13. Founded in 1830, the tavern was bought in 1920 by a famous bullfighter, who hung up his cape to pick up the brush, and took lessons from Ignacio Zuloaga, one of the most successful painters of the day. The walls are covered with Sánchez's portraits of matadors, many of whom stop in and chat with the current owner, himself an ex-*torero*.

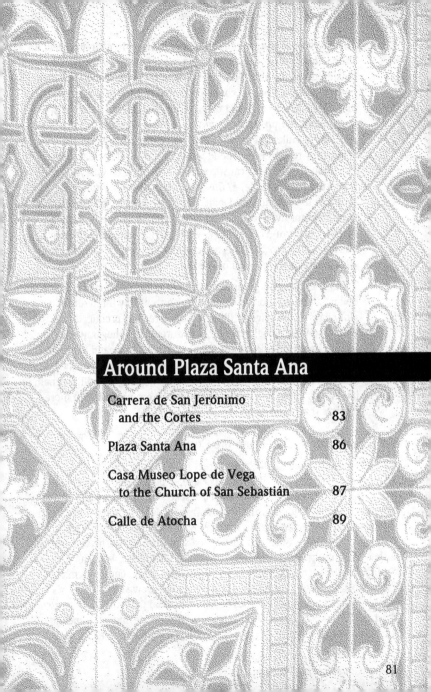

Around Plaza Santa Ana

Carrera de San Jerónimo
    and the Cortes   83

Plaza Santa Ana   86

Casa Museo Lope de Vega
    to the Church of San Sebastián   87

Calle de Atocha   89

This pie wedge of a neighbourhood of narrow dark streets grew up after 1560, just after Philip II made the city the capital. Located outside the walls until 1654, it had low rents (initially) and small houses, and became the congenial home to Madrid's first theatres, its Golden Age writers and playwrights, bordellos and taverns, booksellers and printers and *pícaros*—those out of work soldiers and other landless ne'er do wells whose roguish adventures are colourfully recounted in the Picaresque novels of the day. The neighbourhood's most caustic writer, Francisco de Quevedo, wrote the best of these, *El Buscón* ('The Swindler'),which is probably the second best Golden Age novel after *Don Quixote*, whose author lived just around the corner. A frequent visitor to this part of town was Philip IV, who attended not only the plays, but one of the most famous actresses of the day, La Calderona, who bore him a son, Juan of Austria.

Today the district is sometimes called the Barrio de las Letras or de los Literatos, and the distinction isn't entirely limited to the glory days of the reign of Philip IV: the area has produced two winners of the Nobel Prize for literature, José Echegaray and Jacinto Benavente. But most people call it Huertas and Santa Ana for its most important street and square. Don't expect many museums or monuments here; bars and theatres are still the main landmarks, although in the evenings they are packed with more tourists than *madrileños*.

Carrera de San Jerónimo and the Cortes

East of the Puerta del Sol, the main street to the Prado and the Retiro is the Carrera de San Jerónimo. Laid out as processional route to the royal monastery of San Jerónimo, it is now mostly a dull and respectable row of banks and offices and one essential Madrid institution: **Lhardy**, at No. 8, founded in 1839 by Emilio Lhardy, a friend of French writer Prosper Mérimée. Mérimée was a keen observer of life and art (besides writing the story of *Carmen*, he was France's inspector of historical monuments) and he told Lhardy just what the capital of Spain needed: chocolate éclairs. He was right, and Lhardy soon saw a market for more substantial fare, and his confectioner's soon evolved into the city's best restaurant. The home delivery business was so good that wealthy *madrileños* fired their cooks and built their palaces with only the most rudimentary of kitchens. Lhardys intimate dining rooms upstairs feature French and *muy castizo*

Around Plaza Santa Ana

200 metres
200 yards

Edificio Metropólis
Casino de Madrid
C. DE LA ADUANA
Real Academia Belles Artes
C. MONTERA
C. LA SEVILLA DE ALCALA
New Club
Círco de Bellas Artes
Banco de España
Ministerio Defensa
C. JUAN DE MENA
Banco Español de Crédito
C. ARLABAN
Banco Bilbao-Viscaya
C. DE LOS MADRAZO
Bolsa
Pl. Puerta del Sol
Casa de Correos
CARRERA
C. DE ZORILLA
Teatro Zarzuela
PASEO DEL PRADO
C. ANTONIO MAURA
Pl. Lealtad
C. POZO Canalejas
C. DE
SAN
Cortes
C. DE LA VICTORIA
C. ECHEGARAY
C. VENTURA VEGA
C. STA. CATALINA
JERÓNIMO
Museo Thyssen
Pl. Pontejos
C. CARRETAS
C. ESPOZ Y MINA
C. CADIZ
C. BARCELONA
Pl. de las Cortes
RUIZ DE
Palacio Santa Cruz
PONTEJOS
Pl. BOLSA
C. NUÑEZ ARCE
C. DEL PRINCIPE
C. DEL PRADO
Palace Hotel
Pl. Canovas del Castillo
DE ALARCÓN
Sta Cruz
CONC. JERÓNIMA
Pl. Jacinto Benavente
Hotel Reina Victoria
Teatro Español
C. DE LEON
C. SAN AGUSTIN
Pl. Sta Ana
Casa-Museo Lope de Vega
C. DE CERVANTES
Pl. Jesús
C. DE ATOCHA
C. SEBASTIAN
Pl. Matute
C. QUEVEDO
C. SAN PEDRO
LOPE DE VEGA
Museo del Prado
San Sebastián
San Ildefonso
C. ANIZARES
Pl. Antón Martín
Academia Real de la Historia
C. DE LAS HUERTAS
Pl. Platería Matiñez
Pl. Murillo
C. DE MAGDALENA
Teatro Monumental
Pl. S Juan
C. VERÓNICA
Jardín Botánico
ANTON MARTIN
Ciné Doré
C. DORE
C. DE SAN EUGENIO
COST DESAMPERADOS
GOBERNADOR
C. ALMADÉN
C. ALAMEDA
C. CENICHERO
C. DE SAN NUÑEZ
C. DE ATOCHA
C. FUCAR JESUS
C S BLAS
PASEO DEL PRADO
Hospital San Carlos
C. DE SANTA ISABEL
C. DR MATA
Museo Nacional Centro de Arte Reina Sofia
Pl. Emperor Carlos V
Ministerio Agricultura
ATOCHA
C. DR DRUMEN
Atocha Train Station
C. MENDEZ

Casa Monolos, 7 C/Jovellanos (opposite the Teatro de la Zaruzuela), ✆ 91 521 4516, offers tapas and *churros* in a convivial, old-fashioned atmosphere. *Closed Sun and Mon nights.*

Venencia, C/Echegaray 7, ✆ 91 366 28 59, is an old-fashioned Andalucian bar preserved in aspic from the 1920s; the best place in Madrid for a sherry.

Los Gabrieles, C/Echegaray 17, ✆ 91 429 6261. Once a brothel, it has the most beautiful tile decoration in Madrid; it can get very touristy, and watch out for prices doubling after 5pm.

Viva Madrid, C/Manuel Fernández y González (no phone), used to be favourite of Lorca's and has more lovely ceramics; these depict scenes of Madrid in the 1920s. High ceilings and paddle fans add to the atmosphere of slightly faded elegance.

Cervecería Alemana, Plaza de Santa Ana 6, ✆ 91 429 7033. A German-Spanish bar where Hemingway liked to booze and schmooze, and pretty much unchanged since then. Still a local favourite, despite being on the tourist trail.

Las Bravas, Callejón de Alvarez Gato (behind the hotel Victoria), ✆ 91 532 2620. Birthplace of the very popular tapa, *patatas bravas*—fried potato wedges doused in thick spicy tomato sauce.

La Dolores, Plaza de Jesús 4, ✆ 91 429 2243, just behind the Palace Hotel, is another pretty and popular tiled bar from the 30s, with good beers and excellent canapés to tide you over.

Naturbier, Plaza Santa Ana 9, ✆ 91 429 3918, brews its own German-style beer to traditional recipes. Popular with tourists and students.

Los Gatos, C/de Jesús 2, ✆ 91 429 3067. A veteran bar with a relaxed local ambience and a loyal following among the *torero* crowd.

La Ancha, Zorilla 7, ✆ 91 429 8186, is one of Madrid's finest restaurants, serving excellent traditional cuisine. It is very popular with politicians from the neighbouring Cortes.

La Luiza, Plaza Santa Ana 2, has fantastic displays of pâtisserie and a bar where you can while away the morning with your *café con leche*.

madrileño cuisine; the 'white room' was a 19th-century favourite for trysts, and was practically monopolized by the nymphomaniac Isabel II. Lhardy hasn't changed much in a century, and still keeps its silver samovar full of consommé by the bar downstairs, where clients help themselves and select other sweet or savoury delicacies, and pay at the door.

Just around the corner, colourful bars line Calle de Victoria, including **La Casa del Abuelo**, founded in 1906 and still famous for grandad's sizzling shrimp. In Calle del Pozo is another, even older institution of that most selfless and ephemeral of arts, cake-making: the **Antigua Pastelería del Pozo**, founded in 1830. A third temple to sweet delight, in this case *turrón* (Spanish nougat), is the **Casa Mira**, Carrera San Jerónimo 30, which has been selling the best in Madrid for six generations. Ornate 19th-century buildings line the Plaza de Canalejas; now full of offices, they still retain a stately if faded grandeur with shabby orange awnings festooning the windows.

If you blink you may miss the dowdy **Cortes** (1850), also known as the Palacio del Congreso or the Congreso de los Diputados, the home of the Spanish parliament (*free guided tours on Sat 10–1, except in Aug; bring your passport*). Knots of idle guards toting machine guns and aviator sunglasses are a hint of serious business afoot, but many cities one-tenth Madrid's size have larger and more elegant post offices; from it we can see how little Spaniards thought of their corrupt governments of the 19th century. Today, important sessions of the Cortes are broadcast on the radio, and it was on one such occasion in February 1981 when Civil Guard Colonel Tejero, and his right wing die-hard zealots stormed in, shooting off their pistols while the nation listened (the bullet holes are pointed out on the tour). Tejero held the Cortes hostage for 24 hours, finally surrendering when it became clear that the majority of the army was supporting the King and democracy. The following day saw the biggest demonstration in the city's history, led by the leaders of all the political parties, marching arm-in-arm down Calle de Alcalá. It is an admirable custom, and one that the *madrileños* recently repeated after the ETA assassinated a young politician (Miguel Angel Blanco in July 1997), sending a forceful message out that enough was enough.

The Cortes' most beloved feature are its two bronze lions, made from melted-down Moroccan canons captured by Generals Prim and O'Donnell in 1860. They are named Daoiz and Velarde (after the heroes of the 2 May 1808 uprising) and, judging by their distressed expressions, have just eaten something bad.

Opposite, the Riviera-style **Palace Hotel** offers deputies some of the grandeur and glamour denied by their cramped workplace, with enormous chandeliers and handsomely liveried footmen. In a bizarre juxtaposition, the hotel shares the building with the latest member of the Planet Hollywood chain, which lines its windows with scenes from recent movies. The nearby Plus Ultra building has a little carillon; figures appear on the hour to the mild interest of little bunches of tourists and the total indifference of the *madrileños* themselves. Meanwhile, located just behind the Cortes, the modest, rosy **Teatro de la Zarzuela** (1856), Calle Jovellanos, outsparkles the Cortes architecturally, and (most of the time) for entertainment value as well, with its productions of Madrid's homegrown operetta, ballet, and other music and dance.

Amid the clubs and bars, a couple of serious-minded institutions survive. At Calle del Prado 21, leading south from the Cortes, is the **Ateneo Científico y Literario de Madrid**, founded in 1820 to promote the arts and sciences and as such closed down by the reactionary Ferdinand VII in 1835. When it reopened, it quickly became one of the cultural bastions of the city, with its magnificently shabby patina of scholarship. The delightful old fashioned library with individual reading lamps has a collection of volumes second only to the Biblioteca Nacional; another asset is its popular, very cheap, cafeteria.

Plaza Santa Ana

Just west up Calle del Prado you'll come to the centre of the labyrinth, **Plaza Santa Ana**, one of the main nodes of tourist Madrid; the southern, Calle del Prado side in particular is lined with tiled cafés, bars and restaurants, with tables scattered under breezy trees. It also holds a special place for canine Madrid. *madrileño s* love dogs and this square must be as near to heaven as their furry friends can get, with a big playground just for them.

The square was yet another gift to the city from the 'rey de las plazuelas', Joseph Bonaparte, who demolished the convent of Santa Ana to clear the space. Even predating the convent, however, was the theatre, the Corral del Principe, one of the first in Spain built for the purpose, in 1583; it was rowdy, if not as wild as the *OK Corral* (in Spanish the word conjures up any kind of open-air pen, or court-yard). Madrid's theatre tradition began as soon as Philip II made it the capital; as most of the people in the city lived off the Court, they had plenty of leisure time during the day (most plays began at noon) and it wasn't long before the impromptu dramas held in the courtyards of the larger houses developed into a more professional art form, the profits divided between the performers and play-wrights and the charitable bodies that owned the *corrales.*

Here at the Corral del Principe and at the nearby Corral de la Cruz, which stood just to the west but was demolished in 1859, many of the dramas of the Golden Age were premiered to a famously hard to please audience, attracted in part by the presence of the actresses (unlike in Britain, the female parts were played by women). While distinguished guests sat in the special compartments or balconies along the sides, the cheapest places in the pit were filled by the so-called 'musketeers', the local tradesmen, who came to each performance armed with noise-makers and bells to disrupt a play whenever it failed to meet their approval. If the catcalls were too overwhelming, the playwright in the wings would hastily revise the end. Lope de Vega, in particular, was renowned for paying the musketeers to heckle the works of his rivals. A theatre has stood on the site of the Corral del Principe ever since, currently the **Teatro Español** (1802) decorated with busts of Spanish playwrights. A bird takes flight from the hands of Lorca in a simple statue in front. Yet another statue, of all of Calderón de la Barca this time, stands on the western side of the square, near the Riviera style **Hotel Reina Victoria**, a longtime favourite of visiting *toreros*; a plaque honours one of the greatest, Manolete, while the **Cervezería Alemana**, their (and of course Hemingway's) favourite drinking hole, has a fascinating display of photos and other taurine memorabilia.

Two streets run north of the square. On Calle del Príncipe, the **Teatro de la Comedia** (1875) is one of the best places in Madrid to see the classics of the Golden Age, in a handsome pseudo-Moorish interior. **Calle Echegaray** has a string of old bars, many preserving their beautiful ceramic décor from the 1920s, (*see* p.84 and pp.188–9)

Casa Museo de Lope de Vega

C/Cervantes 11, ℗ 91 429 9216, Ⓜ Antón Martín or Sevilla. Open Tues–Fri 9.30–2, Sat 10–2, closed Sun, hols, all Aug; adm 200 pts, free Sat)

One of the few tangible souvenirs of the Golden Age is the **Casa-Museo de Lope de Vega** where that great and prolific dramatist lived from 1610 to his death in 1635 at age 48, with reputedly some 1,500 plays under his belt, which means, if he started at age 18, he cranked out a play a week. Even more awesome is the fact that he managed to produce so much while leading a singularly messy private life, with assorted scandalous affairs, two wives whom he buried while fathering five children with his mistress, the actress María de Córdoba who went mad while Lope prepared to be ordained as a priest (while having even more affairs). The house has been restored according to an inventory of goods in the house upon his death. One of the rooms is, appropriately, a harem, while another contains personal memorabilia. His little garden has also been diligently restored.

This is also the old neighbourhood of Cervantes (1547–1616). Although he and Lope de Vega were bitter enemies ever since the days they served together in the wars against the Turks (exacerbated by a later rivalry over a *Madrileña* named Elena Osorio), Cervantes lived and died on the same street, on the corner of Calle de León. In spite of much protest at the time, led by historian Mesonero Romanos, his house was knocked down in 1833 and replaced with a plaque. Cervantes held an administrative post for the Crown, and moved here from Vallodolid along with rest of the Court in 1606, having already become famous (but not rich) for the first part of *Don Quixote*. In 1613 he wrote the *Exemplary Novels*, which were also well received, and in 1615 he wrote the second part of *Don Quixote,* understandably vexed after someone forged a mediocre continuation.

For all that, Cervantes was discouraged and destitute when he died the next year, and was buried, somewhere or other in the church of San Ildefonso, in the **Convento de las Trinitarias Descalzas**, a grim and forbidding place with tiny barred windows on Calle de Lope de Vega. Both Cervantes and Lope had daughters who became nuns here. Because of the literary connection, the Spanish academy managed to have the church spared twice when it was threatened with demolition. A jollier place altoghether is the tiny and very old fashioned *frutería,* on the same street at No.14, surrounded with little netted bags of oranges, and bunches of gossiping locals.

Opposite the convent, in Calle Quevedo, a plaque marks the house that sheltered two other literary monsters of the Golden Age, Luis de Góngora and Francisco de Quevedo. Góngora stayed as a boarder until Quevedo, his arch rival, bought the house for the pleasure of booting him out.

To the east, Calle Cervantes crosses the Plaza de Jesús, site of the church of **Jesús de Medinaceli**, one of the ugliest in Madrid. It was built in 1920 to replace the church of the monastery of the Trinitarios Descalzos where the monks devoted themselves to charitable causes, chiefly raising money to liberate Spanish soldiers captured by Algerian pirates. In 1580 they raised the ransom to free Cervantes, who had been captured and imprisoned in 1575 on his way home from serving in Greece.

This was the players' parish church in the 17th century, and Sunday Mass was a high fashion parade as the actresses sought to outdress one another, much to the delight of their followers, and the outrage of the more pious members of society. The church is named for its much venerated 16th-century statue of Jesus, which had also been captured and held to ransom by the Algerians, who demanded its weight in gold. But when the statue was put on the scales, it was miraculously-found to weigh only as much as a single coin. Hundreds of *madrileños* come on the first Friday of each month to kiss its feet.

South of this extends the bar-lined Calle de las Huertas, where not so long ago there were *más putas que puertas* ('more whores than doors'). The numbers were pretty impressive; in the 18th century, there were an estimated 800 brothels in Madrid, for a population of 150,000.

A stiff, disapproving respectability is maintained by the **Academia Real de la Historia** (Royal Academy of History), founded by Philip V in 1738, located to the east on the corner of Calle Léon (*open irregularly, call for information,* © 91 239 8269). The academy's building was designed by Juan de Villanueva in 1788 as a place where the monks of El Escorial could sell their prayer books, but was taken over by the academy a century later. It maintains a small museum with some paintings by Goya, Iberian and Roman antiquities and religious art of the Middle Ages.

Just a block west along Calle de las Huertas, in Plaza Matute, is a more obvious local monument: the beautiful curvaceous assymetrical *modernista* **Casa Pérez Villamil** (No. 10), built in 1906 by Eduardo Reynals. Further up Calle de las Huertas, on the corner of Calle de Príncipe, the **Palacio de Santoña** was built by Pedro de Ribera in 1734. It is ornamentanted with his characteristic ornate portals and now houses the Chamber of Commerce. At the west end of Huertas stands the church of **San Sebastián**, where Lope de Vega was buried in 1635. Like most famous corpses in Madrid, however, his body was lost even before the church was burned down in the Civil War.

Calle de Atocha

Calle de Atocha, running south of Huertas, was blazed as the main route from the Plaza Mayor to the Basílica of Atocha. Now flamboyantly seedy, its northern reaches are a good place to take in a concert at the **Teatro Monumental**. This enormous concert hall, in Plaza Antón Martín, often features performances of the RTVE orchestra and claims the largest organ in Europe, with a staggering 5,000 pipes. Tucked away in the nearby Pasaje Doré, a narrow shop-lined arcade perfumed with the fleshy smells of the surrounding meat and fish stalls, you'll find Madrid's oldest cinema, the **Cine Doré** (1922). Now the **Filmoteca Nacional** shows old art films most nights, and outdoors on the pleasant terrace on balmy summer evenings.

The first part of *Don Quixote* was first printed in 1605 at a printer's that stood at Calle Atocha 87, which may some day be a museum dedicated to the novelist; a plaque at No.94 marks the house of the author of *The Three Cornered Hat*, Pedro Antonio de Alarcón. But what this stretch of Calle Atocha is best known for is the now legendary BIGGEST sex shop in the world, El Mundo Fantástico, with its tempting Las Vegas style entrance and doorman.

...I went to see a regular comedy; there were two English gentlemen in the box with me at the same time. We understood very little of the design of the first act; we saw a king, queen, an enchantress, and many other pretty, delightful sights: but the interlude, with which that act concluded, is, I think, not to be equalled either by Rome or Greece; neither Farquhar, Cibber, or any of our lowest farce-writers, have ever produced any thing comparable to it. The scene was intended for the inside of a Spanish Posada (or inn) in the night; there were three feather-beds, and as many blankets brought upon the stage; the queen and her maids of honour personated the mistress of the Posada and her maids; and accordingly fell to making the beds. After this, there came in six men to lie there, who paid three quarts a piece; one of them being a miser, had rolled up his money in twenty or thirty pieces of paper. Then they undressed before the ladies, by pulling off six or seven pairs of breeches, and as many coats and waistcoats, and got into bed two by two: When behold, the jest was, to see all kick the clothes of one another, and then fight, as the spectator is to suppose, in the dark. The absurdity of this scene, and the incomprehensible ridiculousness of it, made us laugh immoderately. The sight of feather-beds, the men kicking and sprawling, the peals of applause, that echoed through the house, were truly inconceivable; tho', I believe, our neighbours in the next box thought we laughed at the wit and humour of the author. It was a scene that beggars all possible description, and I defy any theatre in Europe, but that of Madrid, to produce such another...

E. Clarke, *Letters concerning the Spanish Nation*, 1763

Paseo del Prado   94

Museo del Prado   94

Casón del Buen Retiro   100

Plaza de la Lealtad   102

Museo Collección
   Thyssen-Bornemisza   102

Behind the Prado   108

The Retiro   110

Plaza del Emperado Carlos V   113

Museo Nacional
   Centro de Arte Reina Sofía   114

Between Atocha Station
   and the Retiro   118

The 'Paseo del Arte' and the Retiro

If the Prado wasn't already enough to make Madrid a major art destination, the re-opening of the Reina Sofía Art Centre in 1990 and the nation's permanent acquisition of the Thyssen-Bornemisza collection in 1992 removed all doubt. Madrid is rightly proud of its showcase 'golden triangle'—three superb museums all within strolling distance of each other, linked by the Paseo del Prado.

The three collections complement each other neatly. The **Museo del Prado** is best known for its hoard of masterpieces of Spanish painting from the 12th to the early 19th centuries, and it also holds rich collections of 15th–17th century Flemish painting, as well as Italian art by the likes of Raphael and Botticelli. Its annexe, the Casón del Buen Retiro, covers the 19th century. The **Museo Nacional Centro de Arte Reina Sofía** picks up the thread with its permanent collection of 20th century art (the centrepiece of which is Picasso's masterwork *Guernica*). The newcomer on the scene, the **Museo Collección Thyssen-Bornemisza**, is a remarkable gathering of work spanning eight centuries. Its highlights include early Italian paintings, 17th-century Dutch works, and paintings by 20th-century masters including Braque, Mondrian, Picasso and Warhol. Fortuitously, it manages to fill in a few of the gaps left by the Prado and the Reina Sofía, with collections of impressionism and post-impressionism, German Expressionists such as Munch, Schiele and Kandinsky, and a restrained but well-informed selection of pop art and geometrical abstracts.

cafés, bars and restaurants

All of the three big **museums** have cafés, but there are plenty of other places just off the Paseo del Prado (also *see* Around Plaza Santa Ana, p.84).

El Botánico, C/Ruíz de Alarcón 27, ✆ 91 420 2342. A relaxing bar directly behind the Prado, with outdoor tables.

Viridiana, C/Juan de Mena 14, ✆ 91 523 4478. The name and décor are dedicated to the films of Luis Buñuel, and the chef dedicated to imaginative cuisine, among the best in Madrid. For lunch as lovely as the art; *around 7,000 pts.*

Jardins Savoy Ritz, Plaza de la Realtad 5, ✆ 91 521 2857. Pamper yourself at Madrid's plushest outdoor tearooms. Also try their restaurant, the **Goya**.

El Cenedor del Prado, Paseo del Prado 4, ✆ 91 429 1561. Delicious Mediterranean cuisine served in luxurious surroundings.

Paseo del Arte

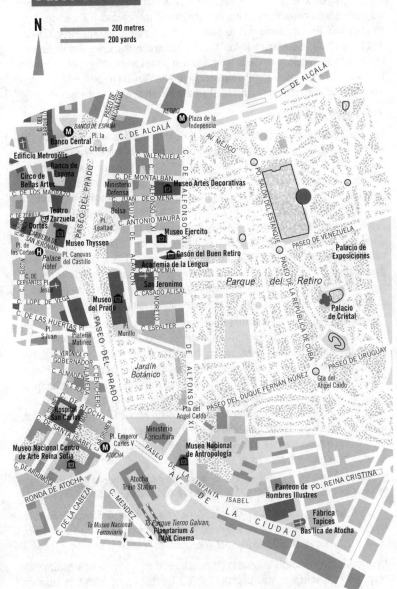

N

200 metres
200 yards

PASEO DE RECOLETOS

C. DEL BARQUILLO

BANCO DE ESPAÑA
Banco Central
Pl. la Cibeles

Edificio Metrópolis

Círco de Bellas Artes

Banco de España

C. DE LOS MADRAZO

C. DE ALCALÁ

C. VALENZUELA

C. DE MONTALBÁN

RETIRO
Plaza de la Indepencia

AV. MÉJICO

C. DE ALCALÁ

PO. SALÓN DEL ESTANQUE

C. DE ZORILLA

Teatro Zarzuela

Cortes

CARRERA DE SAN JERÓNIMO

Pl. de las Cortes

Palace Hotel

C. GUSTIN

C. DE CERVANTES

C. LOPE DE VEGA

Jesús

Ministerio Defensa

Bolsa

Pl. Lealtad

C. JUAN DE MENA

C. ANTONIO MAURA

Museo Thyssen

Pl. Canovas del Castillo

Academia de la Lengua

San Jeronimo

C. CASADO ALISAL

C. ACADEMIA

C. DE ALARCÓN

Museo del Prado

Pl. Murillo

C. ESPALTER

PASEO DEL PRADO

Museo Artes Decorativas

Museo Ejercito

Casón del Buen Retiro

Parque   del   Retiro

PASEO DE VENEZUELA

Palacio de Exposiciones

PASEO DE LA REPÚBLICA DE CUBA

Palacio de Cristal

C. DE LAS HUERTAS

Pl. S Juan

Platería Matiñez

C. VERÓNICA

C. ALMADÉN

C. S. BLAS

GOBERNADOR

ALAMEDA

C. CENICHERO

Jardín Botánico

C. MORETO

C. DE ALFONSO XI

PASEO DE URUGUAY

Gta del Angel Caído

C. DE ATOCHA

Hospital S. San Carlos

C. DE SANTA ISABEL

Museo Nacional Centro de Arte Reina Sofía

C. DE ARGUMOSA

RONDA DE ATOCHA

C. DE LA CABEZA

To Museo Nacional Ferroviario

C. MÉNDEZ

To Parque Tierno Galvan, Planetarium & IMAX Cinema

Pta del Angel Caído

PASEO DEL DUQUE FERNÁN NÚÑEZ

Pl. Emperor Carlos V

ATOCHA

Ministerio Agricultura

Atocha Train Station

PASEO DE AVA

Museo Nacional de Antropología

INFANTA ISABEL

DE LA CIUDAD

Panteon de Hombres Illustres

PO. REINA CRISTINA

Fábrica Tapices

Bas'lica de Atocha

As the Prado, the Reina Sofía and the Thyssen are such near neighbours, many visitors are tempted to hop between them, relishing the change in atmosphere, but risking sensory overload to the third degree. A money-saving *'Paseo del Arte'* voucher will allow you one visit to each of the three big museums for 1,275 pts; don't even think about trying to 'do' the three monsters in a single day unless you are the bionic sightseer, or likely to be satisfied with a mere snippet of each. Add the beautiful gardens of the Parque del Retiro and an assortment of other, but thankfully smaller, museums, this is an area to return to again and again.

The Paseo del Prado

The leafy boulevard that ties the three museums together was laid out by the 'mayor-king' Charles III. As a son of the Enlightenment, Charles was dismayed at the haphazard higgeldy piggeldy way Madrid had grown up, and decided to give his capital a proper broad avenue, lined with worthy scientific institutions. A tree-lined path through the meadow (*prado*) near the Monasterio de San Jerónimo was selected for glory, and in 1775 architect José de Hermosilla laid out the Paseo, a project that involved a massive amount of landfill and levelling. Some of the sweat was provided by speeders: Madrid's first traffic laws were put on the books then, penalizing reckless coachmen with ten day's labour on the Paseo project. In the 19th century, the Paseo became a roaring success—it was *the* place to see and be seen in Madrid, and everyone from all walks of life congregated there in the evening. Six lanes of motor traffic have since changed all that for ever.

Magnificent fountains by Ventura Rodríguez frame what was called the 'Salón del Prado'—from the Fountain of Cybele in the north (see p.124) to the **Fountain of Neptune** in the south, in front of the Prado, with a smaller **Fountain of Apollo** in between. Hermosilla's model was Rome's Piazza Navona, and here, as there, the fountains served the same purpose, as the spina of an ancient circus, for the fashionable carriages to go around and around. Neptune, where the supporters of Atlético de Madrid frolic to celebrate victories, features a statue of the sea god holding his trident; during the 'Hunger Years' of the 1940s, he also sported a sign, added by a local wag: 'Either give me something to eat or at least take away my fork!'

Museo del Prado

Paseo del Prado, © *91 420 2836,* ✆ *91 420 0794,* Ⓜ *Banco de España. Open: Tues–Sat 9–7, Sun and hols, 9–2, closed Mon; adm 500 pts, concessions 250 pts, free Sat after 2.30 and Sun.*

Charles III intended this long, elegant neoclassical structure to be a natural history museum when it was begun in 1785 by the young architect Juan de

Villanueva. But the stuffed elephants never arrived; the museum was just completed in 1808 when the French swooped in like vultures, made it their barracks, and stripped it bare, even taking part of the roof to melt into bullets. And so it rotted forlornly until Ferdinand VII, that most hated of kings, decided to act on an idea first put forth by Mengs, court painter to Charles III. Mengs realized that the paintings adorning Spain's royal palaces added up to one of Europe's greatest artistic treasures, and suggested bringing them all together under one roof. Ferdinand decided that the one roof (once repaired) should be this one and opened the collections to the public in 1819. Even repaired, however, the roof would bedevil the Prado—the museum was always closed on rainy days: even in 1993 there were leaks and buckets in the main Velázquez room.

Although the building itself has been restored several times (the façade is getting the works at the time of writing), the collections have changed little since 1819, outside of the addition in 1868 of a mass of religious works confiscated from Spain's suppressed monastic institutions. Spanish noble families who collected paintings are likely still to have them; the habit of donating to museums never took root as much here as in the rest of Europe. For the best of the Prado we can thank the practised eyes of Charles V, Philip II and Philip IV. Whatever else history can blame them for, they knew good painting when they saw it.

There was considerable disgruntlement when in 1993 the government invested an unprecedented (though bargain) sum in acquiring the Thyssen collection while apparently neglecting the Prado's arguably more pressing needs, in particular its nagging space problem. The exhibition areas are only large enough to display a tenth of the collection, and among the 'unseen' canvases are significant works by a good number of the Spanish Old Masters. At the time of writing, plans are uncertain; there are rumours that the Prado will take over the building currently occupied by the Army Museum (see p.109). Whatever happens, the curators promise that the museum's best known masterpieces will always be on display. Pick up the free, frequently updated leaflet with the floorplan to help you find the paintings you want to see. If you only have time for the highlights, the 1100-pts Quick Guide will direct you to the museum's fifty key works.

Expect crowds, especially at weekends, but don't be dismayed by huge mobs at the entrances; they're likely to be disorganized tour groups counting heads, and you should be able to pass right through. The earlier you go, the fewer of these you'll have to contend with. The best place to begin a comprehensive visit to the collections is to enter at ground level by the Puerta de Goya (Goya gate) at the north end of the main building, the Edificio Villanueva. The grandiose main entrance is closed owing to the restoration of the façade, but there's a secondary entrance (the Puerta de Murillo) at the southern end.

The Collections

A statue of the first great Habsburg collector, Charles V, greets visitors in the main foyer. This was sculpted by a father and son team, León and Pompeo Leoni, who, unbeknownst to the emperor, made his armour removable. Underneath he's nude, at least as the sculptors imagined him, in a rather curious play on the story of the emperor's new clothes.

12th–16th-century Spanish Art

The first ground floor rooms are devoted to medieval religious works. Don't be in too much of a hurry to see Velázquez; some of the best art in the Prado is here, including some 12th-century murals from Segovia and three stunning 14th- and 15th-century *retablos*: the *Archbishop Don Sancho de Rojas* by Rodríguez de Toledo, the *Legend of St Michael* by the Maestro de Arguis, and *The Life of the Virgin and St Francis* by Nicolás Francés. This rich collection of early Spanish painting continues with Renaissance-influenced works such as Fernando Gallego's eerie *Cristo Bendiciendo*. Pedro Berruguete contributes a scene of an *Auto-da-Fé presided over by Saint Dominic* that is almost satirical, with bored church apparatchiks dozing under a baldachin while the woebegone heretics are led off to the slaughter. *San Pedro Martir*, by the same artist, beams beatifically from beneath the meat cleaver splitting his skull. Bartolomé Bermejo's portrait of *St Dominic enthroned as Abbot of Silos* stands out for sheer dramatic realism: the saint is shown seated on a monumental throne surrounded by figures representing the three theological and four cardinal virtues.

Flemish, Dutch and German Schools

Even before Philip II, who valued Flemish art above all others, the Low Countries' close commercial and dynastic ties with Spain ensured that some of their art would turn up here. Today the Prado's collection of Flemish art is almost as unmissable as its Spanish collection. The works are arranged roughly chronologically, beginning with the 15th-century Primitives, including paintings by Robert Campin and breathtakingly detailed work by Rogier van der Weyden. Weyden's *Descent from the Cross* (c. 1435) is astonishing, framed like a scene from a mystery play, in which Gothic stylization is all but forgotten in favour of the realistic visual representation of a whole spectrum of human emotions. Within the tight confines of the composition the figures just float off the surface of the panel. A copy hangs at El Escorial.

The biggest crowds, though, will be around the works of Hieronymous Bosch (1450–1516, known in Spain as 'El Bosco'). His psychological fantasies, including *The Garden of Earthly Delights*, *The Hay Wain*, *The Adoration of the*

Magi and the table in the centre of the room decorated with *The Seven Deadly Sins* are too familiar to need any comment. Philip II bought every one he could get his hands on, and it should not be surprising to find the most complex of all Spanish kings as attracted to this dark surrealism as we moderns are. More works by Bosch can be seen in Philip's apartments at El Escorial. If you like Bosch, you should also get to know his countryman Joachim Patinir, some of whose best work can also be found in this section. Probably no other museum has such a large complement of terror to balance its own beauty; between Goya (*see* below), Bosch and the other northern painters and the religious hacks, a trip to the Prado can seem like a long ride in a carnival funhouse. If you approach it in this way, the climax will undoubtedly be *The Triumph of Death* by Pieter Brueghel the Elder (1525–1569), with its phalanxes of leering skeletons turned loose upon a doomed, terrified world. To Philip II, who is said to have kept a crowned skull on his night table, it must have seemed a deeply religious work. The Dutch, though, in the middle of their war of independence, would probably have been reminded of the horrors of intolerance and militant religion that were searing contemporary Europe—much of it emanating from this very city.

Rubens (1577–1640), a favourite of Philips III and IV, is well represented here, with his epic *Adoration of the Magi* dominating a whole roomful of florid biblical paintings, and his chubby *Three Graces* among other mythological subjects in an adjacent gallery. A room nearby contains the famous collaboration of Brueghel the Younger and Rubens, the *Allegory of the Five Senses*, a complete universe of philosophy in its five enormous canvases. Rubens' works are followed by those of later Flemish masters: delicate portraits by Anton van Dyck (1599–1641), complex studies by David Teniers such as his paintings-within-a-painting work *Archduke Leopold William in his picture gallery*, and, tucked away in a room full of small canvases, one of the greatest works of Brueghel the Younger, the untitled 'snowy landscape'.

The Prado's small Dutch collection consists mostly of 17th-century hunting scenes, still lifes, and the like, but there is one good Rembrandt (1606–69), a dignified portrait of a regal woman thought to be *Artemisia*, wife of King Mausolus. German paintings, too, are few, but they are choice. Albrecht Dürer's rather presumptuous *Self Portrait* (1498), for example, is an interesting work, painted at a time when self-portraits were uncommon (artists were considered unworthy subjects), and composed in a style that is often compared to Leonardo da Vinci's *Mona Lisa* (a copy of which hangs in the Italian section), although it was actually painted five years earlier. Interesting too are Dürer's companion paintings of *Adam* and *Eve*, Hans Baldung Grien's angular Teutonic *Three Graces* and sinister *Three Ages of Man and Death*, and works by Cranach and Mengs.

Italian and French Schools

In the Prado's Italian collection, there are several paintings by Raphael (1483–1520), all religious subjects; from Fra Angelico (1397–1455) an intensely spiritual *Annunciation*; and an unusual Botticelli (1444–1510) trio of scenes from Bocaccio's Decameron, *The Story of Nastagio degli Onesti*. Andrea del Sarto, Mantegna, Antonello da Messina, Veronese, Caravaggio, Tintoretto and Correggio, among the other Italian masters, are all represented, and there are rooms full of Titians, including two portraits of the artist's patron, Charles V, who ruled the biggest empire of all time but paid the painter two hitherto unheard-of compliments for the age: he stooped over and picked up a brush that Titian had dropped, and (on another occasion) knighted him.

Titian (*c.* 1490–1576) never painted anything small, and perhaps his biggest canvas of all is *La Gloria*, a colourful, preposterous cloud-bedecked imagining of the Holy Trinity that gently nudges the boundaries of kitsch. Charles (who is also in the picture, sometimes called his 'Apotheosis'), is said to have gazed upon this picture constantly while on his deathbed. His son, Philip II, was another fervent patron of Titian and apparently spend a lot of time gazing at the sumptuous female nudes in the mythologies, or *poesies*, as he called them. Among the 17th- and 18th-century French works on display are paintings by Poussin and Watteau.

16th–17th-century Spanish Art

To appreciate the genius of Domenikos Theotocopoulos, better known as El Greco (1540–1614), there is no substitute for a visit to the museums of Toledo, but there are some fine examples of what are sometimes called his 'vertical pictures' in the Prado, including *The Annunciation* and *The Adoration of the Shepherds*, mannerist depictions of biblical figures with elongated limbs and faces. El Greco was also a skilled portraitist and his *Nobleman with his Hand on his Chest* is particularly haunting. By the 17th century, the religious pathology of the age becomes manifest, notably in a disturbing painting by Francisco Ribalta of the crucified Christ leaning down off the Cross to embrace St Bernard. Elsewhere, St Bernard comes in for more abuse, this time at the hand of Alonso Cano, who illustrates the old tale of the praying saint receiving a squirt of milk in his mouth from the breast of an image of the Virgin.

Other, uneven, works by Spanish Baroque masters fill a dozen galleries: José de Ribera (1591–1652), Francisco de Zurbarán (1598–1664) and Bartolomé Esteban Murillo (1618–1682) among others. Ribera was a follower of Caravaggio's style and he used dark colours, starkly lit, to suggest pious ascetism, pain, suffering, and earthy sensual pleasure. His paintings of mythological and religious subjects (such as *St Andrew* and *The Martyrdom of St Philip*) are shot through with sinister undercurrents; he was particularly keen on using scruffy urchins and decaying beggars as models in order to inject warts-and-all realism into his work. Zurbarán was a Sevillian contemporary of Velázquez, but was totally unlike him in style. The Prado has some examples of his finely worked still lifes; these have a sacramental quality, with everyday objects laid out like devotional offerings. Murillo churned out plenty of sentimental tosh, some of which has found its way here, but his *Holy Family* (1650) is sweet and un-affected; it is a lovingly painted moment, showing the toddler Jesus playing with a small dog, gently encouraged by his doting parents.

Velázquez

On a day when there are as many Spaniards as foreigners in the Prado, the crowds around the works of Diego de Silva y Velázquez (1599–1660) can be daunting. Many Spaniards consider their countryman to be the greatest artist of all, and you may find the several rooms devoted to him here, the largest Velázquez collection by far, to be a convincing argument. Many of the works have recently been cleaned or restored, making the audacity of his use of light and colour stand out even more clearly. Almost all of his best-known paintings are here: *Los Borrachos* (The Drunkards), *Las Hilanderas* (The Spinning-Women), and *The Surrender of Breda*, which the Spaniards call *Las Lanzas* (the Lances). There are portraits of court dwarves, such as *Francisco Lezcano*, in which he gave his small sitters an air of humanity and dignity generally denied them in daily life (dwarves were employed as court jesters and were treated like children, or worse). Also present are the royal portraits: lumpy, bewildered Philip IV, a king aware enough of his own inadequacies to let Velázquez express them on canvas, appears in various poses—as a hunter, a warrior, or simply standing around wondering what's for dinner. Of his children, we see the six-year-old *Infante Balthasar Carlos* in a charming, mock-heroic pose on horseback, and again at the age of 16. It was this prince's untimely death soon after the latter portrait that gave the throne to the idiot Carlos II. His sister, the doll-like Infanta Margarita, appears by herself and in the most celebrated of all Velázquez's works, *Las Meninas* (the Maids-of-Honour, 1656), a composition of such inexhaustible complexity and beauty that the Prado gives it pride of place. In 1985, a poll of artists and critics voted it The World's Greatest Painting. In it, not only does Velázquez capture eloquently the everyday atmosphere of the Spanish court (the little princess, her bizarre entourage, and, unseen except for in a mirror in the background, her royal parents), he also turns the then-accepted artistic limits of perspective and dimensional space inside out. Velázquez painted himself in the picture (note how he seems to be sizing up us, the viewers, as his subject) but the red cross on his tunic, the badge of the Order of Santiago, was added by King Philip's own hand, as a graceful way of informing the artist of the honour he was conferring on him.

Goya

Like Velázquez, Francisco de Goya y Lucientes (1746–1828) held the office of court painter, in this case at the service of an even more useless monarch, Charles IV. Also like Velázquez, he was hardly inclined to flattery. Critics ever since have wondered how he got away with making his royal patron look so foolish, and the job he did on Charles' wife, the hook-nosed, ignorant and ill-tempered Queen Maria Luisa, is legendary. In every portrait and family scene, she comes out looking half fairy-tale witch, half washerwoman. Her son, later to be the reactionary King Ferdinand VII, is pictured as a teenager, and Goya makes him merely disagreeable and menacing.

Among the other famous Goyas you may compare the *Maja Desnuda* and the *Maja Vestida* (the Naked and Clothed Majas), and the *Dos de Mayo* and *Los Fusilamentos de Moncloa*, the pair commemorating the uprising of 1808 and its aftermath. The latter, much the better known, shows the impassioned patriots' faces caught in the glare of a lantern, facing the firing squad of grim, almost mechanical French soldiers. Nothing like it had ever been painted before, an unforgettable image and a prophetic prelude to the era of revolutions, mass politics and total war that was just beginning, inaugurated by the French Revolution and Napoleon. The setting is Madrid's Casa de Campo, and the spires of the old town can be made out clearly in the background. Representing his early work, Goya's remarkable *cartoons*—designs for tapestries to be made by the Royal Factories for the king's palaces—provide a massive dose of joy and sweetness, with their vivid colours bathed in clear Castilian sunshine. Most, such as *El Quitasol* (the Parasol) and *La Fiesta de San Isidro* are idealized scenes of festivals or country life, and the creatures inhabiting them seem less Spaniards than angels.

In stark contrast are some of the Prado's greatest treasures, its collection of Goya's *Pinturas Negras* ('Black Paintings'), late works painted after his mysterious illness, which are separated from the others by a staircase as if it were feared they would contaminate the sunnier paintings upstairs. All the well-known images of dark fantasy and terror are here: *Saturn Devouring One of his Sons*, *Duel with Cudgels*, *The Colussus (Panic)*, and even a nightmarish vision of the same San Isidro festivies that the artist painted so happily when he was healthy.

Casón del Buen Retiro

C/Alfonso XII 28, ☎ 91 420 2628, ✉ 91 429 2930, Ⓜ Retiro. Closed for restoration at the time of writing, scheduled to reopen in mid-2000. Opening times usually as Museo del Prado, above.

The Prado's collection of 19th-century Spanish art is housed in an ungainly 17th-century building intended as a ballroom for Philip IV's long-lost Palacio del Buen

Retiro, near the entrance to the Retiro Park. The largest and most impressive canvases are hung in the Grand Salon on the ground floor, which also retains its original over-the-top Baroque ceiling on the *Triumph of the Golden Fleece*, painted by Luca Giordano, the Neapolitan court painter to the unfortunate Charles II. The Casón del Buen Retiro is far more famous for the painting it lost (Picasso's *Guernica*) than for the paintings it still holds. Many of these differ little from the bland naturalistic art of the rest of 19th-century Europe, but there are enough little-known gems in the collection to make it worth a visit.

Painters like Mariano Fortuny (1838–1874), Joaquín Sorolla (1863–1923) and the Madrazo family were popular in their day, and are well represented here: the collection opens with a blockbusting neoclassical work by José de Madrazo, his *Death of Viriazo*. Outstanding in a clutch of portraits by Vicente López is a fascinating study of *Goya*, holding his palette and brushes and looking grumpy, and a frank portrait of the blind and decrepit but sweet-faced *Infante Don Antonio*. In each, López expertly captures the essence of the sitter in the set of their facial features, rather than by merely recreating their environment or their pose. On the way upstairs to the Romantic section of the collection is a huge canvas by José Casado del Alisal, *The Surrender of Bailén*, painted in homage to Velázquez' *The Lances*. The Romantic works include paintings by Eugenio Lucas, Leonardo Alenza and Francisco Lameyer, all powerfully influenced by Goya; and Federico de Madrazo's wonderfully wry, flirtatious *Countess of Vilches*, in a room full of stuffy portraits. Among the works by Fortuny is his *Old Man Naked in the Sun*, a study of old age in all its gnarled glory; and Sorolla's sandy-bottomed *Children at the Beach* is a wonderful, luminously lit evocation of boyhood. A few rooms on both the first and the ground floors contain landscapes; of these Santiago Rusiñol's modernist *Garden in Aranjuez* will strike chords in anyone who has visited the gardens of Aranjuez' royal palaces.

The climax of a visit to the Casón del Buen Retiro is without a doubt the Grand Salon, where *Guernica* once hung, now replaced by monumental works by José Moreno Carbonero, Francisco Pradilla, Antonio Gisbert, Eduardo Rosales and others. Carbonero's *Prince Charles of Viana* depicts a cowed prince in a shambolic library, resigned to a hermit-like life having been passed over for the Aragonese throne; and his *Conversion of the Duke of Gandía* shows remarkable emotional control, especially for an artist of only 24 years. Here the putrefying corpse on display is Isabella, wife of Charles V. To say that Pradilla's *Doña Juana the Madwoman* and Gisbert's *Execution of Torrijos and his Comrades* are chilling in their realism does them both scant justice; these are among these artists' finest works. Last in the collection is Juan Gris' *Portrait of Josette*, looking forlorn and left-behind; it should have followed the other 20th-century works to the Reina Sofía but the insistence of its donor, Douglas Cooper, keeps it here.

Plaza de la Lealtad

The large buildings on the circular Plaza de la Lealtad ('Loyalty Square'), just north of the Prado, were designed to blend in with its neo-classical stateliness: the **Ritz Hotel** with its delightful tea garden, built in 1908 at the special request of Alfonso XIII (whose famous wedding was marred not only by a bomb but by the lack of suitably posh rooms in which to lodge his guests); and the **Bolsa de Commercio,** or Stock Exchange, which sometimes has free art exhibitions as well as a permanent one on the institution itself. In the centre, a patriotic obelisk, erected in 1840 to a design by González Velázquez, is the chief monument to the victims of the 2 May uprising—in fact, they are buried in the urn. The gates are usually locked—perhaps to prevent over-curious tourists singeing themselves on the eternal flame that burns in front of the tomb. Across the Paseo del Prado from here is the newest corner of the Triangulo del Arte, the Thyssen Museum.

Museo Collección Thyssen-Bornemisza

Palacio de Villahermosa, Paseo del Prado 8, © 91 420 3944, ✆ 91 420 2780, Ⓜ Atocha or Banco de España. Open Tues–Sun 10–7, closed Mon; adm 700 pts, concessions 400 pts; tickets for temporary exhibitions sold separately, 500 pts. If you want to take a break, make sure you get a stamp ('sello') on your wrist at the information desk.

The directors of the Reina Sofía, reeling from the media response to the controversies surrounding their early policies, were glad to have the spotlight eased off them for a while in 1993, when everyone's attention switched up the road to the Villahermosa Palace. Thanks to the persuasiveness of his wife, Carmen 'La Tita' Cervera, a former Miss Spain, Baron Hans-Heinrich Thyssen-Bornemisza had already decided on Madrid as the temporary home for the cream of his unique collection of art (Madrid having outbid other cities including London, represented by none other than Prince Charles). In 1993, the arrangement was made permanent: the Spanish government purchased the collection for the extremely reasonable sum of 44,000 million pesetas. Despite the recession, and the further millions required to convert the palace into a building to permanently house the paintings, the acquisition seemed to represent an unmissable opportunity to boost Madrid's, and Spain's, already high profile on the international art scene.

The collection, started in the 1920s by the present baron's father, Baron Heinrich Thyssen-Bornemisza, is idiosyncratic, eclectic and fun, and offers a fascinating insight into the personal taste of two men with a magpie-like compulsion. When the elder baron died and the paintings were spread out among his heirs, the present Baron diligently went about buying them back from his kin, and then kept adding and adding, until the collection's old home, the Villa Favorita in Lugano, was bursting at the seams.

Like a prized and precious stamp collection, the museum contains a little of everything—there's an entry on practically every page of art history, from the religious works of 13th-century Italy to the brash output of Europe and the USA in the 1960s and '70s—with the Barons' particular favourites represented in larger quantities (they liked 19th-century American painting; you might not). The present Baron Thyssen is a standard bearer of art for the modern world and his is widely regarded as the world's finest private art collection after that of the British Royal Family. He has claimed that he learned all he knows about art appreciation simply by hanging his pictures up and looking at them; with an approach as honest and pragmatic as this it is wholly consistent that he decided to make it possible for the general public to share his enjoyment of his collection.

The architect Rafael Moneo had a shell of a building out of which to create the gallery spaces, and his finished work, the walls washed in a warm cross between salmon and terracotta (the Baroness's favourite colour–she insisted on it) and bathed in a very pleasing balance of natural and artificial light, is extremely successful. The chronological sequence of works begins on the top floor (reached by the lift or stairs towards the centre of the building) and works its way, anticlockwise, downwards. The sequence was arranged like this so that the modern works could benefit from being hung in the high-ceilinged ground floor rooms. In the basement is a café and a space for temporary exhibitions.

In the entrance, you are greeted by two pairs of full length portraits: of Queen Sofía and King Juan Carlos I, and of the Baron and Baroness, the latter in a remarkable winged cocktail dress with a smudgy canine at her feet.

Second Floor

The collection opens with one of its highlights, a treasure trove of gems of primitive and medieval Italian religious art, including a hauntingly simple and lovely 13th-century statue of the Madonna and Child, and some 14th-century gilded panels of exquisite beauty by the likes of Duccio de Buoninsegna and Simone Martini. These are followed by 15th-century works from the Low Countries, among them Jan van Eyck's stirring and brilliantly executed monochrome *Annunciation Diptych* (c. 1435–1441), depicting the Angel Gabriel and the Virgin Mary with the Holy Spirit fluttering above her head in the shape of a dove. Only rather than show real figures, Van Eyck shows them as stone sculptures, reflected in the shiny black stone behind them: a unique work of the time, of art depicting art. *Clothing the Naked* (c. 1470) by the Master of Saint Gudule offers an interesting illustration of the development of perspective techniques: a court-yard recedes, like a stage set, behind the figures in the foreground. Rogier van der Weyden's tiny, immaculate *Madonna Enthroned* (*c.* 1433), where the Virgin sits in a stone alcove carved with New Testament scenes, is a fascinating point of reference for his large, slightly later work, *The Descent from the Cross*, which hangs in the Prado. Beside this is Petrus Christus' symbolic masterpiece, *Our Lady of the Dry Tree* (*c.* 1450), hung with 15 letter As, each representing an *Ave María*.

The next room contains 15th-century Italian works such as Bramantino's spooky, cadaverous *Resurrected Christ*, and Ercole de' Roberti's charming mythology, *The Argonauts leaving Colchis*, a rarefied work from the Humanist court of Ferrara. Another member of the same school, Cosmé Tura, contributes an almost surreal *St John on Patmos*.

Early Renaissance portraits form another high point of the collection. There are plenty of familiar faces here, including Holbein's *Henry VIII* (*c.* 1534–36), Memling's *Young Man at Prayer* (*c.* 1485), Campin's uncompromisingly crisp *Stout Man* (*c.* 1485) and Antonella da Messina's *Portrait of a Man* (*c.* 1475–76), whose eyes fix you with a direct, intelligent gaze. There is also a *Portrait of Giovanna Tornabuoni* (1488) by Domenico Ghirlandaio, one-time tutor to Michaelangelo, who includes a Latin inscription behind the sitter's elegant neck alluding to the duality of the outer and inner aspects of beauty; it translates as: 'if art could portray character and virtue, no painting in the world would be more beautiful'. Isabella la Católica's favourite painter, the Hispano-Flemish Juan de Flandres, contributes the exquisite wistful *Portrait of an Infanta* (*c.* 1496), a Spanish princess minus all the trappings; it could be Catherine of Aragon, or more poignantly, Isabel's daughter and heir to the throne, the young Juana the Mad.

Rafael Moneo designed the windowed long Villahermosa Gallery, running the length of the building, to recall the gallerias like these in Italian palaces where paintings were hung. Most of the works here are portraits—the special favourite of the first Baron Thyssen. Here another Raphael, *the* Raphael, painted the *Portrait of a Young Man*, believed to be Alessandro de' Medici.

Off the gallery are a row of rooms containing 16th-century paintings. The first room is dedicated to the Italians. Vittore Carpaccio's *Young Knight in a Landscape* (1510) is one of the Thyssen's most famous works, remarkable for its richly detailed allegorical backdrop. Carpaccio's fellow Venetians are here, too: a late *Sacra Conversazione* (1510?) by Giovanni Bellini, a lushly coloured work against a serene background, and *La Bella* (1525) by Bellini's pupil Palma Vecchio, renowned for his talent for painting beautiful women. Venetian

Sebastiano del Piombo's masterful *Portrait of Ferry Carondelet* (1512) was long attributed to Raphael. One of the great quirky painters of the Renaissance, Piero di Cosimo, shows the Virgin and Angel tickling a laughing baby Jesus; in the *Virgin, Child and St John*, Leonardo's pupil Bernardo Luini demonstrates his characteristic *sfumato*, or smoky shadows, while Domenico Beccafumi's *Virgin and Child with SS. John and Jerome* is a near Day-Glo example of the startling colours of Tuscan Mannerism, the same used by Michelangelo on the Sistine Chapel ceiling.

Among the 16th-century German works in the next two rooms are five scenes of a strikingly vivid *Crucifixion* by Derick Baegert, from a painting cut up centuries ago. Dürer's *Jesus among the Doctors* (1506) is a brilliant, oppressively compact composition built around a central motif of two pairs of hands: the youthful ones of Jesus and the sinewy ones of one of the six suspicious-looking priests that seem to be closing in on him. In the same room are a range of works by the Cranach clan: an intense *Virgin and Child with Grapes* and *Portrait of Emperor Charles V* with his huge overbite by the elder Lucas, a sultry *Nymph of the Spring* by the younger Lucas, and the funny cross-dressing *Hercules in the Court of Omphale* by his brother Hans. From the same school is another of the Thyssen's signature works, Hans Baldung Grien's stylish, enigmatic *Portrait of a Woman* (1530), using an extremely limited palette; his *Adam and Eve* shows Adam enjoying Eve's charms right before the Fall.

Dutch paintings from the same century fill the next room, starring Marten van Heemskerck's memorable *Portrait of a Lady Spinning* (1531), and the quirky Joachim Patinir, whose *Rest on the Flight to Egypt* is more concerned with the scenery than the nominal religious subject; his followers would simply leave out the Biblical figures and paint empty landscapes.

The great masters of the 16th-and 17th-century paintings are in the following rooms: a very late *St Jerome in the Desert* (1575) by Titian is an excellent example of his late style, painted with broad brushstrokes and a colour tonalism that was radical for the age and would reverberate down through the late works of Cézanne. Titian's freedom of handling more immediately inspired Tintoretto (*Paradise*, 1583) and El Greco, whose *Annunciation* painted while still in Venice was directly influenced by Titian's and makes an interesting comparison to the one in the same room that he painted for Madrid's Encarnación Convent (*see* pp.143–4).

The Baroque collection kicks off with an early Caravaggio, *St Catherine of Alexandria* (1597), a painting that has been compared to a Flemish still life. His later style, with its revolutionary realistic depiction of biblical figures and dramatic lighting had its greatest followers in José de Ribera (*Lamentation*) and

Mattia Preti (the *Concert*, all in earth tones). These are followed by brighter canvases by Murillo and Claude Lorraine before the collection takes a diversion into 18th-century Venice; there are views by Canaletto and Francesco Gardi, Giambattista Tiepolo's luminous *Death of Hyacynth*, complete with the fatal badminton racket, and one of genre-master Pietro Longhi's most delighful works, *The Tickle* (1755).

Rubens, naturally, dominates among the Flemish and Dutch paintings, which include one of the museum's many interesting juxtapositions: Matthias Stom's *The Supper at Emmaus* (c. 1633–39) and Hendrick ter Brugghen's *Esau Selling his Birthright* (c. 1627). Both lend intense drama to climactic biblical moments by casting them in candlelight.

First Floor

A series of rooms are devoted to 17th-century Dutch painting, the best and most endearing of which show jolly, ribald scenes from peasant life, such as Frans Hals' skittish *Fisherman Playing the Violin* (c. 1630). These are followed by rococo and neoclassical works including a Watteau (*Pierrot Content*) and some of the few English paintings to be found in Madrid outside of the Museo Lázaro Galdiano: a portrait by Sir Joshua Reynolds, and one by Gainsborough. Next comes an even more unusual collection, possibly the only one of its kind in a European museum: paintings by 19th-century American artists. It's a mixed selection, from chocolate-boxy autumnal sunsets by Frederic Edwin Church, John Frederick Kensett and Jasper Francis Cropsey to an innovative still life by John Frederick Peto, *Tom's River* (1905), displaying a bold sense of composition that was way ahead of its time. One curiosity is *Portrait of Washington's Cook* by Gilbert Stuart, whose portrait of the first president adorns American class-rooms across the land. In contrast are the paintings by American painters who lived in Europe most of their lives, James McNeill Whistler and John Singer Sargeant; the latter, a close friend of Sorolla, painted in a similar style of loose brushstrokes shot with light (*The Venetian Onion Seller*).

Among other 19th-century European works are three late Goyas including *Asensio Julià* (1798), a portrait of the artist who worked with him in San Antonio de la Florida, and the delightful laughing *El Tío Paquete*, painted just before Goya left for Bordeaux. There is a fine shimmery late work by Corot, *Setting out for a Walk in the Parc des Lions*, and another by John Constable, *The Lock* (1824), full of silvery highlights and rich colours, a fitting prelude to the selection of Impressionist paintings. This is sadly rather slim (although it does contain a lovely Renoir, his *Woman with a Parasol in a Garden*). The post-Impressionists and Fauve painters are better represented: a gloriously lurid Van

Gogh, a Cézanne *Portrait of a Farmer* (1901–6), relaxing cross-legged in dappled blue shade, Degas' gauzy snapshot-like *Swaying Dancer*, an example of Gauguin's ethnic preoccupations (*Mata Mua*, 1892), a lovely portrait by Toulouse-Lautrec, *The Red Head in a White Blouse,* and some riotously coloured works by Dufy, Derain and Vlaminck.

The Thyssen's collection of Expressionist painting is particularly strong. Some of its leading exponents are here, including Ernst Ludwig Kirchner (1880–1938), Max Beckmann (1884–1950) and Egon Schiele (1890–1918); Schiele's *Houses next to the River* seem to have eyes. The iconic early 20th-century Blaue Reiter movement is represented by typically symbolic horsey works by Franz Marc and August Macke. Although he exhibited with the Blaue Reiter movement, American-born Lyonel Feininger developed an original prismatic Cubism all his own, which he mostly applied to marine and urban scenes; see his *Ships* and *Lady in Mauve* (1902).

The neurotic years of the Weimar Republic led to the final stage of German Expressionism, the Neue Sachlichkeit (New Objectivity); Otto Dix's quasi-photographic *Hugo Erfurth with a Dog* stands out, its precision in tempera a throw-back to the early Renaissance. From Christian Schad there is his discomforting *Portrait of Doctor Haustein* (1928), a tense, psychologically charged work in which the doctor of the title stares out at the viewer, his very smooth hands clasped off-centre, while behind him looms the menacing, distorted shadow of his mistress with a hint of smoke at her lips. Doctor Haustein's infidelity was one of the factors that pushed his wife to suicide; he himself took poison in 1933 rather than be captured by the Gestapo. The same room contains George Grosz' *Metropolis* (1917) with all the frenetic movement of Fritz Lang's famous film of the same name, and Ludwig Meidner's troubling *House on a Corner in Dresden.*

Ground Floor

A radical change in atmosphere marks the beginning of the collection clumped together as the Experimental Avant-gardes. Cubism is represented by its three brightest stars, Georges Braque, Pablo Picasso and Juan Gris, and the individual spin-offs they inspired Légar, the Delaunays, and the Czech master Frantisek Kupka. The Russian pre- and post-Revolution avant-garde are well represented, and there is plenty of space to appreciate the scale of the Mondrians—two of them, *Composition I* (1931), and *New York City, New York*, left unfinished when he died in 1942—and Filonov's astoundingly complex untitled canvas.

A section entitled 'The Synthesis of Modernism' contains Chagall's delightful, dreamlike *The Rooster* (1929), and more paintings by Picasso (the classicizing

Harlequin with a Mirror, 1923) and Braque, plus glittering works by Ernst, Klee, Kandinsky, Léger and Miró, followed by American modernists: Mark Rothko, Georgia O'Keeffe, Jackson Pollock, and emigré Surrealist Arshile Gorky.

Along with a fine Magritte (the *Key to the Field*) and other surrealist works, Baron Thyssen got his hands on an excellent Dalí, his *Dream caused by the Flight of a Bee Around a Pomegranate a Second before Awakening* (1944), but it is the very last section that contains perhaps the most striking works of all: Edward Hopper's *Hotel Room* (1931), a characteristically disturbing Francis Bacon (*Portrait of George Dyer in a Mirror*, 1968); an unforgettable Lichtenstein (*Woman in the Bath*, 1963), in which every dot really is painted by hand to look like a screen print; a Hockney (*In Memoriam of Cecchio Bracci*, 1962), and a startling Tom Wesselmann (*Nude No.1*, 1970) and last of all, one of the best works in the museum: Richard Estes' multi-layered slices of New York (*Telephone Booths*, 1967).

Behind the Prado

This neighbourhood, the Barrio de los Jerónimos (or the Retiro) has been the fashionable centre of Madrid for over a century, and consequently has attracted quite a few museums, devoted to all manner of things. Museums are about all there is to interest the visitor these days for, tasteful as it is, this is one of the duller corners of Madrid.

Its oldest and certainly most woebegone monument is just behind the Prado: the monastery of **San Jerónimo el Real**, founded by Ferdinand and Isabel in 1505, when there was nothing else at all on this side of town. It was here that the local nobles and the Cortes swore their fidelity to the kings of Spain, and its importance as a venue for royal and state ceremonies was the factor that made Philip II build an apartment in the vicinity, which later evolved into a royal palace. Like the palace itself, the monastery took so many licks in the Peninsular War that much of it was demolished in 1868. Only the church and some of the ruined cloister were spared, and the former was completely restored, and given a pair of pseudo-Gothic towers. It remains the setting for royal pageants, most recently the coronation of Juan Carlos in 1975, although it still manages to look worn out and dilapidated.

Opposite is Spain's equivalent of the Académie Française, the **Real Academia Española de la Lengua**, which fits perfectly into the haughty neighbourhood between the Prado and the Casón del Buen Retiro (*see* above, pp.100–1). Both the French and Spanish institutions are devoted to defending the purity of their respective language and writing a dictionary, and both were founded by

Bourbons, this one by Philip V in 1714; the 40 academians of Castellano, however, discreetly refrain from making nuisances of themselves by encouraging national laws to keep out *los hot dogs*.

A block north, the abandoned looking **Museo del Ejército** (Army Museum), C/Méndez Núnez 1, ✆ 91 522 8977, Ⓜ Retiro (*open Tues–Sun 10–2, closed Mon; adm 100 pts, concessions 50 pts, free Sat*) pokes its scores of rusting old cannons menacingly out at the surrounding apartment blocks. Like the Casón del Buen Retiro, the building was originally part of the Palacio del Buen Retiro, a ceremonial annexe called the Salón de Reinos, dedicated to Spain's Empire, and used by Philip IV to hang many of Velázquez's equestrian portraits as well as *The Surrender of Breda*. Most of the exhibits have also seen better days: armour and arms from the conquistadors, and from the nearly invincible infantry that made Spain a European power in the days of the Catholic Kings. One of El Cid's swords is here, and Boabdil el Chico's tunic, among rooms full of shiny military bric-a-brac. The Carlist and Napoleonic wars are covered, and the Civil War, too—you can get the Army's side of the story, to music ranging from the *Flight of the Valkyries* to *Shaft*. At the moment, a question mark hangs over this museum's future, as the building has been earmarked for use by the Prado.

North of this, at the top of the Paseo del Prado at No. 5 is the **Museo Naval**, ✆ 91 379 5055, Ⓜ Banco de España (*open Tues–Sun 10.30–1.30, closed Mon; free*), in a corner of the Ministry of Defence offices. Whatever relics of the age of explorations were not locked away in Seville's Archive of the Indies ended up here. Some of the most fascinating are the maps and charts, not simple sailors' tools, but lovely works in which art and scholarship are joined. The 1375 *Atlas Catalan* is one of these, and Juan de la Cosa's *Mapa Mundi* of 1500 is the earliest Spanish map to show parts of the American coast. Another, made by Diego Rivera just 29 years later, has almost all of the Americas' Atlantic coasts, and some of the Pacific, a tribute to the work Spanish explorers had done in such a short time. Much of the Naval Museum is given over to ships' models. Some are wonderfully detailed and precise, offering real insight into the complexity and artfulness of the age of sail. Columbus' *Santa Maria* is one of these, and it is a reminder of the Admiral of Ocean Sea's achievement to see how small and frail his craft really were.

Two blocks behind the naval museum, a 19th-century mansion houses the **Museo de Artes Decorativas**, C/Montalbán 12, ✆ 91 522 1740, Ⓜ Banco de España (*open Tues–Fri 9.30–3, Sat, Sun, hols, 10–2, closed Mon; adm 400 pts, concessions 200 pts, free Sat after 2 and Sun*), with a comprehensive collection of furniture, costume, ceramics, and work in wood, textiles, gold and silver from the 15th to the 20th century—six floors of it, in fact. Every aspect of Spanish design is covered, with complete rooms—the Gothic hall with leather walls and charming painted *Mudéjar* ceilings (the museum is furnished with fine ones, in every period), as well fine reliquaries, carved chests and a 15th-century ivory horn called the Oliphant. Another curiosity is the raised *estrado*, a platform where noble Spanish women of the 15th and 16th centuries would lounge, doing needlework and playing music. From the 19th century come an array of fans, jewellery, Lalique glass and Art Nouveau furnishings, a little theatre of biblical scenes framed in dried flowers and another collection of holy bone shards. A favourite exhibit is the lovely, tiled 18th-century Valencian kitchen on the top floor, complete with a quorum of naughty cats.

The Retiro

In the mid 17th century, this entire area was a royal preserve, and encompassed a fortress, a palace and this park. In 1636 the Conde-Duque Olivares decreed that this stately pleasure dome be built in order to distract Philip IV while the bankrupt Empire crumbled to pieces. Apart from growing smaller—it once extended westwards to the Paseo del Prado—the Retiro has changed essentially little since; an elegant, formal garden, perfect for the decorous pageants and dalliances of the Baroque era. Good king Charles III was the first to open parts of it up to the public, in 1767, but with a strict dress code: men's hair had to be combed, without capes or hairnets, while women had to wear shawls, but not mantillas. After several decades of repairs following the Peninsular War, the whole Retiro was opened to the public in 1868 and has been the much loved patrimony of the citizens of Madrid ever since. Visit the Retiro in spring, when the tulips and horse-chestnut trees are in bloom; failing that, come on any Sunday, when all Madrid comes to see the flowers, concerts and other impromptu entertainments. If you would like a carriage ride, wait at the little cabin marked '*servicio de simones*' near the entrance opposite Calle Antonio Maura.

The centre of the Retiro is a broad lagoon called **El Estanque**, where you may rent canoes or paddleboats. No king ever did less to earn such a grandiose memorial than Alfonso XII (1874–86), but that's him up on horseback decorating the eastern end of the Estanque. In the 17th century, this was a favourite spot for royal diversions: water pageants and plays. One of the best remembered was a royal performance of Calderón's *Polifemo y Circe* and *Los Incantos de Circe* in 1663; artificial islands were built for the action, while the audience sat around the edge of the Estanque. The whole affair took nine hours, including battles, sea voyages in miniature galleys and Odysseus' trip to the Underworld.

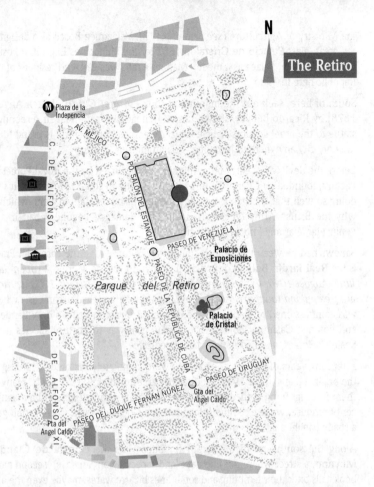

Plaza de la Indepencia

AV. MÉJICO

C. DE ALFONSO XI

PO. SALÓN DEL ESTANQUE

PASEO DE VENEZUELA

Palacio de Exposiciones

Parque del Retiro

PASEO DE LA REPÚBLICA DE CUBA

Palacio de Cristal

PASEO DE URUGUAY

C. DE ALFONSO XI

Gta del Angel Caído

PASEO DEL DUQUE FERNÁN NÚÑEZ

Pta del Angel Caído

C. DE ALFONSO XI

Among the 160-odd hectares (400 acres) of the Retiro are cool fountains, a Japanese garden and, towards the south, a seemingly endless expanse of quiet paths among old shady trees and gardens where you can easily forget you're in the centre of a major metropolis, although the bustlings of busy couples in the privacy of the undergrowth will remind you that you are hardly alone. Among the buildings in the Retiro, all with a regular schedule of cultural exhibits and shows, are the pink **Casa de Vacas** (where cows were once kept in order to provide visitors with the freshest of milk), and the **Palacio de Velázquez** (1883, by Ricardo Velázquez Bosco), designed originally for a mining exhibition, and incorporating the decorated coloured bricks and tiles that the architect would later employ in the Ministry of Agriculture (*see* below, p.113). Velázquez Bosco also designed the great, glass **Palacio de Cristal** in 1887 for the Philippines Exposition, using London's Crystal Palace as a model. Manuel Azaña was elected President of the Republic here in 1936.

South of here, seek out the monument to the ***Angel Caído*** ('Fallen Angel', 1878) by Ricardo Bellver, shown tumbling headfirst from heaven. Erecting a statue to the cruel goddess Cybele is bizarre enough, but Madrid is proud to be the only city anywhere to have one of Satan himself.

Before the devil fell to earth here, this site was occupied by the Royal Porcelain Factory, founded by Charles III in 1760. According to some *madrileños*, it was doing so well that it began to compete with British porcelain-makers, which is why the British Army officiously declared it damaged beyond repair in the Peninsular War and knocked it down.

Sandwiched between the Retiro's southwestern corner and the Paseo del Prado is the **Real Jardín Botánico** (Botanical Garden), Plaza de Murillo 2 (*open daily June–August 10–9, winter 10–dusk; adm 200 pts, concessions 100 pts; there are free guided tours in Spanish only*), a particularly special urban oasis which was commissioned by Carlos III, and developed by architect Juan de Villanueva and botanist Casimiro Gómez Ortega. The goal was to nurture species from Spain's colonies, and find new herbal remedies.

After long years of neglect, the gardens were completely restored according to the original plans in the 1980s, and feature an estimated 30,000 plants, many of them from far-flung corners of the globe; the more exotic flourish in a magnificent hothouse, while ex-Prime Minister Felipe Gonzalez's bonzai collection gets a shady pavillion all of its own.

Along the south end of the Jardín Botánico runs the **Cuesta de Claudio Moyano**, a street where, on fine days (and especially on Sundays), second-hand bookstalls offer their tempting and sometimes bizarre wares, maybe even the one title you've been searching for all these years.

Across Calle Alfonso XII, on a hill towards the south entrance to the Retiro, stands the **Observatorio Astronómico,** a beautiful neo-classical building by Juan de Villanueva. This was also commissioned by Charles III, although he never had a chance to peep through one of its telescopes—after years of neglect and extensive damage caused by the French, it wasn't completed until 1845. The observatory has a dusty collection of old telescopes and astronomical instruments you can peruse (*Mon–Fri 9–2, free*) but if you want to look at the stars you have to make an appointment (© 91 527 0107).

Plaza Emperador Carlos V

From here, the Paseo del Prado ends at the **Plaza Emperador Carlos V**. It's not immediately apparent, but this square represents one of civic-minded Madrid's most significant environmental victories of the 1980s. Relatively recently, the entire plaza was buried under a ghastly, multi-level highway interchange *madrileños* called the 'scalextric' after the model racing car circuit. The scalextric was Mayor Tierno's pet peeve, and he saw it dismantled just before he died, as part of his decade long Operation Atocha.

The traffic is still pretty bad, speeding around another fountain, a replica of the **Fuente de la Alcachofa** designed by Ventura Rodriguez in 1781 for the bottom end of the Paseo de Prado; the original was dismantled and shuttled off to the Retiro when the Atocha station was built. A mermaid and a triton hold the Madrid coat of arms while four children support a granite artichoke, supposedly an allegory of how wisdom lies at the core of a subject and has to be discovered by peeling away the layers.

Wisdom or just a joke, the artichoke offers a proper side dish to the feast of the **Ministry of Agriculture**, where Neo-*Mudéjar* meets Belle Epoque in a shotgun wedding designed by Ricardo Velázquez Bosco in 1893, and decorated with flying horses and colourful ceramics by Zuloaga, one of the masters of the art. Like the frothy and fantastical Palacio de Communicaciones (*see* p.124), it elevates what might seem merely functional to the grandeur assumed by the more outrageous Babylonian potentates.

Trains and their passengers deserve some pizzazz too, and got it in the cast-iron and glass **Atocha station**, designed by Alberto del Palacio in 1892. After 100 years of faithful service it was earmarked for a facelift, including major re-modelling to provide a terminal for the new high-speed Madrid to Sevilla AVE link.

Rafael Moneo was put in charge of the project, and in 1992 the old Atocha station re-opened as a shining new temple to rail travel, complete with an indoor shopping and eating emporium which has as its centrepiece an acclimatized tropical garden, with nervous looking goldfish swimming in pools beneath soaring palm trees. Steam filters down onto this mini urban jungle through ducts in the roof. The effect is spectacular; it's a pity, then, that the glass panels in the ceiling don't let in enough light (this is boosted by banks of artificial lights), and, when planting the garden, the designer chose exotic palms rather than local ones, so many of the trees are struggling to survive.

If you're catching a Cercania train or a slow train to the south, the new Atocha station with its rotunda, also designed by Moneo, is adjacent.

Museo Nacional Centro de Arte Reina Sofía

C/Santa Isabel 52, ✆ 91 467 5062, 📠 91 539 6824, Ⓜ Atocha. Open Mon–Sat 10–9, Sun 10–2.30, closed Tues; free guided tours Mon and Wed, 5pm, Sat, 11am; adm 500 pts, concessions 250 pts, free Sat after 2.30 and Sun; 'Paseo del Arte' voucher allowing one visit to each of the Paseo del Arte museums, 1,275 pts.

With the continuing success of ARCO, Madrid's annual contemporary art fair founded in the early 1980s, and with promising work emerging from local artists, the *madrileños*' active interest in modern art has never been at such a high. It was partly in order to satisfy this popular passion that the Spanish government set about providing their capital with a world-class 20th-century art museum, to replace the old Museo Español de Arte Contemporáneo.

Conversion of the defunct General Hospital, near Atocha station, began in 1980 and the Centro de Arte Reina Sofía was inaugurated by the shy but much loved queen in 1986. Cynics muttered that the timing of the opening was no more than a vote-catching ploy in this, an election year, since the building wasn't actually ready—the air-conditioning, for example, was woefully inadequate. After this abortive inauguration, it was back to the drawing board, and, four years and several more millions of pesetas later, a second opening ceremony was held. The building, graced by its three new landmark glass lifts (or 'crystal towers'), was by now fully equipped to house both temporary exhibitions and a permanent collection of art; all it lacked was a quorum of internationally famous paintings.

It was two more years, however, before the Reina Sofía really made its debut as an art centre to be reckoned with: in 1992, Spain's golden year, Picasso's *Guernica* was moved here from the Prado's annexe, the Casón del Buen Retiro. The move was controversial: Picasso left instructions that New York's Museum of Modern Art should return the painting to Spain when liberty was restored there, and that it should hang in the Prado, as a gesture towards the modernization of that collection. His wish was granted in 1981, and millions of Spaniards made the pilgrimage to the Prado to see a part of their history denied them under 40 years of dictatorship. When the Spanish government proposed the removal of the painting to the Reina Sofía, there were bitter objections from Picasso's surviving relatives, but these were over-ruled in the interests of the fulfilment of a master plan: the Prado was to hold the Old Masters, the Casón del Buen Retiro the 19th-century art, and the Reina Sofía the 20th-century works, with *Guernica*, arguably this century's most famous painting, taking pride of place.

One of the Reina Sofía's greatest assets is the huge amount of space it has at its disposal. As well as having plenty of room for its permanent collection , it has large gallery spaces for temporary exhibitions. There is also an excellent book-shop, a decent café, an oasis of a courtyard garden, a library, a music archive and education unit, and enough supplementary resource areas to fully justify its status as an energetic multimedia community arts centre.

The Main Collection

The Reina Sofía's permanent collection contains works by every one of Spain's most celebrated 20th-century artists, which together amount to solid evidence, if any were needed, to back up the nation's claim to the title of contemporary creative super-power. Pablo Picasso, Salvador Dalí, Joan Miró, Juan Gris, Julio González, Antoni Tàpies, José Gutiérrez Solana and Antonio Saura are all repre-sented. The paintings, sketches and sculptures occupy the second and fourth floors of the building and are grouped chronologically and according to stylistic or conceptual affinity; you'll find you have to weave about a little to follow the intended order of the rooms. The first part of the collection is displayed on the second floor (rooms 1–17) and covers the final years of the 19th century until the end of the Second World War. Later works are upstairs on the fourth floor (rooms 18–45).

The opening rooms set the scene for the avant-garde works to come; Anglada-Camarasa's *Portrait of Countess Pradère* rubs glittering shoulders with the sombre portraits of Ramón Casas. The next room is entirely devoted to the paint-ings of Solana; in his *Tertulia del Café de Pombo* (1920) we are given a sombre glimpse of that typically *madrileño* institution of the late 19th and early 20th century—the *tertulia*, the regular gatherings and discussion of the intelligentsia in the city's cafés. The Café de Pombo on the Puerta del Sol was one of the most famous until the Civil War; Solana includes himself in the coterie.

The curvy, colourful works of Sonia Delaunay, and severely graceful lead sculp-tures of Jacques Lipchitz come next, along with works by other members of the early avant garde. In the adjacent gallery, increasingly mature paintings by Juan Gris line the walls, dominated by the cooly confident *Portrait of Josette*, his wife. A tiny room, not much more than a hallway, displays the superb sculpture of Pablo Gargallo (1881–1934): fluid traceries, deconstructed busts and skin-skele-tons in bronze and iron.

Gargallo's arch *Mask of Greta Garbo with Lock of Hair* flicks an insouciant glance as you pass through to the galleries containing some early, supernatural-looking Miró portraits. These are divided from his later works by a gallery devoted to the remarkable sculpture of Julio González (1876–1942), one of the first to render iron as an artistic medium and to speak as much with void space as with solid material. The space is shared with the delicate sculptures of the American Abstract Expressionist, David Smith, who described González as the 'father of all sculpture in iron in this century'.

It is easy to be distracted from these with *Guernica* just a room away. The lead up to the painting has Picasso's stern-faced *Women in Blue* (1901) presiding over an adjacent gallery of his early work. This painting had a lucky escape from oblivion when Picasso disowned it after it failed to receive much recognition at a show; years later it was discovered by a private collector. Also here is his eerie *Still Life (Dead Birds)* (1912).

Placed dramatically alone along one long wall of the central gallery, *Guernica* gathers a hefty knot of people. Picasso (1881–1973) was commissioned by the Republic to supply a painting for Spain's pavillion at the Paris World Exhibition of 1937. He dallied, unable to decide what to paint, but began work on *Guernica* in May 1937, in immediate, outraged response to the events of the previous month. When the German Condor Legion practised its new theory of saturation bombing on the Basque town of Guernica in April 1937, Franco most likely had not been informed. Nevertheless, the Nationalists were forced to create an elaborate lie—they said the Communists had planted bombs in the sewers—and it became the official version until Franco's death.

As for the painting itself, there are as many interpretations as critics; *Guernica* is much more than a moment of terror caught in the glare of an electric bulb. As can be seen from Picasso's preliminary sketches displayed in the adjoining gallery of his earlier works, the fallen horse and rider in the centre were in the artist's mind from the beginning. In them perhaps we can see the origins of Guernica's destroyers: the man on horseback, the bully, the crusader, the *caudillo*, meeting a bad end from his own designs, while Picasso's primaeval bull looks dispassionately on.

Alexander Calder's (1898–1876) delightful *Constellation* (1948), an airy wood and wire mobile of abstract spheres, floats nonchalantly in a nearby room, along with works from other early surrealists: Jean Arp's bold wood reliefs, André Masson's cerebral paintings and finally, the lyrical paintings of Vassily Kandinsky, founder of Abstract Expressionism.

Dalí's works are also given a whole room to themselves; particularly outstanding are *Girl at the Window, The Enigma of Hitler* and *The Great Masturbator.* Some of his early pantings show him dabbling in the Cubist style—fascinating precursors to the better known pieces. A product of his collaboration with Man Ray, an intruiging, dreamy oil and plaster sculpture, *Portrait of Joella*, sits in the next room along with works by other members of the Surrealist movement, including the bleakly nostalgic Spanish artist, Oscar Dominguez (1906–1957).

Dalí's collaborations with the experimental film-maker, Luis Buñuel (they met as students in Madrid's Residencia de los Estudiantes, *see* p.132)—*An Andalusian Dog* (1929), and *The Golden Age* (1930), co-scripted with Dalí—are screened in Room 12.

Significant numbers of Spanish artists took up residence in Paris between the wars and a selection of their output, including sweetly nostalgic works such as the evocative *Joy of the Basque Country* (1920) by Daniel Vázquez Díaz, are grouped together in a gallery devoted to the various movements which evolved in Spanish art after the First World War. In an interesting juxtaposition, three works—by José de Togores (*Nudes on a Beach*, 1922), Velasco (*Adam and Eve*, 1932) and Balbuena (*Nude*, 1932)—each exhibit an obsessive, almost architectural interest in the smooth rendering of the human form. The unsettling *Accident* (1936), by Alfonso Ponce de León, uncannily presages his own death later that year.

The penultimate rooms of the first part of the museum's permanent collection are given over to the Asturian painter Luis Fernández, also a prolific art theoretician, the slim, elegant sculptures of Alberto Sánchez, and the vivid, schematic compositions of Benjamín Palencia.

The final room on this floor is dedicated to sculpture; although it focuses on Miró's bronzes, including the sublimely simple *Wind Clock* (1967), other notable pieces include Angel Ferrant's mobiles and sculptures made from 'found objects' and Ramón Marinello's wonderful *Figures in Front of the Sea* (1936)— organic plaster and wood reliefs in simple white.

Up on the fourth floor (take the speedy glass lift for wonderful views), the museum picks up the story in the 1940s when the Spanish art scene was characterized by a desire to rebuild and regroup in the wake of the Civil War. Post-war trauma is evident in some of the earliest works exhibited here but, as the Forties gave way to the Fifties, a more liberal mood of catharsis took hold. Among the works from this period are boxy sculptures by Jorge de Oteiza and bristling, spiky pieces by Pablo Serrano, flamboyant, blazing paintings by the Andalucian, José Guerrero, and light, filmy, obscure compositions by Manuel Mompó, as well as the large geometric canvases of the co-operative, Equipo 57.

All these jostling avant garde theories are put into their European context in the next series of rooms. The bathos of Francis Bacon's bleak figures contrasts with the Minimalist showmanship of Yves Klein's slashed canvases and monochrome paintings, while organic Henry Moore sculptures complement the three-dimensional pieces, such as *Spatial Conception. The End of God*, by Lucio Fontana. Antonio López Garcia (1936–), a leading member of the Madrid Realism movement which was instrumental in the renewal of Madrid's art scene in the 1960s and 1970s, has some meticulous urban portraits of Madrid, placed alongside the life-sized sculpted figures of Francisco López Hernández.

Nearby, the sculptures of Eduardo Chillida, Spain's greatest living sculptor, are scooped from wood and terracotta, or wrought from iron and stone. After the ripped, rucked and daubed fabric works by Millares and the turbulent, jolting paintings of Antonio Saura, the series culminates in a room devoted to texture-obsessed Antoni Tàpies, from his early sculptures made out of junk to his later stark monochromes.

The Equipo Crónica group jibe at American mass culture in works such as *Painting is like Hitting* (1964), a Pop Art paintings which has two black and white TV baddies fighting it out amid a shower of paint tubes. Eduardo Arroyo's dark, cartoonish night paintings keep them company. A side room is devoted to the multi-coloured invitation cards to so-called 'concerts' by the quirky, politically provocative Zaj group.

But Minimalism strikes back with the bright clear canvases of Ellsworth Kelly, the huge formal iron cubes of Donald Judd, and Soto's rather staggering *Yellow and White Extension*, before Schnabel's vast, lucid *Buen Retiro Ducks* series, painted as a gift to the Spanish people.

Afterwards, you may want to put your feet up in the museum's inviting, calm inner courtyard, an oasis popular with local workers. It offers a stark contrast to the plaza at the main entrance to the Reina Sofía, with its pair of tall rusting thingamabobs that look like transmitters set in place by an unfriendly star.

Between Atocha Station and the Retiro

Don't go away; there's more. Facing Atocha station's modern clocktower, on the corner of Paseo de La Infanta and Calle Velasco, is the **Museo Nacional de Antropología**, ✆ 91 530 6418, Ⓜ Atocha (*open Tues–Sat, 10–6, Sun and hols, 10–2, closed Mon; adm 400 pts, concessions 200 pts, free Sat pm and Sun am*), which in the merry-go-round of Madrid's museums, was formerly the Museo de Etnología. Few tourists make it here and it is likely you will find yourself alone among the Amazonian shrunken heads, African initiation bonnets, Mongolian tents and subdued cheers of the bored, card-playing guards.

Its permanent exhibitions on physical and cultural anthropology are mostly gleaned from Spain's colonies, with an especially interesting section on the

Philippines; most of the bizarre artefacts, including a stylish Inuit raincoat made from seal intestines and a bell-bedecked bottom pad, good for shimmying, come from the original 19th-century Cabinet of Curiosities of Dr González Velasco, the museum's founder, a surgeon and one of Madrid's most famous eccentrics. According to dark rumour, he embalmed the body of his young daughter and would prop her up in his carriage for rides down the Paseo del Prado.

Paseo de La Infanta Isabel continues past the **Pantéon de Hombres Ilustres**, on the corner of Calle de Julian Gayarre. Founded in Spain's topsy-turvy 19th century, the project of providing a suitable last resting place for the great personalities of Madrid never really got off the ground: between the politically sensitive problems of deciding who was actually rated, and the fact that the remains of most of the neutral candidates like Cervantes, Calderón de la Barca, and Velázquez, were long lost, the project seemed fated never to get off the ground. Designed after Pisa's Campo Santo, the pantheon has a number of elaborate tombs, some of whose residents were, in the age-old Madrid custom, relocated.

Adjacent is the **Real Basílica de Atocha**, a bland, neo-Baroque structure rebuilt after the Civil War. The cult of the Virgin of Atocha is one of the oldest in Madrid; the story goes that a figure of the Virgin was discovered in the esparto grass (*atocha*) shortly after Madrid was captured by the Moors, and became a rallying point among the local Christians. One, Gracián Ramírez, fearing he would be killed in the battles, slit the throats of his wife and daughters to keep them from falling into the hands of the infidels. When he survived, however, he was filled with remorse and went to pray to the Virgin—only to find his family miraculously restored to life. As with the Virgin of the Almudena, the Virgin of Atocha was given a big boost after the Reconquista thanks to the royal patronage of Alfonso VI. A few *madrileños* still keep up the custom of making a special visit here before their weddings, to pray for a happy marriage.

A bit further along, Calle Julian Gayarre leads to a handicrafts workshop fit for kings. In all Madrid's royal residences, as well the Ritz Hotel, hang works of the **Real Fábrica de Tapices** (Royal Tapestry Factory), C/Fuenterrabía 2, © 91 551 3400, Ⓜ Menéndez Pelayo (*open Mon–Fri 9–12.30, closed Sat, Sun, all Aug; adm 250 pts*). Ever since Philip V founded it in the 1710s as Spain's answer to Paris' Gobelins, the weavers of the Real Fábrica have served the Spanish élite's love of fine, pictorial tapestries—not only decorative, but a positive asset to any draughty palace during the chill Castilian winters. Its best-known productions, of course, are those woven to Goya's designs before he became court painter, the cartoons for which are now hanging in the Prado. Much of the work that comes to the factory in these centrally heated days is repairs of older works, which require an impressive amount of skill, matching colours and intricate designs.

You may watch the master weavers (there are only 42 now, compared to 400 before the Civil War) at work on their 18th-century looms any weekday morning, and those with gargantuan bank accounts can even order a genuine tapestry as a souvenir.

Las Delicias

Five blocks south of Atocha station was yet another, the century-old Delicias station, its cast iron skeleton designed by Gustav Eiffel and its name a brave euphemism for a once notably undelightful fleabag corner of Madrid.

The city is busily remaking this whole area into a family attraction, beginning with the station itself, now the **Museo Nacional Ferroviario** (National Railway Museum), Pso. de las Delicias 61, ℗ 91 527 3121, Ⓜ Palos de la Frontera (*open Tues–Fri 10–5.30, Sat–Sun 10–3, closed Mon and hols; adm 450 pts*), with RENFE's oldest and proudest warhorses (some from the 1840s) shined up to look as good as new. The train tracks have been replaced with the **Parque Tierno Galván**, site of the **Planetarium** and the popular **IMAX cinema**, both Ⓜ Menedez Alvaro (*see* 'Children', p.10).

New Madrid

Plaza de La Cibeles   124

Paseo de Recoltas   125

Salamanca   128

Up the Paseo del Castellana   130

Museo Sorolla and
   the Museo Lázaro Galdiano   131

Museo Ciencias Naturales
   to the Museo de la Ciudad   132

When Madrid, a walkable little city while it snug remained within its walls, began to expand in the late 18th century, it was to a different scale altogether. The proportions were set by the Plaza de la Cibeles and, over the next 200 years, the city spread into impossibly wide boulevards and traffic-filled plazas. Most of this is not much fun for walking, and the best approach is to pick out what you'd like to see—and there are some gems—and bus- or metro-hop between them. If you're in the market for a modern office building and want to see what some of the more fashionable Madrid architects have put up in the past two decades, a cruise down the Paseo de la Castellana is in order.

cafés, bars and restaurants

Gijon, Paseo de los Recoletos 21, ✆ 91 521 5425. A legendary haunt for Madrid's intellectuals, the Gijon has been in business since 1888, and still good for breakfast, a set-price lunch, or afternoon tea or coffee.

El Espejo, Paseo de los Recoletos 3, ✆ 91 398 2347. An elegant Paris–style bar (founded in 1978), with high quality tapas, and an elegant reproduction of the old tiled kiosks that once lined the street. The set menu is surprisingly good value.

Embassy, Paseo de la Castellana 12, ✆ 91 576 0080. Since 1931, *the* fashionable tea room in this diplomatic corner of Madrid, with plenty of atmosphere to go with its little sandwiches or cocktails.

Berceo-Le Divellec, in the Hotel Villa Magna, Paseo de la Castellana 22, ✆ 91 587 1234. This is one of Madrid's top gourmet restaurants, with a French chef who really knows his stuff. Excellent seafood. Reservations essential; menu around *5,500 pts.*

Teatriz, C/Hermosilla 15, ✆ 91 577 5379. See and be seen at this fashionable bar/restaurant, designed by Philippe Starck.

Taberna de La Daniela, C/General Pardinas 21, ✆ 91 575 2339. Tiles, tapas and a friendly welcome at this *muy auténtico taberna*.

Ginos, Paseo de la Castellana 85 (just south of AZCA's Plaza Picasso). Wide choice of pastas and pizzas, with good options for vegetarians; in the same building **El Candil,** with a popular *1150-pts* lunch menu that includes an *aperitivo* and wine.

New Madrid

400 metres
400 yards
N

To K10 Towers
Pl. Joan Miró
Pl. de Lima

Urbanación
Pl. de Picasso
AZCA

Pl. de la República Argentina

NUEVOS MINISTERIOS Ⓜ
REP. ARGENTINA Ⓜ

Nuevos Ministerios

PASEO DE LA CASTELLANA

C. DE VITRUVIO

CALLE DE JOAQUIN COSTA

Pl. S. Juan de la Cruz

C. DE SERRANO

C. DEL PINAR

C. CASTELLÓN DE LA PLANA

Museo de Ciencias Naturales Ⓜ

C. DE MARÍA DEL MOLINA

C. DE LÓPEZ DE HOYOS

AV. DE AMERICA Ⓜ

C. DE MARÍA DEL MOLINA

Ⓜ Museo Lázaro Galdiano

Museo Sorolla Ⓜ

Gta. Emilio Castelar

H. BÉQUER

C. DEL GENERAL ORÁA

C. DIEGO DE LÉON

C. DE MALDONADO

C. DE JUAN BRAVO

C. DE VERGERA

C. DE PADILLA

Fundación Juan March

C. DE JOSÉ ORTEGA Y GASSET

Pl. Marqués Salamanca

Salamanca

C. DON RAMÓN DE LA CRUZ

NÚÑEZ DE BALBOA Ⓜ

PASEO DE LA CASTELLANA

C. DE SERRANO

C. DE CLAUDIO COELLO

C. DE LAGASCA

C. DE VELÁZQUEZ

C. DE BALBOA

AYALA

C. DEL PRINCIPE DE VERGARA

C. DE HERMOSILLA

C. DEL CASTELLÓ

SERRANO Ⓜ

C. DE GOYA

C. DE NÚÑEZ

VELÁZQUEZ Ⓜ

La Concepción

Museo de Cera Ⓜ

Pl. de Colón

Biblioteca Nacional

C. DE JORGE JUAN

PASEO DE RECOLETOS

Ⓜ Museo Arqueológico

DE VILLANUEVA

To Plaza de Toros Monumental de las Ventas & Museo Taurino

St Pascal

C. RECOLETOS

C. DEL CID

C. VILLAR

C. CONDE DE ARANDA

COLUMELA

RETIRO

CALLE DE ALCALÁ

BANCO DE ESPAÑA Ⓜ

Palacio de Linares

Banco Hipotecario

Pl. de la Independencia

Pl. de la Cibeles

Palacio de Comunicaciones

Puerta de Alcalá

Parque del Retiro

Banco de España

Plaza de la Cibeles

Three of Madrid's most important streets, the Paseo del Prado, the Paseo de los Recoletos and Calle de Alcalá meet at Madrid's grandest roundabout, the **Plaza de la Cibeles** (⓾ Banco de España), where streams of traffic swirl around Ventura Rodríguez' **fountain** (1780) of the great mother goddess Cybele in a carriage drawn by lions. Although it often dismantles and moves them, Madrid loves its fountains. This one is a special favourite of Real Madrid supporters, who celebrate their club's victories with total immersion baptisms and high jinks that in 1994 resulted in the breakage of one of Cybele's arms. One wonders if they would have dared to take such liberties if they knew that Cybele's cult was famous in antiquity for requiring self-castration by her priests. These days whenever Cybele is threatened by a Spanish football victory, she is given full police protection.

The plaza is *la madrileñísima* (the most Madridy), perhaps because it's the most unlike any other square in Spain, or perhaps anywhere on the planet. One reason for this is the elaborate fantastical marble pile on the southeastern side, which is nothing more than the city's main post office, named, appropriately enough, the **Palacio de Comunicaciones**, by Antonio Palacios (1904). The *madrileños* have been making fun of what they immediately dubbed 'Nuestra Señora de Comunicaciones' ever since it was built, but buying a stamp has never felt so glamorous, and posting a letter through one of the magnificent slots, one for each region of Spain, offers a quaint sense of satisfaction of civic order and well being in a cockamamie world (the world outside Madrid's post office, that is). You can bask a little longer in the old world magic at the post office's **Museo Postal y de Telecomunicaciones** (*open Mon–Fri 9–2 and 5–7, Sat 9–2, free*) with a huge collection of stamps, old phones and switchboards, and postal employee uniforms through the ages.

The three other buildings that share the Plaza de la Cibele with the post office weigh nearly as much: one, the Palacio de Buenavista on the northeast corner, was built for the Duchess of Alba in 1777 but now contains the army. Spain's central bank, the **Banco de España** (1882, by Eduardo Adaro), with the elaborate façade, fancy clock and a rich art collection, has works ranging from the 16th to the 20th centuries, but they are visible only if you write in advance to the bank's Chief of Protocol. The third, the **Palacio de Linares**, dignified by a row of droopy flags mounted despondently on a piece of astroturf, is one of the last of many extravagant mansions that made the Plaza de Cibeles–Paseo de Castellana axis a Millionaire's Row in the early 1890s. It was built by a banker, the Marquis de Linares, who had the curious misfortune of falling in love with and marrying his half sister, a fact he only learned in his father's deathbed confession. Accorded the special dispensation of the Church, the two were permitted to live under the same roof but in separate quarters, and the palace was designed to give each spouse a floor of their own. Long boarded up and forlorn, the palace was refurbished and re-opened as part of the 1992 celebrations as the **Casa de América**, a venue for concerts, movies and exhibitions of works from Latin America.

East of here, Calle de Alcalá continues to Plaza de la Independencia, which has for a centrepiece the stately Baroque **Puerta de Alcalá** (1798), one of Madrid's symbols, a sort of triumphal arch with no triumph to commemorate. Before Madrid's last set of walls was demolished in the last century, this was the actual gate on the road to the university town of Alcalá de Henares, which was also the same road from which foreign travellers entered Madrid. A good first impression was in order and, after rejecting several designs, Charles III finally chose one by Francesco Sabatini. Actually he absentmindedly chose two designs and, not wanting to offend, Sabatini used both, one on each side, although even today most *madrileños* who pass it daily remain unaware of its asymmetry. The granite of the body contrasts nicely with the white Colmenar stone decoration, and it shines at night under the floodlights.

Once past the gate, Calle de Alcalá skirts the Retiro Park, passing an equestrian **statue of General Espartero**, hero of the first Carlist War, astride his famously well-endowed horse. Nearby is one of the finest neo-*Mudéjar* buildings in Madrid—the **Escuelas Aguirre** with its tower (1887), designed by Emilio Rodríguez Ayuso.

Ayuso also designed the other Madrid landmark on Calle de Alcalá (although it's a good kilometre walk), the almost winsome neo-*Mudéjar* **Plaza de Toros Monumental de Las Ventas** (1929): the busiest and most prestigious, the biggest (with seating for 23,000) and, according to the *madrileños* at any rate, the most beautiful in Spain, with its colourful tile decoration. Around the back by the stables is the recently re-arranged **Museo Taurino**, Pza. de Las Ventas, Patio de Caballos, ✆ 91 725 1857, Ⓜ Ventas (*open Tues–Fri 9.30–2.30, Sun 10–1, closed Sat and Mon; free*), the largest and most complete museum of bullfighting, with special exhibitions on famous *toreros* like Manolete, who met the horn in this ring in 1947.

Paseo de Recoletos

North of Cibeles, the **Paseo de Recoletos** was planned as an extension of the Paseo del Prado back in the 1770s but was only laid out as a proper street in the 1830s and 1840s. Along its shady flanks you can see a few of the fancy mansions that once stood here (Nos.13 and 15) as well as one of Madrid's most celebrated cafés, **Café Gijón** (No.21, *see* 'cafés, bars and restaurants' above). The Gijón, founded in 1888 and last refurbished in 1948, was a favourite haunt for spies during World War I (Spain was neutral, and the embassies of the main players are all nearby). In the 1920s, the spies were replaced by writers, and it became legendary for literary *tertulias* that attracted the likes of Lorca and Neruda. After the Civil War, the Gijón was the one place where politicians and the intelligentsia from both sides felt free to meet and talk; this *tertulia* tradition continues today, in the late afternoon, at some of the specially reserved tables. All the chat has spawned some fine literature, including *The Hive*, a novel about its regulars, by Nobel-Prize winner Camilo José Cela. In 1951, the Café Gijón Short Novel literary prize was established, and since then a number of books have appeared about the goings-on at these tables.

The church near here, **San Pascal**, once belonged to a convent on this site, but was rebuilt in the 1850s. It's as nondescript as any in Madrid, but is known for its statue of St Clare, patron saint of television (owing to a TV-like vision she once had in Assisi), who has an enviable reputation for finding parts in TV dramas for her devotees.

In the Madrid of the 19th century, architectural tastes favoured the grandiose. One prime example is the primrose yellow stucco **Banco Hipotecario**, set back from the road across the street; built on the site of the Convent of the Recoletos, this was the former residence of Madrid's most flamboyant speculator of the era, the Marquis de Salamanca (*see* below, p.128). When it was finished in 1850, it housed his dazzling private art collection, not to mention the first private flush toilet in Madrid.

Even more florid is the pile built by Isabel II that houses the **Biblioteca Nacional** (National Library), Pso. de Recoletos 20, ✆ 91 580 7823, Ⓜ Serrano or Colón (*open Mon–Fri 9–9, Sat 9–2*). Known as the 'Prado of Paper', its collection includes every work printed in Spain since 1716 as well as rare ancient manuscripts, drawings by the Grand Masters, and the first ever Spanish grammar (Spain was the first language to have one, back in 1492). It has recently opened a **Museo del Libro** (*same hours, free*) dedicated to the history of books and the media.

Sharing the building is the **Museo Arqueológico Nacional**, entrance C/Serrano 13, ✆ 91 577 7915 (*open Tues–Sat 9.30–8.30, Sun 9.30–2.30, closed Mon; adm 400 pts, concs 200 pts, free Sat after 2.30, Sun*). By any measure, this is the only comprehensive archaeology museum in the country. If you can read a little Spanish, the explanations posted around the exhibits will provide a thorough education in the obscure comings and goings of Spain's shadowy prehistory. Not that the museum is limited to Spain—there is a surprisingly good collection of Greek vases, and an Egyptian room full of mummies and gaping school-children, along with some very fine jewellery and engraved seals. Many of the Greek and Egyptian relics were actually found in Spain, testimony to the close trade relations ancient Iberia enjoyed with the rest of the Mediterranean world.

A visit to this museum, however, is really a pilgrimage to the first and greatest of the great ladies of Spain, *La Dama de Elche*. Nothing we know of the history and culture of the Iberians can properly explain the presence of this beautiful 5th-century BC cult image. As a work of art she ranks among the finest sculptures of antiquity. Pre-Roman Spain was one of the backwaters of the Mediterranean and, while it would be sacrilege in Spain to suggest that this lady was the work of a foreign hand, the conclusion seems inescapable. The dress and figure are reminiscent of some eastern Mediterranean image of Cybele, and the Greeks could often capture the same expression of cold majesty on the face of an Artemis or Ariadne or Persephone. Elche, where the bust was discovered, was then in the Carthaginian zone, and that meant easy access to all the Mediterranean world; an artist from anywhere could conceivably have turned up to execute the high priests' commission. Nevertheless, many experts disagree, and find in *La Dama*'s unapproachable hauteur something distinctly Spanish. She holds court these days from a large glass case on a pedestal in the museum's main hall; when the hordes of school-children run up, pressing their noses on the glass and shouting, as thousands of them do every day, you will see the lady's expression intensify into a look of chilly disdain that is a wonder to behold. She shares the room with her less formidable cousins, the very few other Iberian goddesses that have ever been found, including the 4th-century *Dama de Baza* and the *Dama de Cerra de Los Santos*.

The Iberians of the Bronze Age were at least up-to-date in metalworking, and the collection of small expressionistic bronze figurines shows a fine talent; these are similar in many ways to the famous bronzes from the same period found in Sardinia. Spain's entry into the literate world is chronicled in a host of inscriptions from all over the country. Scholars think the language was related to modern Basque, and not surprisingly they haven't completely deciphered any of them. From the Romans, there are indifferent mosaics and copies of Greek sculpture, along with larger-than-life statues of emperors. The bronze tablets from AD 176, inscribed with the laws and orations of Septimus Severus, would have been set up in public places—a landmark in the development of political propaganda. The practice was begun by Augustus and used by several of the more energetic emperors that followed. There are also working models of the Roman catapult and ballista (a kind of gigantic crossbow) if you've ever wondered how they did the business.

Spanish early Christian art is one of the museum's surprises. The architectural sculpture and mosaics show a strong and original sense of design, and a tendency to contemplative geometry that seems almost Islamic. The Visigoths haven't much to offer outside the Treasure of Gurrazar, a collection of vigorously barbaric bejewelled crowns and crosses, all in solid glittering gold, that were found in the Visigothic capital, Toledo. King Reccesvinth's crown (*c.* 650), the richest of all, has his name dangling from it in enamelled golden letters; to the mainly illiterate Visigoths, these must have seemed like magic symbols. A small number of Moorish and medieval Christian works complete the collection.

Outside, near the gate, a small cave has been dug to house replicas of the famous Upper Paleolithic paintings of Altamira, Cantabria: flowing and vigorous bisons, bulls, and other animals in red and black from the same 'school' as Lascaux. The museum has gone to great lengths to copy the atmosphere of the real cave (which is now, except by special arrangement, closed to the general public)—the lighting is so realistically dim, you can barely make out the pictures.

As an antidote to the overall good tastefulness of the area, there awaits Madrid's wax museum, the **Museo de Cera**, Paseo de Recoletos 41, © 91 308 0825 (*open daily; adm 1,500 pts, concessions 100 pts; wax museum only 900 pts, concessions 600 pts,* with a score of tableaux that will whip you through the whole history of Spain. Gluttons for punishment can take the terror train and ride the virtual reality flight simulator.

Recoletos ends where its old gate once stood, in the broad crossroads of the **Plaza del Colón**, dedicated to Genoese seaman Cristoforo Colombo, who used the alias Colón once he reached Spain. The upper part of the square, the **Jardines del Descubrimiento** is one of Madrid's new parks, and the great blocks of sandstone decorating it are all part of an interesting modern **Monument to Columbus**, carved with reliefs and quotes from the explorer's journals. Below the gardens, with an entrance underneath the waterfall-at-the-end-of-the world is the **Centro Cultural de la Villa**, a municipal arts centre with a theatre. Behind is a neo-Gothic monument to Ferdinand and Isabella's Admiral of the Ocean Sea from 1885.

Salamanca

The Paseo de los Recoletos runs along the west end of the fashionable **Barrio de Salamanca**. When the last city walls were knocked down in the 1860s and the spacious grid of streets of the *ensanche* (extension) was laid out, the response to all the new building sites was decidedly underwhelming; no one had the money to do anything, with the exception of the city's most famous speculator, the aforementioned toilet-possessing Marquis de Salamanca (1811–83), who reigned supreme as Madrid's first and probably most roguish robber baron and sometime Finance Minister (*see* p.126). The Marquis built Spain's first railroad, the train to Aranjuez, and dabbled in banking and the stock market—not always following the rules. He went bankrupt twice as a result of his shady dealings, and was forced to leave Spain under a cloud. At one point it got so bad that the Carlists mutilated his gold-plated private railway car.

But the Marquis was a survivor, 'twiced ruined and three times rich' and on his third comeback from financial and political exile, he invested tremendous sums in his slice of the *ensanche*, building houses that were the last word in luxury at the time—complete with lifts and indoor plumbing—all linked to the Puerto del Sol with Madrid's very first tram. On one famous occasion, when he was showing important investors around, an employee warned him that there was an embarassing flaw in the cement of the house he was about to visit. The Marquis turned the potential embarassment into a public relations coup by pointing out the fault and burning the house down in front of everyone.

Much of Salamanca's cheerless waffle iron of swanky avenues bears an eerie resemblance to the neighbourhoods around New York's Park Avenue, with a scattering of old mansions with a certain Victorian panache, trendy show-offs peering in the windows of the Calle de Serrano boutiques, illegally parked cars with diplomatic licence plates, and concierges walking other people's Pekineses. If you're wandering around this well-dressed quarter, its landmarks are equally on the pompous side, with the exception of the 19th-century church of the **Purísima Concepción**, on Calle de Goya, where Art Nouveau meets neo-Gothic, with numerous references from the great cathedral of Burgos (the fretwork spire and the star vaulting in the interior, for example). Opposite is the **California café** (C/Goya 47), a ghastly Salamanca institution that refers to itself as an 'American-style drugstore', replete with a great angled glass facade and decorated with elaborate nautical references.

Just east at Calle Velázquez you can shop in post-modernist design splendour at **Ekseption** (No.28), created by fashionable Barcelona bar designer Eduardo Samsó, or continue up to Calle Velázquez 63, where a mansion of 1908 (now a bank) served as Madrid's City Hall during the Republic, and later as general headquarters for the International Brigades. In the evening, return to dine or have a drink at **Teatriz,** Calle Hermosilla 15, designed in 1989 by the French master of nocturnal architecture, Philippe Starck, who converted the interior of the Teatro Beatriz into a suitably theatrical and trendy refuge for the *barrio*'s gilded youth. The loos, with their marble slabs and mirrors, take the Marquis de Salamanca's famous flush toilet on to another plane altogether.

North, the **Plaza del Marqués de Salamanca**, the one and only square in the *barrio*, is presided over by a statue of the district's founding father. Just up from here, the **Fundación Juan March** (C/Castelló 77, Ⓜ Núñez de Balboa, *open Mon–Sat 10–2 and 5.30–9, Sun 10–2*), was established in 1955 by Barcelona's equivalent of the Marquis, the tycoon Juan March, who was also one of the great financiers of the Nationalist cause in the Civil War. Unlike the Marquis, however, March's swindles eventually caught up with him in the 1970s and he served time. Besides an excellent permanent collection of contemporary Spanish art, the foundation organizes major retrospectives and exhibits throughout the year.

When people say Madrid resembles the capitals of Latin America, the Paseo del Castellana is one reason why. Although the word *paseo* evokes the leisurely promenades of the last century, when the street was lined with fancy mansions, today's Castellana is designed for thundering herds of cars, a kind of trophy thoroughfare, where banks, insurance offices and corporate internationals vie to upstage one another in headquarters by the latest architects. It wasn't exactly planned as such: the Castellano grew up from Charles III's genteel Paseo del Prado, and naturally kept its width and pretensions as it became the Paseo de Recoletos. Then it followed the expanding city north, bursting forth like a mighty shoot, but sadly stripped of its trees in recent decades. In the summer, the business of business is swept aside in the evenings as the *terrazas* take over, some of the more elaborate outdoor bars doubling as night clubs for poor wretches who can't get away to Ibiza.

The Castellana starts in the Plaza de Colón. Just up on the left, the parade of headquarters kick off with the **Torres Heron** (by Antonio Lamela, 1967–76), twin towers built from the top down in a then-experimental technique, and recently joined together under a green crown. Further up, you'll find such gems as the brick and stone **Bankinter** at No.29, with a 1976 extension by Rafael Moneo and Ramón Bescos. To its left squats a truncated pyramid on a lawn, another imaginative work by Lamela.

Opposite, at No.24, the **Banco Santander** headquarters spreads across three 19th-century apartment buildings that once housed royalty, but now contain one of the most exciting contemporary interiors in Spain, designed by Hans Hollein in 1993 (you can peek into the atrium from the Calle Ortega y Gasset entrance, or brazen your way in past the guards into the entrance hall, graced with El Greco's *Adoration of the Shepherds*). Next to this at No.34 is the cupola-crowned Andalusian-style **ABC building** (1926), former headquarters of the conservative newspaper, but since 1995 a fancy pants shopping centre, adroitly combining three buildings with another pair of façades on Calle Serrano; the restaurant (entrance Calle Serrano) with its leaded art nouveau roof lights is especially pretty. The slim, slick black building across the Castellana is **La Unión y el Fénix** insurance headquarters (1968) by Madrid's most prolific architect of the Franco years, Luis Gutíerrez Soto.

Up at No.41, the **Museo de Escultura al Aire Libre**, or Museum of Outdoor Sculpture (Ⓜ Ruben Dario), was a project set up in the 1970s when the highway engineers who designed the Calle de Juan Bravo overpass thought the extra space they created on the edges should be filled in with sculpture. Works were duly donated by Miró, Henry Moore and Julio González, and Eduardo Chillida, whose

Stranded Mermaid, a six-ton cube suspended by the fly-over, steals the show. The nearby area is packed on summer nights, with an array of cheerful summer bars and *terrazas*.

The overpass leads to the leafy district of Chamberí, a part of the *ensanche* that grew up at the same time as Salamanca, with fewer pretensions but just as many embassies. The west extension of Calle Juan Bravo, Paseo Eduardo Dato, is the address of the striking neo-Moorish style **Museo e Instituto Valencia de Don Juan** (visits by appointment, ✆ 91 308 1848) with a collection of ceramics and paintings, including a formidable portrait of Quevado in black rimmed spectacles by Velázquez.

Museo Sorolla and Museo Lázaro Galdiano

One of Madrid's most congenial museums is a couple of blocks north, to the west of the Paseo del Castellano in Chamberí. The delightful **Museo Sorolla**, Calle Gen. Martínez Campos 37, ✆ 91 310 1584, Ⓜ Iglesia (*open Tues–Sat 10–3, Sun 10–2, closed Mon; adm 400 pts, concs 200 pts; free Sat after 2 and Sun*), takes you back a century in the Valencian painter's home, with its refreshing Moorish garden. Joaquin Sorolla (1863–1923) was one of the most fashionable international painters of his day, specializing in large highly coloured sun-filled outdoor scenes in the country or by the beach, often with his wife and family as models, all dressed in billowing white, to which his broad, vigorous brushstrokes were especially adapted. His house and studio have remained very much as he left it when he died, and offer a charming insight into the man, his times and his art.

The next big node on the Castellana, **Glorieta Emilio Castelar**, claims both the fountain, the **Fuente Castellana**, that gave the street its name, and a monument to Castelar. A famous speaker, he briefly became prime minister during the First Republic in 1873, a tenure he used to abolish slavery. The monument (1908) was paid for by public subscription, and shows Castelar speaking to a distinguished audience that includes the suitably impressed figures of Demosthenes and Cicero. Showcase bank and insurance buildings surround the *Glorieta*, including Madrid's first experiment in architectural high-tech, the rusty **Bankunión** (José Antonio Corrales and Ramón Vázquez Molezún, 1972), rated one of the finest from that decade. Two from the 1980s are by Federico Echevarría: the asymmetrical blue-tinted **Banco Europa** and the **Compañía Nacional Hispánica**. Best of all, set back on an embankment, are the cantilevered prisms of the **Catalana Occidente Building** (1987) by Rafael de la Hoz, a pioneering work of four-dimensional architecture. In an engineering *tour de force*, the outer floor is suspended on steel cables from the concrete roof slab. The floating lightness of the building is enhanced by walls made of two layers of glass that deflect the sunlight and heat.

A block in on the east side of the Castellana, at Calle Serrano 75, you'll find the only building that really stands out in Salamanca: the **US Embassy** (1955) done in that style only possible to American embassies, half fortress and half kitchen appliance.

Just up from here you'll find the excellent if often rather lonely **Museo Lázaro Galdiano**, C/Serrano 122, ☎ 91 561 6084, Ⓜ República Argentina or Avda. de América (*open Tues–Sun 10–2, closed Mon and all Aug; night-time tours available in the summer; adm 300 pts*). The founder, who died in 1948, had a better eye and deeper pockets than the other Madrid collectors whose homes have been turned into museums. Among the 37 rooms of art, he assembled one work by nearly every important Spanish painter, including beautiful 15th- and 16th-century triptychs by the masters of Astorga and Ávila, a self-portrait by the excellent Pedro Berruguete, an apocalyptic *Vision of Tondal* and *St John of Patmos* by Hieronymous Bosch, a *Descent* by Quentin Metsys, two works by Magnasco, a Rembrandt portrait and, something you won't see much of in any other Spanish museum, English paintings, including works by Gainsborough, Turner and Reynolds. There's nearly a whole room of Goyas, including two of his first 'Black Paintings', which originally hung in the Duchess of Osuna's El Capricho (*see* below, p.136). Galdiano's tastes were remarkably eclectic and, on the ground floor, articles from the Moors, Byzantines, Persians and Celts share space with medieval enamels, swords and armour, little Renaissance bronzes, early clocks and watches, and two exceptional treasures: the gold and enamel *Gran Sagrario de Limoges* (*c.* 1300) and an engraved goblet made for one of the nuttiest Habsburgs, Rudolph II of Prague.

Just around the corner from the museum, at Calle del Pinar 23, stands the rather plain brick building of the celebrated **Residencia de Estudiantes** (1911), or '*resi*' as everyone called it, which features frequent exhibitions (☎ 91 563 6411). Founded by Alberto Jímenez Fraud to offer an open university education to all and a forum for writers, academics and artists, the revolutionary *resi* soon became the most important institution of its kind in Spain, publishing its own magazine and attracting notice from intellectuals and artists around the world, who lectured or performed here. Under Franco, the Residencia became part of the CSIC, a scientific research council; in the 1980s, it decided, along with the Ministry of Education and Culture, to re-create Fraud's original vision.

Museo de Ciencias Naturales to Museo de la Ciudad

Back on the Castellana, you'll find the building that threw down the design gauntlet to the other banks and insurance companies, the audacious upside-down pyramid of **La Caixa** at No.61, designed by José María Bosch Aymerich in 1968. Just beyond, a giant hand by Botero rises out of the median to greet passing commuters while, still on the east side of the Castellana, an equestrian statue of Isabel la Católica guards a landscaped oasis around the last relic of Madrid's 1881

Exhibition of Industry and the Arts, a brick building with an iron skeleton crowned with a round neo-Renaissance dome. Two of its pavillions house the **Museo de Ciencias Naturales**, or Natural History Museum, entrance C/José Gutiérrez Abascal 2, © 91 411 1328 (*open Tues–Fri 10–6, Sat 10–8, Sun and hols 10–2.30; adm 400 pts, concs 300 pts*), with all sorts of buttons to push and other kinds of interactive educational doodads that children love, although in Spanish only. Among the bones of dinosaurs and other extinct creatures is a stuffed Indian elephant named Pizarro, who travelled around America and Spain in a carnival show, defeating every bull and other animal pitted against it, and losing a tusk in the process. In 1863, the mayor of Madrid offered Pizarro the old botanical gardens (then used as a zoo) for his retirement. On one memorable occasion when he found his feed uninspiring, Pizarro walked into the street and raided a nearby shop.

Until 1930, the next square, **Plaza de San Juan de la Cruz**, marked the end of the Castellana. The Republic's Minister of Public Works, Indalecio Prieto (whose statue was erected here in 1984), carried the street through by knocking down a race course that stood in the way, making room for the long grey bunker of the **Nuevos Ministerios**, which contains three ministries in a building as outscale as Spain's first lesson in totalitarianism, El Escorial. Planned by dictator Primo de Rivera and his wonderfully named architect Secundino Zuazo, building began during the Republic; when Franco came to power, Zuazo returned from exile to rework the project to fit in the with the régime's more conservative mindset. The park in front, originally designed for people, has been given over to cars; the recently glassed-in gallery in front holds exhibitions on architecture. A recent statue of Largo Caballero (prime minister during the Republic) stands on the sidewalk outside, honouring his role as Minister of Work from 1931–37, while an equestrian statue of Franco, the last one in Madrid, stands closer than the two men ever did in life, at the west end of Plaza de San Juan de la Cruz. Caudillo intended this to complement his triumpal arch by the University City, but changed his mind after a spate of student protests, fearing that his monument to himself might be desecrated by young hot-heads.

Anyone still intruiged by architectural perversity might consider a 15-minute walk west of the Nuevos Ministerios, down Calle de Raimundo Fernández Villaverde, to the **Hospital de Maudes**, designed in the 1920s by Antonio Palacios. The architect of the Palacio de Comunicaciones is one of those architects who re-invented his style for every commission, but this is one of his least successful avatars: his hospital is in the shape of a cross, decorated with all kinds of chunky thingamabobs, brightened by a few coloured tile blotches. After standing empty for years, the place is now used as offices by the Comunidad de Madrid, which has weirded the building even more; the French speak of *mal de pierre*, but this is halitosis. Check out the lurid chapel if it's open.

If you like cities as cities, there's a much happier and more urbane project waiting a 10-minute walk east; **El Viso**, 'the vantage point', a garden community of Art Deco two- and three-storey houses laid out in the 1920s and 30s, when this was the outskirts of Madrid. A bit further east, is **Museo de la Ciudad**, C/Príncipe de Vergara 140, © 91 588 6599, Ⓜ Cruz del Rayo (*open Tues–Fri 10–2 and 4–6, Sat–Sun 10–2, closed Mon; adm free*), a permanent exhibition tracing Madrid's evolution as a city, past, present and future, including videos, 3D reconstructions and interactive displays. Despite the modern gadgetry the museum's content is all rather dry but it hosts regular, more interesting, temporary exhibitions on topical issues. Madrid is also proud of its new Auditorio Nacional de Música (José Maria García de Paredes, 1988) just up at No.146, its forbidding exterior of brick and Colmenar limestone concealing a pair of naturally lit and acoustically excellent halls, home base of the Orquesta y Coro Nacionales de España.

Urbanización AZCA

North of the Nuevos Ministerios on the west side of the Castellana is the quarter of Cuatro Caminos, best known for holding the liveliest and best market in Madrid, the **Mercado de Maravillas**, at Calle Bravo Murillo 122 (Ⓜ Alvarado).

On another scale altogether, back in the mid 1950s, the government came up with a project with the inedible name of Urbanización AZCA (*Asociación Zona Comercial A*, Ⓜ Nuevos Ministerios or Lima) as a centre for business intended to relieve some of the congestion in the centre. The inspiration came from the United States: self-contained traffic-free plazas on various levels, combining offices, housing shopping, and public areas, with a full array of bars, restaurants and clubs to keep it hopping at night.

The plan hibernated until the 1970s, when the first skyscrapers sprouted up. As commercial interests soon took over and the original scheme of building in harmony went by the board, as did much of the planned housing. AZCA does, however, have plenty of shopping, including an enormous El Corte Inglés department store patronized by Madrid yuppiedom, and a smattering of restaurants, cafés and discos. The **Plaza Picasso**, originally designed to hold a modern opera house, has a monument to the artist and a garden where office workers sit out during lunch, pouring out the AZCA's three skyscrapers: the **Banco Bilbao-Vizcaya** of 1980, with its genteely rusty awnings, designed by one of Madrid's most influential architects, Sáenz de Oíza. This is the only one in the city equipped with shock absorbers in its foundations, to counter the vibrations of the Atocha–Chamartín train tunnel underneath. Madrid's tallest building is here as well, the slim white aluminum clad 43-storey **Torre Picasso** (1988), the last work by Minori Yamasaki, the same Japanese architect who also built the World

Trade Center in New York. A helipad on top does a brisk trade, although the entrance resembles a giant mouse-hole. The cylindrical **Torre de Europa** on the north end of AZCA (1982, Miguel Oriol e Ibarra), home of the Caja de Madrid, has an art exhibition space underneath, the **Fundación Mapfre Vida**, open daily. On the opposite side of the Castellana, another eye-catcher is the office block (No.110) topped with a glass pyramid hat, where the managers of the Abu Dhabi Investment Agency deliberate.

Just north of AZCA, where the Castellana meets Avenida General Perón, you'll find a brightly coloured mural by Miró crying out for a scrub, decorating the **Palacio de Congresos**, built by Franco in 1964 to commemorate his 25 years in office, but now a bit overshadowed by Bofill's newer congress centre (*see* below, p.136). Opposite this is the striking **Estadio Santiago Bernabéu**, the home of Real Madrid since the late 1940s, when Franco heavily supported the club to give the *madrileños* something to be proud of during the years of hunger (and to trounce arch-rival Barcelona). The stadium was expanded and given a muscular concrete case in 1982, when Spain hosted the World Cup. It can hold 105,000 fans, and often does.

The most controversial and attention-grabbing of all the projects along the Castellana are up past a rather long dull stretch of offices, in the Plaza de Castilla: **KIO Towers**, ⑩ Plaza de Castilla (or more properly these days, the **Puerta de Europa**, as the Kuwait Investment Office, embroiled in a financial scandal, was unable to finish the project), completed in 1996. You can't miss them—the pair tilt towards one another like blind grubs in love, 15 degrees off true, dwarfing the fountain, roundabout and new bus depot below. Designed by the New York firm Burgee and Associates, diehard modernists may find them facile, grossly commericial and inelegant (not to mention a copy of a project in Toledo, Ohio) but the *madrileños* are quite fond of them. Even if you don't agree that they represent the 'New Spain', they do signal a revival of the 12th-century knack for building leaning towers (besides the most famous examples in Pisa and Bologna, in Italy, there's a good tilting church, Santa María del Sar in Santiago de Compostela). It's fun to watch the towers' window-washers in action, inching along a purpose-built metal bar that fits into the aluminum tracks that run up the corners of the towers.

The Periphery: Parque Juan Carlos I, the Caprichio de Osuna

Now that the Paseo del Castellano is all filled up, Madrid's developers are concentrating their attention on the region northeast of the city towards Barajas airport. The centrepiece of the area is the vast **Parque Juan Carlos I**, at the Campo de las Naciones (bus 122, but soon to be linked on the new metro line to the airport). Built around an olive grove, it has an artificial river, fountains and canals, 'cybernetic water displays' on summer evenings in front of the amphitheatre, sculptures, and lots of young trees that will make it a shady refuge in about 20 years. Near here on the M40 is the brightly-coloured **Feria de Madrid** trade fair, a building in the Centre Pompidou mould designed by Jerónimo Junquera, Estanislao Pérez-Pita and Sáenz de Oíza in 1991, a venue for a wide range of events, including the enormous ARCO art fair. The Catalan neo-neo-classical architect Ricardo Bofill designed the **Palacio Municipal de Congresos** (1993), on Avenida Capital de España Madrid, a typical grandiose building in the Bofill mode, with mega-tons of marble and giant Ionic columns and interior atriums, hidden behind the poky entrance doors.

Lost among all this is one of the prettiest gardens in Madrid, **El Capricho de Osuna**, Paseo de la Alameda de Osuna, ⓜ Canillejas or Campo de Naciones, bus no.101 (*open Sat, Sun and hols 9–6.30, till 9pm from April–Sept*). A residence was founded here in 1783 by the Duchess of Osuna, the most cultured woman of her age, who hired Pierre Mulot, architect of the gardens of the Petit Trianon, to design her gardens. The Duchess, a friend of Goya's and rival to the Queen Maria Luisa and the Duchess of Alba, was famous for her parties. After the death of the dissipated last Duke of Osuna in 1882, the house was demolished and the gardens abandoned and neglected until they were purchased by the Comunidad de Madrid in 1974. Now beautifully restored, they are an oasis of romantic coolness in the brash new developments.

Convent de las Descalzas Reales 140
San Ginés 142
Convento de la Encarnación 143
Plaza de Oriente and the Teatro Real 144
Palacio Royal (Palacio Oriente) 145
South of the Palace 147
Ermita de la Virgen del Puerto
and the Campo del Moro 148

Royal Madrid: The West End

PL. ESPAÑA

Edificio Carrión (Capitol)

GRAN VIA

C. C. DE LEGANITOS

C. ISABEL

SAN VICENTE

C. DE FOMENTO

C. RELOJ

Palacio del Senado

Pl. Maria Española

C. TONJA

STO DOMINGO

Jardins de Sabatini

C. ROLLAND

ENCARNACION

C. C. BOLA

C. STO. DOMINGO

Convento de la Encarnación

Jardines Cabo Noval

C. FELIPE V

Palacio de Gaviria

Pl. de Oriente

Teatro Real

OPÉRA

C. CARLOS III

C DE ARENAL

DE BAILÉN

C. LEPANTO

C. FUENTES

C. REQUENA

Pl. Ramales

C.NOBLEJAS

C. UNIÓN

C. ESCALINATA

Pl. Herradores

Palacio Real

Pl. de la Armería

C. CRUZADA

C. SAN NICOLAS

C.S. LUZÓN

C. INDEPENCIA

PO. DE LA VIRGEN DEL PUERTO

C. BIOMBO

Campo del Moro

C. FACTOR

C. J. HERRE

Mercado de San Miguel

C. ALM/DENA

Casa de la Villa

Pl. Villa

Pl. C. S. Miguel

Ermita

Catedral de Santa María Real de la Almudena

C. TRAVIESA

C. MALERA

C. CORDON

C. ROLLO

C. PUÑONROSTRO

Convento de los Carbonero

Parque Emir Mohamed I

C. SACRAMENTO

Basílica de San Miguel

Pl. Cruz Verde

Pl. Pta Cerrada

PTE. DE SEGOVIA

C. DE SEGOVIA

C. VERDE DE SEGOVIA

RONDA DE SEGOVIA

C. BEATRIZ GALINDO

CTA CIEGOS

C. DE BAILÉN

C. MORERIA

Pl. G. Miró

C. YESEROS

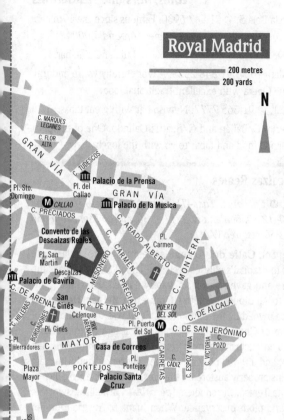

Royal Madrid

200 metres
200 yards

N

C. MARQUES LEGANES
C. FLOR ALTA
GRAN VIA
C. TUDESCOS
Palacio de la Prensa
Pl. Sto. Domingo
Pl. del Callao
CALLAO
GRAN VÍA
C. PRECIADOS
Palacio de la Musica
Convento de las Descalzas Reales
C. ABADO ALBERTO
Pl. Carmen
C. CARMEN
Pl. San Martín
Pl. Descalzas
C. MESONERO
C. MONTERA
Palacio de Gaviria
C. PRECIADOS
C. DE ARENAL
San Ginés
Pl. C. DE TETUÁN
PUERTO DEL SOL
C. HILERAS
Celenque
IRV. ARENAL
C. DE ALCALÁ
C. BORDADORES
Pl. Ginés
Pl. Puerta del Sol
C. DE SAN JERÓNIMO
C
POZO
Pl. Herradores
C. MAYOR
Casa de Correos
C. CARRETAS
C. ESPOZ Y MINA
C. VICTORIA
Plaza Mayor
C. PONTEJOS
Pl. Pontejos
C. CÁDIZ
Palacio Santa Cruz
C. DE LOS CUCHILLEROS

Madrid was founded, in part, because of the strategic value of this easily defensible ridge over the Mazanares. The Moors built their castle, or Alcázar, here in the 9th century. Under the Christian kings, this Alcázar would go through countless alterations and refurbishments, until much to Philip V's delight it caught on fire and could be replaced by a mastodonic royal palace. Throughout the ages, the royal presence here was a magnet for other prestigious institutions, including two remarkable convents, the Senate, opera house, and most recently Madrid's new Cathedral.

Taberna La Bola, C/de la Bola 5, © 91 547 6930. Famous since the 19th century for its traditional *cocido*, served only at lunchtimes. *Around 3,000 pts.*

El Anciano, C/Bailén 19, © 91 559 5332. A famous old tile and zinc bar.

Casa Marta, C/Santa Clara 10, © 91 548 2825. A wonderfully warm and intimate restaurant behind the Opera with excellent traditional food.

Pantumaca, C/Mayor 31, © 91 365 7777. Newish bar with great tapas.

Terraza Vistillas, corner of C/Bailén and C/Beatriz Galindo. One of the most traditional *terrazas*, with good food and tapas to go with the lovely views.

Convento de las Descalzas Reales

> © *91 542 0059*, Ⓜ *Sol, open Tues–Thurs and Sat, 10.30–12.30 and 4–5.30, Fri 10.30–12.30, Sun and hols, 11–1.30, closed Mon; adm 650 pts, concessions 250 pts, free Wed.*

West from the Puerta del Sol, **Calle del Arenal** is the main thoroughfare into Royal Madrid, and one of the capital's oldest streets: its name ('sandy') recalls the stream that once ran here and gave Madrid its watery name. Just to the right, Calle San Martín leads to fabulously wealthy **Convento de las Descalzas Reales**. Originally a palace owned by the kings of Castile, it was the birthplace of Juana of Austria, daughter of Charles V, who, widowed at age 19, decided to make the palace over into an exclusive convent for blue-blooded nuns. The first building dates from 1556, and although it was substantially renovated in the late 1700s, the convent remains properly austere on the outside; it's a branch office of the order founded by Santa Teresa, the shoeless (*descalza*) Carmelites, sworn to poverty, sandal-wearing and pious observance. When Juana of Austria took her vows, however, fashion was not far behind, and the Royal Barefoots soon became the richest prestige nunnery in Christendom, full of works of art and relics donated over the centuries by nuns not quite prepared to leave it all behind. To this day it maintains a large garden and orchard, smack in the centre of Madrid. In the 1980s, the residents (now 23, and no longer all royal, although the convent remains under the patronage of Juan Carlos I) converted a section of their convent into a museum that won an award as the top European Museum of 1988.

To visit, however, you'll have to submit to a guided tour in rapid fire Spanish. This begins at the grand staircase, decorated with excellent *trompe l'oeil* frescoes from the mid 1600s by José Ximénez Donoso and Claudio Coello, in which Philip IV and his family (including the Infanta Margarita, the little girl of *Las Meninas, see* p.99) appear to be looking down from a balcony.

The enclosed, two-storey cloister (in 1999, the restorers uncovered some of its original fresco decoration) is lined with precious chapels: one has a gory recumbent Christ with a gaping jewelled hole in his side, where the Host is placed when the statue leads the Good Friday procession. One tiny, low chapel is especially designed for the little girls sent to live in the Convent, with miniature Nativity items for them to play with; another chapel, dedicated to the Virgin of Guadaloupe, has 68 oil paintings on glass depicting the strong women from the Bible. Another contains a Puerto Rican baby Jesus (look closely, the guide will proudly assure you, even the teeth and tongue are perfect!)

The Ante-choir has one of the convent's most curious statues: a St Joseph holding the Child converted into a St Anthony who has ended up with two left hands. Two of Charles V's daughters are laid to rest here, including the Empress María in the nuns' choir, her tomb surrounded by disembodied arm candelabras, like those in Cocteau's film *La Belle and La Bête*. Beneath, a famous statue of the *Virgen Dolorosa* by Pedro de Mena has eyes that seem to ready to brim over with tears. The nuns have several centuries' accumulation of rich tapestries, including a magnificent series woven in Brussels, the *Triumph of the Eucharist* designed by Rubens and donated to the convent by the Infanta Isabella Clara Engenia, governor of the Netherlands, as a votive offering for the Spanish victory at Breda in 1626. When the nuns were starving in the 1830s, they considered selling these most precious tapestries in order to eat, only to be forbidden by the abbess, who declared they must belong to the convent until the end of time. There are also several paintings in the tapestry room—one of *St Ursula and the 11,000 Virgins arriving in Cologne* (the Convent has their relics stowed away somewhere—the mind boggles at the size of the reliquary) while another painting, a Flemish-inspired *Presentation in the Temple* was painted on both sides, visible thanks to the one and only mirror permitted in the convent.

Another room has a case with spiked shoes (the only kind the discalced sisters ever wear) and knotted ropes for mortification. Another is lined with royal portraits; one of the little Infantas, daughters of Philip II, shows a rare depiction of the long lost Alcázar in the background. There is a full length portrait of an adolescent Sebastian of Portugal, whose timely death enabled his uncle Philip II to claim the crown of Portugal (*see* p.79). On the back wall hangs a portrait of the emperor's sister Eleanor, the one François I agreed to marry. You'll see what changed his mind.

The Chapterhouse has 16th-century frescoes of the life of St Francis and the convent's finest sculptures: two other weepy Virgins, one by Pedro de Mena, who also did the ultra-realistic *Ecce Homo*. The dramatic *Magdalen* in the case is attributed to Gregorio Fernández, a work that looks forward to the Addams Family, while over the door is the symbolic mural of the *Crucified Nun*. The next room, the Hall of the Kings, preserves some of the original palace features, including a stucco frieze under the ceiling, and more portraits, including many royals dressed up as saints (they fooled everyone until their recent restoration). Note the charming spiral stair in the corner, a short cut to the upper cloister. This is followed by the Flemish painting room, featuring an unusual 16th-century allegory called the *Ship of the Church* by a follower of Bosch, with the Pope at the helm and a crew consisting of the founders of the religious orders. The royal family paddles up in a couple of long boats while various sins try to waylay the ship, and Jesus and a courtly group of saints wait in the Port of Salvation. Most of the other paintings are copies of famous works displayed elsewhere, with the exception of a beautiful *Adoration of the Magi* by Brueghel the Elder. The Italian and Spanish rooms have a *Christ Carrying the Cross* by Sebastian del Piombo, a gloomy *St Francis* attributed to Zurbarán, and the *Tribute Money* by Titian, who signed his name on the Pharisee's collar.

The convent's church, designed by Juan Bautista de Toledo, was much altered over the centuries, especially after a disastrous fire in 1862. One feature that survived is the tomb of the foundress Juana (d.1573), in a burial chapel designed in part by Juan de Herrera and hidden off to the right of the presbytery; the marble figure of Juana praying is by Pompeo Leoni, who sculpted the similar statues of the royal family for San Lorenzo de El Escorial.

San Ginés

Back on Calle del Arenal, at No.9 is the sumptuous **Palacio de Gaviria** (1851) built by the eponymous Marquis to entertain Isabel II; although the exterior is no longer what it was, some of the rooms inside are intact and contain music bars. The **Eslava Club** on the same street occupies the Teatro Eslava of 1872, famous for its premier of Lorca's first (and disastrous) attempt at drama in 1920, a saga of cockroach love called *The Butterfly's Evil Spell.*

The little church of **San Ginés** was founded shortly after the Reconquista, but like all the others was given the 17th-century treatment, which in turn was restored after fires. Originally a society church in the reign of Isabel II, it is now dark, very quiet, run by the Opus Dei and filled with the pungent smell of incense. One chapel, dedicated to the Virgen de los Remedios, has a little dried out crocodile, dedicated by a certain Alonso de Montalbán who, like Captain Hook, was chased by one across the Caribbean until the Virgin delivered him from its jaws. San Ginés' chief prize is in the adjacent **Capilla de Cristo,** entered by way of Calle Bordadores: El Greco's *Expulsion from the Temple*, although you have to come during Mass to see it. At the other times, especially in the wee hours, you can take consolation dipping a *churro* in chocolate at the **Chocolatería San Ginés**, in Pasadizo San Ginés.

Calle Arenal ends at the back of the operahouse, in Plaza Isabel II. The **statue of Isabel II** was erected in 1850, but the queen, in an unusual gesture of royal deference, had it withdrawn, saying that the *madrileños* could put it back after her death, if they found her reign satisfactory. Actually they didn't—they ousted her in the end—but it seemed unkind to leave her statue rotting in a warehouse.

Convento de la Encarnación

Plaza de la Encarnación, ✆ 91 542 0059, guided tours only (Spanish only), Tues, Wed, Thurs and Sat 10.30–12.45 and 4–5.45, Sun and hols 11–1.45; adm 425 pts, concs 225 pts, free for EU citizens Wed.

The area north of Calle Arenal has another convent for blue-blooded nuns, the **Convento de la Encarnación**, founded by Philip III and his wife and cousin Margarita de Austria, in 1611. The nuns at the Encarnación get by with fewer treasures than their cohorts at the Descalzadas, and their home has gone through more turmoil, condemned to disappear several times in the 19th century, and partially demolished. The convent does, however, have its share of royal portraits and paintings. One, the charming anonymous *The Exchange of Princesses on the River Bidasoa* depicts the famous big league Franco-Hispanic princess marriage trade off during the Twelve Year Truce of 1615: Louis XIII got Anne of Austria, daughter of Philip III, and Philip IV got Elizabeth (Isabelle) of France, daughter of Henry IV. The issue, in the next generation, led the Bourbons winning the throne of Spain in the War of the Spanish Succession. Other paintings include a *St Isidro*, the city's patron (while he naps, two angels plow; Spaniards say it's a fitting allegory for a capital that lives off the rest of the country); a portrait of Philip III by his court painter, Bartolomé González, and a rather beautiful *St John the Baptist* with an earnest sheep, by Ribera.

In the sculpture room, pride of place goes to the wooden polychrome statues by Gregorio Fernández, master of the 17th-century Spanish blood and guts school of religious art (although he has plenty of rivals): his recumbent, green-faced Christ distorted in rigor mortis lies in one corner and is viciously flagellated in another. The next hall is lined with portraits of Habsburgs, all copies of works now in the Pitti Palace in Florence (there were a pair of Medicis in the woodpile: the sister of the convent foundress married the Grand Duke of Tuscany and Marie de' Medici was the mother of Elizabeth of France, in the famous princess exchange).

The tour continues to the cloister and choir, which also doubles as the convent cemetery; one nun buried here is Luisa de Carajal, a great friend of the first abbess, who died in the Tower of London in 1614 after going to England to fight against Anglican reform. Note the Herreran walnut stalls (complete with their little Herreran balls) and portraits of the seven archangels with their attributes.

The more fleshy aspects of the faith reach a unique epiphany in the convent's **Reliquario**, a small ornate room with a frescoed ceiling, and an altarpiece of the *Nativity* by Leonardo's pupil, Bernardino Luini. It is lined with wooden cases that could belong in a cosy study but instead hold a world record-breaking collection of relics, skulls, teeth, toes, hair, fingernails, you name it, with a bit or bob from nearly every saint on the calendar, wrapped up in little boxes with flowers like expensive chocolates, most of them rescued by the Habsburgs from Protestant lands during the Counter Reformation. The nuns are proudest of a droplet of blood from St Panteleon, a 4th-century Greek doctor, which apparently liquifies on the day of his martyrdom (27 July) or whenever Spain is in danger. (Incidently, he's also a good saint to appeal to for lottery numbers; in Rome, if you go through the proper rigamarole, he'll come at night with the winning numbers written on a piece of paper. Only he's a tricky saint, and hides it).

The tour continues to the church: in spite of the sombre, boxy granite façade attributed to Juan Gómez de Mora it turns out to have a graceful interior, one of the prettiest in Madrid, dating from a remodelling by Ventura Rodríguez in the 1700s, decorated with stuccoes and frescoed ceiling on the *Life of St Augustine*. If you like organ music, the Sunday 11.30 Mass is reputedly a treat, played with all the stops out on the original 17th century instrument, but the church bells are charmingly flat.

Just north, up Calle de la Encarnación, is the **Palacio del Senado**, which also began as a convent in 1581, only to be converted in 1820 into a neoclassical home for the Senate. In 1991, the Senators, who actually have very little political power in Spain, caused a stink by building themselves a modern palace around back, complete with all the amenities, including an indoor pool. Around the corner, the hedonistic senators can take their post prandial strolls through the **Jardines Sabatini**, a section of the royal gardens that has seen better days.

Plaza de Oriente and the Teatro Real

The **Plaza de Oriente** was the largest space cleared by 'the king of squares' Joseph Bonaparte, although it wasn't laid out properly until 1844; its name, confusingly, refers to the fact that it is on the east side of the Royal Palace, even if it's on the west side of Madrid. Now pedestrianized and rather frenchified with cafés, it makes a dignified front lawn for the Royal Palace, lined with the rather woebegone statues of Hispanic Roman emperors, Visigothic and Spanish kings and queens who were intended to go on the palace roof. Precisely why they aren't is a subject of some controversy: some say Philip V's second wife Isabel Farnese had them removed after a dream that there was an earthquake and they fell on her head; others believe they were removed by Charles III with the excuse that they were too heavy.

The equestrian **Statue of Philip IV** in the centre original stood in the Retiro Park and has an interesting history: the original design, by Florentine sculptor Pietro Tacca, was deemed too unheroic by Philip's favourite, the Conde Duquee de Olivares, who asked Velázquez to paint a portrait of the king on a rearing horse and send it to Florence to show the sculptor just what was required. Tacca was startled; no one had ever cast a rearing horse before and so he went to Galileo for some advice on the technical problems of balance (make the rear quarters of the horse solid, and the front hollow, said Galileo). From then on, every monarch had to have a rearing horse. If Tacca's king and horse look a bit wooden, it could be Velázquez's fault; his genius balked at equestrian portraits; even those in the Prado look like stage props.

The centrepiece of the Plaza del Oriente, the **Teatro Real Opera** (*guided visits 500 pts, concessions 300 pts*) reopened in 1997 after a 72-year break. Begun in 1810 but completed only in 1850, in time for Isabel II's 20th birthday gala, the theatre then closed in 1925, supposedly for refurbishment. Civil war followed by 40 years of Franco (who couldn't even be bothered to finish the nearby cathedral) puts the delay into context. Political infighting delayed reconstruction for more than a decade while costs soared, hitting the 21 billion peseta mark. From the outside, the building is little changed, but its innards now boast state of the art acoustics and an overall cubic area greater than the Telefónica building on the Gran Vía, at least according to its architects. The opera house offers a varied programme, and seat prices are, by British and American standards, reasonable, with top seats weighing in at 20,000 pts, and a seat in the gods for 800 pts.

Palacio Real (Palacio de Oriente)

C/Bailén, ☎ 91 542 0059, Ⓜ Opera. Open, summer, Mon–Sat 9–6, Sun and hols 9–3; winter, Mon–Sat 9.30–5, Sun and hols 9–12; adm 850 pts (includes the Farmacia), concessions 350 pts, free to EU passport-holders on Wed. Optional tours are given in English and other languages for an extra 100 pts.

Any self-respecting Bourbon had to have one. Philip V, who commissioned it in 1738, chose the most reputed architect of the day, Filippo Juvarra, who came up with a model four times larger than what was actually built, then abruptly died. The project was inherited by his pupil, Giovanni Battista Sacchetti, who reduced the scale when Philip's wife Isabel Farnese convinced him that 2,800 rooms would probably meet her needs. As it was, the first king to live in the finished structure was Charles III, while Alfonso XIII was the last king to use the Palace as a residence. Juan Carlos' tastes are much more modest; he lives quite comfortably at the suburban Zarzuela Palace, without any semblance of an old-style court.

Originally this was the site of the Moorish Alcázar, converted by Henry IV into Madrid's first Royal Palace. It was here that Velázquez lived and painted for Philip IV, and many of his works are infused with the atmosphere of its old, dark chambers. A great fire on Christmas 1734 destroyed the Alcázar and its great paintings, including some by Velázquez, and occasioned the 18th-century replacement, very much in the style of Versailles and other contemporary palaces.

The entrance to the palace is by way of the Plaza de la Armería, a courtyard big enough to hold the entire Plaza Mayor, buildings and all. If you're around at noon on the first Wednesday of each month (*except July, Aug and Sept*) you can watch the **changing of the guard**, complete with a military band and some impressive horsemanship, all done in early 1900s style. Fortunately, not take all 2,800 rooms are open, but even so expect a mild delirium after the first three dozen—each room with its tapestry from the Real Fábrica, portraits of bewigged sycophants, a nice inlaid table, a half-ton chandelier, and indolent mythological deities painted on the ceiling by the likes of Francisco Bayeu, best remembered these days as Goya's master, and the German, Anton Rafael Mengs.

Some rooms do stand out: the **Grand Stair**, frescoed by Corrado Giaquinto of Naples, and the ceilings frescoed by Giambattista Tiepolo, the last great Italian fresco painter, in the **Salón de los Halbardiers** (*Venus Commanding Vulcan to forge arms for Aeneas*) and in the **Throne Room**, where the enormous *Apotheosis of Spain* was frescoed over a period of eight years. This was the last major project of Tiepolo's life, painted at the invitation of Charles III in 1762, although it is hardly his best work: some say the subject matter was too much of an oxymoron at the time for even the agreeable Tiepolo to swallow. The old man, aged 66 when he arrived in Madrid, also had to put up with the jealous rivalry of Mengs, who in 1770 connived to have Tiepolo's last paintings for the royal chapel of Aranjuez replaced with his own work. (Tiepolo died shortly thereafter, probably of chagrin. In his native Venice he would have got a fancy tomb, but in Madrid his remains shared the fate of all famous men—they've been lost.) Another room, the **Antécamara de Gasparin**i, has two pairs of paintings of Charles IV and his wife Maria Luisa by the artist who superseded Tiepolo, Goya (although the originals now hang in the Prado); the next room, the **Salón de Gasparini**, is a rococo masterpiece of chinoiserie, designed by Charles III's court painter. One room is full of gold clocks collected by Charles IV and, if you happen to be there at noon, you can hear them all go off, a delicate symphony of bells and chimes. There are violins by Stradivarius and other fabulous musical instruments, and a **state dining rooom** wrapped in frescoes by Bayeu and Antonio González Velázquez, with a table capable of seating 145, some of the Middle East peace talks in 1992 took place here.

The **Farmacia**, on the east end of the Plaza Armeria, contains many fittings and jars of the original, founded by Philip II in 1594. Bar codes with the Royal crest, wrapped around the necks of the flasks, add a quaint supermarket touch.

Tickets are sold separately for the **Armería Real** (Royal Armoury), if it's ever reopened after restoration. Charles V, living in an age when the medieval manner of warfare was rapidly becoming obsolete, had a truly Quixotic fascination for armour. His collection makes up most of what you see today, and includes his favourite suit, the one he wore at the Battle of Mühlberg and when he posed for Titian. Even the royal dog could be suited up in a full metal jacket in a chivalrous version of Dr Who's K 9. One sword in the collection got a real workout—it belonged to El Cid. A third museum, out in the park of the Campo del Moro, the **Museo de Carruajes** (Museum of Carriages) has been undergoing a major restoration for the past nine years and seems to be in no danger of re-opening.

South of the Palace

Amazingly, despite its four centuries as capital of Catholic Spain, Madrid does not have a single church worth going out of your way to visit. For centuries part of the diocese of Toledo, it didn't even have a proper cathedral until the official opening in 1992 of the **Catedral de Santa María Real de la Almudena**, C/Bailén, ☎ 91 542 2200, Ⓜ Opera (*open Mon–Sat 10–1.30 and 6–8.45, Sun 10–2 and 6–8.45; mass daily at noon and 8pm, Sun at 11, 12, 1.30 and 8*). It was Emperor Charles V who had the idea to make the old parish church here into a cathedral, back in 1518. The project finally got underway in 1883 and took over 100 years in the building; besides the interruption caused by the Civil War, the delays were political and bureaucratic and the cathedral is not quite the stunning culmination of *madrileño* religious passion its builders had hoped for. Nevertheless, its dedication in June 1993 was marked with some ceremony, with the Pope on hand to bless the new cathedral, fêted by enthusiastic *madrileños* who showered him with yellow and white confetti, made, true to Madrid's public commitment to recycling, from chopped-up phone directories. Founded on the site of the old Almudena Mosque, the most beautiful part of this bulky, ungainly building is its high ceiling of triangular panels painted with Moorish-inspired patterns in muted earthy reds, browns and greens. Overall, the cathedral feels light and airy, but empty, in spite of all the chapels (as awful as you might expect); the abstract stained glass adds much needed splashes of colour.

South of the Cathedral is the only surviving bit of Moorish Madrid, a winsome fragment of wall in **Parque Emir Mohammed I**, named after the founder of Mayrit, and now surrounded with the detritus of Madrid's current restoration fervour. Facing it and overlooking a small and shabby square, a copy of the statue of the Virgin of the Almudena (from *almud*, or granary) stands in a niche, the raison d'etre for the cathedral and subject of a *muy loco* pious story that claims the image was brought to Spain by St James the Greater, and hidden on this spot by a blacksmith in 712 when Madrid was taken over by the Moors. After the Reconquista, in 1085, Alfonso VI led the faithful here to find the statue, unforgotten after all these years, and when all requests for divine assistance failed, a woman claiming to be a descendent of the original statue-hiders, declared she would give her life in exchange if they could only find the Virgin. At once part of the town wall fell on top of her, but revealed the statue hidden inside. The statue enshrined in the cathedral, however, is not the miraculous one, but a copy of the original that went missing again in the 16th century and has yet to reappear.

Calle Bailén south of here gives on to a handsome concrete viaduct over the Calle Segovia, built in the 1930s and once Madrid's favourite suicide leap (to such an extent that the sides have been glassed in).

Ermita de la Virgen del Puerto and the Campo del Moro

From the Cathedral you can walk downhill through a slightly seedy run-down park to the Paseo de la Virgen del Puerto, which at its southernmost end has one of the city's prettiest churches, the brick **Ermita de la Virgen del Puerto**, built by Pedro de Ribera in 1718 and topped with a striking octagonal slate roof. Blown to smithereens in the Civil War, it was rebuilt as exactly as it was in 1951.

On the way you can also admire the **Puente de Segovia**, a once-majestic bridge designed by Juan de Herrera in 1584 for Philip II, to allow him to make a quick escape to El Escorial. It dwarfs the Mazanares in the way that parents buy their children clothes a size or two too large knowing that they will someday grow into them. Over the centuries the bridge and river (which used to dry up completely in the summer) have been a soft target for jokes: Lope de Vega advised Madrid to sell the bridge or buy a river; a German ambassador named Rhebinor declared that the Mazanares was the best river in Europe, because one could navigate it in a horse and carriage. The villa Goya that purchased in 1819, La Quinta del Sordo ('the villa of the deaf man') once stood very near here, and in spite of suggestions at the time to preserve it as a Goya museum it was demolished, although the murals, the famous 'Black Paintings', were transferred to canvas and hence to the Prado.

At the north end of the Paseo de la Virgen del Puerto you'll find the entrance to the largest of the formal parks that make up the grounds of the Palacio Real, the quiet **Campo del Moro** (*open until 8pm*). Its name recalls the Moorish encampment of 1109, when the Muslims made their last unsuccessful attempt to recapture Madrid. Planted like an English park in 1842, the Campo del Moro was opened to the public in 1931, but was closed by Franco and only reopened in 1983; it has lovely views up to the palace.

Madrid of the Bright Lights

The Real Academia de Bellas Artes
de San Fernando   152

Down the Calle Alcalá   154

The Gran Vía   156

Malasaña   157

Chueca   159

Las Salesas   162

Gran Vía, Malasaña and Chueca

N

200 metres
200 yards

Gta Ruiz Jiménez

CALLE SAGASTA GÉNOVA

C. DE MONTELEÓN
DE RUIZ
C. MANUELA MALASAÑA
C. SAN ANDRÉS
C. DE CHURRUCA
C. DE LARRA
C.GALERIA ROBIES
C. DIVINO PASTOR
APODOCA
BARCELÓ
C. DAOIZ
Pl. Dos de Mayo
C. VELARDE
Jardines Arquie. Riv.
Iglesias de las Maravillas
C. DE LA PALMA
C. DE SAN BERNARDO
C. DOS DE MAYO
C. SANTA LUCIA
C. DE SAN VICENTE
ESPÍRITU
TRIBUNAL
Museo Municipal
C. S. MATEO
C. SANTA ÁGUEDA
C. MAINS
C. DEL TESORO
C. STA. BRIGIDA
C. POZAS
C. DEL MARQUES DE SANTA ANA
C. JESÚS DEL VALLE
C. MADERA
CORREDERA ALTA DE SAN PABLO
C. FARMACIA
Pl. ESPAÑA
Edificio Carrión (Capitol)
C. VELARDE
C. DEL PEZ
C. ESCORIAL
C. M.
Pl. Ildefonso
C. HERNÁN CORTES
C. PIZARRO
Convento de San Plácido
C. AUGUSTO FIGUEROA
C. DE LA LUNA
C. S. ROQUE
CORREDERA
San Antonio Alemanes
C.PÉREZ GALDOS
C. C. DE LEGANITOS
C. DE FOMENTO
G R A N   V Í A
C. ESTRELLA
C. PUEBLADA
VALVERDE
Pl. Melia
C. RELOJ
C. ISABEL
C. MARQUES LEGANES
Pl. Soledad
C. CORREDERA
C. BARCO CORREDERA
DE HORTALEZA
C. FLOR ALTA
C. TUDESCOS
C. INFANTAS
C. TONJA
STO DOMINGO
C. G. ROLLAND C. BOLA
Pl. Sto. Domingo
Palacio de la Prensa
GRAN VIA
Teléfonica
C. STO. DOMINGO
CALLAO
C. PRECIADOS
Pl. del Callao
Palacio de la Música
GRAN VIA
Convento de las Descalzas Reales
Pl. San Martin
C. ABADO ALBERTO
C. CARMEN
Pl. Carmen
Casino de Madrid
C. PRECIADOS
C. MONTERA
C. DE LA ADUANA
Real Academia Belles Artes
PUERTO DEL SOL
Banco Español de Crédito
C. LA SEVILLA
Pl. Puerta del Sol
Casa de Correos

This is central Madrid's main shopping and business area, busy around the clock and replete with awkward skyscrapers, grand imperial cinemas with enormous hand-painted billboards, hamburger joints, banks, and unyielding traffic swarms. Part of the excitement comes from its wildly eclectic array of early 20th-century architecture along the Calle de Alcalá and Gran Vía. North of the Gran Vía are the two flavoursome old districts of Malasaña and Chueca, once seedy and druggy but now two top night-time destinations: Chueca is now firmly established as the city's gay district.

CALLE SAGASTA GÉNOVA

C.A. FLORES
C. SERRANO ANGUITA
C. MEJIA LEQERICA

Pl. Alonso Martínez

CALLE SAGASTA GÉNOVA

Museo Romántico

Pl. Sta. Bárbara

C. CAMPOMOR
C. S. MATEO
TRV. S. MATEO
C. JUSTINIANO
C. DE ARGENSOLA
C. GEN. CASTAÑOS
C. M. ENSENADA

Pl. Villa de París

C. S. LORENZO
C. STA. BRIGIDA
C. DE HORTALEZA
C. FERNANDO VI
C. REGUEROS
BELÉN

San Anton

C. LUIS GONGORA
C. PELAYO
C. BÁRBARA BRAGANZA

GRAVINA
C. PIAMONTE
C. CONDE DE XIQUENA

C. DE CHUECA
C. AUGUSTO FIGUEROA

C. ALMIRANTE

C. DE PRIM

Pl. Mella
C. S. MARCOS
LIBERTAD
C. DEL BARQUILLO

PASEO DE RECOLETOS

C. INFANTAS

Casa de las Siete Chimenas

BANCO DE ESPAÑA

Banco Central

Pl. la Cibeles

GRAN VÍA

Edificio Metropólis

Casino de Madrid

C. DE ALCALÁ

New Club

Círco de Bellas Artes

Banco de España

C. DE LOS MADRAZO

Banco Bilbao-Viscaya
C. ARLABÁN

Chicote, Gran Vía 12, ℗ 91 532 6737. The oldest, best and most famous cocktail bar in Madrid.

Del Diego, C/de la Reina 12, ℗ 91 523 3106. A stylish cocktail shake away from Chicote, and founded by one of Chicote's barmen, inventor of the 'Diego' (vodka, kirsch, lime, and peach).

Artemisia, C/Tres Cruces 4, ℗ 91 521 8721. One of the friendliest vegetarian restaurants in Madrid.

Café Commercial, Glorieta de Bilbao 7, ℗ 91 521 5655. North of the Municipal Museum, and an institution among the locals and intelligentsia. It has cushy old leather seats for prolonged sitting and reading.

Café Acuarela, C/Gravina 10, ℗ 91 522 2143. Antique chic and a lively atmosphere at this trendy gay café.

Bar Santander, C/ Augusto Figueroa 25, ℗ 91 522 4910. Famous for a hundred different tapas.

Salvador, C/Barbieri. A famous neighbourhood place, serving stalwartly traditional and cheap food.

The Real Academia de Bellas Artes de San Fernando

> ℗ 91 522 1491, Ⓜ Sol or Sevilla (*open Tues–Fri 9–7, Sat–Mon and hols, 9–2.30; adm 300 pts, concessions free. Note how the guards get to read books rather than look bored and follow you about*).

One of the ten streets radiating from Sol (*see* pp.55–60), broad, dignified **Calle de Alcalá** sweeps out past the Hotel Paris to the northeast. In the Middle Ages it was blazed by shepherds, herding their massive flocks between Extremadura and the summer pastures in the north. By the 18th century, however, this transhumance trail was considered one of the most elegant streets in all Europe, lined with *elegantísimo* palaces, and even today it maintains its panache—at least here on its west end, even though many of the private mansions were replaced with plush and pompous bank buildings in the late 19th century.

At No.5, the Ministry of Finance occupies the former **Customs House**, another project of Charles III, designed by Francesco Sabatini in 1769, who borrowed rather heavily from the Palazzo Farnese in Rome for the façade. In 1944, it was extended and given a door by Pedro di Ribera, from a destroyed palace. Next to it, at No.13, stands the Palacio Goyeneche, the fancy home of a banker designed by José de Churriguera in 1720, but shorn of all its Baroque froo-froos in 1773, when it became home of the **Real Academia de Bellas Artes de San Fernando**. The Enlightened academians found them distinctly old-fashioned.

Founded by Philip V in 1752, the academy has a collection of art that makes a fine appetizer or dessert to the feast served at Madrid's Big Three. And like the Prado and Thyssen, the personality of the collectors shines through in unexpected ways: the academians, in short, may have been enlightened, but their tastes weigh very much towards the unusual, the whimsical and the downright funny. Start in the courtyard in the belly of the building, presided over by a statue of Cervantes: Madrid's main monument to Spain's greatest novelist in Plaza de España is silly enough, but here he presides over parked cars with a menacing quill-wielding hand stretched over his head like an awning.

The collection spans the last five centuries of Spanish painting, beginning with a room full of moody, dramatic Riberas and Alonso Canos, nearly all on religious themes, including a rather unorthodox *Assumption of the Magdalen*, who by most accounts never assumpted anywhere. Cano also weighs in with the *Death of a Franciscan*, a sombre scene, at least on the earthly plane; thanks to the artist we see the friar riding off merrily to his reward in a chariot drawn by white horses. There are five remarkable life-size portraits of monks by Zurbarán, beautiful works full of early Renaissance precision; in contrast, there's his *Blessed Alonso Rodriguez*, a busy picture in which the subject is being branded by Jesus and Mary, sitting in heaven and holding their hearts out like ray guns. Then there's *La Abundancia*, by Martin de Vos, in which one child frolics with a fiery salamander and another holds a miniature triceratops in his hand—probably the first instance of a dinosaur in art.

Along with the quirky works there are fine paintings by Murillo, El Greco and Velázquez (*Portraits of Philip IV* and *Mariana of Austria*), and dark works by the Bassano family, who specialized in nocturnal scenes. One room has small paintings by Bellini and Correggio, next to the delightful *Spring*, a portrait of a man entirely composed of flowers, the only work in Spain by Italian proto-Surrealist Arcimboldo, who painted for the Habsburgs in Austria and Prague.

In Rubens' *Suzanna and the Elders*, the dirty old men are not content to stare, but pinch her doughy pink Rubenesque flesh, while the same artist's peculiar *St Augustin between Christ and the Virgin* shows the Virgin doing some self-pinching of her own, while Augustine rolls his eyes in disbelief or ecstasy. It's hard to tell. Jans Jannsens' *Roman Charity* (a theme taken up again by Steinbeck at the end of *The Grapes of Wrath*) is equally memorable, with a loving rendition of the old man's dirty feet. The last two paintings in the room are by that most uncanny of 17th-century painters, Alessandro Magnasco, who used his precocious quick stroke technique to highlight the nightmares of his diseased age. One painting looks like a self portrait in a wizard hat, and the other, the *Capitulo de Franciscanos*, shows the friars apparently writhing and dissolving in a whirlwind St Vitus dance.

None of this really prepares you for the anti-Christmas crib at the top of the steps. Like the Italians, the Spaniards love elaborate Nativity scenes populated by a host of extras, but it took a genuine sicko like Charles IV, who wanted to achieve the ultimate 5,950 piece display in the Palacio Real, to commission José Gines to sculpt figures illustrating the Massacre of the Innocents. At least the maddened mothers seem to be getting their own back, as they bite, stab and tear the eyeballs out of the cruel men. As an antidote, there are charming sun-filled paintings by Sorolla, Andrés Segovia's guitar, a goofy Greek fantasy of the *Colossus of Rhodes* by M. Degrain, the *Family of Skeletons* by J. Lopez, all happily holding hands, and Mengs' *La Marquessa del Llana with Parrot.*

Best of all are the excellent Goyas, including two self portraits (one young, one troubled and deaf), one of *Ferdinand VII*, looking silly on a horse two sizes too small for him, and another of the detested minister *Manuel Godoy*, slumped contemptuously in a chair in the middle of a battle. There are also haunting scenes in his 'Black Style': a *Bullfight, Inquisition, Flagellantes*, a *Madhouse*, and his famous and rather eerie *El Entierro de la Sardina*, on the riotous fiestas that mark the end of carnival. 'The Burial of the Sardine' continues to this day in Madrid, with a mock funeral party that bears a coffin containing a large papier-mâché sardine through the streets to the Casa de Campo, where it is set alight to commemorate the occasion when the starving townspeople of Madrid received a long-awaited consignment of fish only to discover on arrival that it was completely rotten, and the only thing to do was burn it on the spot. More Goyas—some of his original plates—are in the **Calcografía Nacional**, on the first floor of the same building; it also holds frequent exhibitions of etchings.

Down the Calle de Alcalá

Just up from the academy you'll find the sumptuous Riviera-style **Casino de Madrid**, built in 1910 as a private club for men, a purpose it still serves (women can enter as guests). If you ask nicely at the door they may just let you have a peek at Madrid's most extraordinary flowing stairway; you almost want to join the club or compromise your virtue with a member to swan down it at least once.

Many of the members used to hold court in the equally grand bank and commercial buildings opposite that in the 19th century made up the heart of Madrid's financial district. Although business fashion has since relocated to the Paseo de la Castellana, their original headquarters here prove that a taste for the flamboyant is nothing new among Madrid's movers and shakers: the building squeezed into the sharp corner opposite, now housing the **Banco Español de Crédito**, was designed in the 1880s by Catalan José Grasés Riera, who introduced some of Barcelona's *modernista* curves and whimsy into a city more used to Castilian symmetry. This was the first major commercial block in Madrid; next to it, the **Banco Bilbao-Viscaya** (1910, Ricardo Bastida) supports not one, but two bronze quadrigas straight out of *Ben Hur*, ready to fly over the Calle d'Acalá in an airborne circus. Further down, on the corner of Calle Cedaceros, the **New Club** (1899) was the first private English-style club in Madrid, designed by Grasés Riera in one of his tamer moods.

Next on the street is the massively domed church of the convent of **Las Calatravas**, built in 1670 for nuns of the eponymous military order; one of Madrid's better Baroque churches, it still possesses one last overwrought altarpiece by José Churriguerra. Further along, at the point of the 'v' where Calle de Alcalá meets the Gran Vía, stands the **Edificio Metropólis**, performing the same landmark task as the Flatiron building in New York. Designed in 1905 by Jules and Raymond Fevrier in the French Belle Epoque bathyscope style, the Metropólis set the snazzy tone for future projects along the Gran Vía, with its cylindrical prow of Corinthian columns, ring of statues and dome picked out with gilt faldirol, topped by a Winged Victory, waiting to crown the winning charioteer on the BBV building. On street level, the vaguely Mae West bronze flower seller is La *Violetera*, heroine of one of Madrid's favourite *zarzuelas*.

Opposite is another attention grabber: the asymetrical **Círculo de Bellas Artes**, Calle Alcalá 42 (*exhibitions open Tues–Fri 5–9, Sat 11–2 and 5–9, Sun 11–2, closed Mon; café open 9am–2am, till 4am on Fri and Sat; adm 100 pts*). This is one of Madrid's best, if most eccentric, Art Deco structures, concocted by Antonio Palacios (1919–26), architect of the cream cake Palacio de Communiciones (*see* p.124). Originally another private club devoted to the arts (hence the statue of Athena) the Círculo is now open to the public for a small fee. Its cool vanilla marble interior has a delightful airy bar, while the other floors feature exhibition halls, theatres, a lavish ball room and classrooms.

Further along is another, less exotic work by Palacios: the **Banco Central-Hispano** (1910), while opposite, the brick church of **San José** (1742) was the last work of Pedro de Ribera and is famous for having witnessed the wedding in 1802 of Spain's future nemesis, the great liberator Simon Bolívar. Just behind it, in Plaza del Rey, the reputedly haunted **Casa de las Siete Chimeneas** (the House of the Seven Chimneys) was built by Juan Bautista de Toledo and Juan de Herrera as a country retreat in 1577, when Madrid ended at the Puerta del Sol. The ghost is a young lady in white, and her skeleton with some late 16th-century coins was found hidden in the walls during a 19th-century restoration. Among the famous who have stayed here, in 1623, was the future Charles I of England, coming down for a preview of the Infanta Maria (*see* p.46). The house is now used as an annex of the Ministery of Culture; the sculpture in the square is by Eduardo Chillida.

The Gran Vía

Ploughed through 14 pokey medieval streets of old Madrid between 1910 and 1930, the **Gran Vía** was a smash hit from the start with the *madrileños*. Planned as an elegant Parisian boulevard in the Hausmann mode it became instead a quirky cosmopolitan architectural *ratatouille,* reminiscent of big commercial streets in Latin America, full of offices and big hotels and music halls. To this day it's lively and bustling, even on Sundays, when everyone heads over for an afternoon or evening at the cinema. Many of these old movie palaces hide behind elephant-sized handpainted posters; the artists, a specialized guild, use housepaint and can crank them out in a couple of days. The fact that the Gran Vía isn't straight as was originally planned (two church properties in the way forced it to have an elbow) adds to the visual impact. And don't forget to look up: there is a plethora of giant doodads, as if the bric-a-brac cabinet of Gargantua had spilled out on top of them.

The aforementioned Metrópolis building at the corner of Calle de Alcalá was echoed just up at the next wedge-shaped corner, Gran Vía 1, in a building of 1916 belonging to Madrid's most prestigious jewellery makers, **Grassy**, with its big sign for Piaget. Downstairs, it has a small museum dedicated to Art Nouveau clocks (*open Mon–Sat 10–1 and 5–8*). No.2 served as the headquarters of the citizens' militia in the Civil War—a small act of vengeance after members of the exclusive men's club inside had tried to make Franco a member in the 20s.

Another 'museum' on the Gran Vía is **Chicote** at No.12, Madrid's premier cocktail bar, designed in 1931 by Luis Gutíerrez Soto, who would go on to build many of Franco's showcase buildings; the interior, down to the seats and even some of the waiters, remains as intact as ever. Famous as the only bar in Madrid that never closed during the Civil War, it was the favourite oasis of war correspondents, of Hemingway, and of every celebrity who ever passed through Madrid. The *museo* on the sign was a collection of bottles from around the world, but it was recently sold off.

Next up, at No.28 is the **Telefónica** skyscraper, Madrid's first, designed in 1929 by American Lewis Weeks and Ignacio de Cárdenas and rising 266ft, complete with little Herreran turrets just to remind us that we're in Madrid. In the 1920s, dictator Primo de Rivera hired the Bell Telephone company of America to construct a state-of-the-art phone system for Spain. During the Civil War, it proved its worth when commanders from both sides could ring up their front lines to see which villages had been captured. A small **museum** (entrance on Calle Fuencarral, *open Tues–Fri 10–2, 5–8, Sat, Sun 10–2, closed Mon*) is devoted to the history of telephones and the occasional contemporary art exhibitions. Opposite, note the 1904 building, covered with busts.

The Telefónica today lies at the crux of another combat zone—the streets to the south, especially Calle Montenera, are Madrid's red light district. If you take this street and turn immediately to the left, you'll come to one of the churches that caused a crick in the Gran Vía, the neo-classical **Oratorio del Caballero de Gracia**, designed in late 18th century by Juan de Villanueva (who also built the Prado), with a handsome basilican interior.

This humming mid-section of the Gran Vía. completed under the Republic, has a pair of buildings by Palacios, the office building at 27 and the Hotel Avendia. There are more fine Art Deco works, the **Palacio de la Música** (No.35), the brick **Palacio de la Prensa** (No.46), and the **Callao Cinema**, with its lavish interior and exterior resembling flocked wall paper. Best of all is the Edificio Carrión (No.78) better known as the **Capitol**, for the cinema it houses, a lovely streamlined Art Deco building of 1932 by Luis Martinez Feduchi and Vicente Eced. South of Plaza de Callao, the busy pedestrian-only **Calle de Preciados** links the Gran Vía to the Puerta del Sol with its boutiques, buskers and beggers and branches of the omnipresent El Corte Inglés and FNAC chains.

The last segment of the Gran Vía has fewer pretensions; Calle Liberoros, off to the north, is famous for its second hand book shops. Around the corner, on Calle Flor Alta, is a grand if dilapidated neo-classical façade designed in 1722 by Ventura Rodríguez for the Count of Altamira. But it was all that was ever completed.

Malasaña

To the north of the Gran Vía and east of the once-grand Calle San Bernardo lies the piquant neighbourhood of **Malasaña**, a jumble of crowded streets, which by day are home to locals, and by night thronged with revellers. In the past this was one of the poorest districts in the city, called the Barrio de Maravillas, 'of Marigolds', but also more whimsically, 'of Wonders'. Under Franco it hit rock-bottom and was at the point of being bulldozed, when the residents rallied in protest; in the 1960s, its ridiculously low rents combined with the convenient location began to attract hippies and other alternative types. Although quiet by day—it is one of the last genuine residential areas in the centre—Malasaña still lives off its reputation as the epicentre of the *movida* years, and every other doorway seems to be a club. The town hall has cleaned the place up recently, and cleared out many of the badly parked cars, turning the area into a more or less pedestrian zone.

From the Gran Vía, one of its first landmarks is the church of **San Placido** (take Calle Silva to Calle San Roque). This is the church of a convent founded in 1623 by a frisky noblewoman who wanted to become a nun while keeping her lover, the powerful and extremely wealthy Jerónimo de Villanueva, state minister to

Philip IV. Villanueva built a love-nest next door, linked by a secret passageway. This hanky-panky was only the beginning of a scandal worthy of *The National Enquirer*: the passage was used by the amorous king himself when he fell in love with a beautiful young nun, Sor Margarita de la Cruz, who only managed to deter his unwanted attentions by laying in a coffin, clutching a crucifix and pretending to be dead. It gave Philip IV the shock of his life, but led to his commissioning Velázquez to paint the *Christ on the Cross*, which Philip then donated to the convent (it now hangs in the Prado). Before long the shenanigans inside the convent attracted the attention of the Inquisition, which sent a messenger to Rome with the tale of royal indiscretion. He didn't make it; the indefatigable Conde Duque de Olivares, Philip's right hand man, had him kidnapped along the way. The convent's father confessor, who used sex to exorcise nuns supposedly possessed of the devil, fared less well and was imprisoned by the Inquisition for life. The church, rebuilt in the 20th century, may no longer have its Velázquez or lusty nuns but it does have a gory Recumbent Christ by Gregorio Fernández, an *Annunciation* by Claudio Coello, and polychrome saints by Manuel Pereira.

Perhaps there's some poetic justice in the fact that this is now a red light district. Calle del Pez ('of the fish', named for the ponds that were here in the 16th century) leads to the district's other church, the brick Baroque **San Antonio de los Alemanes**, founded as part of a hospice by Philip III to care for the many down and out Portuguese who immigrated to Madrid in search of work, when Portugal was under the Spanish Crown (1580–1640). It was later given to the Germans who accompanied one of the unfortunate brides of the unfortunate Charles II. To this day it retains its charitable mission and is run by the Hermandad del Refugio. The interior is entirely frescoed: the *Apotheosis of St Anthony* in the dome was painted by Francisco Rizzi and Juan Carreño de Miranda, and the walls are by Luca Giordano, with more on St Anthony, mingled with a handful of royal portraits.

A few blocks north, the heart of Malasaña is the **Plaza de Dos de Mayo**, named for the famous events that took place that day in 1808. The square was the site of Montleón artillery barracks (only the entrance arch survives); after the French fired on the crowd protesting the apparent abduction of the royal family in the Puerta del Sol, a young officer, Pedro Velarde, ran here and convinced Captain Daoiz to disobey the French order that closed all the barracks and to distribute weapons to the citizenry to defend themselves against the French. A fierce, desperate fight of several hours ensued against the Napoleonic troops. One of the casualties was a local 17-year-old seamstress, Manuela Malasaña, who was summarily shot for defending herself with her scissors (according to the most popular account); the district now bears her name. The square with its classical statues of Velarde and Daoiz (both of whom were killed in the battle) is lined with pleasant *terrazas*. It is a popular late night party rendez-vous and fills up pretty quickly in the evenings, but in the daytime it almost reverts to its Dr Jekyll normality and niceness, with just a few flecks of graffiti to betray its night-time antics. The church just to the south of the square, the **Iglesia de las Maravillas**, has a Virgin with marigolds (*maravillas*) on the altar.

Like any good *barrio* in Madrid, Malasaña has its quirky shops, and quirky shop signs. Masterpieces of the genre, in tiles, may be found at Calle de San Vicente Ferrer 28: the **Laboratorio de Especialidades Juanse**, with its advertisements from 1925 of ailments that the Juanse crew promised to relieve (unfortunately no longer available) and the adjacent **Antiqua Hervería** (the 'Old Eggery'), where the tiles show contented chickens. The next street south, Calle Espiritu Santo has a fine old neighbourhood feel; in the 17th century it was famous for its brothels, which were impressively decimated one night by a bolt of lightning.

Chueca

East of Malasaña, its sister *barrio* of **Chueca** has prospered in its role as the capital's gay district. It too has an older name, the *Barrio de los Chisperos*, which referred to the area's many blacksmiths, although the word later became synonymous with any low class, low down inhabitant of Madrid. In the heyday of the *movida*, Chueca gained a sinister reputation for hard drugs. Madrid's gay community have managed to clean it up, and famously co-exists with the elderly residents who have stuck here through thick and thin, and its trendy bars, restaurants and fancy and quirky shops (not all of which are exclusively gay by any means) are among the hippest in the city.

During the day there are things to see as well. Colourful Calle de Fuencarral, just a couple of blocks east of Plaza Dos de Mayo is one of the main streets, a slice of real Madrid, and a perfect setting for the excellent **Museo Municipal** (Municipal Museum), C/Fuencarral 78, ✆ 91 588 8672, Ⓜ Tribunal (*open Tues–Fri 9.30–8, Sat–Sun, 10–2, closed Mon and hols; adm 300 pts, concessions 200 pts, free Wed*). Housed in the 18th-century Hospicio de San Fernando, with an exuberant, almost orgasmic Churrigueresque portal by Pedro de Ribera, the museum has been renovated and greatly expanded in recent years. More *madrileños* come here than tourists, and you can sense their growing civic pride as you watch them scrutinizing the old maps and prints, pointing out landmarks and discussing how their city has changed. The collection is large, and you can learn as much as you care to about Madrid; exhibits go right back to

Paleolithic times. There are paintings of the city from various periods, and the excellent 1656 street plan of Madrid, by Pedro Texeira. Spaniards love to make room-sized models of their cities, and there is a remarkable one here, commissioned by Ferdinand VII from Colonel León Gil de Palacio, that accurately reproduces the Madrid of the 1830s on a scale of 1:864, complete with every balcony and window, fountain and garden, closed in by walls with twelve gates. Also here are Pedro Berraguete's limpid *Virgin and Child* and the Renaissance-Plateresque burial effigies of the ubiquitous Beatriz Galindo ('La Latina'), Isabella's enormously influential Latin teacher, and her husband, Francisco Mirez, equally specialized (in bombardments) and known as 'El Artillero'.

Then there's Goya's *Allegory of Madrid*, which has a history that demonstrates the interesting times he lived in. In the original version, commissioned by the city in 1810 to preside over its sessions, Goya painted a portrait of then king Joseph Bonaparte in the oval frame supported by the angels, next to Madrid's coat of arms. In 1812, when Joseph took to his heels, the city asked Goya to replace the portrait with a book labelled the Constitution of 1812. When Joseph returned in 1813, Goya was asked to repaint him. In 1814, the king was replaced again by the Constitution, but this had to be smudged out and replaced by one of Goya's followers with a portrait of the hated Ferdinand VII (in the same year Goya was lucky to be exonerated from the charge of 'accepting employment from the usurper' but only because he never wore the medal Joseph Bonaparte had given him; he further patched things up by painting his famous *Dos de Mayo* and *Tres de Mayo* paintings in the Prado). As for the Allegory, it had to be repainted in 1829 after a soldier stabbed the painting with his bayonet. In 1841, when the Liberals took power, the Constitution re-appeared. Studying the layers of paint, the mayor of Madrid in 1861 asked that they all be scraped off to reveal Goya's original. But when the restorers reached the portrait of Joseph Bonaparte, it was too much to stomach and and he replaced it with the words *'Dos de Mayo'*. And so it has remained.

Behind the museum, Ribera's **Fuente de la Fama**, the fountain equivalent of his doorway, was moved here to serve as his monument. Another monument here is the **Pacha**, a celebrity nightclub housed in Luis Gutiérrez Soto's Cine Barceló of 1930, one of the buildings that hint of the cool, streamlined architecture Madrid might have had if the Depression, Civil War and Dictatorship had not intervened.

Close by you'll find Chueca's second museum, the **Museo Romántico**, C/San Mateo 13, © 91 448 1045, Ⓜ Tribunal, *open Tues–Sat 9–3, Sun and hols 9–2, closed Aug; adm 400 pts, concs 200 pts*), an atmospheric down-at-heel place founded by the Marquis de Vega-Inclán in 1924 with the aim of recreating a typical abode of the early 19th century (the building actually goes back to the mid 1700s). He didn't do a bad job, with a collection of paintings from the period, including a *St Gregory* by Goya and other works by the *costumbrista* painters who, like Goya, delighted in scenes of festivities. You can also peruse the personal memorabilia of the Romantic poet Mariano José de Larra, who cut a great potential career short at age 27 by shooting himself in 1837 with the pistols on display.

Just east, the main street of Chueca, **Calle Hortaleza**, links the Gran Vía to the old gate in Plaza Santa Barbara; its name recalls the gardens that once lined it. Cross Hortaleza for Calle Fernando VI, to see Madrid's best and most beautiful Art Nouveau building, the Palacio Longoria, now better known as the **Socieded de Autores**, for the association of writers and artists who own it. Designed in 1902 by Catalan architect José Grasés Riera for a banker, the undulating structure eschews all right angles and straight lines, with a result that looks ever so creamy and edible. If the door man will admit you, step inside to see the wonderful spiralling stairway, inset with a rainbow-hued, domed, stained-glass ceiling, the colours echoed in the daisies, inset with coloured glass petals, which seem to grow out of the banisters.

Now a good place to buy muscle enhancer, glittering disco balls, a ceremonial sword, a safe, or a fluffy alien, Calle de Hortaleza also has another church by Pedro de Ribera, **San Antón**, although later architects have stripped away his signiature lavish stone frosting. St Anthony Abbot is always depicted with a pig, and this is a good place to be on the saint's day (17 January), where the millions of *madrileños* with dogs, and a surprising number of other household pets, show up to have them blessed.

East of this, Calle Gravina leads to **Plaza Chueca**, the symbol of the neighbourhood's revival, where the local transvestites walk their poodles and stop off for a *vermut aperitivo* at the zinc and tile **Taverna de Angel Sierra**.

Colourful Calle de Barbieri crisscrosses the square, address of the funky **San Antón** market; on the corner here, of Calle de Augusto Figueroa, is the famous **Tienda de Vinos**—not a wine store, but a renowned scruffy restaurant famous and beloved for selling every dish at the same low price—hence its more popular name, **La Comunista**. Near the bottom of the street is the Art Deco **Hotel Mónaco**, a famous kitsch palace, converted in 1919 by a Frenchman into a lovers' hideaway before it turned into Madrid's society brothel, frequented by King Alfonso XIII; the favoured royal room at No.30, had not only mirrors and paintings, but enough space to include a string quartet to serenade his amours.

Las Salesas

To the east, the atmosphere changes again in the *barrio* known Las Salesas, tucked behind the big barracks on Plaza de la Cibeles. Only a couple of blocks east of Plaza Chueca, **Calle Almirante** is snobby and full of trendy boutiques and art galleries, including the **Moriarty Gallery**, a hot spot during the *movida*. North of here, on Calle Marqués de la Enseneda is another building by Grases Riera, the **French Institute** (1902), adorned with his favourite elephant head motifs, although much of the building had to be rebuilt after a fire.

Around the corner here on Calle Bárbara de Braganza, is the church that gave the neighbourhood its name, **Las Salesas Reales**, originally part of a convent founded in 1747 by Barbara de Bragança, the wife of Ferdinand VI, and built by a French architect, François Carlier. The Queen wanted to establish a cosy niche for her widowhood (only she died first) and spent so much money on the project that the *madrileños* say '*Bárbara reina, Bárbara obra, bárbaro gusto, bárbaro gasto*' (Barbara queen, Barbara work, barbaric taste, barbaric waste). The adjacent convent is now Madrid's law courts, but the church survives in its original sumptuous rococo state (if you're lucky enough to find it open), with much green marble and frescoes and the tombs of Barbara de Bragança (because she bore no children, she could not be buried in the Escorial) and Ferdinand VI, designed by Sabatini, and that of General O'Donnell, one of the many military men prominent during the topsy turvy reign of Isabel II.

Plaza de España   166

Museo Cerralbo   167

Parque del Oeste   168

Ermita de San Antonio de La Florida
    (Goya Pantheon)   168

Casa de Compo   169

Argüelles, Moncloa and
    the *Ciudad Universitaria*   170

Madrid's Parklands

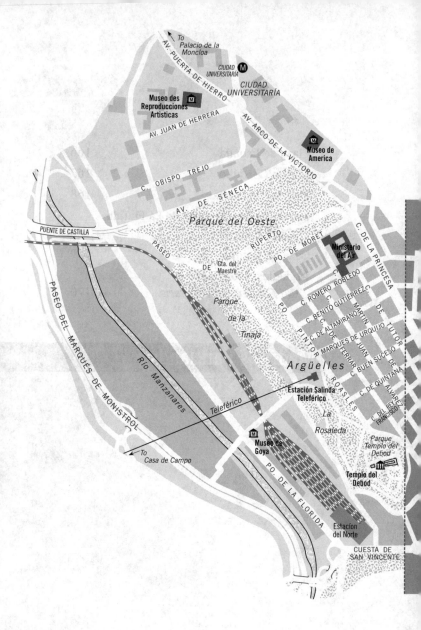

To
Palacio de la
Moncloa

AV. PUERTA DE HIERRO

CIUDAD
UNIVERSITARÍA

CIUDAD
UNIVERSITARÍA

Museo des
Reproducciones
Artisticas

AV. JUAN DE HERRERA

AV. ARCO DE LA VICTORIO

Museo de
America

C. OBISPO TREJO

AV. DE SÉNECA

Parque del Oeste

PUENTE DE CASTILLA

RUPERTO

PO. DE MORET

PASEO

DE

Gta. del
Maestro

Ministerio
del Air

C. DE LA PRINCESA

C. ROMERO ROBLEDO

PO.

C. BENITO GUTIERREZO

Parque
de la

C. DE ALTAMIRANO

DE TUTOR

C. C. C. DE

PINTOR

C. MARQUES DE URQUIJO

MARTIN

Tinaja

C. FERRAR

DE JUAN

C. BUEN SUCESO DE

Argüelles

ROSALES

C. DE QUINTANA

Teleférico

Estación Salinda
Teleférico

La

C. DEL REY
FRANCISCO

Rosaleda

Parque
Templo del
Debod

Río Manzanares

PASEO DEL MARQUES DE MONISTROL

To
Casa de Campo

Museo de
Goya

Templo del
Debod

PO. DE LA FLORIDA

Estación
del Norte

CUESTA DE
SAN VINCENTE

The west end of Madrid has its largest parks, where you'll find most of the trees that substantiate its claim to be the second most wooded city in the world. It also has one of Goya's masterpieces, in San Antonio de la Florida, large bulky ugly-pieces by the Franco regime, and some surprises: an excellent museum of pre-Columbian art, a genuine Egyptian temple, the Tornado and other scary rides, a packrat museum with the most delightful ballroom in Madrid, a lighthouse without a light, and yet another royal palace.

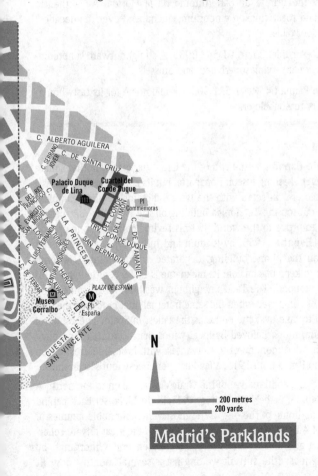

Madrid's Parklands

cafés, bars and restaurants

There are lots of good, small restaurants around the lake in the Casa de Campo. Here are a few more ideas:

Bruin, Paseo del Pintor Rosales 48, © 91 541 5921. Long-established and excellent purveyor of ice cream and other refreshments, near the *teleférico*.

Café Rosales, Paseo del Pintor Rosales 36, © 91 547 7166. Elegant sandwiches and drinks, and outdoor tables.

Casa Mingo, by the Ermita de San Antonio de la Florida. An authentic Austrian *sidreria* and roast chicken emporium, unchanged over the decades, with plenty of outdoor tables.

El Cangrejero, C/Amaniel 25, © 91 548 3935. A straightforward, unpretentious neighbourhood bar serving superb beer and mussels.

El Mano, C/de la Palma 64, © 91 521 5057. Well-known for its tasty homemade tapas and very reasonable prices.

Plaza de España

The broad **Plaza de España**, at the end of the Gran Vía, is yet another square created by the convent-bashing Joseph Bonaparte, but its current appearance is a legacy of the Franco era. Infected with the typical dictator's edifice complex, Franco wanted to out-top the Telefónica building on the Gran Vía (*see* p.156) with a skyscraper to prove to the world that his regime could get one up: the resulting **Edificio España** (1953, by Joaquín and Juilián Otamendi), is even more Baroque than the phone building, decorated with its dinky Herreran towers, like spikes to keep pigeons off; its nickname is El Taco, although in this case it means 'the stopper'. The Taco's neighbour was built in the same style, and it was no sooner completed when the same fraternal duet produced the ugly **Torre de Madrid** to take over the kudos as the tallest in Spain. The centre of the Plaza de España, much beloved by local winos, has a fountain and olive grove and a back-handed monument to Cervantes, with bronze figures of Don Quixote and Sancho Panza from 1915, a favourite for cheesy tourist snapshots.

Busy Calle Principesa, a continuation of the Gran Vía carries on to the north. A short walk, up at No.20, is the 18th-century **Palacio de Liria**, set back behind the trees. This is the home of the one of the most venerable noble families of Spain, the Dukes of Alba, who have accumulated one of the great private collections of Spanish art and allow visitors to see it only on Friday mornings, by advance written request (the current waiting list is several months long). It houses works by Fra Angelico, Titian, Andrea del Sarto, Rembrandt, Rubens, and the famous full length portrait by Goya of the 13th Duchess of Alba, where she is seen pointing to the words 'Only Goya'.

Behind the palace, the former royal barracks, the gargantuan **Cuartel del Conde Duque**, was designed in1717 by Pedro de Ribera with his signature grandiose doorway. After years of fires and decline it was purchased and restored by the city in the 1980s and now hosts a lively culture centre, providing an anchor for the renewal of the entire quarter. Just to the east of this, Plaza de las Comendadoras is named for the church of the **Comendadoras**, whose chivalric nuns are the ladies' auxillary of the knightly Order of Santiago—hence the red cross on their habits. The convent was designed by Sabatini and given old-fashioned Flemish Habsburg towers. There are several references to the patron saint of the order, St James the Moor-Slayer, including a large painting over the altar by Luca Giordano. Another church, **Santa Maria la Real de Monserrat**, just down Calle de Quiñones, was founded in 1642 by Philip IV for monks from Monserrat in Catalonia, when they were forced to flee their own monastery during a separatist revolt. Due to financial difficulties, the church took so long to build that it mostly bears the imprint of Pedro de Ribera, who completed the door and ornate tower. Its treasure is a rather eerie *Christ* made out of hide and human hair, like the famous Buffalo Jesus in Burgos.

Museo Cerralbo

© 91 547 3646. *Open Tues–Sat 9.30–2.30, Sun 10–2, closed Mon and hols; adm 400 pts, concs 200 pts, free Wed and Sun.*

The northwest corner of the Plaza de España is occupied by the luscious Art Nouveau **Casa Gallardo** apartments; just past this, at Calle Ventura Rodríguez 17, is the **Museo Cerralbo**. One of Madrid's more accessible private collections that have become museums in their original settings—in this case, the home of a world -travelling magpie Marqués who died in the 1920s. As instructed by his will, the curators have displayed the collection in exactly the gloriously cluttered state he left it: there are minor paintings by Ribera, Tintoretto, Palma Giovane, Magnasco, Zurburan, Valdes Léal, and a fine *St Francis* by El Greco. An intricately decorated *Sala Arabe* has suits of western and Japanese armour, and an ornate opium pipe, with instructions for use. There are also very beautiful bathroom fixtures, and a picture of the Marquis in a curious collage of lottery tickets; a very cosy little library and dining room where guests could enjoy paintings of porcupines and vipers, and lots of ambient bric-a-brac, furniture, some awful chandeliers, and scores of ticking clocks.

The highlight of the museum are the two delightful rooms frescoed by otherwise little known Máximo Juderías Cabellero in 1891–93, now restored to their full glory (as of October 1999): the Salón de Confianza, where the Marquis would play bridge amid scenes of the Four Seasons, with nymphs observing from the ceiling; and a superb ballroom, dedicated appropriately to dance, a whirl of gilt stuccoes and remarkable mix of realistic-historical-mythological scenes.

Parque del Oeste

Around the corner from the museum is the beautifully landscaped Parque del Oeste, with its unexpected ornament: a sandstone Egyptian temple of the 4th century BC. The **Templo de Debod**, ✆ 91 409 6165, ⓜ Ventura Rodríguez or Plaza de España (*open Tues–Fri 10–2 and 6–8, Sat–Sun 10–2, closed Mon and hols; from Oct–Mar Tues–Fri 9.45–1.45, 4.15–6.15, Sat and Sun 10–2; adm 300 pts, concs 200 pts, free Wed*) is nothing very elaborate, but it is genuine. The Egyptian government sent it, block by block, as a token of appreciation for Spanish help in the relocation of monuments during the building of the Aswan dam. However far it has strayed from the Nile, the little temple seems cheerfully at home, facing a reflecting pool, surrounded by palms, orientated to the same sunrise, looking over the peculiar city below. Inside some of the reliefs and a later altar dedicated by Cleopatra's dad have survived the temple's various vicissitudes: it was moved at least twice before arriving in Madrid, and spent a number of years under water, which washed out its murals.

In July 1936, this spot was occupied by the Montaña Barracks, scene of one of the earliest and bloodiest events of the Civil War. When the government decided to arm the popular militias, they found that the bolts for most of the rifles available were locked away in the barracks, held at the time by a group of rebellious officers and Falangists. After a brief siege, some miners from Asturias managed to blow a hole in the walls, and the barracks were stormed by a mob, who killed most of those inside, throwing many alive from second-storey windows.

North of the temple you'll find the *teleférico* (*see* p.170) to the Casa del Campo and, below the temple, **La Rosaleda** where international rose exhibitions are held in spring each year (and will reopen after an overhaul in spring 2000).

Ermita de San Antonio de la Florida (the Goya Pantheon)

Pso. de la Florida 5, ✆ 91 542 0722, ⓜ Príncipe Pío. Open Tues–Fri, 10–2 and 4-8, Sat–Sun, 10–2, closed Mon, hols; adm 300 pts, free Wed.

From the centre of the Parque del Oeste, Calle Francisco y Jacinto Alcántara descends to the train tracks, passing by way of the National Ceramics School, next to a little garden with a ceramic copy of Goya's *Tres de Mayo*, marking the first burial place of the 43 victims of the execution. A pedestrian flyover through the railyards of the woebegone Estación de Príncipe Pío will take you to the narrow island between the tracks and the river (the big letters spelling GOYA hint that you're getting close) where two identical neoclassical chapels stand, both dedicated to the same St Anthony. The one you want is opposite the seated statue of the painter; the other is a replica, built when the original was made into the Goya Pantheon. The replica is the focus of the week-long *verbena* around the 13th of June, dedicated to Anthony, when the *paseo* is closed off for the festivities.

The original church was designed by Felipe Fontana for Charles IV, and contains one of the milestones of Spanish art. In 1798, Goya was commissioned to do a series of frescoes on the upper walls, ceiling and dome, and the genius of 'magical atmospheres', did them in a way never seen before in any church. St Anthony, in the dome, is clearly recognizable (he is bringing a corpse to life to bear witness in a dispute) but that is Goya's only concession to the usual conventions of religious art. The scores of figures with which he covered the ceilings have the same faces from his celebrated cartoons, only instead of angelic *madrileños* they have become angels in fact. Every one has the quality of a portrait; the peaceful rapture expressed in their faces has at its source nothing the Church could give, but a particular secret perhaps known only to Goya. He painted the whole thing in 120 days; the restorers in 1996 took three times as long, but the frescoes are now more beautiful than ever; an audiovisual guide offers surprising close-ups. Goya is buried here—his body was brought back here from Bordeaux and the church has become his monument. His body, that is, but not his head: legend has it that he asked the executor of his will to separate his skull and bury it in a secret place with the foot of the Duchess of Alba, who predeceased Goya by 26 years. Goya died in 1828 and, when the body was moved from Bordeaux in 1880, the head was already missing. Like many famous *madrileños*, the Duchess's tomb has vanished; the church she was buried in was demolished, along with the frescoes that Goya painted around her tomb, of men carrying her body to its last rest. In the frescoes she was said to have resembled his famous *Maja.* Or so they say.

From the church, it's a short walk to the Puente Reina Victoria, spanning the **Manzanares**. After centuries of ridicule by locals and visitors, and more recently, decades of pollution and neglect, soft-hearted, nature-loving Mayor Tierno Galván decided to take the 'ditch learning to become a river' as Quevedo called it and give it some respect (and water, borrowed from the Sierra). Thanks to Tierno Galván, there's even a pleasant walk along its banks for a mile or so.

Casa de Campo

When the Habsburgs decided to make Madrid their capital, they didn't give much thought to amenities. One of their tricks was to chop down every tree of the forests that once surrounded Madrid; they sold them as firewood all over

Castile, and used the money to embellish their palaces. Philip II, an avid hunter like most of his kin, soon regretted this, and he had this tract of several square miles reforested. There was no altruism in Philip's motives. He simply wanted a place to hunt, but the Casa de Campo was the happy result, a stretch of quiet , green countryside for picnics and outings, in spite of a slightly shady reputation for illicit goings-on, just a short walk (or bus or metro ride) from the centre of the city.

The most interesting views of this park—and of the Manzanares and the Palacio Real with the city beyond—are from the cable car (**teleférico**, *open daily, weekdays 11–3 and 5–8.30, Sat 11–3 and 4–9.30, hols 11–3 and 4.30–8.30; single 365 pts, return 520 pts*) that runs there from the Parque del Oeste. Within the Casa de Campo's boundaries are a fairground, which hosts some interesting alternative events such as the International Tatoo Convention, as well as the permanent **Parque de Atracciones** funfair and amusement park, ☎ 91 526 80 30 (*open daily, in winter Sun–Fri noon–11pm, Sat noon–1am; in summer, Sun–Thurs noon–11pm, Fri–Sat noon–3am*) where the admission fee includes most of the rides, including the 'Flume Ride', 'Top Spin' and 'Looping Star' rollercoasters. The new 'Tornado', a triple loop-the-loop roller coaster where punters are strapped in without a proper floor, is one of the scariest in Europe.

The Casa de Campo also has the **Parque Zoológico**, ☎ 91 711 9950 (*open daily, in summer 10–9.30; in winter 10–7.30; adm*), the star of which is Chulín, the first panda to be born in captivity in the West. Although rarely visible, the panda's surroundings are at least roomy, which is more than can be said for most of the zoo's inhabitants. The zoo also has a new 1.8 million-litre tropical aquarium, complete with hammerhead, and other sharks.

Argüelles, Moncloa and the *Ciudad Universitaria*

From the *teleférico* station, Calle Marqués de Urquijo leads back into the prosperous residential and shopping area of **Argüelles,** named like La Latina for another of Isabel I's tutors, in this case Augustin Argüelles. A fancy suburb in the early 1920s, it was the last home of the great chronicler of Madrid, Benito Perez Galdos, who died here in poverty in 1920; another resident was the Chilean poet, Pablo Neruda.

The neighbourhood's biggest building is at the top of Calle de la Principessa, the **Ministry of Air**, designed by Luis Gutiérez Soto in 1942 after designs by Hitler's architects, but adjusted after the Fürer's defeat into something that looks so much like the Escorial that it was immediately dubbed the 'Monasterio del Aire'. Although Franco adored it, Soto found it extremely embarrassing in later years; in the next decade he would be the first architect in Madrid to embrace functionalism and modernism after a visit to the States. Opposite this unwieldy pile is an eagle-topped monument to Franco's war dead, and at the top of the square, the triumphal **Arco de la Victoria** built by the man they called the 'Sphinx' to celebrate his victory in the Civil War. It also has a practical purpose: inside are the archives of the **Universidad Complutense**, the campus of which begins just beyond.

Miguel Primo de Rivera always liked to think of himself as a great benefactor of education, and it exasperated him that Spain's university students spent most of the 1920s out in the streets calling him names. He began this sprawling, suburban campus in 1927, partly to appease them but mostly to get them out of town. This institution, the nation's largest, began as the Complutensian University, founded by Cardinal Cisneros in Alcalá de Henares. After it moved to Madrid, its buildings were originally north of the Gran Vía. Primo de Rivera's new campus was unfinished when the Civil War broke out; in the battles for Madrid, the University found itself in the front line, providing a potent symbol of the nature of the war as Franco's artillery pounded the halls of knowledge to rubble. Franco rebuilt them after the war in a stolid, authoritarian style. Today the campus is well-kept but as dull to visit as it must be for the students who attend it.

There are two museums near here, at the southern end of the Ciudad Universitaria. The Art Deco **Museo de América**, Avda. Reyes Católicos 6, © 91 549 2641, **Ⓜ** Moncloa (*open Tues–Sat 10–3, Sun and hols, 10–2.30, closed Mon; adm 400 pts, concessions 200 pts, free Sat after 2 and Sun*), emerged like a butterfly in 1994 after a renovation programme lasting 12 years. In its new incarnation the museum is cool, elegant, and beautifully designed. On display is one of Europe's largest collections of artefacts from the Aztecs, Incas, Maya, and other indigenous New World cultures, many of them plundered in the time of the conquistadors, but many more acquired much later by more honourable means. Among the most beautiful are gold ornaments from Colombia and Costa Rica, some over 1,000 years old, and ancient Peruvian and Chilean textiles. The museum holds an extremely rare post-Classic Mayan codex, the Códice Tro-Cortesiano, a document relating in symbols (*glyphs*) news of the Spanish arrival, and a replica of this is on display. Spanish engravings depicting indigenous South Americans as fantastical giants, headless monsters or cheerful cannibals give a fascinating insight into the popular state of mind at the dawn of the Age of Exploration, and a series of 16th- to 18th-century maps illustrate graphically the rapid growth of Western knowledge of this alien territory. The museum also covers aspects of contemporary Latin American culture; film showings highlight current social and cultural issues in the context of the past.

Just outside the Museo de América is the **Faro de Madrid** (*open, summer, daily, 10.30–1.45 and 5–7.45; winter, daily, 10.30–1.45 and 4.30–7.15; adm 200 pts, concessions 100 pts*), an inland lighthouse designed by Salvator Pérez Arroyo to be exactly 92 metres high, opened as part of the 1992 celebrations. A lift will whizz you up to the observation platform for fine 360° views, but buy your beer or soda from the vending machine before you ascend, as the top of the Faro is the one dry spot in this city of bars.

Nearby, just off the Avenida de la Victoria, is the not terribly compelling **Museo des Reproducciones Artisticas**, Avda. Juan de Herrera 2, ℂ 91 549 6618, **Ⓜ** Moncloa (*open Tues–Sat, 10–6, Sun and hols, 10–2, closed Mon*), formerly the Museo Español de Arte Contemporáneo before its paintings were moved off to new quarters at the Reina Sofía. The building won the National Architecture prize in 1969. The official residence of the Prime Minister of Spain, the Palacio de la Moncloa, is just behind, while beyond is the pretty iron gate, the **Puerta de Hierro** (1753) that once marked the beginning of El Pardo.

From the Faro you can see the woodlands of El Pardo, and if you're tempted, bus no.83 from Paseo de Moret near the Moncloa metro leaves every 10-15 minutes for the rural village of El Pardo and the **Palacio Real de El Pardo**, Ctra. de El Pardo, ℂ 91 549 0059 (*open Mon–Sat 10.30–6, Sun and hols 10–1.40; closed when used by a visiting head of state; adm 650 pts, concs 250 pts, free Wed*). El Pardo offered the richest hunting grounds in central Castile, and first hunting lodge on this site was built by Henry III in the 1390s. Charles V and his son Philip made this into a palace, apparently the first in Spain to sport slate Flemish towers. It was burned down and rebuilt by Sabatini for Carlos III, and part of it is hung with Goya's sweet tapestries. Now used to lodge visiting presidents and princes, El Pardo was used by Franco as his residence throughout the dictator-ship, and the palace offers the only glimpse of how the dictator worked, with his office left as it was when he died, which you can compare with the famous *despacho universal*—Philip II's poky hole of an office in El Escorial. The beau-tiful hills and woodlands are still full of game, and mostly off limits to visitors. As a footnote, *pardo* means dun, and got the name from a huge dun-coloured bear killed there by King Alfonso XI, which made such an impression, according to some, that it was placed on the coat of arms of Madrid.

The current king of Spain, Juan Carlos I, and his family live on a simpler scale nearby in the **Palacio de la Zarzuela** (*no access*); the original palace, where Philip IV was entertained by the ancestors of Madrid's famous operetta, was burned during the Civil War but was rebuilt in the 1950s to house the heir to the throne.

Art	174
Archaeology and Ethnology	175
Historical	175
Military	175
Science and Technology	176

Madrid Museums

Like most capital cities, Madrid has a lion's share of the nation's art and cultural artifacts, ranging from the famous treasures of the Prado to a special museum for the blind. Most, but not all of these are described in the text—there are some rather specialized ones—and most have free days and/or concessionary discounts for students and EU citizens over 60. But admission fees are reasonable across the board, compared to what you pay in other cities. The following list is to help you find what you crave.

Art

Museo del Prado, Paseo del Prado, ✆ 91 420 2836, Ⓜ Banco de España. One of the greatest art galleries in the world, with a collection of Spanish and international masterpieces from the 12th to the early 19th centuries (*closed Mon*), *see* p.94.

Casón del Buen Retiro, C/Alfonso XII 28, ✆ 91 240 2628, Ⓜ Retiro or Banco de España. Annex to the Prado, housing its 19th-century collection (*closed Mon*). Closed for refurbishment until mid-2000, *see* p.100.

Museo Thyssen-Bornemisza, Paseo del Prado 8, ✆ 91 420 3944, Ⓜ Banco de España or Atocha. Holds over 800 paintings from the 13th century to the present day (*closed Mon*), *see* p.102.

Museo Nacional Centro de Arte Reina Sofía, C/Santa Isabel 52, ✆ 91 467 5062, Ⓜ Atocha. 20th-century Spanish and international art, including Picasso's *Guernica*. Also has impressive library (*closed Tues*), *see* p.114.

Real Academia de Bellas Artes de San Fernando, C/Alcala 13, ✆ 91 522 1491, Ⓜ Sevilla. Delightful museum with works spanning five centuries by Goya, Rubens, El Greco, Murillo, Sorolla, and Bellini (*open daily*), *see* p.152.

Museo Sorolla, C/Gen. Martinez Campos 37, ✆ 91 310 1584, Ⓜ Iglesias or Rubén

Darío. Charming museum displaying the artist's collection of oil paintings and sketches (*closed Mon*), *see* p.131.

Panteón de Goya, Pso. de la Florida 5, ✆ 91 542 0722, Ⓜ Norte. The small chapel where Goya is buried, with frescoes on the walls, ceiling, and dome painted by the artist (*closed Mon*), *see* p.168.

Palacio de Liria–Fundación de la Casa de Alba, Ⓜ Plaza de España, a collection belonging to the Duchess of Alba, including works by Goya, Zurbarán, Renoir and Titian (*visits by appointment only*). Ask at the Tourist Information office, *see* p.166.

Convento de Las Descalzas Reales, Plaza de las Descalzas Reales, ✆ 91 542 0059, Ⓜ Opera. An award-winning museum containing a rich collection of fabulous tapestries, paintings, holy relics and *trompe l'oeil* frescoes (*closed Mon*), *see* p.140.

Convento de la Encarnación, Plaza de la Encarnacion, ✆ 91 542 0059, Ⓜ Opera. Religious paintings and sculpture of the 17th century, curious and well-stocked *reliquario*. (*open Wed and Sat*), *see* p.143.

Museo Nacional de Artes Decorativas, C/Montalbán 12, ✆ 91 522 1740, Ⓜ Banco de España. Furniture, textiles, costume and ceramics spanning six centuries (*closed Mon*), *see* p.109.

Museo Cerralbo, C/Ventura Rodríguez, ℗ 91 547 3646, Ⓜ Ventura Rodríguez or Plaza de España. A private collection of archeological artefacts, porcelain, tapestries and paintings from different periods (*closed Mon*), *see* p.167.

Museo Lázaro Galdiano, C/Serrano 122, ℗ 91 561 6084, Ⓜ Núñez de Balboa. Eclectic collection of Grand Master paintings, clocks, furniture, jewellery, gold, silver, ivory and enamel objects (*closed Mon and Aug*), *see* p.132.

Archaeology and Ethnology

Museo Arqueológico Nacional, C/Serrano 13, ℗ 91 577 7912, Ⓜ Serrano or Colón. This is the only comprehensive archaeology museum in Spain, with replicas of the famous Altamira rock-paintings (*closed Mon*), *see* p.104.

Museo de America, Avda. Reyes Católicas 6, ℗ 91 549 2641, Ⓜ Moncloa. One of Europe's largest collections of artefacts from the Aztecs, Incas, Maya and other indigenous New World cultures (*closed Mon*), *see* p.171.

Museo Nacional de Antropología (formerly the Museo de Etnologia) C/Alfonso XII, ℗ 91 530 6418, Ⓜ Atocha. A 'Cabinet of Curiosities' containing bizarre artefacts from all seven continents (*closed Mon*), *see* p.118.

Historical

Palacio Real, C/Bailén, ℗ 91 542 0059, Ⓜ Opera. Magnificent 18th-century palace, opulently furnished and decorated. Also incorporates the Palace Gardens (or Campo del Moro, *see* p.148), the Royal Armoury (*currently closed for restoration*), the *Farmacía*, and the Museum of Carriages (*closed indefinitely for restoration*). *Palace open daily*, *see* p.145.

Museo de la Ciudad (City Museum), C/Principe de Vergara 140, ℗ 91 588 6599, Ⓜ Cruz de Rayo. Interactive displays outlining the history of Madrid from its origins until the present day. Also hosts temporary exhibitions (*closed Mon*), *see* p.134.

Museo Municipal, C/Fuencarral 78, ℗ 91 588 8672, Ⓜ Tribunal. Recently expanded museum containing paintings, drawings, models and documents illustrating the city's development (*closed Mon*), *see* p.159.

Museo Romántico, C/San Mateo, ℗ 91 448 1045, Ⓜ Alonso Martínez or Tribunal. Atmospheric 17th-century building containing furnishings and paintings from the Romantic period (*closed Aug*), *see* p.160.

Casa Museo de Lope De Vega, C/Cervantes 11, ℗ 91 429 9216, Ⓜ Antón Martín or Sevilla. Restored house and garden where dramatist and poet Lope de Vega lived and died (*closed Mon*), *see* p.87.

Military

Museo del Ejército/Army Museum, C/Méndez Núñez 1, ℗ 91 522 8977, Ⓜ Colón. Displays of arms, uniforms and insignias of the Spanish Armed Forces, armour and arms of the conquistadors (*closed Mon*), see p.109.

Museo Naval, Paseo del Prado 5, ℗ 91 379 5055, Ⓜ Banco de España. Relics of the age of exploration, models, maps and charts. (*closed Mon, Aug*), *see* p.109.

Science and Technology

Museo de Ciencas Naturales, C/José Guttiérez Abascal, ℂ 91 411 1328, Ⓜ Nuevos Ministerios. Two permanent and interactive exhibitions on the history of life and the history of the earth (*closed Mon*), *see* p.133.

Fundación Arte y Tecnología de Telefónica, C/Gran Vía 28, Ⓜ Gran Vía. A permanent collection of historical and technological exhbits. There is also a collection of contemporary art (*closed Mon*), *see* p.156.

Acciona-Museo Interactivo de la Ciencia, Pintor Murillo, Parque de Atracciones, Alcobendas, ℂ 91 661 3909, a hands-on science museum in the northern dormitory town of Alcobendas (about 20 minutes away by bus: take Interbus 151, 152, 153, 154, all of which leave from Plaza Castilla).

Ciencia y Technologia, Pso del las Delicias, ℂ 91 530 3121, Ⓜ Delicias. Microscopes, experiments, and other science projects designed for children (*closed Mon.*)

One-offs

Museo Taurino/Bullfighting Museum, Plaza de Las Ventas, Patio de las Caballos, ℂ 91 725 1857, Ⓜ Ventas. The art and history of bullfighting in drawings, sketches and prints (*open Tues–Fri*), *see* p.126.

Museo Nacional Ferroviario, Paseo de las Delicias 61, ℂ 91 527 3121, Ⓜ Delicias. A collection of old railway paraphernalia and model trains in an old train station (*closed Mon, Aug*), *see* p.120.

Observatorio Astronómico, C/Alfonso XII, ℂ 91 527 0107, Ⓜ Atocha. Small, dusty collection of telescopes and astronomical instruments (*closed weekends*), *see* p.112.

Real Fábrica de Tapices, C/Fuenterrabía 2, ℂ 91 551 3400, Ⓜ Menéndez Pelayo. Fine pictorial tapestries, drawings, rugs and carpets weaved by master craftsmen (*closed Sat, Sun, Aug*), *see* p.119.

Casa de la Moneda, Doctor Esquerdo 36, ℂ 91 566 6544, Ⓜ O'Donnell. Collection of coins from ancient Greece, Rome and Al Andalus (*closed Mon*).

Museo de Cera, Paseo de Recoltas, ℂ 91 308 0825, Ⓜ Colón.Waxworks and thrills, *see* p.128.

Museo Tifloóglico, La Coruña 18, ℂ 91 589 4200, Ⓜ Estrecho. A museum specially designed for the blind and visually impaired, with works of art by blind artists, models of monuments, and more; the sighted will find plenty of interest as well (*closed sun, mon*).

Templo de Debod, Parque de Oeste, ℂ 91 409 6165, Ⓜ Plaza de España. Contents and engravings in a real Egyptian temple (*closed Mon*), *see* p.168.

Museo Postal y Telecomunicaciones, Plaza de las Cbeles, Ⓜ Banco de España. Postage stamps and telecommunications history (*closed Sun*), *see* p.125.

Museo del Libro, Pso. de Recoltas 28, ℂ 91 580 7823, Ⓜ Colón. Multi-media look at the rare books housed in the Biblioteca Nacional (*closed Mon*), *see* p.126.

Museo del Aire, Ctra. de Extremadura km 10.5, train station Cuatro Vientos, ℂ 91 509 1690. Historic planes and memorabilia (*closed Mon*).

Museo Ángel Nieto, Avda del Planetario 4, ℂ 91 468 0224, Ⓜ Méndez-Alvaro. On the career of the champion motorcyclist (*closed Mon*).

Eating Out	178
Madrid Specialities	178
Tapas Bars	179
Restaurants East of the Castellana	179
Restaurants South of Puerta del Sol	180
Restaurants North of Puerta del Sol	183
Vegetarian Restaurants	185
Open-Air Eating	185
Cafés, Bars and Interesting Places to Drink	185
Madrid Specialities	185
Spanish Wines	186
Other Spanish Tipples	187
Café Society	187

Food and Drink

No place in Spain, except perhaps the Costa del Sol, can offer such a wide choice. Besides the country's best gourmet restaurants, you can sample the cuisine of every region of Spain and a score of other lands without straying half a mile from the Puerta del Sol. Most of the old well-known establishments are in Old Madrid.

Eating Out

Between restaurants and *tascas* (tapas bars, *see* below) are **comedores** (literally, dining-rooms) often tacked on to the backs of bars, where the food and décor are usually drab but cheap, and **cafeterías**, usually those places that feature photographs of their offerings of *platos combinados* (combination plates) to eliminate any language problem. Others are self-service, and most tend to be dreary bargains. **Asadores** specialize in roast meat or fish; **marisqueras** serve only fish and shellfish. Keep an eye out for **ventas**, usually modest family-run establishments offering excellent *menús del día*. If you take a day-trip (see pp.215–262), try and visit one in the country on a Sunday lunchtime when all the Spanish families go out to eat and make merry. There are also many **Chinese restaurants** which are fairly good and often inexpensive, and although about 98 per cent of the **Italian restaurants** are dismal, you can get a good pizza in many places. Vegetarians are increasingly well catered for (*see* below).

Menu and restaurant vocabulary are included in the 'language' section at the end of the book (see pp.271–272). Note that unless it's explicitly written on the bill (*la cuenta*), service is *not* included in the total, so tip accordingly.

Price categories are based on a two-course meal with wine:	
expensive:	7,500 pts and up
moderate:	3,500–7,500 pts
cheap:	1,500–3,500 pts

Madrid Specialities

Traditional Madrileño cuisine is a reflection of the cooking of Castille; roast meats and heavy stews. The pinnacle of the capital's culinary arts is *cocida*— part soup, part meat and two veg. The meal, chickpeas and vegetables are cooked in broth, then removed and set aside. Added to the broth is *fideuá* pasta, which is then served as the first course of a *cocido completo*. In winter, most restaurants offer a *cocido* on their Tuesday *menu del día* (Thursdays is traditionally paella). Even the capital's most expensive restaurants offer their version of the dish.

Callos a la Madrileña might just convince you to give tripe a go. Cooked in a rich spicy sauce based on *pimenton*, or sweet red pepper, the tripe is manageable, having been cut into bite-sized pieces.

Despite its location in the middle of a desert, Madrid ranks among the world's main consumers of seafood and fish. Oysters are readily available throughout the winter months, as are all other manner of crustacea, shipped down overnight from Galicia, along with *pulpo*, or octopus, a firm favourite in the capital's bars.

Tapas Bars

If you are travelling on a budget you may want to eat one of your meals a day at a **tapas bar** or **tasca**. Tapas means 'lids'. They started out as little saucers of goodies served on top of a drink and have evolved over the years to form a main part of the world's greatest snack culture. Bars that specialize in them have platter after platter of delectable titbits, from shellfish to slices of omelette or mushrooms baked in garlic or vegetables in vinaigrette or stews. All you have to do is pick out what looks best and order a *porción* (an hors d'oeuvre) or a *ración* (a big helping) if it looks really good. It's hard to generalize about prices, but on average 1,000 pts of tapas and wine or beer really fill you up. You can always save money in bars by standing up; sit at that charming table on the terrace and prices can jump considerably. Another advantage of *tapas* is that they're available at what most Americans or Britons would consider normal dining hours. Spaniards are notoriously late diners; in the morning it's a coffee and roll grabbed at the bar, a huge meal at around 2pm, then after work at 8pm a few tapas at the bar to hold them over until supper at 10 or 11pm. After living in Spain for a few months this makes perfect sense, but it's exasperating to the average visitor. On the coasts, restaurants tend to open earlier to accommodate foreigners (some as early as 5pm) but you may as well do as the *madrileños* do.

East of the Castellana: Castellana itself, Salamanca, Retiro

tapas

Casa Braulio, Avenida de los Toreros 43, ℗ 91 356 1182. A must if you fancy a quick tapa before or after attending the bullfights at Ventas, which is just round the corner. Braulio has been packing them in for 60 years, lured by the home cooking. They'll also prepare snacks to take into the ring.

El Espejo, Paseo de los Recoletos 3, ℗ 91 398 2347. An elegant Paris–style bar (founded in 1978), with high quality tapas, and an elegant reproduction of the old tiled kiosks that once lined the street. The set menu is surprisingly good value.

La Tierruca, General Diaz Porlier 55, ℗ 91 402 8769. Tucked away in the heart of Salamanca is this tiny bar with some of the best fried sardines and prawns in the capital. Every customer is treated as though a life-long regular. A great place to watch football, as the owners are Atlético de Madrid fans.

Nicolas, Villalar 4, ℗ 91 431 7737. Unpretentiously post-modern, Nicolas keeps the food imaginative, but based on sound principles of home cooking. Eating here is a leisurely affair, so take your time.

El Olivo, General Gallegos 1, ℗ 91 359 1535. It took a Frenchman, Jean Pierre Vandelle, to make Spaniards appreciate the finer points of olive oil. Mediterranean cuisine at its best, with Jean Pierre always on

La Taberna de la Daniela, General Pardinas 21, ℗ 91 575 2329. Don't even think of just turning up. If you want to enjoy one of the best *cocido madrileños* in the capital (and this is all they offer, aside from sea bream in the evenings), then you'll have to book. If you can't get a table, pass by to try the tapas.

El Espejo, Paseo de Recoletos 31, ℗ 91 398 2347. Despite its location, and the elaborate (but fake) 1920s decor, El Espejo offers excellent food at affordable prices.

Not far away, but a little more upmarket, is **El Cantabrico**, Padilla 39, ℗ 91 402 5042. Excellent draught beer, with a variety of fresh seafood. A great place to meet, or to start the evening.

restaurants: expensive

hand to advise. Aside from the myriad oils, one of the best selections of sherry in the capital.

Viridiana, Juan de Mena 14, ℗ 91 523 4478. Although a symbol of the economic boom of the late eighties, Viridiana is no nouveau riche hang out. One of the best wine cellars in the capital, faultless but discreet service, and imaginative but classical dishes make for a memorable meal.

restaurants: moderate

The secret is a set menu, which varies according to the time of year. Wine is apart, but it's more than possible to dine amid elegant surroundings and fine service for well under 5,000 pts a head.

L'Entrecote, Claudio Coello 70 and 41, ℗ 91 435 3517/℗ 91 577 7349. Don't waste your time looking at the menu. Start with a green salad, move on to the entrecote, with the best chips in town, and finish with any of the homemade pies on offer. Number 70 is the original of the two.

South of Puerta del Sol: Plaza Mayor, Santa Ana, Lavapiés

tapas

Las Bravas, Alvarez de Gato 3, ℗ 91 532 2620. Nothing less than an institution. The name comes from the hot sauces poured liberally on their deep-fried potato chunks.

Excellent tortillas, as well as *pulpo*, and *oreja* (pig's ear). The ideal stopping-off point to take on tasty carbohydrates as you make your way through the many bars dotted around the Puerta del Sol.

Pantumaca, Mayor 31, ✆ 91 365 7777. A taste of Barcelona in Madrid, this newish establishment takes its name from that Catalan staple—country bread spread with fresh tomato and garlic, which are then piled high with cold meats.

La Moderna, Plaza de Santa Ana, ✆ 91 420 1582. Probably the best of the half-a-dozen or so tapas bars which line the south side of the Plaza Santa Ana. Hemingway did not drink here, which means that the proprietors make an effort to provide a good range of wines and imaginative tapas.

La Dolores, Plaza de Jesus 4, ✆ 91 429 2243. Tucked away behind the Palace Hotel, this relic from the 1930s owes its fame to the sublime canapes it serves, alongside a beautifully pulled *caña*.

La Ancha, Zorrilla 7, ✆ 91 429 8186. Chances are you'll be rubbing shoulders with an errant MP taking it easy after a hard day at the nearby parliament. The formula is simple: impeccable service, the finest ingredients and wines, and dishes that know their limits, based on traditional cuisine.

Currito, Pabellon de Vizcaya de la Casa de Campo, ✆ 91 464 5704. In summer, this is quite simply the best open air place to eat in Madrid. It's not bad inside either. It might seem like a long trek from the

Viuda de Vacas, Cava Alta 23, ✆ 91 366 5847. This is the third generation of the Canovas family keeping Castillian cooking alive. Something of a mecca for the unpretentious foody—the restaurant has engendered many of the wine bars and restaurants which now populate the increasingly trendy Austrias area.

Casa Montes, Lavapiés 40, ✆ 91 527 0064. Easily overlooked, but one of the longest-running bars in Lavapies. Genial Don Cesar pours some excellent wines, and serves fine tapas such as *mojama* (cured tuna fish), anchovy canapes, and delicate cured ham.

If you're rooting round the Rastro on a Sunday morning, a stop at **Casa Amadeo**, Plaza de Cascorro 18, ✆ 91 365 9439, is obligatory. Few bars in Madrid still serve snail stew, but Amadeo, who came to the capital in 1942, knows the secret.

Muddy's, C/Alameda 6, ✆ 91 420 3484. An old favourite, close to the myriad bars near Atocha.

restaurants: expensive

centre, but it's not that far to savour excellent roast meats and fish (or better still barbecued), along with more modern dishes, and all accompanied by fine wines.

Errota Zar, Jovellanos 3, 1st floor, ✆ 91 531 2564. From outside you might be put off from entering this Basque cultural centre. Don't. Upstairs is one of the capital's best-kept secrets. This is Basque cooking at its best, with superb meats and fish, usually grilled. You'll find cheeses and cured meats from the region, along with a sublime wine list.

restaurants: moderate

La Bola, Bola 5, ✆ 91 547 6930. Known for its peculiar version of *cocido madrileño* —served in a clay urn—La Bola's old world interior is very much the place for a hearty meal on a cold winter's evening.

El Caldero, Huertas 15, ✆ 91 429 5044. Lined with bars and restaurants, it can be difficult to know where to go in Huertas. El Caldero offers rice and vegetable dishes from Murcia, and has been packing 'em in for 25 years. Try the Sangria de Cava.

Casa Hortensia, Olivar 6, ✆ 91 539 0090. The emphasis is very much on the food, so don't be put off by the lack of decor. Asturian cooking at its best, with a *fabada*—bean stew—famed throughout the city, served with traditional cider poured from shoulder height by the waiters.

Casa Marta, Santa Clara 10, ✆ 91 548 2825. Just behind the opera, this intimate restaurant offers superb service, a relaxed atmosphere, and some beautifully prepared dishes, such as El Bacalao Marta, or Duelos y Quebrantos—a stew mentioned in El Quijote. Very reasonable prices.

El Estragon, Plaza de la Paja 10, ✆ 91 365 8982. Following the square's restauration, the Plaza de la Paja has seen a mushrooming of new bars and restaurants. El Estragon is vegetarian, with some 20 odd tables distributed throughout different levels. The clientele is young, often expat, and the mood relaxed.

Hogar Gallego, Plaza Comandante las Morenas 3, ✆ 91 559 6404. A candidate for the capital's best-kept-secret. Just off the Plaza Mayor, but behind anonymous walls, sits this traditional Galician restaurant, which has been packing them in since 1940. The seafood is brought from Galicia, and although the terrace gets crowded in summer, it's worth booking a table and sitting back to watch the locals.

Champagnería Gala, C/Moratín 22, ✆ 91 429 2562. The splendidly luminous interior patio of Gala and their single price menu paella with sangria has beendrawing the crowds for a decade now.

Lion, Bordadores 4, ✆ 91 365 3005. Book a late table—the kitchen is open till one in the morning, and aside from the excellent seafood, much of it with a Catalan feel, you'll get the bonus of the owner tickling the ivories as you dine into the wee hours.

Palacio de Anglona, Segovia 13, ✆ 91 366 3753. Open till one in the morning, the Palacio de Anglona attracts a young, smart set. Imaginative dishes based on Spanish classics. If you're looking for a quieter evening, ask for a table upstairs.

Posada de la Villa, C/Cava Baja 9, ✆ 91 366 1880. A restored lodging house, this is the first of several traditional restaurants which line Cava Baja. Although popular with tourists, the food is excellent, and the building spectacular.

Mara, C/Cava Baja 5, ✆ 91 365 5586. Don't be put off by the somewhat modern decor; the food is more than worth it. Sensible fare, with more than a touch of the Basque and some fine Rioja wines.

La Bodeguita del Caco, C/Echegaray 27, ✆ 91 429 4023. The Caco in question is moderately famous salsa singer Caco Senante, who is often on hand—though not to sing. The cuisine is Canarian, and combines Caribbean spice with Spanish bulk.

La Burbuja Que Rie, C/del Angél 16, ✆ 91 366 5167. Recently opened, the laughing bubble presumably refers to the gargantuan quantities of cider—albeit still—poured here. Excellent value, and often crowded. Reservations on Tuesdays, Wednesdays and Thursdays only.

restaurants: cheap

La Vega, C/Ventura de la Vega 13, ✆ 91 429 0807. Dating back to 1950, this has long been a favourite with students and struggling artist-types, drawn by the generous portions of home cooking. Thursday is *cocido* and not to be missed.

tapas

Falafel, Valverde 8, ✆ 91 448 5520. If you're wandering through Malasaña, you could do worse than try the best falafel and kebab in the capital, along with Mediterranean salads and side dishes, all served by expat Israeli Giora Gilead.

La Vendimia, Pza. del Conde del Valle de Suchil 7, ✆ 91 445 7377. Set in one of the capital's lovliest and overlooked squares, this neoclassical celebration of all that is best about modern Basque cooking is an absolute treat. Try the *Txangurro*, a type of lobster, in its many forms.

La Gastroteca de Stephane y Arturo, Pza. de Chueca 8, ✆ 91 532 2564. A pleasant surprise in Chueca. Arturo will tell you the night's recommendation—try

Bonar, Cruz Verde 16, ✆ 91 521 2602. A taste of León in the heart of Madrid. The portions are more than generous, with a good range of quality meats and fish cooked simply but well. In the summer they put tables and chairs out on the pavement.

Carmencita, Libertad 16, ✆ 91 531 6612. Steeped in history, Carmencita has played host to Spain's literati and politicians since 1850. The place was given a more modern feel in the late eighties, and the food is clearly Basque influenced, while still retaining a traditional Madrid feel.

Cornucopia, Flora 1, ✆ 91 547 6465. Tucked away in the ground floor of a 19th-century palace, just off the Calle Mayor,

Santander, Augusto Figueroa 25, ✆ 91 522 4910. If you're ambling round Chueca and smitten suddenly with hunger, then Santander is the place to go. More than a hundred tapas, all well priced. Among the highlights are the *Choux de langostinos* and the cod chunks.

restaurants: expensive

the house speciality of ray, or go for other fish favourites.

Robata, Reina 31, ✆ 91 521 8528. Given that Madrid boasts the third largest fish market in the world (after Tokyo and San Francisco), little wonder that there should be so many good Japanese restaurants. Robata, just off Gran Via, has a sushi bar, normal tables or a Japanese salon. Not as fancy as Suntory, but better value.

restaurants: moderate

can be found this gem of a restaurant. International cuisine with a slight American flavour, backed up by affordable but well-chosen wines. If you're packing in the meals, then there's a very reasonable midday menu.

Extremadura, Libertad 13 and 31, ✆ 91 531 8958/91523 3503. The name says it all. If you want a taste of this western, and still largely remote region, then this is the place. *Migas* (breadcrumbs with bacon and grapes), and winter salads, backed up by roast goat, and finished off with home-made *orujo* (schnapps), of varying flavours—with the addition of a snake or a lizard in the bottle.

Gula Gula, Gran Via 1, ☎ 91 522 8764. Essential to book. Another of Madrid's gay crossover successes. Drag queen waitresses, loud, this is a place to see and be seen. The food is good, with a set menu, or a salad bar.

Mi Paisano, Gravina 18, ☎ 91521 3763. Madrid is finally waking up to Peruvian food. This latest addition sits opposite one of the first—El Inca. Start things off with a fine *pisco* sour, and move on the house specialty, *cebiche*—raw seafood, marinated in lime juice. A fine selection of local dishes such as *seco de cordero*—a lamb stew, all at a reasonable price.

Sarrasin, Libertad 8, ☎ 91 532 7348. With its policy of a fixed price menu, and a limited choice of dishes based on simple but tasty ingredients, this is one of the more enjoyable and affordable of the many (mainly) gay restaurants now flourishing in Chueca.

Al Hoceima, C/Farmacia 8, ☎ 91 531 9411. One of the longest-established Moroccan restaurants in the capital, Al Hoceima is close to the Malasaña area and offers well-priced dishes such as couscous and other North African specialities.

Cantina Mexicana, C/Tesoro 31, ☎ 91 522 0416. The first Mexican restaurant to open its doors here, back in 1982, the cantina has built up a loyal following for its extensive range of well-priced tacos and other Mexican delights; all served with Mexican beers and tasty cocktails.

Casa de Valencia, Paseo del Pintor Rosales 58, ☎ 91 544 1747. Rice rules here, with more than 14 different paellas, and a range of *fideuá* (paella done with macaroni), all washed down with a stunning range of Cavas. The lunchtime menu is a steal at 2,500 ptas.

El Chivito de Oro, Plaza de Chamberí 2, ☎ 91 448 7893. A modest Uruguayan establishment with a terrace in summer and autumn. Good quality beef, at reasonable prices.

Restaurant Zara, C/Infantas, ☎ 91 532 2074. Great Cuban food, a friendly neighbourhood atmosphere (if you smile hard enough at the waitress), and the best frozen daiquiris in town.

restaurants: cheap

Kekutin, C/R icardo Ortiz 47, ☎ 91 356 9124. Just across the M30 ring road from the bullring at Ventas, Kekutin is very much a neighbourhood restaurant. Home cooking at its best, with the emphasis on roast meats, soups, and other traditional Castilian dishes. The lunchtime menu, at 1,500 ptas is unbeatable.

Las Batuecas, Reina Victoria 17, ☎ 91 554 0452. A little off the beaten track, and don't be put off by the modest exterior. Inside awaits some of the best-priced food in the capital. The house speciality is Spanish omelette topped with tripe stew. Not for the faint hearted.

Salvador, C/Barbieri (no phone). A famous and endearingly scruffy neighbourhood hang out, serving stalwartly traditional, cheap and cheerful food.

Vegetarian

Madrid used to be a veggie's nightmare. Things have changed, and the capital boasts a wide selection, many of them excellent value.

El Granero de Lavapiés, C/Argumosa 10, ℗ 91 467 7611, Ⓜ Lavapiés, only opens for lunch.

Artemisa, C/Ventura de la Vega 4, ℗ 91 429 5092, Ⓜ Sevilla, is one of the capital's oldest, with a branch at Tres Cruces 4, ℗ 91 521 8721, Ⓜ Gran Vía, although the menu is not overly imaginative.

El Estragón, Plaza de la Paja 10, ℗ 91 365 8982, Ⓜ La Latina, is a new addition, with a relaxed, American feel, and a distinctive, creative menu.

La Mazorca, Paseo de Infanta Isabel, ℗ 91 501 7013, Ⓜ Atocha, is a homely place with a chimney which offers a good respite from the hustle and bustle of the nearby Reina Sofia musuem.

Vegetalía, C/Flor Baja 5, ℗ 91 542 7317, Ⓜ Santo Domingo. Recently opened vegetarian, with the emphasis on international cuisine. Try the wines made from organically grown grapes.

Open-air Eating

Eating out in the open is an option in the Spanish capital right through the year. Try any of the restaurants around the lake in the Casa de Campo, Ⓜ Lago, for lunch.

El Urogallo is a short walk up from the lake, still in the Casa de Campo, and has recently opened. An Asturian restaurant with a beautiful terrace opening out onto views of the Madrid skyline.

La Plaza de Chamberí, Plaza de Chamberí 10, ℗ 91 446 0697, Ⓜ Bilbao, is a delight on a summer's evening.

El Viajero, Plaza de la Cebada 11, ℗ 91 366 9064, Ⓜ La Latina, serves the finest Uruguayan beef, as well as good salads and crêpes and puts tables outside in the summer.

Cafés, Bars and Interesting Places to Drink

Madrid Specialities

The *aperitivo*—a quick drink in a bar before lunch or dinner—forms an integral part of daily life in Spain, and the capital is no different.

Never having produced any wines of distinction, Madrileños have never acquired much of a taste for quality *vino*. The traditional tipples of the capital are beer, sherry, and vermouth. Beer should typically be served *al metodo antiguo*, which involves a fast initial pour, letting the *caña* settle, and then topping it up. The result is a creamy, refreshing glass.

Fino and *manzanilla* are the sherries of choice for the capitals inhabitants. Unlike the warm furniture polish which passes for sherry in Britain, *fino* is served ice cold, and typically accompanied by a couple of *gambas a la plancha*, or prawns.

Vermut is similar to Martini Rosso, and has been popular with the working classes in Madrid since the last century. It should be served *al grifo*, or on tap, in a small glass with soda and no ice, and can be found in the dwindling number of *tabernas* in the city. Perhaps because of the poor quality of local grapes, Madrileños have no problem in mixing red wine. The result in summer is the delicious and refreshing *tinto de verano*; red wine over ice and lemon, with a healthy measure of lemonade. Cheaper restaurants offer red wine and lemonade as standard with their *menu del dia*.

Spanish WInes

No matter how much other costs have risen in Spain, **wine** has remained refreshingly inexpensive by northern European or American standards; what's more, it's very good and there's enough variety from the various regions of the country for you to try something different every day. There are 30 areas in Spain under the control of the *Instituto Nacional de Denominaciones de Origen (INDO)*, which acts as a guide to the consumer and keeps a strict eye on the quality of Spanish wine.

Catalunya is best known for its wines from Penedés and Priorato, the former producing excellent whites and some fine reds (try *Gran Caus '87*). One of the most typical Catalunyan whites is *Blancs en Noirs* and, like the dry white wines of Tarragona, is excellent with fish, or as an *aperitivo*. Some of the best sparkling wines (*cava*) come from Sant Sadurni d'Anoia, near Barcelona; *Mestres Mas Vía* can rival any standard champagne.

Navarra has some excellent reds (*Magaña Merlot '85*). Navarra's neighbour, La Rioja, is the best known and richest area for wine in Spain, producing a great range from young whites to heavy, fruity reds; its *vino de gran reserva* spends three years ageing in oak barrels, and another in bottles, before release to the public.

In La Mancha, Valdepeñas is Spain's most prolific area; its young, inexpensive table wines are sold everywhere, and make even a potato tortilla something special. Valencia has some fresh, dry whites and an distinctive rosé (*Castillo de Liria*). Euskadi is known for its very palatable 'green' wine, *Txacoli*, while Galicia's excellent *Ribeiro* resembles the delicate *vinho verde* of neighbouring Portugal; other good wines from the region are *Rías Baixas* and *Valseorros*, pleasant light vintages that complement the regional dishes, seafood in particular.

Andalucía is best known for Jerez, or what we in English call sherry. When a Spaniard invites you to have a *copa* (glass) it will nearly always be filled with this

Andalucían sunshine. It comes in a wide range of varieties: *manzanillas* are very dry, *fino* is dry, light and young (the most famous is *Tío Pepe*); *amontillados* are a bit sweeter and rich; *olorosos* are very sweet dessert sherries, and can be either brown, cream or *amoroso*.

Other Spanish Tipples

Spanish brandy is extremely palatable; the two most popular brands *103* (very light in colour) and *Soberano*, both drunk extensively by Spanish labourers and postmen at 7am. *Anís* (sweet or dry) is also quite popular. *Sangría* is the famous summertime punch of red wine, brandy, mineral water, orange and lemon with ice, but beware—it's rarely made very well, even when you can find it. Each region has its wine and liqueur specialities and nearly every monastery in Spain seems to make some kind of herbal potion. The north of Spain, where apples grow better than vines, produces cider, or *sidra*, which can come as a shock to the tastebuds. Ground almonds whipped to create *horchata de chufa* are refreshing in the summer.

Many Spaniards prefer **beer**, which is also good though dearer by degree than wine. The most popular brands are *San Miguel* and *Cruzcampo*—most bars sell it cold in bottles or on tap; try *Mahón* Five Star if you see it.

Café Society

Café society in Madrid includes everyone who cares to participate. With one bar for every 96 inhabitants, according to the last census, there's always somewhere to go, from beloved ancient holes in the wall which haven't been decorated since the time of Alfonso XII, to chic boulevard cafés where the Madrileñan *jeunesse dorée* discuss movies and modern art. You'll find one close to your hotel in which you'll happily send an entire afternoon down the drain, but here are some of the most interesting and famous.

The **Café Gíjon**, Pso. de Recoletos 21, © 91 521 5425, Ⓜ Banco de España, dates from 1888 and is seeped in history: it is here that Madrid's writers, artists, philosophers and political theorists have always gathered to engage in the discussion meetings that became known as *tertulias*.

Other legendary haunts of Madrid's intellectual class include the **Café Comercial**, Glorieta de Bilbao 7, © 91 521 5655, Ⓜ Bilbao, a veritable institution which, like the Gijón, is over a century old, with devoted regulars; and **Chicote**,Gran Vía 12, © 91 532 6737, Ⓜ Gran Vía, an Art Deco haven which never closed during the Civil War, and, in recent years, has had its original 1940s furnishings immaculately restored. Chicote was famous for his cocktails and this was his bar.

Madrid's celebrated fine arts centre has a large café, the **Café de Círculo de Bellas Artes**, C/Marqués de Casa Riera

2, Ⓜ Banco de España, which looks rather like a cross between a ballroom and an old-fashioned dentist's waiting room, but is one of the most relaxed places to linger in the city centre. It has an ostentatious *terraza* on the Calle de Alcalá which is open all year. The centre itself houses exhibition spaces and a library, and the annual masked ball held in the upstairs banqueting rooms is one of the highlights of the Madrileñan social calendar (for information on shows, workshops and events, call Ⓒ 91 531 7700).

It's all too easy to let the hours slip by at the **Nuevo Café Barbieri**, C/Ave María 45, Ⓒ 91 527 3658, Ⓜ Lavapiés, a beautiful old café, yellowed with age, with huge, Baroque wall mirrors, and a civilized atmosphere. Soothing by day (symphonies play in the background and there are speciality coffees and infusions to enjoy over a newspaper) and quietly sophisticated and sociable by night, this café also offers occasional film screenings. It's in the Lavapiés district, itself apparently barely touched by the ravages of the 20th century, and full of traditional local bars and cafés.

An excellent tea-time hideout in the very centre of Madrid is **La Mallorquina**, Puerta del Sol 8, Ⓜ Sol—while the busy shop downstairs sells pastries and gaudily wrapped sweets, upstairs there's a salon which is just the place to sip a cup of something in comfort and quietude while gazing out over the hubbub of the Puerta del Sol below.

La Luiza, Pza. Santa Ana 2, Ⓜ Sol, is cool for cakes, with broad glass-fronted displays of *pastelerías* and *bollerías*, and a bar where you can sit and dunk the leg of a croissant in your coffee.

Chueca's gay crowd favour the **Café Figueroa**, C/Augusto Figueroa 17, Ⓒ 91 521 1673, Ⓜ Chueca, a chatty, relaxed turn-of-the-century café.

One of the most pleasant places to watch the sun go down is the **Café Moderno**, Pza. de Comendadores, Ⓜ Noviciado, on a traffic-free square with a playground in the middle; as the light fades and the children are bundled away to supper, locals mellow out over their *copas*.

Meanwhile perhaps the most glorious views in all Madrid, particularly at sunset, are to be had from the shady terrace of **El Ventorillo**, C/Bailén, Ⓜ La Latina, which overlooks the Jardines de Las Vistillas, Nuestra Señora de la Almudena and the Campo del Moro, with the sierra in the distance, and which serves good, simple meals. There are also lovely views of green parkland and the distant Guadarramas from the *terrazas* along the Paseo del Pintor Rosales, on the east side of the Parque del Oeste.

Not far away from El Ventorillo is **El Anciano**, C/Bailén 19 (across from the Palacio Real), Ⓒ 91 559 5332, Ⓜ Opera, a very old and picturesque wine shop.

Another very *típico* old bar near the centre is **Casa Manolo**, C/Jovellanos 7, Ⓜ Sevilla (near the Teatro de Zarzuela). Tapas and *churros* in a convivial and old-fashioned atmosphere.

The **Bodega Ángel Sierra**, C/Gravina, Pza. de Chueca, Ⓜ Chueca, is also a classic place to drink—it's a traditional *vermut* bar, with house vermouth on tap.

The Plaza Santa Ana area is always full of high-spirited drinkers and a favourite place to meet people is **Viva Madrid**,

C/Manuel Fernández y González, Ⓜ Sevilla, one of Lorca's old haunts, which retains its gorgeous tiled façade; inside there are more coloured tiles, carved wood, and caryatids, plus the obligatory free-flowing beer taps.

Equally popular is **Los Gabrieles**, C/Echegaray 17, ✆ 91 429 6261, Ⓜ Sevilla, a handsome, cool, ancient (19th-century) bar, lined with decorative tiles, and full of loud music and lively company. Note that the prices here double after 5pm.

Or there's **La Venencia**, C/Echegaray 7, ✆ 91 429 7313, Ⓜ Sevilla, an ancient sherry bar with a macho atmosphere, serving countless varieties of sherry from rows of bottles and vats.

Near here is **No se lo digas a nadie**, C/Ventura de la Vega 11, ✆ 91 429 7525, Ⓜ Sevilla, a multi-purpose venue with a café/disco/bar which was once almost exclusively women-only but now welcomes lesbians and gays; it hosts private parties, drag shows, and other entertainments, and it doubles as an occasional meeting place for militant action groups.

Back on the Santa Ana trail is the **Cervecería Alemana**, Pza. Santa Ana 6, ✆ 91 429 7033, Ⓜ Sol, a perfect German-Spanish beerhall and one of Hemingway's many old watering holes.

Further north, the **Cervecería Santa Bárbara**, Pza. Santa Bárbara 8, ✆ 91 319 0449, Ⓜ Alonso Martínez, is packed with twenty-somethings at weekends.

C/Reina is host to two of the capital's best cocktail bars: **Cock**, at C/Reina 17, ✆ 91 532 2826, is hideously expensive, but unique in its 1920s fake country house décor, while **del Diego** has attentive service and imaginative food and drink.

The **Palacio de Gaviria**, Arenal 9, ✆ 91 526 60 69, is a 19th-century palace turned into macro venue, its many salons are home to a range of moods and musics. It attracts an international crowd.

The **Centro Cubano**, Claudio Coello 41, ✆ 91 575 8279, Ⓜ Serrano, boasts an excellent restaurant behind its anonymous doors. Its bar also serves the best *mojitos* and *daiquiris* in town. Not for lovers of Fidel, though.

Malasaña has undergone gentrification in recent times, and is no longer the rough and ready area it once was. It still largely attracts an under 30s crowd though, drawn to such famous bars as **Louie Louie**, C/de la Palma 43, Ⓜ Noviciado, where you'll have to knock to get in, or **La Vía Lactea**, C/Velarde 18, Ⓜ Tribunal, still stuck in an early eighties timewarp, but none the worse for it.

Malasaña also has some lovely cafes to while away the hours: **Cafe Ruiz**, C/Ruíz 11, ✆ 91 446 1232, Ⓜ Bilbao, or **Café Isadora**, C/Divino Pastor 14, ✆ 91 445 71 54, Ⓜ Bilbao. The Art Deco **Café Manuela**, San Vicente Ferrer, Ⓜ Tribunal, holds story-telling nights.

Cocido (serves six)

Ingredients:

3 litres water
200g ham
500g stewing beef
1 marrow bone
100g salt pork
500g garbanzos, soaked
1 turnip, cut in quarters
1 small stewing hen
1 stalk celery, cut in sections
2 leeks, cut in sections
1 onion, spiked with 4 cloves

3 carrots, halved lengthwise
6 medium potatoes, peeled and halved
3 cloves garlic, chopped
salt and pepper
1 small cabbage, coarsely chopped
150g chorizo sausage
150g morcilla sausage
200g fine noodles or rice or bread
parsley or mint
a spicy tomato sauce

Method:

Bring water to boil in a large pot, and add the ham, beef, bone, and salt pork. Skim off all the scum that rises to the surface, then turn down the heat, cover and simmer for two hours. Then add the garbanzos, turnip and hen and simmer for another 40 min. Then add the celery, leeks, onion, carrots, potatoes, garlic, salt and pepper, and cook until the vegetables are soft.

While this is cooking, boil the cabbage, chorizo and morcilla in a separate pot, and drain. In a frying pan, heat the oil and fry the cooked cabbage.

Strain the broth into another pot and boil. Cook the noodles or rice in it and serve as soup for the first course, sprinkling a bit of parsely or mint on the top. If you use bread instead, cut into thin strips, put in the bowls and ladle the soup on top. For the second course, cut the meat and sausages into pieces and serve on a platter, with the vegetables on a second platter. Serve the tomato sauce separately, to be added to the meats or vegetables as each diner chooses.

Where to Stay

North of Puerta del Sol   192
East of the Castellana   194
South of Puerta del Sol   196
Accommodation Agencies   198

With some 50,000 hotel rooms in Madrid, there are always enough to go around. Regrettably, few are at all interesting. If it's reliability or familiarity you're looking for, there are all the world's big chains to choose from, even a Holiday Inn, off an avenue named after General Perón (★★★★**Holiday Inn Madrid**, Pza. Carlos Trías Bertrán, ⓒ 91 597 01 02, ⓐ 91 597 02 92, Ⓜ Lima), or you could stay at any of a hundred other three, four- or five-star hotels—all pleasant and well-staffed, and all pretty much the same. Many are along the Gran Vía and other major streets; convenient but often intolerably noisy.

At the top end of the scale, Madrid has well over a third of all the luxury hotels in Spain. You could always pamper yourself at the Ritz, but only, needless to say, if money is no object—if you'd be inclined to wonder whether any hotel suite can possibly be worth 176,000 pts a night (the 'royal suite' is even more expensive) then this is definitely not your kind of place. At the other extreme, finding a good, cheap room for the night is not a problem if you're prepared to share a bathroom; otherwise you'll be hard pressed to find a double for under 4,000 pts.

The price categories for a double room are as follows:

luxury:	40,000 pts and up
expensive:	25,000–40,000 pts
moderate:	12,000–25,000 pts
inexpensive/cheap:	5,000–12,000 pts

North of Puerta del Sol: Opera, Chueca, Malasaña, Gran Vía

luxury

★★★★★**Hotel Santo Mauro**, C/Zurbano 36, ⓒ 91 319 6900, ⓐ 91 308 5477, Ⓜ Rubén Darío. Built as a palace late last century, the classicism of the public areas of this small-but-perfectly-formed recent arrival to Madrid's luxury class contrasts with the contemporary post-modernism of the rooms. Tucked away in a residential neighbourhood, this opulent but tasteful hotel is frequented by the rich and famous who also like their privacy.

★★★**Hotel Tirol**, C/Marqués de Urquijo 4, ✆ 91 548 1900, Ⓜ Argüelles. Slightly off the beaten track, and for that reason better value than many hotels only marginally more central. Spacious, airy rooms, clean, and close to the lovely Parque del Oeste.

★★★★**Gran Hotel Conde Duque**, Plaza de Conde del Valle Suchil 5, ✆ 91 447 7000, ✉ 91 448 3569, Ⓜ San Bernardo. Located in a residential square in the Chamberi area, and frequented by students and well-to-do families, the Gran Hotel Conde Duque is a good choice for the traveller who prefers to see how Madrid really lives. The professional and attentive staff and pleasant, refurbished rooms are the selling point.

★★★★**Hotel Emperador**, Gran Vía 53, ✆ 91 547 2800, ✉ 91 547 2817, Ⓜ Callao. Home to the only remaining roof-top hotel pool in Madrid, commanding stunning views up and down the Gran Vía, the Emperador is at the heart of the capital's traditional shopping centre. Just a short walk from Sol and Plaza de España, its large, well-decorated rooms are much in demand all year round.

★★★★ **Gaudi**, Gran Vía 9, ✆ 91 531 2222, ✉ 91 531 5469, Ⓜ Gran Vía. A good choice for business travellers, this small, bright modern hotel has excellent facilities including a sauna and a gym.

★★★**Hotel Zurbano**, C/Zurbano 79, ✆ 91 441 5500, ✉ 91 441 3224, Ⓜ Gregorio Marañon. North of the centre, near to the shopping and office complexes which line the Paseo de la Castellana, this unabashedly modern, spacious hotel is popular with businesspeople during the week. As a result, discount rates on weekends add up to a great deal for a break away from the usual tourist route.

★★★**HR Galiano Residencia**, C/Galiano 6, ✆ 91 319 2000, Ⓜ Colón. The peculiarities of the Spanish system of categorizing hotels makes this a hostal, albeit a three star one. However, this charming former palace knocks spots off most of the city's hotels with its intimate old world feel.

★★★★**HR Mayorazgo**, Flor Baja 3, ✆ 91 547 2600, ✉ 91 541 2485, Ⓜ Pza. de España, offers stylish, international—if anonymous—comfort.

★★★★**Style Santo Domingo**, ✆ 91 547 9800, ✉ 91 599 2216, Ⓜ Santo Domingo. In the buzzing heart of the Gran Vía, this stylish establishment is well placed for the area's nightlife.

★★**HSR Santa Bárbara**, Pza. Santa Bárbara 4, ✆ 91 446 93 08, ✉ 91 446 23 45, Ⓜ Alonso Martínez, is on one of central Madrid's most pleasant squares.

★★**Hostal Barajas**, C/Augusto Figueroa 17, ✆ 91 532 4078, Ⓜ Chueca/Tribunal. More upmarket than most of the *hostales* in the area, it is still quite relaxed, with the fashionable neighbourhoods of Chueca and Malasaña right on the doorstep.

★★**Hotel Trafalgar** C/Trafalgar 35, ✆ 91 445 6200, ✉ 91 446 6456. Ⓜ Iglesia. Popular for not being on the beaten track, this hotel has simply furnished, pleasant rooms.

*Hotel Monaco, C/Barbieri 5, ✆ 91 522 4639, 📠 91 521 1601, Ⓜ Chueca/Gran Vía. A hotel for the last forty years, the Monaco used to be one of the city's best-known brothels frequented famously by King Alfonso XIII. The atmosphere persists in a leather and marble lobby where a neon sign points to the miniscule bar and in the more elaborate of the mirror-filled rooms, complete with canopies and raised baths.

**Hostal Sil, C/Fuencarral 95, ✆ 91 448 8972, 📠 91 447 4829, Ⓜ Bilbao. At the end of Fuencarral away from the Gran Vía, this family-run *hostal* is kept spick and span by the pleasant couple who own and run it. With private baths and air conditioning, the TV- and telephone-equipped rooms are really good value for a stay during Madrid's sweltering summer.

**Hostal Rico, C/Fuencarral 22, 1° derecha, ✆ 91 531 9587, Ⓜ Tribunal. Simple but clean, well staffed by English speakers, this family run establishment is also ideally located for those in search of nightlife in Chueca and Malasaña.

**HSR América, C/Hortaleza 19-5°, ✆ 91 522 6448, 📠 91 522 6447, Ⓜ Gran Vía. Walk up C/Fuencarral or C/Hortaleza and you'll find an enormous choice of low-cost *hostales*. This is one of the classier cheap places at the noisy, grubby Gran Vía end of the district, high enough up for you not to be aware of the buses thundering by below. It has a clean, lived-in atmosphere and a jolly, efficient landlady; there's a TV lounge and a sunny balcony off the entrance hall.

Pensión Romero, C/León 13-3°, ✆ 91 429 51 39, Ⓜ Antón Martín. The landlady is very amiable; this too is a family flat, complete with small excitable dog.

**Hotel Tirol, C/Marqués de Urquijo 4, ✆ 91 548 1900, 📠 91 541 3958, Ⓜ Argüelles. A fairly basic but clean and pleasant hotel in the studenty part of town, convenient for the Plaza de España, and the Gran Vía. Very good value.

East of the Castellana: Castellana itself, Salamanca, Retiro

*****Hotel Villa Magna, Pso. de la Castellana 22, ✆ 91 360 8000, 📠 91 360 8100, Ⓜ Rubén Darío. The Villa Magna's modern—albeit bland—surroundings are more than made up for by the quality of service and facilities on offer at this hotel away from the city centre. The establishment of choice for many visiting sports stars and celebrities, the Villa Magna is also home to one of Madrid's most famous, and justly so, restaurants.

*****Hotel Wellington, C/Velázquez 8, ✆ 91 575 4400, Ⓜ Principe de Vergara. Discreetly upmarket, and well-placed for the expensive shops that line Velázquez and nearby Serrano, the Wellington's success is based firmly on good old-fashioned service. Enter its portals and leave behind your cares. Downstairs is the Zambra flamenco *tablao*, and—unusual in Madrid—there is also a swimming pool.

****Hotel Castellana Inter-Continental**, Paseo de la Castellana 49, ℗ 91 310 0200, Ⓜ Rubén Darío. Having undergone redecoration, this well-located—albeit unattractive from the outside—hotel is perhaps the best value at the top end of the scale. The best rooms overlook the interior garden; itself one of the capital's best-kept secrets, with live jazz in summer. The rooftop gym terrace bar offers wonderful views.

****Hotel Los Galgos Sol**, C/Claudio Coello 139, ℗ 91 561 7662, Ⓜ Nuñez de Balboa. Modern, comfortable, with excellent facilities, and certainly well-located. Unusual for a Spanish hotel, it even has no-smoking floors.

****Hotel Serrano**, C/Marqués de Villamejor 8, ℗ 91 435 5200, Ⓜ Metro Rubén Darío. If you want to be in the smart, Salamanca area, this is probably as good value as you're going to find. Generally chic and immaculate, some rooms are a bit basic.

****Hotel Alcalá**, C/Alcalá 66, ℗ 91 435 10 60, ℗ 91 435 1105, Ⓜ Príncipe de Vergara. Friendly staff provide a warm welcome at this popular hotel, and many longtime visitors to Madrid wouldn't dream of staying anywhere else. The courtyard garden looked on to by the quieter interior rooms is a verdant reminder of the nearby Retiro.

***Hotel Zurbano**, C/Zurbano 79, ℗ 91 441 5500, ℗ 91 441 3224, Ⓜ Gregorio Marañon. North of the centre, near to the shopping and office complexes which line the Paseo de la Castellana, this unabashedly modern, spacious hotel is popular with businesspeople during the week. As a result, discount rates on weekends add up to a great deal for a break away from the usual tourist route.

****Hotel Bauza**, C/Goya 79, ℗ 91 435 7545, Ⓜ Goya. Fully refurbished, this well-appointed hotel has earned itself an extra star in the process, and offers excellent value.

***Rafael Ventas**, C/Alcalá 269, ℗ 91 326 1620, ℗ 91 926 1819, Ⓜ Carmen. Bright, breezy, and very modern, this hotel is near the bullring and attracts a number of *toreros*. The staff are very helpful and the rooms are light and airy.

***Style Excultor**, ℗ 91 310 4203, ℗ 91 319 2584, Ⓜ Rubén Darío. This small hotel is fairly basic, but comfortable nonetheless. It is set in one of Madrid's most exclusive residential areas, not far from the delightful Museo Sorolla (*see* p. 131).

***Meliá Confort Galgos**, C/Claudio Coello 139, ℗ 91 562 6600, ℗ 91 561 7662, Ⓜ Núñez de Balboa. Perfectly located for shopping on one of the area's most fashionable areas, this hotel provides efficient, if slightly impersonal, service.

*HSR Coruña, Pso. del Prado 12-3°dcha, © 91 429 2543, Ⓜ Banco de España, and ***HSR Sudamericana**, Pso. del Prado 12-6°izqda, © 91 429 2564, Ⓜ Banco de España, are two of the friendliest and quietest lodgings in Madrid, occupying the same fine old building with leafy views towards the Prado.

**HSR Corberó, C/Cervantes 34-1°izqda, © 91 429 4171, Ⓜ Banco de España, has small doubles with bathroom and TV, and, in the next door block, mini-apartments with living room and kitchenette, which sleep up to four and are excellent value.

South of Puerta del Sol: Plaza Mayor, Santa Ana, Lavapiés

luxury

*****Hotel Palace, Pza. de las Cortes 7, © 91 360 8000, ✉ 91 360 8100, Ⓜ Banco de España. In a perfect location between the Prado and Sol, turn-of-the-century architecture meets the latest facilities in one of Madrid's largest luxury hotels. But it's far from impersonal, and reasonably priced restaurants and bars in the stunning public areas make the Palace a bustling, friendly place to stay or just to be.

*****Hotel Ritz, Pza. de la Lealtad 5, © 91 521 2857, ✉ 91 523 8776, Ⓜ Banco de España. Consistently rated among the best hotels worldwide, a stay at the Ritz is all about being pampered. From the renovated and sumptuous rooms, to the fabulous restaurant and 'place-to-be-seen' garden terrace, the hotel is close to the Prado and is just a stone's throw from the Retiro and the boutiques lining the streets of Salamanca.

expensive

****Gran Hotel Reina Victoria, Pza. Santa Ana 14, © 91 531 45 00, ✉ 91 522 03 07, Ⓜ Sol. Well-established, convenient and comfortable, this hotel is a bullfighters' favourite. Minibuses carrying clutches of them, resplendent in their fighting regalia, regularly pull up outside the wedding-cake façade. The nicest rooms overlook the Plaza Santa Ana.

****Hotel Tryp Ambassador, Cuesta de Santo Domingo 5–7, © 91 541 6700, ✉ 91 559 1040, Ⓜ Santo Domingo. Right in the centre but tucked into a quiet street between the Palacio Real, the opera house

and Gran Via, this luxurious establishment is arguably the capital's best-kept secret. Attractive patio garden and glass atrium make the hotel an oasis of light and calm in the summer months.

*****Hotel Villa Real, Plaza de las Cortes 10, © 91 420 3767, ✉ 91 420 2547, Ⓜ Banco de España. Although only built in 1990, the Villa Real has captured the neo-classical feel of the elegant neighbourhood. It's ideally situated for the main museums, and the Puerta del Sol and Atocha station.

★★Hotel Asturias, C/Sevilla 2, ✆ 91 429 6676, Ⓜ Sevilla. Just up from Sol, and well placed for the Huertas/Santa Ana areas. English spoken by friendly staff. Outside rooms have good views, but can be noisy.

★★★HR Reyes Católicos, C/Angel 18, ✆ 91 265 8600, 🖷 91 265 9867, Ⓜ Puerta de Toledo. Set in a very nice old neighbourhood near the basilica of San Francisco El Grande; small, personal, and a good bargain for the services offered.

★★★Carlos V, C/Maestro Vitoria 5, ✆ 91 531 41 00, 🖷 91 531 37 51, Ⓜ Sol. Family-run and friendly, this is an otherwise unexceptional place, popular partly, no doubt, thanks to its location—a mere hop from El Corte Inglés.

★★★Style Excultor, ✆ 91 310 4203, 🖷 91 319 2584, Ⓜ Rubén Dario. This small hotel is fairly basic, but comfortable nonetheless. The staff are efficient and very friendly. It is set in one of Madrid's most exclusive residential areas, not far from the delightful Museo Sorolla (*see* p. 131).

★★★Hotel el Prado, C/Prado 11, ✆ 91 429 0234, 🖷 91 429 2829, Ⓜ Antón Martín. Near the Cortes, this hotel is a bit bland but offers some plush comforts, including private parking and satellite TV in all the rooms.

★★Hotel Mora, Pso del Prado 32, ✆ 91 420 1569, 🖷 91 420 0564, Ⓜ Atocha. Clean and functional, the Mora is good value, and well located opposite the Prado.

★★★Hotel Inglés, C/Echegaray 8, ✆ 91 429 6551, 🖷 91 420 2423, Ⓜ Sevilla, Sol. With 150 years of history under its belt, this family-run hotel lies equidistant from the shopping areas of Preciados and Carmen and the bars of Santa Ana. Relaxed and very comfortable atmosphere in public areas and sunny rooms, but those giving onto Eche garay itself can be noisy on weekends.

★★★★Hotel Suecia, C/Marqués de Casa Riera 4, ✆ 91 531 6900, 🖷 91 521 7141, Ⓜ Sevilla, Banco de España. Tucked away in a quiet corner of the old city, the Suecia has a pleasant terrace on the 7th floor for sunbathing and relaxing.

★★Hotel Paris, C/Alcalá 2, ✆ 91 521 6491, 🖷 91 531 0188, Ⓜ Sol. The velvet-lined lobby hotel is as packed with character as it is with china bric-a-brac, but the friendly staff soon make visitors feel right at home. Two steps away from the Puerta del Sol, the best of the wooden-floored rooms look onto the courtyard garden and keep the sound of traffic at bay.

★★Hotel Santander, C/Echegaray 1, ✆ 91 429 9551, 🖷 91 369 1078, Ⓜ Sevilla, Sol. High-ceilings, a jumble of furniture from all over and the light-filled, although sometimes noisy, exterior rooms make the Santander a firm favourite of many budget travellers. Obliging staff and a great location close to shops and bars in the centre of the city mean it's best to call ahead and reserve.

★★Hostal Cervantes, C/Cervantes 24, ✆ 91 429 8365, 🖷 91 429 2745, Ⓜ Antón Martín. In a quieter sidestreet close to the bas and clubs of the busy Huertas and Santa Ana area, an easygoing ambience is the tonic in this small owner-managed hotel. All the rooms have plenty of natural light and en-suite bath facilities.

inexpensive/cheap (cont'd)

Hostal Madrid, C/Esparteros 6, 2°, ✆ 91 522 0060, Ⓜ Sol. Centrally located, with friendly owners more than happy to provide info on what's on and how to get there.

★★HSR La Torre, C/Espoz y Mina 8-3°, ✆ 91 532 4303, Ⓜ Sol, is probably the best value option in this area, a bright, squeaky-clean *hostal* which includes large twin rooms with fabulous balconies, giving views, opposite, of rooftop gardens, and, down the street to the left, the Puerta del Sol's landmark Tío Pepe advert.

★★HS La Macarena, Cava de San Miguel 8, ✆ 91 365 9221, ✉ 91 364 2757, Ⓜ Opera, just off the Plaza Mayor. One of the most atmospheric places to experience Madrid, tucked in a street full of ancient bars and restaurants (including fake Mexican eatery El Cuchi, whose awning proclaims, memorably, 'Hemingway Never Ate Here'), and tall buildings pitched at such a slope they look as though they'll topple over at any minute.

★HSR Santa Ana, Pza. Santa Ana 1-2°dcha, ✆ 91 521 3058, Ⓜ Sol, is a small and clean if slightly tatty *hostal* right on the square. The owner, Marta, and her huge Siamese cat are both very friendly, and some rooms have lovely sunny balconies.

★HSR Vetusta, C/Huertas 3-1°, ✆ 91 429 64 04, Ⓜ Sol, has a balcony dripping with geraniums, and good value rooms (some for *4000 pts*).

Accommodation Booking Agents

If you haven't got the time or the inclination to find accommodation yourself, there are a couple of agencies who will work it all out for you:

The **Brújula Agency** at Calle Princesa 1, ✆ 91 559 9705, books accommodation in Madrid and the surrounding region for a fee of 300 pts. They will also provide you with a map and directions for getting to the hotel. It is usually best to show up in person, as it can be difficult to get through on the phone. There are branches at Atocha station (✆ 91 539 1173) and Chamertín train station (✆ 91 315 7894), and the airport bus terminal at the Plaza del Col (✆ 91 575 9680).

Viajes Aira offer a similar service at Terminals 1 and 2 of Barajas Airport, ✆ 91 305 4224/ ✆ 91 393 6867. There is no booking fee, but they only offer hotels in the moderate range and don't provide maps or directions.

Entertainment and Nightlife

Classical Music and Zarzuela

The opening of the Teatro Real in 1997 has done much to reinvigorate Madrid's classical music scene; by freeing up other venues, and by attracting top level visiting orchestras and companies. Check the listings section in the daily papers.

Light opera fans will want to take in a *zarzuela*, Spain's answer to Gilbert and Sullivan, or Offenbach. The season lasts from June to September, although the Teatro de la Zarzuela and the Auditorio Nacional stage winter productions. The open-air performances staged in the Lavapiés district at the Corrala, C/Tribulete 12, are not the most polished, but the tenement setting and festive mood more than compensate. Performances start at 10pm, and the box office opens one hour before.

Auditorio Nacional de Música, C/Principe de Vergara 146, ℗ 91 337 0100. Home to the Orquesta Nacional de España, the auditorio also stages some jazz events. The concert season is October to June, with guest orchestras. Getting tickets can be difficult, though, due to the season ticket policy.

Teatro Monumental, C/Atocha 65, ℗ 91 429 8119. The venue for most of state radio and television company Radio Television Española's recorded concerts. Tickets are reasonably priced and usually available, but programming tends to be more traditional.

Fundación Juan March, C/Castelo 77, ℗ 91 435 4240, has a tiny concert hall which offers free admittance to its noon events on Sat and Mon, and at 7.30pm on Wed. There are also art exhibitions upstairs.

Dance

Strangely enough, Spain's rich flamenco culture tends not to merge with the mainstream dance scene. Thus, flamenco dance remains part of the flamenco world. For flamenco dance venues, *see* section on flamenco, below.

There are two main dance companies in Spain, the **Compañía Nacional de Danza** and the **Ballet Nacional de España**. However, the capital boasts its own **Ballet de la Comunidad de Madrid,** led by Victor Ullate, with the emphasis on well-known Spanish and French works.

The capital hosts several dance events and festivals throughout the year, many of them at the Teatro Albeniz (*see* below) and the Teatro Pradillo. Keep an eye open for posters and check the listings pages, as well as the following venues:

Teatro Real, Plaza de Oriente, ℗ 91 516 0660. The newly renovated Teatro Real, also known as the Opera, is where you'll catch Natcho Duato's Compañía Nacional de Danza—when they are in Madrid.

Teatro de Madrid, Avenida de la Ilustracíon, ℗ 91 740 5274. Out in the Barrio del Pilar neighbourhood, this modern theatre often features dance.

Teatro de la Zarzuela, C/Jovellanos 4, ℗ 91 524 5400. A beautifully restored mid 19th-century miniature La Scala with a varied programme which now takes in much more *zarzuela* than before.

Film

Cinema going remains popular in Spain, perhaps because at around 750 ptas it's still so cheap compared to other European capitals. Spanish cinema has had its ups and downs over the years, and the glory days of state funding ended with the arrival of a conservative government. In creative terms, the director of 'Women on the Edge of a Nervous Breakdown' Pedro Almodóvar still casts his shadow large over the scene, and his style of post-modern *costumbrista* is much copied.

The Callao metro stop at Gran Vía is the mecca for big-screen Hollywood-import fans, with the occasional local big budget production drawing in the crowds. Down the Gran Vía at Plaza España are four multi-screen cinemas specializing in subtitled foreign language movies. Madrid has no film festival, preferring not to compete with San Sebastián's annual jamboree. For listings information, the *Guía del Ocio* is the most complete, covering all aspects of entertainment and nightlife. The two main newspapers, *El País* and *El Mundo*, have complete daily listings. For foreign language entries look under the 'versión original' heading.

Mainstream

Although usually showing Hollywood imports, these three cinemas are worth a visit if only for their pre-war opulent decor.

Capitol, Gran Vía 41, ✆ 91 570 6633.
Gran Vía, Gran Vía 66, ✆ 91 570 6633.

Palacio de la Música, Gran Vía 35, ✆ 91 521 6209.

Foreign Language

Alphaville, Martín de los Heros 14, ✆ 91 559 3836. One of the capital's first art house cinemas, Alphaville boasts a café and bookshop. Like its neighbour Renoir, however, the policy of non-numbered seats can lead to giant queues round the block—first to buy your ticket, then to get into your film.

Princesa, Princesa 3, ✆ 91 541 4100. Round the corner from Alphaville, and with six screens, Princesa is more comfortable than most multi-cines, and they let you take drinks in.

Multicines Ideal, Doctor Cortezo 6, ✆ 91 369 2518. With numbered seats and advanced booking, Ideal has the edge over the competition. Eight screens mix the best in imports with independent Spanish efforts.

Open Air

Madrid's summer festival, the Veranos de la Villa, offers two screenings a night throughout July, August, and the first two weeks of September at a giant open-air screen in the Parque de la Bombilla, on the Avenida de Valladolid, close to the church of San Antonio de la Florída. Not for serious cinema fans, but it certainly allows you to mix with the locals.

The Filmoteca

Spain's national film theatre is not overly well-funded, but this turn-of-the-century cinema offers interesting seasons, a good bookshop, a café, and in summer a rooftop open-air screen.

Flamenco

Those looking for flamenco in its purest form should head to the **Peña Chaquetón**, C/Canarias 39, ☏ 91 671 2777, one of the capital's oldest, and last, *peñas*. This is a world away from the *tablaos*, with an almost scholarly approach on the part of the *aficionados* who turn up to hear some of the finest singers and guitarists in the country.

Despite its touristy feel, **La Soleá**, C/Cava Baja 27, ☏ 91 365 3308, attracts some good amateurs, and singers and guitarists make their way here to try their hand and see if they have that special something. Also a favourite for neighbourhood locals who just fancy the flamenco equivalent of a good singsong down the pub.

Casa Patas, C/Cañizares 10, ☏ 91 369 0496, attracts some of the best performers, with dance a regular feature. The bar/restaurant is separate from the performing area, and famous faces from the flamenco world are often seen there.

Of the *tablaos*, the better are **Café de Chinitas**, C/Torrija 7, ☏ 91 547 1501, and **Corral de la Morería**, C/de la Morería 17, ☏ 91 365 8446. Aside from their house artistes, they regularly attract top names. You'll be lucky to get away with less than 6,000 ptas a head once you've had something to eat and drink.

Suristán, C/de la Cruz 7, ☏ 91 532 3909 (*see also* under 'Rock, Blues and Jazz'), also hosts flamenco on Wednesday nights.

If you want to mingle with players and other figures from the flamenco world—as well as their hangers-on—then a late-night drink at **Candela,** C/del Olmo 2, ☏ 91 467 3382, is a must.

Nightclubs and Bars

First-time visitors to Madrid are often surprised at just how late the capital's inhabitants stay out. Indeed, if you're only here for a short stay and plan to do culture by day and clubbing by night, you'll need to fit a siesta in, because things don't really start happening here until around midnight.

Another feature of the capital's nightlife is the way certain areas have developed a scene of their own, with dozens of bars within walking distance, all catering to a particular social set or age group. This to some extent explains the lack of venues offering only live music: people want to go out and wander round different places, meeting up with friends at agreed rendezvous 'later on'. All of the venues listed in the rock music section double as clubs, for example. The Salamanca neighbourhood for example is distinctly upmarket, and mainly for the over thirties. Malasaña

and Lavapiés are still distinctly grungy, although smartening up
overwhelmingly gay, and Argüelles is for the under eighteens. H\
Ana attract the widest range, with bars to suit every taste.

The **Malasaña** neighbourhood is filled with so many bars, and so
similar, that it's hard to recommend any in particular. Head for t\
Mayo, and take in the atmosphere from any of the open-air tables. After that, a
wander up C/de la Palma, and round back up San Vicente Ferrer gives as good a
feel of the flavour of the place as you'll need.

The warren of narrow streets that makes up the **Austrias** area between the
C/Segovia and the market at La Latina is the capital's oldest district, but is
smartening up. Several wine bars now offer the opportunity for a night-time tour,
with suitable pauses for refreshment and tapas.

Try the following as starting-off points: close to the C/Segovia is **La Taberna de
los Cien Vinos**, C/del Nuncio 16; **Casa Paco**, Plaza de Puerta Cerrada 11; **El
Almendro 13** at that address. Over towards the La Latina market, start at **El
Viajero**, Plaza de la Cebada 11, and head down to **El Tempranillo**, C/Cava Baja
38, or **Matritum** on C/Cava Alta 17.

Spaniards are not as exclusive as the British: most bars still play an eclectic mix of
music, and few apply any sort of dress code—except for the Salamanca area, where
many places don't accept sneakers. As said, the rule generally is to settle on an
area, and then wander from bar to bar until the wee hours, ending the revelries
with a hot chocolate before collapsing into bed.

Discos

Joy Eslava, C/Arenal 11, ✆ 91 366 3733.
The capital's best-known and best loved disco
is a classic, with pounding music, lights,
scantily clad go-go dancers of both sexes. It
attracts a varied fauna, from businessmen to
drag queens and camp revellers.

Kapital, C/Atocha 125, ✆ 91 420 3964.
With seven floors of fun, including cinema,
karaoke bar, and chill-out areas the idea is
you don't need to go anywhere else. At
2,000 ptas to get in, you'd better be sure.
The rooftop terrace bar has fantastic views.

Palacio de Gaviria, C/Arenal 9, ✆ 91 526
6069. Located in a former palace, Gaviria's
labyrinthine and ornate interior offers a range
of ambiences, and attracts a mixed crowd.

Torero, C/de la Cruz 26, ✆ 91 523 1129.
The smart set still hang out here, and getting
in on a Saturday can be tricky, so the smarter
and wealthier you look, the more chance of
just breezing in. Ground floor is a bar, and
downstairs offers a mix of house, flamenco
and latin music.

/Bars

Comedia, C/Principe 16, ☏ 91 521 5164. Its location in the heart of the Huertas Santa Ana district means it's always full, but a spacious interior and good natured young crowd makes it a good starting off point for the night.

La Boca del Lobo, C/Echegaray 11, ☏ 91 429 7013. Again, conveniently situated in the Santa Ana area, this old-time cellar bar plays old-time music from the thirties up to the sixties, and attracts a cheerful, pleasantly mixed crowd.

Cardamomo, C/Echegaray 15, ☏ 91 369 0757. In many ways this relaxed club sums up the capital's approach to going out: an eclectic mix of music, taking in flamenco, salsa, ethnic, and even house—but most importantly, a relaxed mood as revellers come and go throughout the night.

Davai, C/Flor Baja 1, ☏ 91 547 5711. Influenced by the British drum'n'bass scene, Davai has nevertheless established a distinctly Spanish identity, with the emphasis on techno, house, and as the evening wears on, virtually anything.

El Sol, C/Jardines, ☏ 91 532 6490. Endearingly scruffy, Sol occasionally puts on live gigs, but most of the time offers late night funk, seventies and eighties to an eclectic crowd more interested in having a good time than being seen.

Soma, C/Leganitos 25, ☏ 91 521 0708. Over the years this former flamenco *tablao* has taken on many guises. Currently housing a techno club, its tiled decor and labyrinthine interior offers a cool escape from steamy summer nights.

Teatríz, C/Hermosilla 15, ☏ 91 577 5379. Now something of an institution, Teatriz's Eighties designer interior still packs the Salamanca smart set in. Restaurant, disco and bar all in one former theatre.

Viva Madrid, Manuel Fernandez y Gonzalez 7, and its nearby neighbour Los Gabrieles, are two of the capital's best-known bars, close to the Plaza Santa Ana. Expensive, crowded, and to some extent touristy, they are at least a good starting-off point for the evening, and somewhere everybody knows.

Gay

El Mosquito, C/Torrecila del Leal 13. On the edge of the Lavapiés district, and close to Huertas/Santa Ana, Mosquito is typical of many nominally gay bars in the capital, and is very much a mixed venue. Also, one of the few places with a genuinely political agenda.

La Lupe, next door, attracts gay men and women to its coffee bar by day. In the evening it's relaxed, with good music and, like Mosquito, distinctly uncamp.

The **Acuarela Café**, C/Gravina, ☏ 91 522 2143, has a comfy mixture of shabby-chic furniture, candelabra, angelic cherubs and velvet cushions. Again, it crams in a mixed clientele and is very relaxed. It is tiny and can get pretty packed.

In Chueca itself, the **New Leather Bar**, C/Pelayo 42, ☏ 91 308 1462, is, as its name suggests, tending towards the heavier side. There are shows every night, and it is very much part of the circuit.

In a similar vein and nearby are: **Cruising**, C/Pérez Galdós 5, ☏ 91 521 5143, which also allows women in upstairs; **Blanco y Negro**, C/Libertad 34, ☏ 91 531 1141, which attracts older men in search of younger men to its disco.

If you're looking to lose yourself, then head for **Strong Center**, C/Trujillos, between Opera and Sol. Its darkroom is legendary, and very, very large...

Shangay Tea Rooms, C/Mesonero Romanos, ✆ 91 531 4827. Without a doubt the best tea dance in Madrid. Also plays great disco music and has shows every weekend.

Lesbian

Medea, C/de la Cabeza 33, allows men at weekends, and is perhaps the capital's best-known lesbian disco.

Ambient, C/San Mateo 21, serves food and attracts a relaxed crowd, and is a good starting place if you want to know what's going on.

In Chueca, **Truco**, C/Gravina 10, ✆ 91 532 8921, offers a terrace bar, and is open to men and non-lesbian women.

No evening is complete without a hot chocolate to end things off, accompanied by the traditional *churro*—deep-fried batter sticks. **Chocolatería San Ginés**, Pasadizo de San Ginés 11, tucked away in a narrow alley behind Sol, and next door to the Joy Eslava disco, doesn't close until 7am, and is nothing less than an institution. It is open every night of the year except Christmas Eve.

Rock, Blues and Jazz

Madrid manages to attract its share of super-acts, despite lacking a decent indoor super-venue; the climate allows for summer open-air concerts in any of the capital's large football stadia. An enthusiastic jazz and blues following means big names come to Madrid, particularly in late summer, when the northern cities of San Sebastián, Bilbao, and Vitoria all host jazz and blues festivals, allowing artists to fit in a couple of extra dates. The problem is that the venues concerned are small, and with a guaranteed public, hence advertising is minimal. Also, most venues double up as bars or clubs. Forget the listing section of the newspapers, and buy the pocket-sized, weekly listings guide, the *Guía del Ocio*.

The following venues are worth checking out for a feel of the local music scene.

Café de la Palma, C/de la Palma 62, ✆ 91 522 5031. Part bar, part chill-out zone, part music venue, the Palma has carved a niche for itself as a relaxed club offering local talent a showcase. Everything from flamenco to blues, taking in Cuban *trovadores*.

Downtown, C/Covarrubias 31, and **La Coquette**, C/de las Hileras 14, are a must for blues fans, with live music weekends and a smokey late-night feel.

Café Central, Plaza del Angel 10, ✆ 91 369 4143. Voted among the world's best jazz venues by *Wire* magazine, Café Central attracts world-class names to a genuine café setting. By day it's a lovely place to sit and read the paper and enjoy a coffee. Just down the road is **Populart**, at C/Huertas 22, ✆ 91 429 8407, which attracts local players, with the emphasis on a rowdy good time. It can get a little too crowded at weekends.

If you're in the **Malasaña** neighbourhood, try the **Triskel Tavern** at C/San Vicente Ferrer 3, ✆ 91 523 2783, which pulls in some excellent local players for its late-night jam sessions.

Suristán, C/de la Cruz 7, ✆ 91 532 3909, is the capital's only club dedicated to world music, attracting African, Cuban, Brazilian and North African artists. Spacious, with a table area, the mood is relaxed.

Salsa took Madrid by storm in the early nineties. The fever has cooled off somewhat. But if you're looking to dance the night away, then try **Café del Mercado**, Ronda de Toledo 1, ✆ 91 365 8739. It's in the by now almost abandoned market at the end of C/Toledo, but continues to attract top-class bands and plays hot tracks.

Oba Oba, C/Jacometrezzo 4, just behind the Callao cinema area, is a Brazilian cellar bar with the best *caipirinhas* in town and some excellent live music.

Sports and Activities

Spectator Sports

With their great sense of occasion, Spaniards flock to large sporting events, and the capital's two main **soccer** stadia, belonging to Real Madrid and Atlético Madrid, regularly play host to 50,000-plus fans. Given Spanish teams' success in Europe, there are games on televison every night of the week except Friday.

Basically, Real Madrid is the wealthier and more successful of the capital's two teams, attracting a more fashionable, upmarket fan to its giant stadium, the Estadio Santiago Bernabéu, C/Concha Espina and Paseo de la Castellana, ✆ 91 398 4300. Atlético de Madrid's ground, down by the river at Estadio Vicente Calderon, Paseo de los Melancolicos, ✆ 91 366 4707, may not be as smart, but the team's fans pride themselves on their working-class credentials.

Bullfighting continues to pack in the crowds, and is worth an estimated billion pounds a year. The spring San Isidro festivities see the biggest names at the Ventas bullring, while August and September's holidays—many in the villages around the capital—draw large crowds to impromptu *corridas*. If you really must take in what the Madrid columnist Franciso Umbral has called a national shame and the reason why the rest of Europe will continue to think of Spain as essentially barbaric, head for the Plaza de Toros de las Ventas, C/Alcalá 237, ✆ 91 726 4800. Between March and October there are *corridas* every Sunday afternoon.

Basketball is the other most popular spectator sport, and the capital boasts two top teams: Estudiantes, and Real Madrid. The Palacio de Deportes de Madrid in the Salamanca area is home to both, at the pedestrian shopping street Avenida de Felipe II (✆ 91 401 9100).

Activities

Madrileños make good use of the many sports centres which dot the city, offering five-a-side football, martial arts and swimming. For the visitor, a day out at a municipal open-air **pool** in summer offers a fascinating slice of Spanish life: discreet gays, topless grannies, gypsies and their guitars, Moroccans showing off, and preening adolescents. The open-air pool at the Casa de Campo, by the Lago metro stop, offers all of the above, and is open from mid-May to mid-September, from 10.30am to 8pm daily.

Joggers and **cyclists** are not advised to try the city centre. If you can organize the transport, get out to the Casa de Campo. It's got acres and acres of largely unvisited woodland. Some areas are frequented by prostitutes and there is a gay cruising area up by the *teleférico* cable car, but they all tend to keep themselves to themselves, and incidents are all but unknown. Besides which, the police patrol the area heavily.

There are a number of **golf** courses in the metropolitan area, none of them cheap, the best equipped being the Club de Campo Villa de Madrid, Ctra. de Castilla km 3, ℘ 91 357 2132.

Theatre

Madrid has never been able to establish as confident a thespian self-image as its rival Barcelona. With no national theatre as such, however, writers are very much on their own when it comes to getting productions mounted, and there is a clear lack of contemporary quality drama. Nevertheless, even with drastic cutbacks in state and local government funding a wide range of theatre remains on offer.

Classical and Contemporary Theatre

Spain's equivalent of the Royal Shakespeare Company is the **Compañía Nacional de Teatro Clásico**, which puts on works from the Golden Age by such luminaries as Calderón de la Barca, Tirso de Molina, and Lope de Vega.

Teatro de la Comedia, C/Principe 14, ℘ 91 521 4931.

The **Teatro Español**, just up the road at C/Principe 25, ℘ 91 429 6297, is worth a visit if only for its mid 18th-century interior, although its productions of early 20th-

century Spanish works have won international acclaim.

So have the productions at the **Centro Dramático Nacional**, based at the Teatro María Guerrero on Tamayo y Baus 4, ℘ 91 319 4769.

Teatro Albeniz, C/de la Paz 11, ℘ 91 531 8311. The Albeniz is the centrepiece of the autumn festival, and puts on a wide range of dance and music, showcasing visiting international companies, as well as domestic contemporary productions.

Alternative

Perhaps the best-known and consistently creative fringe theatre in Madrid is the **Sala Triángulo** in the Lavapiés district on Zurita 20, ☎ 91 530 6991. The theatre hosts a couple of festivals every year, as well as children's events.

Teatro Alfil, C/del Pez. Something of a institution on Madrid's alternative scene, the Alfil is a comfortable-sized theatre with a cabaret feel lent by the in-house bar and tables and chairs. Recently rescued from closure by internationally known comedy group Yllana, the focus is increasingly on humour, and the theatre is venue to one of Europe's best comedy festivals in spring.

Cuarta Pared, C/Ercilla 17, ☎ 91 517 2317. Again, tucked away in the Lavapiés area, the Cuarta Pared offers dance, as well as some of the capital's best new writing.

English language works can often be found at the **Ensayo 100**, C/Raimundo Lulio 20, ☎ 91 447 9486, as well as at the **Teatro de las Aguas**, C/las Aguas 8, ☎ 91 366 9642.

El Canto de la Cabra, C/San Gregorio, ☎ 91 310 4222. One of the more experimental theatre groups, featuring the work of contemporary writers, both Spanish and international. In summer, they perform outdoors on the adjoining square.

El Montanargas, C/Antollón, ☎ 91 526 1133. A lively cultural association which runs a wide range of events, including children's shows, cabaret, workshops and very creative theatre.

Fashion   210
Books, Records and News   211
Specialities   211
Sweet Nuns   212
Markets   213
Sweet Treats   213
Oddments   214

Shopping

Fashion

Madrid has not one fashion centre, but several, each with its own distinctive character. For designer labels, the streets to head for are those criss-crossing the self-confidently prosperous Salamanca district, north of the Retiro: Serrano, Goya, Claudio Cuello, Velázquez and Ortega y Gasset (Ⓜ Serrano, Velázquez, Núñez de Balboa). Spain's best-known names are here, including **Adolfo Domínguez**, Serrano 18, ✆ 91 577 82 80, Ⓜ Serrano, with sober, beautifully cut clothes for men and women; **Agatha Ruiz de la Prada**, Goya 4, ✆ 91 577 27 11, Ⓜ Serrano, offering more expressive, outgoing designs; and **Sybilla**, C/Jorge Juan 12, Madrid's legendary fashion trail-blazer, who keeps on creating exciting collections. Here too are the international fashion celebrities, such as **Chanel**, **Kenzo**, **Giorgio Armani** and **Gianni Versace** (all on C/Ortega y Gasset).

No trip to Madrid is complete without taking in **Loewe**, Serrano 26, ✆ 91 435 30 56, Ⓜ Serrano. Among the best designed, and most expensive, leather goods in Spain, along with dinky, more affordable accessories for men and women. For delicate underwear, **Meye Maier**, Jorge Juan 12, ✆ 91 575 36 54, Ⓜ Retiro.

For affordable mainstream fashion for men and women, the Calle de la Princesa between Argüelles and Moncloa metro stations is the best hunting ground, with particularly rich pickings at sale time. Shoe shops abound: **Bravo**, C/Princesa 58, for quality designs; **Camper**, C/Princesa 75, for more rugged styles; and **Iris**, C/Princesa 70, for rock-bottom prices. There is a branch of the department store **El Corte Inglés** here, near Argüelles metro, and branches of Madrid's favourite fashion chains, such as **Mango**, C/Princesa 68, selling relaxed fashions with individual touches, and **Zara**, C/Princesa 45. Most Madrileñan women have at least one or two Zara outfits in their wardrobe though not all would admit it—the shop specializes in young fashions and designer copies at affordable prices.

Madrid's more *outré* street fashion shops are more scattered. At **Buggin**, Pza. de Cascorro 7 (Ⓜ La Latina, *open on Sundays to catch the nearby Rastro trade*), the assistants bop about to pounding techno among the display of club clothes—currently tiny T-shirts and dayglo mini backpacks. **Marihuana**, C/Duque de Alba, Ⓜ Tirso de Molina, sells biker fashion—heavy metal band shirts, skull hip flasks and goblets, chunky watches, and Harley Davidson branded gear. Finally, if you're planning a night on the town and nothing less than a skin-tight zebra print skirt will do, make a bee-line for **Glam**, C/Hortaleza 62, Ⓜ Gran Vía.

Marks & Spencer is big in Spain. The four-floor emporium on Serrano 52, ✆ 91 520 0000, Ⓜ Serrano, has everything from undies to chicken tikka sandwiches.

Books, Records and News

La Casa del Libro, Gran Vía 29, Ⓜ Gran Vía, claims to be Spain's largest book-shop—there are several floors of it, including an English language section. For scholarly and obscure matters about Spain in any language, try **Meissner**, C/Ortega y Gasset, Ⓜ Núñez de Balboa. The charming little **Most Madrid** book-shops have a small selection in English. For English titles, the capital's best shop is **Booksellers**, José Abascal 48, ✆ 91 442 7959, Ⓜ Ríos Rosas. There is an excellent travel bookshop, **Añosluz**, C/Francisco de Ricci 8, Ⓜ Argüelles, which will have any specialized books on Spain as well as guides and maps to all cities.

The French chain **FNAC** has a characteristically massive branch off the Puerta del Sol at C/Preciados 28, Ⓜ Callao, Sol, with row upon row of CDs, videos, video games, books, magazines and newspapers, and a concert ticket agency. **Madrid Rock**, Gran Vía 25, Ⓜ Gran Vía, is also large but somehow less overwhelming.

Foreign newspapers are sold at the larger stands around the Puerta del Sol, Gran Vía, Calle de Alcalá, Plaza de Cibeles, and in the Salamanca district.

Specialities

If you don't make the trip to Toledo, which has almost as many tacky gift shops as tapas bars, you can simulate the experience in Madrid at two neighbouring shops, **El Escudo de Toledo**, Pza. Canovas del Castillo 4, and the self-deludingly named **Objetos de Arte Toledano**, Pso. del Prado 10, Ⓜ Banco de España, by splurging on decorated swords, penknives, and souvenir ashtrays. All branches of **El Corte Inglés** have a souvenir department. **Monsy**, Plaza Mayor 20, ✆ 91 548 1514, also piles up the tourist tack, and even offers replicas of the sword of El Cid.

For something genuinely Spanish, original and tasteful, the porcelain produced by Galician cooperative **Sargadelos**, C/Zurbano 46, ✆ 91 310 4830, is among the most distinctive anywhere, and notable for its lovely deep blues and translucent whites. Its modern designs are based on traditional themes. **El Caballo Cojo**, C/Segovia 7, ✆ 91 366 4390, Ⓜ Sol/Opera, has an attractive 19th-century shop-front, behind which you will find an astonishing range of exquisite ceramics, handicrafts and furniture.

For the widest selection of flamenco recordings, as well as books on the subject, and even those dancing shoes you now need, **El Flamenco Vive**, C/Unión 4, ✆ 91 547 3917, Ⓜ Opera, is essential.

Those who have acquired a taste for salt cod can stock up at **La Casa del Bacalao**, C/Marqués de Urquijo 1, Ⓜ Argüelles, a tiny, traditional, marble-floored emporium of the stuff. The best place for olive oil is the exhaustively stocked **Patrimonio**

Comunal Olivarero, C/Mejía Lequerica 1, Ⓜ Tribunal. The **Aceite di Oliva Virgen,** on the corner of C/Meija Lequica and C/de Hortaleza is another fine place to pick up excellent olive oil, although it is notorious for its haughty staff.

For *turrón*, the almond nougat that was once made by Toledo's religious communities, you can do no better than **Casa Mira**, Carrera de San Jerónimo 30, Ⓜ Sol, an ancient shop which also sells all sorts of other luscious goodies.

For an incredible array of delicious *embutidos*, hams and cheeses, try **Jamonería Ferpal** C/Arenal 7, Ⓜ Sol, or one of the five branches of the **Museo del Jamón**, such as the one at Carrera de San Jerónimo 6, Ⓜ Sol, which feature spectacular displays of suspended hams. You can taste them at the counter or in one of their vast cafeterias. **El Palacio de los Quesos**, C/Mayor 53, Ⓜ Sol/Opera, is an atmospheric old shop which, in addition to its exhaustive range of cheeses, also sells fine wines and other Spanish delicacies.

Casa Seseña, C/Cruz 23, Ⓜ Sol, with its incredible window displays, is the place to go for traditional *madrileño* velvet-lined capes, *mantillas* and beautifully embroidered Manila shawls; Spanish guitars are made at the **Guitarrería Manzano**, C/Santa Ana 12, Ⓜ La Latina, and sold at **Garrido-Bailén**, C/Bailén 19, Ⓜ Opera, which has a stock of musical instruments from all over the world. For both traditional and modern ceramics and tiles from some of Spain's best craftsmen, head for **Cerámica El Alfar**, C/Claudo Coello 112, Ⓜ Núñez de Balboa, or **Antigua Casa Talavera**, C/Isabel la Católica 2, Ⓜ Santo Domingo.

Madrid has surprisingly few shops devoted to ethnic *artesanía* from Latin America, but it's worth paying a visit to **Ayllu**, C/Sombreretel, Ⓜ Lavapiés, for textiles and jewellery, or to **El Quetzal de las Indias**, C/Mayor 13, Ⓜ Sol; for something rather special, the shop at the **Museo de America**, Avda. Reyes Católicos 6, Ⓜ Moncloa, has a small but beautifully chosen selection of gifts.

Sweet Nuns

The cloistered nuns in Madrid still earn their way in the world by baking and selling their goods on revolving drums that preserve their privacy. The **Convento de Las Carboneras,** C/Codo off Plaza de la Villa, Ⓜ Opera or Sol, make a choice of 11 different sweets, including almond pastries, tasty dry biscuits called the 'bones of Fray Escobas', *mantecados* (butter cakes) and *tocinitos de cielo* ('heavenly bacon'—a rich caramel custard). The **Salesas**, C/de San Bernardo 72, Ⓜ San Bernardo, make delicious *pastas de Santa Eulalia*, a pastry invented by one of the nuns, as well as plum cake, tea biscuits and *mantecados*. For similar delicacies, as well as marmalade, honey, and candies made in convents across Spain, visit **El Torno**, at Joaquín María López 28, Ⓜ Moncloa.

Markets

Madrid's most celebrated flea market is **El Rastro**, which takes over the La Latina district every Sunday morning, starting at Plaza de Cascorro and flooding down the Calle de Ribera de Curtidores and into the neighbouring streets and squares. The best time to visit is early in the morning, from autumn to spring: in summer the crowds are thicker and the spread of stalls thinner, and by mid-morning it's already hot. Once devoted solely to antiques and curios (this is the speciality of many of the permanent shops in this district), there are now stalls selling all sorts of junk— cheap shoes, jewellery, belts and bags; second-hand, ethnic, and new-age fashions; plants; household goods; pirate tapes; and rack after rack of sunglasses. If it's antiques and curios you're after, head for the Calle Mira el Río Baja and its neigh- bours. There are good bric-a-brac stalls in the Pza. del General Vara de Rey, and a few more upmarket shops in the sadly characterless **Mercado Puerta de Toledo**, Ronda de Toledo 1. The Pza. del Campillo del Mundo Nuevo is the place for plants and old books. Now that the Rastro has become as popular with tourists as with *madrileños*, the bargains are harder to come by, but if you've the time, and room in your suitcase, the shops and stalls are worth a look. Remember to keep an eye on your belongings. The lively **Mercado de las Maravillas** (*see* p.134) is just north of the Nuevos Ministerios (Ⓜ Alvarado).

The **Mercado de Antón Martín**, C/Santa Isabel 5, Ⓜ Antón Martín, is one of the most central of Madrid's bustling *castizo* food markets, with two floors of perma- nent stalls selling all manner of fresh produce (*open 9–2 and 5.30–8.30*). The **Mercado de San Miguel**, Pza. de San Miguel, Ⓜ Sol, also very central, is smaller but worth visiting for a glimpse of its bizarrely ornate ironwork exterior. Market shoppers should be aware that the melée round a busy stall is actually the *madrileño* version of an organized queue. The convention is that each new arrival calls out *¿Quién es el último?* ('Who's last?') in order to find out their place in the serving order—often the cue for a great deal of good-natured argy-bargy and verbal jostling for position. Nobody would dream of standing in line.

Sweet Treats

Madrid is full of shop windows piled high with goodies that will make your mouth water. **Viena Capellanes**, C/de Genoa 4. Deliciously rich cakes, fine wines and coffees. **Felipe Sanchez**, Pza. del Humiladero, is a traditional, endearingly shabby establishment with all manner of nuts, caramels and sweets lined up in great bas- kets and drawers lining the walls. The **Viena Capellanes**, C/de Génova 4, Ⓜ Alonso Martínez, sells deliciously rich cakes, fine wines and coffees, and **El Riojan**, C/Mayor 10, Ⓜ Sol/Opera, has a deservedly high reputation for sump- tuous *pâtisserie*.

Oddments

Just in case you haven't found anything that really catches your eye, the following is a list of some of Madrid's more unusual establishments:

Matys, C/Victoria 2 (near church of St Gínes), everything for the serious flamenco dancer, from castanets in different woods and sizes and low wide-brimmed black hats, to *mantillas* and exquisite haircombs.

Nueva Parisien, C/Montera, is a tiny old fashioned shop with exquisite little costume buttons, diamante and feathers.

Simón, C/de Hortaleza (just of the Gran Vía). Every kind of sword from teeny weeny ones to samurai-sized hulks.

Narciso Martínez, C/Espos y Mina 18, is one of the world's top specialists in moustache combs.

Articulos de Ballet, C/de Pria (by Plaza del Oriente). Tiny flouncy tutus for baby ballerinas.

PROVINCIA
DE
MADRID

BUZON 6

Living and Working in Madrid

Long Term Residence
and Finding a Job   216

Finding Somewhere to Stay   217

Help and Services   217

Madrid poses less problems than most other European cities when it comes to finding work and somewhere to live. Indeed, in a country with more than 20 per cent unemployment, English-speaking foreigners will often find it easier to get started here than Spaniards arriving from the provinces.

The capital boasts a substantial ex-pat community, many of whom were lured here in the middle and late 1980s by the Movida, the cultural and economic boom which followed the arrival into office of the socialists. English teaching and translating work are not difficult to find, and in a city where eating and drinking is a way of life, there is plenty of work to be found in bars and restaurants.

However, Spanish bureaucracy can be tiresome. Anybody thinking seriously about setting up here, even if just for a year or so, should hire the services of a *gestor*, who will deal with all the paperwork involved in registering, through to your tax return, VAT, driving licence, and even your flat rental. English speaking *gestors* are listed below; or else look in the Yellow Pages or ask anybody already living here to recommend somebody.

Long-term Residence and Finding a Job

For visits of under three months, EU, American, Canadian and New Zealand citizens do not require a visa. Those intending to stay longer are required by law to register with the police within fifteen days of arrival to begin the process of obtaining a *permiso de residencia*, or **residency permit**. However, as passports are no longer stamped on entry, just when you begin this process effectively depends on you.

The police office dealing with foreigners' **registration** is located at the Comisaria de Extranjería at C/Los Madrazo, 9, © 91 521 9350. To work legally, you must have a residency permit.

If you do not have a firm offer of work, or better still, a contract, then you must either show proof of being able to support yourself during your stay, or register as an *autonomo*, or self-employed. Again, the first step is the *permiso de residencia*. You then head for the tax office, where you will have to declare the nature of your profession.

From there the next stop is the Seguridad Social, or social security. Here things can get a little complicated, and the advice of a *gestor*—a combination of a solicitor and a notary public—is useful in determining the best tax bracket to register in. You will be required to make a yearly tax declaration, and if you wish to use the public health system, to pay a monthly contribution.

American citizens be warned. It is best to consult the Spanish consulate in your home town or state. Otherwise you may have to make a return trip for such documents as a statement from the local police vouching for your good conduct.

One final point. Once you have residency and you wish to drive, you are required to exchange your driving licence for a Spanish one. If you wish to avoid doing this, then when driving, always carry your passport, and never show you residency permit as proof of identity when stopped by the police. The down side of this is that you are required to pay all fines on the spot.

Finding Somewhere to Stay

Shared accommodation is common in Madrid. If you're here for the first time, it offers a cheap, quick solution, with the added benefit of plugging you in to a social scene which can often lead to work. Flat shares can be found on notice boards in the city's numerous Irish pubs, as well as in *Segundamano*—a thrice weekly publication offering all types of rented accommodation, jobs and second-hand goods.

If you prefer to live alone, again, *Segundamano* is the best source. Avoid agencies unless you are prepared to pay a month's rent in commission. Another method is to find the area you want, and trek round looking for small advertisements in windows, or asking the porter in apartment blocks.

The most sought-after accommodation is in the 65,000 ptas to 100,000 ptas, which should bring you a one- or two-bedroomed flat reasonably close to the city centre. However, if you're prepared to travel half an hour by bus or metro, you can get a lot more for your money. Most apartments are still furnished, *amueblado*. As a rule of thumb, the south of the city is the cheapest, the north and north west the most expensive. Bargains can be found just over the river, west of the centre.

Increasingly, landlords ask either for a *nomina*, or work contract, or an *aval bancario*, proof from your bank that you can pay the rent; one month in advance, and a month's deposit is the norm. Contracts are legally valid for a five-year stay, renewable on a yearly basis at your discretion. Anybody stipulating a shorter period than five years is liable to offer a discount. Rents can only legally be increased on a yearly basis, in accordance with inflation. Again, if you are thinking about a long stay, a *gestor* will check the contract for you.

Help and Services

Gestorias: Gestoria Calvo Canga, Plaza Tirso de Molina 12, ✆ 91 369 3503, is as good a place to start as any in acquiring your residency, as well as dealing with tax problems. Work Manager, Bravo Murillo 3, ✆ 91 593 9622, is run by women, friendly, and among the least expensive.

Computers: Micro Rent, General Yague 10, 6F, ✆ 91 597 3282, rents both Apple and PCs on a daily, weekly or monthly basis. Also has a range of other office equipment. Bitmailer, Juan Bravo 5, ✆ 91 402 1551, *www.bitmailer.com*, provides internet service with good backup.

Couriers: UPS Centro de Transportes de Madrid, Carretera de Villaverde a Vallecas, km 3.5, ✆ 91 507 0888, has an overnight international and national courier service. Call by 5pm for a 7pm pickup.

Language courses: International House, Zurbano 8, ✆ 91 310 1314, is the best-known and has a solid reputation. Courses to suit all needs.

Messengers: Trebol, Esperanza 3, ✆ 91 530 3232, offers a cycle messenger service that is fast, cheap and environmentally friendly. They also offer international and national deliveries at competitive prices.

Moving: SIT Transportes International, SA, Gran Vía 66, ✆ 91 541 9494, provide a door-to-door service throughout the world.

Translation services: CL Servicios Linguisticos, Fuencarral 123, ✆ 91 448 5861, will handle anything from a conference to letters (English, German and French).

El Escorial	224
Valle de los Caídos	228
Segovia	229
Ávila	238
Alcalá de Henares, Guadalajara and Sigüenza	224
Aranjuez	249
Toledo	251

Day Trips

Beyond the caprice of Charles V and Philip II, Madrid's location made it the logical site for Spain's capital. Not only is it roughly central to the country as a whole, but its growth filled a vacuum at the centre of a region containing many of the most important cities of 16th-century Spain. Philip's new capital thus had a sort of ready-made Île-de-France around it, a garland of historic and lovely towns, each with something different to offer the

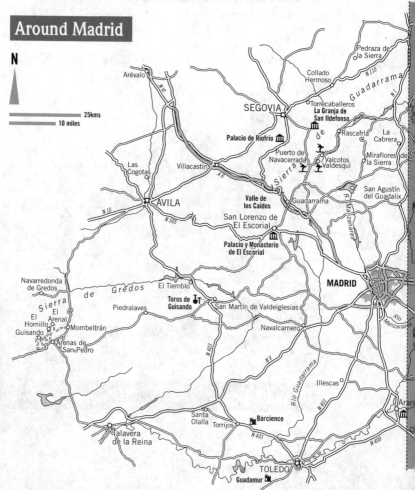

Around Madrid

N

25kms
10 miles

Pedraza de la Sierra

Collado Hermoso

N 110

N I

Guadarrama

Arévalo

N VI

SEGOVIA

Torrecaballeros

La Granja de San Ildefonso

Rascafría

La Cabrera

Palacio de Riofrío

Sierra

Puerto de Navacerrada

Valcotos Valdesquí

Miraflores de la Sierra

Las Cogotas

Villacastín

A 6

de

San Agustín del Guadalix

R. Manzanares

ÁVILA

N 10

N 505

Valle de los Caídos

Guadarrama

San Lorenzo de El Escorial

Palacio y Monasterio de El Escorial

MADRID

Navarredonda de Gredos

Sierra

de

Gredos

El Tiemblo

Toros de Guisando

San Martín de Valdeiglesias

El Hornillo

El Arenal

Mombeltrán

Piedralaves

Navalcarnero

Río Manzanares

Guisando

Arenas de San Pedro

N 403

N V

Río Guadarrama

Illescas

Aran

Santa Olalla

Torrijos

Barcience

N 401

N 400

Talavera de la Reina

N 403

TOLEDO

Guadamur

visitor and easy to escape to whenever Madrid's traffic, cacophonous nightclubs and endless museum corridors become too much. Everyone goes to **Toledo**, of course, and romantically beautiful **Segovia** also comes in for its share of travellers. But beyond these, you may also conveniently use Madrid as a base for visiting **Ávila**, resolutely medieval behind its famous walls, the distinguished old university town of **Alcalá de Henares**, quiet, seldom-visited **Sigüenza**, the royal palaces at **Aranjuez**, or **El Escorial**.

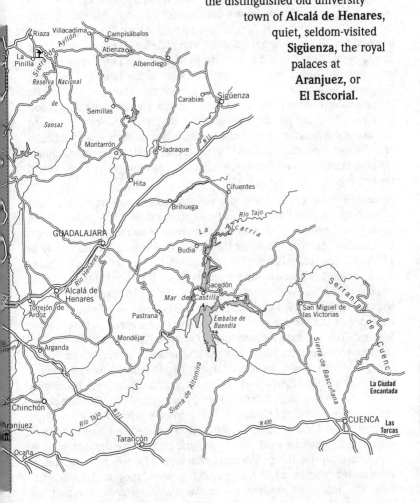

El Escorial

The Spaniards aren't shy; they matter-of-factly refer to Philip II's combination palace-secretariat-monastery-mausoleum as 'the eighth wonder of the world'. Any building with a façade 660ft wide and 2673 windows is entitled to some consideration, but it's not so much the glass and stone of the Escorial that make it remarkable, but the neurotic will of the king who conjured it up. This is the vortex of Spain, full of magnificence and poison, a folly on an imperial scale. To the Protestants of northern Europe, hard pressed to keep Philip's armies and priests at bay, this building was a diabolic horror, the seat of evil on earth. Philip himself would have calmly disagreed (for he was always calm), explaining that what he really had in mind was the re-creation of the Temple of Solomon. Despite all the effort Philip expended in stamping out heretical opinions in his long reign, he seems to have entertained on the sly quite a few of his own, possibly picked up during his years spent in the Low Countries. He found geomancers to select the proper site for the millennial temple, astrologers to pick the date for laying the corner stone, and hermetic philosophers to help with the numerical mysticism that is supposedly built into every proportion of the building.

An *escorial* is a slag-heap. There once was some sort of mine on this site—and so the proper title of Philip's dream-house translates as the Royal Seat of the Royal Saint Lawrence of the Slagheap. The reasons for the dedication to San Lorenzo are unclear. Supposedly Philip won a victory on the saint's day in 1557, at St Quentin in Flanders, and vowed to build him something in return; this is unlikely, as the dedication wasn't made until 10 years after El Escorial was completed. An even less probable tale has Philip's architects planning this rectangle of buildings and enclosed courtyards as an echo of the saint's gridiron attribute (San Lorenzo was roasted alive on one; he is supposed to have told the Romans: 'You can turn me over now; I'm done on this side'). While San Lorenzo is not one of the most popular saints, there's an obscure legend that he brought the Holy Grail to Spain, and this may help to explain the tangled web of esotericism behind Philip's work. Philip's original architect, Juan Bautista de Toledo, had worked on St Peter's in Rome; you may find that these two chilly, overblown symbols of the Counter-Reformation have much in common. Work commenced in 1563, but Bautista died four years later, and the Escorial was entrusted to his brilliant pupil, Juan de Herrera, who saw the task through to its completion in 1584. It kept him busy; even though Herrera had little time to spare on any other buildings, his reputation as one of the great Spanish architects was made. By creating the *estilo desornamentado*, stripping the Renaissance building to its barest essentials, he captured perfectly the nation's mood of austere militancy. Philip was more than pleased, and as he contemplated the rising work from the spot on the hills above the Escorial still called 'King Philip's Seat' he must have dreamed just a little of the dawn of a new classic age, where Christianity and Renaissance achievement were combined in the spiritually perfect world empire of Spain.

If you come to the Escorial for a classic revelation, you'll have to settle for dry classicism; those who have read too much about the dark side of Philip's Spain and come expecting a monkish haunted house will be equally disappointed. As huge as it is, there's nothing gloomy or menacing about the Escorial. Its crisp lines and soft grey granite combine for an effect that is tranquil and airy both inside and out. Everything is remarkably clean, as if dust and age had been banished by royal decree; somehow the Escorial looks as bright and new as the day it was completed.

Getting There

By train: Trains to El Escorial (Cercanías line C 8a or Regionales line R 1, direction Ávila) start from Madrid-Atocha, and also stop at Madrid-Chamartín. The journey takes about an hour, and there are usually hourly departures in the daytime, and more at peak times, so it would be possible to combine Ávila with El Escorial for a slightly hectic day-trip. The trains arrive at the neighbouring village of El Escorial and are met by local buses for San Lorenzo and the monastery. The alternative to this short bus ride is a gentle 2km walk uphill from the station, along a fragrant avenue shaded by chestnuts and pines, past the Casita del Príncipe (*see* below). RENFE information, Madrid: ℗ 91 328 9020; El Escorial: ℗ 91 850 5390.

By bus: Keep in mind that the proper name of the town beside the monastery is San Lorenzo de El Escorial, and it appears that way in bus schedules. The bus, nos. 661 and 664, is faster than the train, and is run by Herranz, ℗ 91 543 3645 or ℗ 91 850 5390, from bay 3 of the Intercambiador de Transportes (bus interchange) next to the Moncloa metro stop in Madrid, to the stop in Pza. Virgen de Gracia in San Lorenzo, very near the monastery (*buses every half hour in the morning, every hour thereafter, daily, journey time 1hr*). Herranz also has a once-daily service from San Lorenzo to the Valle de los Caídos, allowing enough time to see the place (the journey takes 20mins). Tickets are sold from a little office in a bar on C/Reina Victoria; the bar also has bowling lanes, so you can get in a few frames while reflecting on Habsburg eccentricity.

By car: From Madrid take the NVI (Ctra. de La Coruña) northwest, then the M505.

C/Floridablanca 10, ✆ 91 890 1554, near the bus station.

Palacio y Monasterio de San Lorenzo el Real de El Escorial

Open Tues–Sun 10–7; closed Mon; adm exp; free for EU passport holders on Wed.

El Escorial is managed by the Patrimonio Nacional. They sell tickets, guidebooks and souvenirs inside the north entrance. They also run guided tours, in various languages, for which there is no extra charge; if you want to join one, you may be asked to wait for a large enough group to gather. If you prefer, you can explore the complex independently, in any order you like (the official tour route is clearly sign-posted). However, without any guidance, you may miss out on a lot of intriguing details, such as the many manifestations of Philip's obsession with mystical patterns in designing and building the place. You may also find, as you make your way from chamber to chamber and up and down dim stone staircases, that you quickly lose all sense of direction, and fail to appreciate, for example, the strategic location of the royal mausolea and Philip's apartments in relation to the Basilica. (James Michener was not ashamed to admit he came here twice without realizing it had a church, though a 13,000 sq m basilica with a 90m-high dome would else-where be hard to miss.) Admission to the Basilica only is free—you can walk right in, through the monumental western entrance, under the statue of San Lorenzo with his gridiron, and from here, along the central axis of the complex, the sym-metrical grandeur of Bautista and Herrera's plan will begin to unfold.

Palacio de los Borbones and Nuevos Museos

The official tours begin in the northeastern quarter of the Escorial, a quarter never used by Philip II, but converted by the Bourbons Carlos III and Carlos IV into a royal residence. These two do not seem to have had any interest in Philip's conception of the Escorial, but used it only as a sort of glorified hunting-lodge. Not surprisingly, they refurbished these rooms as a similar, though smaller version of the Bourbon Royal Palace in Madrid. The **Bourbon Apart-ments,** with their tapestries after works by Goya and others, have now been restored to their former splendour, and they form a pleasant contrast to the aus-terity of their surroundings. Sadly, one of the most interesting rooms, the **Hall of the Battles**, with its fresco nearly 62m long representing every detail of the 1431 Battle of Higuerela, a victory of King Juan II over the Moors of Granada, is under restoration and closed to the public.

Downstairs there is an exhibition of some of the machinery and tools used to build the complex, plus architectural drawings and scale models tracing the progress of the construction work through its various stages of completion. Upstairs again, the **New Museums** occupy a long corridor along the eastern walls, with windows looking out over intricate knot gardens. Much of Philip's collection of paintings is displayed here, including works by Bosch, Patinir and Dürer; later additions include a Velázquez.

Palacio de Philip II

Such is the reputation Philip earned for himself—the evil genius of the Inquisition and all—that it comes as a genuine surprise to visit the little palace he tacked onto the back of the Escorial for himself. Few kings anywhere have ever chosen a more delightful abode: a few simple rooms reminiscent of the interiors from paintings of Vermeer, with white walls, Delft-blue tiles, and big windows opening to gardens and forests on all sides. These rooms suggest that Philip's famous self-isolation had less of the monkishness about it than the desire of a cultured, bookish monarch to ensure the necessary serenity for the execution of the royal duty he took so seriously. Philip did not like courtiers, and he didn't care to go out. Alone with his trusted secretaries, he governed the affairs of his empire meticulously, reading, re-reading and annotating vast heaps of documents and reports. Aesthete and mystic, he approached politics with the soul of a clerk, and each of all the long list of mistakes he made was decided upon with the greatest of care.

It was here that Philip received nervous, respectful ambassadors on a throne 'hardly grander than a kitchen chair'. Here, in his perfect temple, where the wisdom of Solomon was to be reborn, they brought him the news of the Armada's disaster, the national bankruptcies, the independence of the Netherlands, and all the little pinpricks in between. Here he endured the wasting disease that killed him, stinking so badly that neither servants nor visitors could bear his presence. He made sure his bed was situated right above the High Altar of his Basilica, and had a spy-hole cut in the bedchamber wall so that he could observe the endless Masses and bad art down below. With only that crowned skull on his night table to keep him company, here he awaited the reward of the virtuous.

The art and furnishings of the apartments may not necessarily be an accurate representation of Philip's tastes, but there is a copy Philip had made of Bosch's *Hay Wain*, one of his favourites, the original of which hangs in the Prado. In the throne room, be sure to see the marvellous inlaid wood **doors**, decorated with *trompe-l'oeil* scenes and architectural fantasies, done by an anonymous German artist of the 16th century; they are among the most beautiful things in the entire Escorial.

Mausoleums, Sacristy, Chapter House and Library

An opulent but narrow staircase leads down to the **Panteón Real**, situated beneath the Basilica's High Altar. All manner of stories have grown up around this pantheon of bad kings. Carlos II, it is said, spent whole days down here, ordering the gilded marble tombs to be opened so that he might gaze on his mummified ancestors. As in the Basilica, the most expensive stone from around the Mediterranean was used in its construction; the red jasper of the pavement and pilasters is so hard it had to be cut with diamond-tipped saws. The adjacent room is called, charmingly, the **Pudrería**, where Habsburg and Bourbon potentates spent 20-odd years mouldering until they became sufficiently dried out for their interments. Royal relations fill a maze of corridors beyond the Pantheon of the Kings, guarded by enormous white heralds with golden maces. Don Juan, victor of Lepanto, is the best known of them, though the tomb everyone notices is the tall, marble wedding-cake that was built to hold 60 baby princes and princesses; it is now more than half full. Don Juan, the father of the current king, Juan Carlos I, is the most recent addition. Don Juan got in, despite never having ruled, largely on the say so of his son. Beyond are the **Sacristía** (sacristy) and **Salas Capitulares** (chapter houses), which house some of the Escorial's collections of religious art.

One other section that may be seen is the **Biblioteca** (library) entered by a stair near the Escorial's main gate. Philip's books meant as much to him as his paintings. His librarian, Benito Arias Montano, contributed much to the esoteric conception of the Escorial, and he built Philip one of the largest collections of Greek, Hebrew and Arabic philosophical and mystical works in Europe. His agents watched over all the book-burnings of the Inquisition, and saved from the flames anything that was especially interesting. That his hoard of 40,000 volumes survives almost unchanged since Philip's day is due only to the benign neglect of the generations that followed; 18th-century travellers reported that the monks watching over the collection were all illiterate. The frescoes of 1590–2 that cover the vaulted ceiling, by the Italian Pellegrino Tibaldi, are an allegory of the seven liberal arts, portraying seven of the famous philosophers and scientists of antiquity. The large globe of nested spheres in the centre of the library is Philip's orrery, used in making astronomical calculations.

Basilica and Patio de los Reyes (Patio of the Kings)

Once inside the huge, square church, you will quickly become aware of the heightened atmosphere of a holy-of-holies. With very few windows, the Basilica was purposely kept dark as a contrast to the airiness of the rest of the Escorial. No church in Spain is colder inside; even in the hottest days of July the thin air seems pure distilled essence of Castile. Just inside the entrance, in the narrow **lower choir**, note the unusual ceiling and its 'flat vaulting', an architectural trick of very shallow vaulting that creates the illusion of flatness. It was far too daring for Philip II, who ordered Herrera to support it with a column. The architect complied, but in wood and plaster, which he dramatically kicked away in the presence of the king to prove his skill, only to earn his famous scolding from Philip: 'Juan de Herrera, Juan de Herrera, with kings one does not play games.'

From here, the eye is drawn to the bright *retablo*, framed in darkness. Its paintings are by several then-fashionable Italian artists, including Pellegrino Tibaldi, who like Juan Bautista was a pupil of Michelangelo. Above them all is a golden figure of Christ on the Cross, and at its foot a tiny golden skull that stands out even across the great distance; its hollow eyes seem to follow you as you pass through the Basilica. These are really only of gilded bronze; if they weren't, they wouldn't be here. Originally the Basilica was full of real gold ornaments, and the precious stones of the Tabernacle were some of the most valuable that the Spanish royal house possessed. Napoleon's troops did a thorough job of looting El Escorial in 1808, making off with them all. Connoisseurs that they were, they left the artwork in peace. Notable are the gilded bronze ensembles to the sides of the altar, the families of Charles V and Philip II (with all three of his wives) at prayer. Beneath the high altar is the *primera piedra*, the cornerstone of the Escorial. The west doors of the Basilica open onto the **Patio de los Reyes**, which is the Escorial's main courtyard, named after sculptures by Monegro representing six mighty Kings of Judah which adorn the church's western façade. On the far side of the courtyard is the west gate, the main ceremonial entrance to the Escorial, and to the right and left are the *colegio* and the monastery, which are both still in use, and are not open to the public. The two statues in the centre represent David and Solomon.

Beyond the Monastery

Two little country houses within walking distance of the Escorial are included in the admission ticket. The **Casita del Príncipe** and the **Casita de Arriba** (also known as the Casita del Infante), both built in the 1770s for Carlos IV, are tasteful, cosy and full of pretty pictures, and worth a visit if you just can't get enough of those Bourbons or you have time to kill before the bus comes. The Casita del Príncipe has neat, well-tended gardens in typically Spanish style, with box hedges laid out in knot patterns, and roses and shrubs flourishing among the fruit trees in the ancient orchards. It's worth taking a field guide to European trees on the walk down to the Casita del Príncipe: the **bosquecillo** has some magnificent examples, many well over 100 years old. Fans of Romantic architecture will enjoy a walk round the **Terreros** neighbourhood which runs down behind the Victoria Palace Hotel: there are several good value restaurants around here which cater to locals with summer houses in the area.

San Lorenzo de El Escorial

Since the building of the Escorial, a pleasant little town has grown up here. San Lorenzo has held on to its village atmosphere despite having an air of sophistication thrust upon it thanks to the presence of a private university and an influx of well-to-do settlers. *Madrileños*, keen to escape their city of baking concrete, are drawn here not only by the palace but also by the beauty of the setting in the cool, forested foothills of the Guadarramas. San Lorenzo is a much more attractive commuter base than any of Madrid's fringe of new-town suburbs, and, for urbanites, it's a popular summertime resort. The town boasts a tiny, exquisite theatre, the **Real Coliseo**, which was founded by Carlos III. It's a short walk from the Escorial at C/Floridablanca 20, ℗ 91 890 4411.

Eating Out

Beef from the Sierra de Guadarrama has been given its own denomination of origin, and if you're a meat-eater, there's nothing finer. Steeped in tradition, **Charolés**, C/Floridablanca 24, ℗ 91 890 59 75 (*expensive*) is the town's best. Its *cocido* takes some beating, and it offers excellent baked fish.

On the pretty Plaza de la Constitución, the **Fonda Génara**, Plaza San Lorenzo 2 (*moderate*), offers a terrific midday menu at around 1000 pts.

The **Erriuga**, Ventura Rodriguéz 7, ℗ 91 890 6136 (*moderate*), is a pleasant wine bar/restaurant which attracts a mainly local crowd. The cooking here is lighter, with the emphasis on game and fish.

Valle de los Caídos

Death is the patron saint of Spain.

Váldez Léal

If you're one of those who came to the Escorial expecting freakishness and gloom, don't be disappointed yet. From the town, there's a regular bus service to Francisco Franco's own idea of building for the ages. The **Valley of the Fallen** is supposedly meant as a memorial to soldiers from both sides of the Civil War, but it was old Republicans and other political unfortunates languishing in Franco's jails who did the work in the 1950s, blasting a 245m tunnel-like church out of the mountainside, and erecting a 150m stone cross above. The crowds of

Spaniards who come here in a holiday mood on any weekend seem to care little for history or politics; they linger at one of Spain's most outrageous souvenir stands, then take the children up the funicular railway to the base of the cross. For local colour, there'll be a few ancient widows in black who come every week, and perhaps a pair of maladjusted teenagers in Falangist blue shirts. If you find yourself in the area around 20 November, make the trek: it's the anniversary of the **Generalisimo's** death, attracting a strange mixture of followers.

The **cross**, held up by faith and structural steel, is claimed to be the largest in the world. Around its base are a series of titanic sculptured figures in some lost, murky symbolism: lions, eagles and pensive giants lurch out above you. The view takes in the hills and valleys for miles as well as the monastery Franco built for the monks who look after the **basilica** below.

This cave church is impressive, in the way the palace of a troll-king might be. The nave goes on and on, past giant, disconcerting Fascist angels with big swords, past dim chapels and holy images, finally ending in a plain, circular altar. José Antonio Primo de Rivera, founder of the Falangists, is buried here. His original interment in the royal crypt of the Escorial was too much even for many of Franco's supporters, and he eventually had to be moved here. Franco is here too; the company he chose for his last resting-place is perhaps the last word on what kind of man he really was. **Franco's tomb** is a plain stone slab on the floor near the altar, opposite José Antonio's. The gentlemen behind you in sunglasses and Hawaiian sports shirts are, if you haven't guessed, plain-clothes policemen, waiting for someone to try and spit on the old Caudillo.

Segovia

Segovia is within easy reach of Madrid as a day-trip, though as one of the most beautiful cities of Spain it is a place where you may wish to spend more time. Three distinct cultures have endowed this once-prominent town with three famous monuments. The Romans left Segovia a great aqueduct, and the age of Emperor Charles V (Carlos I of Spain) contributed an equally famous cathedral. The third, Segovia's Alcázar, should be as well known. Though begun by the Moors and rebuilt in the Middle Ages, its present incarnation is pure 19th-century fantasy, a lost stage set from a Wagnerian opera. Segovia has its other monuments—a unique style of Romanesque church, and the *esgrafiado* façades of its old mansions, but the memory the visitor takes away is likely to be mostly a fond impression. The delicate skyline silhouetted on a high narrow promontory between two green river valleys gives the city the appearance of a great ship among the rolling hills of Castile. To enter it is to climb into a lost medieval

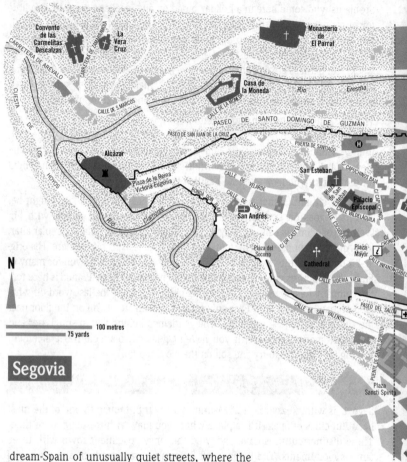

dream-Spain of unusually quiet streets, where the buildings are all of a single, lovely shade of warm, tan stone, making all old Segovia seem a single work of art.

When the Emperor Trajan built the aqueduct in the early 2nd century, Segovia was already a venerable city. Under Rome, and later the Visigoths and Moors, it attained little distinction, but it survived. After it fell to the Christians in the 11th century, Segovia blossomed in the great cultural and economic expansion of medieval Castile. Its Romanesque churches and palaces were built on the profits of an important textile industry, and by the time of the Catholic kings it was one of the leading cities of Spain.

Like most of Europe's medieval cities that have survived intact, Segovia's present-day serenity hides a dark secret. The economic policies and foreign wars of Charles V and Philip II ruined Segovia as thoroughly as the rest of Old Castile, and it is only the four centuries of stagnation that followed that allow us to see old Segovia as it was.

Getting There

By train: Unless you've a hankering for slow, uncomfortable train journeys, Segovia is better reached by bus. There are nine trains every weekday and seven daily at weekends from Madrid-Atocha (Regionales line R 2, via Villalba de Guadarrama), leaving at two minutes past the even hours, plus 3.02pm. The journey takes just over 2hrs. All trains pass through Madrid-Chamartín about 15mins after leaving Madrid-Atocha. The journey takes you through some rugged, craggy scenery, and there are good views of the huge cross of the Valle de los Caídos as the train approaches Los Molinos. Trains back to Madrid leave Segovia at 55 past the even hours. Segovia station is in the modern part of town, about 20 minutes' walk from the old city, or a short ride by local bus. RENFE information, Madrid: ✆ 91 328 9020, Segovia: ✆ 921 42 0774.

By bus: La Sepulvedana, a comfortable, modern fleet, runs 15 buses every weekday (fewer at weekends) from Paseo de la Florida 11, Madrid, to Segovia's bus station on the central Paseo Ezequiel González. The buses are much quicker than the train, taking around an hour, but cost a little more. La Sepulvedana information, Madrid: ✆ 91 530 4800, Segovia: ✆ 921 42 7707.

Segovia also has bus connections to Ávila (twice on weekdays, once each on Sat and Sun), Valladolid, La Granja, as well as all the villages in Segovia province.

Tourist Information

The main tourist office is at Plaza Mayor 10, ✆ 921 46 03 34, ✉ 921 44 27 34; even if it's closed, there's plenty of information posted up on the doors and windows outside. There's another office by the viaduct at Plaza del Azojuego 1, ✆ 921 44 02 05, ✉ 921 42 09 08.

Plaza Mayor and the Cathedral

Although new districts have grown out past the Roman aqueduct to the south and east, the **Plaza Mayor** (the former Plaza Franco) remains the centre of the old town, with its arcades and cafés. From here, the **Cathedral** (*open daily in summer 9–7; in winter Sun–Fri 9.30–1 and 3–6, Sat, hols, 9.30–6*) is just a stone's throw away. This has been called the 'last Gothic cathedral' of Spain; most of the work was done between 1525 and 1590, though parts were not completed until the 18th century. Segovia's old cathedral had been burned during the Comunero revolt, and Charles V contributed much to its replacement as an act of reconciliation. Juan Gil de Hontañón, who designed the Catedral Nueva at Salamanca, carried further here the tendencies of his earlier work. Segovia is finer in form and proportion than Salamanca, and less encumbered with ornament, expressing the national mood of austerity in grandeur in much the same way as El Escorial. The best parts of this cathedral are the semicircular eastern end, where an exuberant ascent of pinnacles and buttresses covers the chapels behind the main altar, the unique squarish bell-tower and an elegant dome over the choir. The latter two are Renaissance elements that fit in perfectly; in an age of architectural transition it was the greatest part of Juan Gil's accomplishment to make a harmonious combination of such diverse elements. The architect chose to be buried in the spare, well-lit interior. There's little to see on the inside—a comment on the hard times 16th-century Segovia had come into—and the small **museum** (*adm 200 pts*) inside is almost painful to visit. See the **cloister**, though, if it's open; this is part of the original cathedral, built in the Isabelline Gothic style by Juan Guas and moved here and reassembled after it survived the fire.

Alcázar

Open summer, 10–7, winter, 10–6; adm.

The **Alcázar**, jutting out on its cliffs over the confluence of the Río Eresma and the smaller Clamores, was one of the great royal residences of Castile when Segovia was at the height of its prominence. Alfonso the Wise spent much of his reign here, as did other kings of the 12th and 13th centuries. By the 19th, though, the old, forgotten castle had declined into a military school; in 1862, some young cadets set fire to it, in the hope they might be transferred to Madrid. No one, it seems, bothered to record the name of the architects who oversaw the Alcázar's restoration in the 1880s. Even worse, some writers have sniffed that the job they did is 'not authentic'. Just because these forgotten heroes of the picturesque saw fit to turn the Alcázar into a flight of fancy worthy of the Mad King Ludwig, with pointed turrets and curving crenellated walks, some people find fault. The German tourists look puzzled, and a little disappointed to find a castle on the Rhine in Castile; still they admit it's a very good Rhine castle. The Alcázar is *better* than authentic.

As if the architects had ordered them for effect, sombre ravens perch on the turrets and walls. The people of Segovia who look after the castle have joined in the fun, fitting out the interior in a fashion that would make the characters of any Sir Walter Scott novel feel quite at home. There are plenty of 14th-century cannons and armour, an harquebus or two, stained glass and dusty paintings of Visigothic kings. Some of the interiors survived the fire; there are fine *artesonado* ceilings in the Sala de Las Piñas and in the throne room, built by Enrique IV but furnished as it might have been in the days of Ferdinand and Isabel. The **Plaza** at the Alcázar's entrance, with old mortars left over from the days of the military school, was the site of Segovia's original cathedral.

Old Quarters and Romanesque Churches

Between the Cathedral and Alcázar lies the oldest district of Segovia. The *esgrafiado* work on some of the houses is a local speciality; a coat of stucco is applied, then scraped away around stencils to make decorative patterns. In a small plaza just west of the Cathedral stands the finest and most representative of Segovia's Romanesque churches, the 13th-century church of **San Esteban**, with a lively bell-tower in the Italian style. The arcaded porch around two sides of the church is the trademark of Segovia's Romanesque architecture. Porches like this adorned all the old churches, and most likely the old cathedral as well; in the Middle Ages they were busy places, serving as the centres of business and social life the way arcaded streets and squares do in other Spanish towns. Across the plaza is the **Palacio Episcopal** (Archbishop's Palace), its plain façade enlivened only by the reliefs of a serpent-woman and other curious medieval fancies over the entrance.

Within Segovia's walls, the streets meander languidly; to meander along with them is a treat, and fortunately the old town is small enough so that you will never get entirely lost. The medieval parish churches are everywhere: **San Andrés**, a solid, simple work from the 12th century on the Plaza Merced; the church of **La Trinidad** on the Plaza de Doctor Laguna, off Calle de la Trinidad, with an interior restored to something like its original appearance; **San Martín** on Calle Juan Bravo and **San Juan de los Caballeros** on the Plaza de Colmenares, both smaller versions of San Esteban (though both are older) with the characteristic arcades and towers. Calle Juan Bravo is named after the Segovian military leader of the Comunero revolt, who was executed after the defeat at Villalar in 1521. Segovia remembers enough of its ancient pride and liberty to keep him as a hero to this day, and his statue can be seen in the plaza. Nearby, the **Casa de los Picos** is another Segovia landmark, a 14th-century mansion with a façade like a waffle-iron, with protruding stone diamonds, a style copied in many later buildings in Spain and even one famous church in Naples.

One of Segovia's finest churches is outside the walls, near the centre of the new town on Avenida de Fernández Ladreda. **San Millán** is also the oldest, but the capitals of its arcade, charmingly sculpted with scenes from the Bible and from everyday life, have survived much more clearly than at the other churches.

The Aqueduct

Nothing else remains from Roman Segóbriga, but for the city to have merited such an elaborate water-supply it must have had nearly as many inhabitants as modern Segovia's 50,000. Trajan, one of the Spanish emperors of the Roman Empire, most likely ordered its construction. Its two-storey arcade rises 39m over the busy Plaza Azoguejo below, making it the tallest surviving Roman aqueduct.

The Romans, antiquity's master plumbers, did not build it there just to show off. An aqueduct's purpose is to bring water from a distant source, in this case the Río Frío, several kms to the east. Over the length of it a constant downward slope must be maintained to sustain the flow, and wherever it crosses a valley like this an arcade must be built to keep the flow level. The actual water-course, a channel cut into the stone and lined with lead, is at the very top. What you see here is only a small part of the system; the Romans built an underground water course from here to the Alcázar, and from the other end you can follow the arcade, ever shallower as the ground rises, up Calle Fernán García from the Plaza Azoguejo and right out of the city.

Note the notches cut into the rough stone on the arcade; these allowed for attaching scaffolding for the higher levels, and for block and tackles to hoist up the heavier stones. The Romans never cut corners; this was built for the centuries to come, and most likely would have survived unchanged had not several of the arches been destroyed in a siege by the Moors in the 11th century. Some 400 years later, Queen Isabel hired the monks of El Parral monastery to oversee the reconstruction, and when they had finished, they replaced the little statue of Hercules that had stood in a niche over the centre with an image of the Virgin Mary.

A Templar Church and a Rogue's Retreat

Do not by any means leave Segovia without a walk through the valley of the Eresma. Through either of the old *mudéjar* gates in the city's northern walls, the road leads down to the river through willow and poplar woods dotted with wild flowers. Following the road under the walls of the Alcázar, you cross the river and arrive at the church of **La Vera Cruz** (*open summer, Tues–Sun 10.30–1.30 and 3.30–7; winter, Tues–Sun 10.30–1.30 and 3.30–6, closed Mon and all Nov; adm*), one of the most interesting surviving Templar foundations, standing on a low hill in open countryside.

The church was built in 1208, and with the dissolution of the Templars in 1312 it became a regular parish church. The last few centuries have seen it abandoned, and its relic of the True Cross (*la vera cruz*), a sliver of wood, moved to the little village of Zamarramala, 1.6km away. Today the church is used by a Catholic brotherhood that grandiosely styles itself the 'Knights of St John'. Like many Templar churches, this one is round, with 12 sides; at its centre is the two-storeyed chamber, the 'inner temple' where the Templar secret rites took place, as opposed to the 'outer temple' which belonged to the common Church rituals.

None of the paintings or furnishings are as old as the Templars, but one 15th-century picture of the Last Supper, with the apostles seated at a round table, is worth a look. You may climb the bell-tower for one of the best views of Segovia and the Alcázar, taking in a number of churches and monasteries nearby in this holy valley, now largely unused. The closest, the 17th-century **Convento de las Carmelitas Descalzas** (*open daily 10–1 and 4–7*) has the tomb of the gentle St John of the Cross—or what's left of him since, like that of any Spanish saint, his corpse was chopped up finely for holy relics.

To reach the most interesting of the monasteries, **El Parral** (*open daily 10–12 and 4–6.30*), retrace your steps from the Vera Cruz to the river and continue up the opposite bank. On the way you'll pass the remains of the **Moneda**, or mint, where American gold and silver were turned into coins before 1730. El Parral's founder, Juan Pacheco, Marqués de Villena, ranks among the slipperiest of all Castilian court intriguers. A protégé of the famous favourite Álvaro de Luna during the reign of Juan II, he played a role in the wars between the partisans of Isabel and Juana la Beltraneja by taking first one side, then the other, and occasionally both. He apparently chose this site because it had brought him luck—he had killed three men here in duels. In its day, El Parral was famous throughout Spain for its woods and gardens. The place is still lovely, and the long-neglected church has been restored, with a number of interesting tombs of famous Segovians (and some of the Marqués' illegitimate children).

Another Bourbon Palace: La Granja de San Ildefonso

Open summer Tues–Sun 10–6; winter Tues–Sat 10–1.30 and 3–5, Sun 10–2; closed Mon; adm, no charge for EU passport holders on Wed; gardens open summer 10–8; winter daily 10–6.

La Granja ('the farm'), 11km southeast of Segovia and linked by bus, is one of the works of Philip V, he of the insatiable appetite for palaces. The building has a certain rococo elegance of the sort American millionaires love to copy, but its fame has always been its **gardens**. Philip originally conceived La Granja as a scaled-down version of Versailles (his father, Louis XIV's, palace) and the gardens, laid out in the 1740s, completed the picture. There are some 28 hectares (70 acres) of them, with remarkable fountains everywhere, decorated with pretty pagan deities. However, there is only one day of the year when they all work, and it's worth watching them come alive: 25 August.

The palace itself is furnished in 18th-century French style, and contains an impressive collection of Spanish and French tapestries and some spectacular cut-glass chandeliers. You can visit the Crystal Factory where these were made, in the village of **San Ildefonso** (La Real Fábrica de Cristales, *open Wed–Sun 11–8, closed Mon and Tues; adm*).

Eating Out

More than anywhere else in Castile, Segovia takes dining seriously, and the streets around the Plaza Mayor and the Aqueduct are packed with dimly lit *típico* restaurants, each with a window heaped with a luxuriant display of fresh fish, furred and feathered game, bunches of thyme, rosemary and lavender, glistening heaps of offal, and, taking pride of place, a freshly butchered piglet. Here master *asadores* of reputation, bedecked in ribbons and medals, serve up Spain's best *cochinillo* (roast sucking-pig, traditionally only 21 days old and so tender that you can cut it with the blunt edge of a plate), along with roast milk-fed lamb and other formidably heavy Castilian specialities.

Heading the list for 50 years or so now has been the **Mesón de Cándido** Pza. Azoguejo 5, ✆ 921 45 59 11 (*expensive*), with its picturesque exterior (shown on most of Segovia's tourist brochures) beside the aqueduct. The late Señor Cándido was the expert—he used to write cookbooks on Castilian cuisine—and he played host to all the famous folk who have ever passed through Segovia (autographed photos on the walls, of course, to prove it). Dinners here will set you back *4000 pts*.

The young contender in Segovia is the **Restaurante José María**, off the Plaza Mayor at C/Cronista Lecea 11, ✆ 921 46 11 11, ✉ 921 46 0273 (*moderate*), where everything is first-rate (try the breaded frogs' legs, another local treat) and the prices kept relatively low. José María, who started his career as an apprentice under Cándido, is passionate about Castilian wines; he is the man responsible for bringing Segovia's excellent Ribera del Duero reds into the spotlight by serving them as his house wine, and he now owns his own vineyard, not far from the legendary vineyards of Pesquera and Vega Sicilia.

Other renowned *asadores* hold court at the **Casa Duque**, C/Cervantes 12, ✆ 921 43 0537 (*expensive*), **La Oficina**, C/Cronista Lecea 10, ✆ 921 43 1643 (*moderate*), and **El Bernardino**, C/Cervantes 2, ✆ 921 43 3225 (*moderate*). If, however, you fancy something a little more creative, try **La Cocina de Segovia**, Paseo Ezequiel González 26, ✆ 921 43 7462 (*moderate*).

Less expensive restaurants abound, in the same central areas, like the **Restaurante Lazaró** on C/Infanta Isabel (cheap *menú del día*, but you can get *cochinillo* here, too), and similar places on Calle Juan Bravo and the Plaza de San Martín. Sensitive souls should lay off the *sopa castellana* (spicy garlic soup served with a poached egg), especially in the cheaper places, where it's made with enough grease to lubricate a locomotive. It's not bad, though.

If all that roast flesh from Segovia is palling, then it's worth thinking about lunch in La Granja. **Zaca**, © 921 47 00 87 (*moderate*) is a small eatery only open at midday. Stews are the speciality. *Booking is essential at weekends.*

Ávila

For two cities so close together and with so much history in common, Segovia and Ávila could hardly appear more unlike. Chance, with a little help from the geography, has made them into stone images of complementary sides of the Spanish character. Secure on its natural hilltop fortress, Segovia had the leisure to become a city of kings and merchants, aesthetic and relaxed and full of trees. Ávila stands more exposed, and it has always had the air of a frontier camp, coarse and ugly, a city first of soldiers, and later of mystics.

Ávila's **walls** are its main attraction, the only complete circuit of fortifications around any Spanish city. Though medieval, they rest on Roman foundations, and their rectangular layout is the classic form of the Roman *castrum*. For Rome, this was a frontier post against the Celtic tribes they had displaced from the area, and after the 8th century Ávila found itself performing the same role in the constant wars between Moor and Christian. Through most of the 11th century it was the front line, often changing hands, until Alfonso VI decided in 1088 to construct these walls, built between 1090 and 1099, and make the town a secure base for further Christian advance.

Except for Saint Teresa, who was a native and spent much of her career as a writer and monastic reformer behind Ávila's walls, the town has been heard from but little since. For a proper view of the walls, though, you'll have to cross the River Adaja, leaving town on the Avenida de Madrid, and onto the N501, turning right over the bridge.

Getting There

Ávila is a little under 2hrs from Madrid by train or bus.

By train: Unlike Segovia, a train journey to Ávila is worth the effort, with spectacular scenery and a quicker ride. Trains on the Regionales line R 1 from Madrid, running roughly once an hour from Atocha and more frequently from Chamartín (via Villalba de Guadarrama and El Escorial) arrive at the station in the new town on Avda. José Antonio, a 10-minute walk from the city's old walls. Most of the trains to and from Galicia, Asturias, Salamanca and even the Basque provinces and Burgos pass through here. RENFE information, Madrid: ✆ 91 328 9020; Ávila ✆ 920 25 02 02.

By bus: The city bus station is nearby on the Avenida de Madrid. Buses from Madrid are run by Automóviles de Ávila, ✆ 91 530 3092, twice a day from Estación Sur, C/Méndez Álvarez (🚇 Méndez Álvarez) (✆ 91 468 4200); and by Empresa Larrea, ✆ 91 530 4800, three times a day from Pso. de la Florida 11. There are regular bus connections from Ávila to Segovia.

Tourist Information

Pza. de la Catedral 4, across the square from the cathedral, ✆ 920 21 13 87, 📠 920 25 37 17.

San Vicente

Modern Ávila has almost completely forsaken the old walled town. The bus and train stations are out in the eastern extension, and however you arrive you are likely to approach the historic centre from this direction. Here, just where the Avenida de Portugal reaches the walls, is the Romanesque **Basílica de San Vicente** (*open summer, Tues–Sun 10–1 and 4–7; winter, Tues–Sun 4–6, closed Mon*), the most interesting of Ávila's churches. Parts of it are as old as the late 12th century, including the fine sculptural work on the west portal. San Vicente was another native of Ávila, who was martyred along with his sisters, SS. Sabina and Cristeta, during the persecutions of Emperor Diocletian in 306. There's more graphic, vigorous sculpture inside, where scenes of San Vicente on the rack and suffering other tortures decorate his sarcophagus. The church, probably succeeding an earlier Visigothic structure, was built over the site of the martyrdom, and if the attendant will agree to take you down to the crypt you can see the rock where the Romans did them in.

Watch out for snakes; there's a legend of a serpent who guarded the saints' graves while Ávila was occupied by the Moors. A custom grew up whereby the people of Ávila would come down here to make bargains and swear oaths; if they lied, the serpent would come out and sting them (the only recorded victim was a bishop). Also down in the crypt is a much-venerated icon called **Nuestra Señora de la Soterana** (Our Lady of the Underground).

Los Verracos

This part of town, just east of the walls, is really as old as anything inside. A block from the walls, at Pza. de los Navillos 3, just off the Plaza de Italia, an old ecclesiastical residence called the Palacio de los Deanes has been converted into Ávila's very good **Museo Provincial** (*open Tues–Sat 10–2 and 5–8, Sun 10–2, closed Mon*), with a folk-costume and crafts collection, Roman artefacts and some fine local medieval pictures—displayed where you can see them much more clearly than in Ávila's dim churches.

The museum provides a good introduction to an interesting aspect of Ávila's ancient history. Ávila was a busy place when the Celts lived here, something as close to a capital or religious centre as this determinedly non-urban people cared to have. Remains of their castles and monuments can be seen all over the countryside, as well as hundreds of unique stone grave-markers called *verracos* (boars), carved in the shape of boars or bulls. These continued to be erected under Roman rule, as late as AD 300, and some carry Latin inscriptions, such as 'to the gods Manes and Titillo'.

Two blocks south, outside the **Puerta de Alcázar**, main gate of the old town, is the **Plaza de Santa Teresa**, the only really lovely corner of Ávila, with most of the modest restaurants and hotels nearby. The church here with the lovely rose window is **San Pedro**, from the 13th century.

The Walls

Calle San Segundo runs along the eastern side of the fortification, towards the Puerta de Alcázar. In this section of the walls, you will see some stones with Roman inscriptions, and a good many others with a rectangular niche and a groove cut into them. These were the bases of the *verracos*, and the niches held the ashes of the departed chiefs and warriors. The Castilians dragged in dozens of them to help build their walls, with 88 towers and nine gates. (A few *verracos* can be seen in the Plaza Calvo Sotelo, just inside the Puerta de Alcázar.) Though simple, the walls were up-to-date for the military needs of the 11th century; an engineer from Rome was called in to help with the design. The distinctive rounded towers, typical of ancient Roman fortifications, are called *cubos*, but the biggest bulge, facing Calle San Segundo, comes as a surprise. It is the apse of Ávila's cathedral, built right into the walls as if to symbolize the Church Militant of Old Castile, helping man the battlements of the Reconquista.

It's a pleasant 2.4km walk around the walls; on the southern and western sides they face open country, and the setting is sufficiently medieval to have been used for the shooting of several movies. On the narrow west end, they overlook old bridges spanning the River Adaja and the 12th-century church of **San Segundo**, yet another local saint, who supposedly converted Ávila in the 1st century. If you wish to have a look at Ávila from the top of the walls, the only entrance is in the garden of the *parador*, inside the northern face of the walls.

The Cathedral

Open summer, daily 10–1 and 3–6; winter daily 3–5.

It isn't much, though one of the earliest Gothic churches in Spain, and though a king of León (Alfonso IX, 1188–1230) once lived here in sanctuary during a civil war. From the front it has no character at all, apart from the two bizarre stone wild men with clubs, added in the 18th century, who guard the portal. Ávila's cathedral, half-church and half-fortress, does however have a little stage presence. The critics like to speak of Gothic architecture at its best as an eloquent argument for the Christian faith; this church was for a people who needed no convincing. Strong and plain, it has the air of an outsized chapel for warrior knights. The men of the Reconquista adorned it richly inside as if it were their treasure-house, and they lined its walls with niches for tombs where they expected to be buried.

Some of the sculpted tombs are among the best works in the cathedral, and there are some good reliefs in the north portal, and paintings and sculpture inside from quieter times when the wars of the Reconquista had passed on. One work very famous in Spain is the tomb of a learned 15th-century bishop named Alfonso de Madrigal (better known as *El Tostado* for his swarthy complexion), with a statue of the bishop deep in his books, wearing robes carved with finely detailed scenes from the scriptures.

Although Ávila has been a backwater for many centuries, a wander round the walled city is revealing. Like many a city in Castile, Ávila is quietly prosperous, and a host of ironmongers, gentlemen's outfitters and corner shops testifies to an economy which has little need of tourists—although they are more than welcome. And, little by little, its weedy lots and ruins are being restored. Avila's summer fiestas, which take place between 17 and 25 July, do liven the place up though, and its high altitude make it a pleasurably cool place in July and August. October 15th sees processions and festivities in honour of Saint Teresa.

In her writings, Santa Teresa had little kind to say about Ávila; apparently it was not a place where reforming ideas were very welcome. Nevertheless, Ávila is happy to show off memories of her life in a number of convents about town. On the spot where she was born they built the **Convento de Santa Teresa** (*open daily 9–1 and 3.30–8.30*), just inside the southern gate. There is a squat church in the Herreran style, with a collection of relics and paintings of imagined scenes from the saint's life. More of these can be seen at the **Convento de la Encarnación** (*open summer, Wed–Mon 9.30–1 and 4–7; winter, Wed–Mon 3.30–6; closed Tues*) where she lived for 27 years, just north of the walled town on Calle de la Encarnación, and at the **Convento de Las Madres** on Calle del Duque, three blocks east of the Plaza de Santa Teresa.

Ávila's Doctors of the Soul

The people of Ávila celebrate Santa Teresa de Ávila's memory as ostentatiously as the Corsicans do Napoleon's. Even if it were possible to escape hearing about her for a while, there would still be the ubiquitous, nasty, candied egg-yolks called 'Yemas de Santa Teresa' to remind you. A traditional speciality of the local nuns, they are sold in every shop in town.

Teresa Sánchez de Cepeda y Ahumada was born into a wealthy family of Jewish converts in 1515. She got religion young; at seven, after reading the *Lives of the Saints* she talked her brother into running away with her to be maryred by the Moors. An old stone cross called *Las Cuatro Postes*, just across the Adaja from the town, is the spot where their uncle caught the children and brought them back. Teresa had to wait until she was 18 before she took her vows as a Carmelite, and she lived 22 uneventful years in her convent until she had the famous vision that set her off on her career as a mystic—an angel pierced her heart with a burning arrow during prayer—unforgettably depicted in Bernini's statue in Rome, portraying Teresa in a state of eternal orgasm.

Usually Teresa's union with God was more down to earth. Shortly after her first mystical experience, she had a second while praying at the chapel of Nuestra Señora de la Soterana in San Vicente, which bade her to reform the lax Carmelite order and return it to its original regime of poverty and simplicity. The subterranean Virgin also had her take off her shoes, and wearing sandals became the symbol of the new *descalzada* (shoeless) Carmelites. Teresa then spent much of her life on the road, founding and reforming 32 convents in Castile and Andalucía. Her first male convert was a 21-year-old theology student from Fontiverós, near Ávila, named Juan de Yepes, who became Teresa's confessor and the spiritual director of the *descalzadas.* One of the best things he did was order Teresa to write her autobiography, the frankest, most spontaneous, humorous and likeable account composed by any saint on the calendar.

In 1578 still-shod (Calced) Carmelite timeservers, who spitefully labelled Teresa 'the roving nun', denounced both her and her confessor Juan to the Inquisition. Both were confined to Toledo, separately, and wrote to each other daily—the disappearance of their correspondence is considered one of the greatest losses in Spanish letters. For it was in Toledo that the two wrote their classical works of mysticism: Teresa's *Inner Castle* was based on her vision of a glittering castle of seven abodes, each a stage that the bride/soul must pass on the road to heaven to the ultimate union with God. The Church disapproved of her books when she died in 1582, but it saw fit to canonize her in 1622, repackaging the honest mystic into a miracle worker and an object of popular devotion whose chopped-off fingers soon became prized holy relics.

Juan—the future St John of the Cross—suffered far worse indignities. The Calced members of his Order imprisoned him in a dungeon for nine months, a period of forced reflection that resulted in his first poem, *En una Noche Oscura (The Dark Night of the Soul)*—one of the masterpieces of Spanish literature. Like all his poetry, *The Dark Night* was ripe for misinterpretation because of its several levels of meaning, including the carnal; Juan assigned religious concepts genders and used often ambiguous erotic imagery to make potent poetic points with an extraordinary economy. He wrote fewer than 1000 lines in his whole life but into those fit a complete exposition of Catholic mysticism, expressed allegorically in unrivalled songs of love and nature, poems that create moods rather than merely describe them.

Although Juan managed to escape from prison when the Calced and Discalced Orders were officially separated, he met an obscure end in 1591, dying from abuse and starvation after years of suffering in the monastery at Úbeda, persecuted even on his deathbed by the prior, who had nuns sign affidavits against him. He and his poetry were vindicated when he was canonized in 1726 and made a Doctor of the Church in 1926, an honour St Teresa herself became the first woman to enjoy in 1970, putting Ávila in the record books as the only town to produce two Doctors of the Church.

Eating Out

Ávila is full of good, solid, inexpensive restaurants: more than you would expect in a small town with lots of tourists. Most are near the eastern end of the walls, inside or out. At **El Rincón**, Pza. de Zurraquín 15, ✆ 920 21 3152 (*moderate*), you can get *cochinillo* and other Castilian specialities for a reasonable price.

Others worthy of mention are **Doña Guiomar**, C/Tomás de Victoria 3, ✆ 920 21 37 89 (*moderate*), for inventive cooking and friendly service; **Casa Patas**, C/San Millán 4 (*cheap*), just off the Plaza de Santa Teresa, for tapas and simple meals, and **Los Leales**, Plazuela de Italia, ✆ 920 21 1329 (*moderate*), near the museum.

For some classy, classic Castilian food, try the **Mesón del Rastro**, Pza. del Rastro 1, ✆ 920 21 1218 (*moderate*)—here they serve authentic local dishes such as veal, pickled trout, roast lamb, and *judías de Barco* (bean casserole with *chorizo*).

Outside the city walls, on the banks of the Río Adaja, **El Almacén**, Ctra. de Salamanca 6, ✆ 920 21 1026 (*expensive*) also serves regional favourites, as well as imaginative variations on traditional themes.

Alcalá de Henares, Guadalajara and Sigüenza

The railway line that trundles out of Madrid in the direction of Zaragoza and Barcelona follows the course of the Río Henares all the way to its source, near the provincial border of Guadalajara and Soria. Trains passing this way stop at towns which have stood on the river for centuries, such as **Alcalá de Henares**, famous for its ancient university, and **Guadalajara**, in the heart of the Alcarria. Northeast of Guadalajara the line cuts through dazzling fields of sunflowers on the way to the graceful town of **Sigüenza**. It's a pleasant journey, through plenty of open countryside which, thanks to the river, is splashed with green even in the driest of summer months.

Getting There

By train: There are six or seven trains a day to Sigüenza on the Regionales line R 9b from Madrid-Chamartín; some of these stop at Madrid-Atocha, and all pass through Alcalá de Henares and Guadalajara. The journey to Sigüenza takes around 2hrs. Alcalá and Guadalajara are also served by Cercanías trains from Madrid-Chamartín and Madrid-Atocha, four times an hour for Alcalá and every half hour for Guadalajara.

RENFE information, Madrid: ✆ 91 328 9020; Alcalá de Henares: ✆ 91 888 0196; Guadalajara: ✆ 949 21 2850; Sigüenza: ✆ 949 39 1494.

By bus: This is one case where the train is so convenient that you needn't worry about buses, unless you're based near the terminus at Avenida de América 34, from which Continental Auto, ✆ 91 533 0400, runs a frequent service to all three towns.

Alcalá de Henares: at Callejón Santa María 1, ✆ 91 889 2694.

Guadalajara: at Pza. Mayor 7, ✆ 949 22 0698.

Sigüenza: at C/Cardenal Mendoza 2, ✆ 949 39 1262.

Alcalá de Henares

Anyone from the Arab world would recognize the name's origin straightaway—
al-qalat, a fortress—and it was the Moors who began this town, on the site of the
abandoned Roman city of Complutum. In the 12th century, warrior bishops
from Toledo captured it for Christianity and built it up; the long tradition of
Church control may be one of the reasons Cardinal Jiménez de Cisneros founded
his great Complutensian University here in 1508, an institution that almost
immediately rivalled Salamanca as the foremost centre of learning in Spain.

In 16th-century Castile, it was possible for a man like Cisneros to be on one hand
an imperialist and a disturbingly fierce religious bigot, and on the other a champion of the new humanist scholarship that was sweeping Europe. For a brief,
brilliant period the University became one of the intellectual lights of the conti-
nent; its great achievement, indeed its main reason for being, was the creation of
the Complutensian Polyglot Bible, the first authoritative scholarly edition in
modern Europe, with Latin, Greek, Hebrew and Aramaic originals in parallel
columns. Even today it remains the standard work for biblical scholars; in its day
it created an academic revolution. Among the University's graduates in Spain's
golden age can be counted Calderón, Lope de Vega and Ignatius Loyola.

Through the 17th and 18th centuries the University's degeneration was gradual
but complete, and half its buildings lay in ruins by 1837, when the sad remnants
were moved to Madrid. Some of the old colleges were used as the Communist
headquarters during the Civil War.

Economic recovery in the 1970s and 1980s brought a change of fortune to
Alcalá, which became one of the fastest growing cities of Spain, through industrial growth and the presence of a huge US air base nearby at Torrejón (a popular
rendezvous for anti-NATO protesters from Madrid). Many of the old academic
buildings were restored, and the university re-opened its doors to students in
1977. Cisneros would have been delighted—the re-establishment of his university brought Alcalá's dormant intellectual and cultural interests back to the
surface and made it a lively city once more.

Alcalá's centre is the leafy, pleasant **Plaza de Cervantes**, with a bandstand at
one end and gossipy cafés at the other. Touching its edge is the arcaded **Calle
Mayor**, Alcalá's busy, pretty, old main street, which comes alive with yet more

café tables after the shops shut on summer evenings. The University buildings are spread all over town, but the best of them, the **Colegio Mayor de San Ilde-fonso**, is just off the Plaza de Cervantes; it has a wonderful Plateresque façade by Rodrigo Gil de Hontañón (the architect who also worked on the cathedrals of Segovia and Salamanca), with the arms of Cisneros (note the swans—*cisnes*).

Inside are the **Capilla Universitaria**, a Plateresque chapel, and a famous hall called the **Paraninfo** with an *artesonado* ceiling, used for graduation cere-monies and other congregational occasions. Other noteworthy buildings are the **Colegio de la Palma** on Calle de los Colegios and the **Casa de los Lizana**, with its brave stone lions, on Calle Postigo. Most of the University colleges are built in a very austere, Herreran style, as are Alcalá's churches.

On the Calle Mayor is a small museum devoted to Alcalá's most famous son, Miguel de Cervantes. The **Museo Casa Natal de Cervantes** (Cervantes' Birthplace) (*open Tues–Fri 10.15–1.45 and 4.15–6.45; Sat–Sun, 10.15–1.45, closed Mon*) is a lovingly kept reconstruction of the house in which the author was born. It's furnished to look like a mid 16th-century family dwelling, and in an upstairs room there is a display of rare editions of Cervantes' works and other ephemera.

Modern Alcalá's only monument is on the street leading from the railway sta-tion. The **Hotel Laredo** or *Quinta de la Gloria* is an incredible confection of brick Moorish arches and turrets piled up by some forgotten madman of the 19th century. Its style is not really 'neo-*Mudéjar*' as the sign says, but more honestly 'hyper-*Mudéjar*'.

Guadalajara

The next stop up the rail line from Madrid, this once great town of New Castile was almost completely wrecked during the long battles for Madrid during the Civil War, but rebuilt as a modern, industrial city. The only reason to stop is the **Palacio de los Duques del Infantado**, Pza. de los Caídos 1 (*open Tues–Sat 10.15–2 and 4–7, Sun 10.15–2, closed Mon*) built by Juan Guas in 1461 for the founder of what was to become one of Spain's most powerful noble houses, the Mendozas. Among its members it counted statesmen, authors, even a Viceroy of New Spain. The palace, in the Plateresque style, has a façade and courtyard florid enough to please any duke. Most of the palace has been restored or rebuilt, and it now houses a provincial art museum.

Sigüenza

The cathedral is worth the trip, but what makes Sigüenza a pleasant excursion from Madrid is its setting in the hills around the Henares. From the quiet, arcaded Plaza Mayor you can walk through a little gate into the marketplace on the cliffs above the valley, and from there pass directly into the lovely forested hillsides that surround the town. Sigüenza is altogether much too cosy and charming to be in Castile.

The Cathedral has a good deal in common with the one in Ávila; both were built at about the same time and both show the influence of the French Gothic with a distinctive Castilian twist. Like Ávila's it stands honest and foursquare—a castle with rose windows. They are very good rose windows, especially over the north portal, but the best things are inside. In the chapel of the Arce family is the tomb of Martín Vázquez de Arce, a young man who died in the wars with Moorish Granada in 1486. An unknown artist carved his figure in alabaster on the top of the sarcophagus, gently smiling and musing over a book. The image, as evocative of the medieval world as any passage from Tennyson, has become so well known it is referred to simply as El Doncel de Sigüenza. Doncel, in this case, means a king's page; Arce was an attendant of Ferdinand and Isabel. His crossed legs are not just an expression of nonchalance. It was a convention of Spanish medieval art, used to show that the deceased had died while fighting for the faith.

To stroll through the rest of Sigüenza will require a little climbing up narrow streets to the **castle** that dominates the town. Like Guadalajara, Sigüenza suffered greatly in the Civil War. The castle, now a *parador*, and the Plaza Mayor have been almost completely restored, but plenty of bullet scars can still be seen on the cathedral tower. Several other Romanesque and Gothic churches, all quite plain, have also been restored, including the 12th-century San Vicente on Calle del Jesús. Across the Plaza Obispo Don Bernardo from the cathedral there is a museum, the Museo Diocesano del Arte Sacro, with works by El Greco and Zurbarán and some early religious art. The second Sunday in May sees a spectacular *romería*, or religious procession, from Sigüenza 7km to the sanctuary of Barbatona.

Eating Out

Alcalá de Henares

The town has one restaurant so well-known that it attracts a regular clientele from Madrid. The **Hostería del Estudiante**, C/Colegios 3, ✆ 91 888 0330 (*expensive*) is a *parador* restaurant in an annexe of the Colegio Mayor, faithfully restored to recreate a 16th-century atmosphere, right down to the oil lamps and uncomfortable chairs. Traditional Castilian cuisine is studiously maintained, and if you're up to spending a small fortune on dinner in this corner of Castile, this is the place.

Lower-priced alternatives, both of which serve good quality, inspired meals, are **La Cúpola**, C/Santiago 18 (*moderate*), in a converted 17th-century convent, and **La Parilla**, Pza. de los Santos Niños (*inexpensive*).

Visitors to the Colegio Mayor, Pza. de San Diego, are at certain times able to eat at its superior **Cafetería Rectorado**, ✆ 91 855 4140 (*cheap*), perhaps Alcalá's best-value eatery; in this glassed-off corner of the historic Patio de los Filósofos, generous platefuls of standards such as *gazpacho*, salads, grilled *merluza* and chicken roasted in wine cost next to nothing.

For those with a sweet tooth, a visit to the **Convento de San Diego**, Calle Beatas 7, is a must. The nuns of the Santa Clara order make the most exquisite *almendras garapiñadas*: almonds, toasted in thick chewy toffee, made fresh every week.

Guadalajara

The finest ingredients go into creative variations on classical cuisine at **Amparito Roca**, C/Toledo 19, ✆ 949 21 4639 (*expensive*), and Castilian favourites are normally on the menu at **Casa Victor**, C/Bardeles 6, ✆ 949 21 2247 (*moderate*).

Other places to seek out local specialities such as *cabrito a la barreña* (spit-roast kid), garlic soup, and *bizcochos borrachos* (rum babas) are plentiful around the Plaza Mayor and Plaza Bejanque areas.

Sigüenza

Visitors to the town are often directed to the **Restaurante Calle Mayor**, C/Mayor 21, ✆ 949 39 1748 (*moderate*), where the house specialities include *chipirones rellenos* (stuffed squid), *cabrito al ajo* (kid with garlic), and *cordero asado* (roast lamb).

Other good places to try the local lamb are the **Restaurante Medieval Segontia Asador**, C/Portal Mayor 2, ✆ 949 39 32 33 (*moderate*), and the **Mesón La Cabaña**, Ctra. de Soria Km 5, ✆ 949 39 1615 (*moderate*).

El Laberinto, Pso. de la Alameda, is always full of locals and has an unusually wide choice of dishes on its set menu; there are plenty of cafés and bars on this street, and in the ancient and rather lovely Alameda Park itself.

Aranjuez: Yet Another Bourbon Palace

Palaces open summer, Tues–Sun, 10–6.15, winter, Tues–Sun 10–5.15; closed Mon; adm exp, free for EU passport holders on Wed; gardens open summer, Tues–Sun 8–8.30; winter Tues–Sun 8–6.30, closed Mon.

There has been a royal residence in Aranjuez since the days of Philip II. His palace, built by Bautista and Herrera, the architects of El Escorial, burned down in the 17th century, and we can only wonder what sort of pleasure-dome those two grinds could have created. Philip V began the replacement at the same time as he was building his palace at La Granja. It is hard to tell the two apart. Like La Granja, Aranjuez is an attempt to emulate some of the grandeur of Versailles; it isn't surprising, with Louis XIV meddling in Spain's affairs at every step, that the junior Bourbon wanted to show that he, too, was somebody. Aranjuez is a natural location for a palace. The water of the Río Tajo makes it an oasis among the brown hills, on the threshold of La Mancha. Centuries of royal attention have given the area more trees than any other corner of Castile, and even today it is famous in Spain for its strawberries and asparagus. A small town has grown up around the palace since the 16th century.

The first week of September sees spectacular fiestas based around the *motín de Aranjuez*. This celebrates the uprising of 1808, when, in the face of the French invasion, the locals rose up to overthrow the then prime minister, Godoy, who had advised Carlos IV to flee to America as part of his own evil schemes to gain power. The mob attacked Godoy's palace in Aranjuez, and the king was forced to sack him and then abdicate in favour of his son. This is considered the inspiration for the uprising in Madrid which followed on 2 May of that year. The fiestas attract big crowds, many dressed in period costume.

Getting There

By train: Cercanías line C 3 trains from Madrid (Atocha) run to Aranjuez roughly every half hour and takes 45mins. To make a special outing of it, you could pay the extra to take the **Tren de la Fresa** (strawberry train), a real steam train that chuffs from Atocha to Aranjuez and back weekends from mid-May to October and once a day during the summer months, leaving at about 10. A local bus will take you right from Aranjuez station to the palace; if you'd rather walk, turn right out of the station, then left down the avenue. RENFE information, Madrid: ✆ 91 563 0202, Aranjuez: ✆ 91 891 0202.

By bus: Buses from Madrid, run by AISA, ✆ 91 527 1294, leave hourly from Estación Sur, C/Méndez Álvaro, Ⓜ Méndez Álvaro. Buses from Madrid to Chinchón are run by La Veloz, ✆ 91 409 7602, from a stop near their office at 49 Avenida Mediterráneo (Ⓜ Conde de Casal). Departures in both directions leave hourly on the hour on weekdays and Sat, and roughly every 90mins on Sun. The journey takes 50mins.

Tourist Information

Plaza de San Antonio 9, ✆ 91 891 04 27.

As at La Granja, the prime attractions here are the **gardens**, full of sculptural allegory, and fountains in the most surprising places, shady avenues and walks along the Tajo, even an informal garden of the sort that were called 'English gardens' in the 18th century. They'll drag you through a guided tour of the **Palacio Real**, packed full of chandeliers and mirrors, with collections of porcelain, fancy clocks and court costume of the period. Among the gardens is another small palace, the **Casa del Labrador**, modelled after the Petit Trianon, and along the river a **museum of boats**; the conscientious Carlos III built the structure as part of a forgotten project to make the Tajo navigable, but his successors turned it into a boathouse, and their pleasure craft are on display.

Eating Out

Aranjuez

Such has been the boom in tourism over the last decade that most restaurants can't get local strawberries and asparagus; nevertheless, that's what people come here to eat. And they figure prominently on most of the town's restaurant menus. Most of them are expensive, though, and you may settle for *fresas con nata* (strawberries and cream) from one of the little stands around town, although the cream won't be real either. Many restaurants have elegant settings along the riverfront, like **La Rana Verde**, C/Reina 1, ✆ 91 891 32 38 (*moderate*), where paying the extra for one of the fish or game specialities is preferable to the simple set menu.

Casa Pablo, C/Almíbar 42, ✆ 91 891 14 51 (*moderate*) takes the cuisine and the wine a little more seriously, and is a little more expensive. Casa Pablo makes a welcome change from the usual fare, with inventive, international, *nouvelle*-inspired cuisine making it very popular. The recommended place for very fresh fish and seafood as well as wood-fired roasts is **El Molino de Aranjuez**, C/Príncipe 21, ✆ 91 892 4215 (*expensive*), a restaurant in the wing of an ancient palace.

No city in Spain has seen more, or learned more, or stayed true to itself for so long through the shifting fortunes of a discouraging history. Under the rule of Madrid the usurper, though, the last 400 years have been murder for Toledo; its pride humbled, its talents and achievements dried up, this city with little political or economic function is entirely at the mercy of the tourists. It would be a ghost town without them.

It isn't Toledo's fault that it has become a museum city, but it carries out the rôle with considerable grace. Its monuments are well-scrubbed, its streets lively and pleasant, and the city summons a smile and a welcome for even the most befuddled package tourist. No matter how you come to Toledo, you'll be glad when you finally arrive. The surrounding countryside, once all irrigated farmland or forest, is a desolation, a desert with a tinge of green. Toledo has a beautiful setting on a plateau above the Río Tajo, and its little plazas and narrow streets are like an oasis in brick and stone.

History

Toledo was a capital of sorts when the Romans found it, a centre for the local Celtiberian tribes called the Carpetani. As a Roman town, Toletum did not gain much distinction, but scanty remains of temples and a circus, still visible just north of town off the Avenida de la Reconquista, indicate it must have been fairly large. The Visigoths made it their capital in the 6th century; their palace may have been on the site of the Alcázar, but they were not great builders, and relatively little is left from their two centuries of rule.

King Roderick and the Tower of Hercules

Toledo is full of stories. One of the oldest speaks of a tower, built by Hercules, that stood on the edge of the city. No one knew what was in it, and it became a tradition for every Spanish king to add a new padlock to the scores of them that already secured the tower's thick brass door.

Roderick, that scoundrel who was to be the last of the Visigoths, neglected this, and was confronted one day by two magicians in mysterious dress to remind him of his duty. Roderick's curiosity was piqued, and instead of carrying on the old custom he resolved to find out what was inside the ancient tower. The bishops and counsellors did their best to dissuade him, but in the end Roderick had the centuries' accumulation of locks pried off, one by one, and threw open the brass door. An air as chill as death issued

Toledo

Circo Romano

CALLE OCAÑA

AVENIDA DE CARLOS III

AVENIDA DE LA RECONQUISTA

CALLE ESCALONA

AVENIDA DEL DUQUE DE LERMA

CALLE LA DIPUTACIÓN

AVENIDA DE LA DIPUTACIÓN

PASEO DEL CIRCO ROMANO

PASEO DE CANÓNIGOS

Paseo de Merchán

PASEO DEL CRISTO DE LA VEGA

PZA. ALFONSO VI

AVENIDA PUENTE DE LA CAVA

Puerta de Bisagra

C/ LA CARRERA

C. ALFONSO VI

PUENTE DE LA CAVA

CUESTA DE LA GRANJA

Santiago del Arrabal

REAL DEL ARRABAL

CALLE AZA

Puerta del Cambrón

CALLE REAL

LAS CARMELITAS

LA MERCED

Puerta del Sol

C/ CARRETAS

Monasterio de S. Juan de los Reyes

SANTA LEOCADIA

PZA. STA. CLARA

PZA. CARMELITAS

Mezquita del Cristo de la Luz

PINTOR MATÍAS MORENO

COLEGIO DE DONCELLAS

PZA. PADILLA

NÚÑEZ DE ARCE

LOS REYES CATÓLICOS

ESTEBAN ILLÁN

PZA. S. VICENTE

LOS ALFILERITOS

C/E RÍOS MENORES TOLEDO DE OHIO

Museum of Contemporary Art

S. CLEMENTE

Post Office

PUENTE DE SAN MARTÍN

CALLE ÁNGEL

LAS BULAS

Museo de la Cultura Visigótica

PZA. AMADOR DE LOS RÍOS

C/ SAN ROMÁN

Sinagoga de Sta. María la Blanca

PZA. BARRIO NUEVO

PZA. DE VALDECABALLEROS

NÚÑEZ VIEJO

Santo Tomé

STO. TOMÉ

ALFONSO X EL SABIO

NUNCIO VIEJO

C/ COMERCIO

PZA. MAGDALENA

Sinagoga del Tránsito and Museo Sefardí

Río Tajo

JUAN DE DIOS

TRÁNSITO

LA TRINIDAD

Palacio Arzobispal

Cathedral

PLAZA MAYOR

Casa Museo de El Greco

Palacio de Fuensalida

DEL MORO

Taller del Moro

TALLER

PLAZA AYUNTAMIENTO

SIXTO

JUAN LABRADOR

CUESTA DE CAR

PASEO DEL TRÁNSITO

Ayuntamiento

POZO AMARGO

Posada de la Hermandad

PZA. CABEZA

CALVARIO DESCALZOS

PZA. DE SAN CRISTÓBAL

AVE. MARÍA PLEGADERO

PZA. SAN JUSTO

CUESTA DE SAN JUST

PZA. DEL REY D. PEDRO

PZA. FUENTES

SAN LORENZO

PZA. DE STA. CATALINA

C/ SACRAMENTO

LAS RECOGIDAS

CARRERAS DE SAN SEBASTIÁN

PZA. DON FERNANDO

PZA. DE SAN LUCAS

San Lucas

PASEO DE LA CANDELA

PZA. ANDAQUE

N

300 metres

300 yards

from inside, but the king entered, alone, and climbed a narrow stair to the top of the tower. There he met the figure of a bronze warrior, larger than life, swinging a great mace back and forth and barring his entrance to the tower's inner chamber. Still undaunted, the king commanded it to stop and it obeyed. Behind it lay a chamber with walls covered in gold and precious stones, empty save for a small table bearing a small chest. This the king opened greedily, finding nothing inside but a large folded linen scroll. He saw that it was covered with scenes of battle; as he unrolled it the figures on it came to life, and Roderick saw his own army go down to defeat at the hands of unknown invaders in outlandish costume. While he blinked in astonishment at the moving pictures, a loud crash like thunder sounded from the depths of the tower; he dropped the linen scroll and hurriedly fled, escaping just in time to see an eagle with a burning brand in its claws soaring over Hercules' tower. With a scream it dropped the flame directly over it, and in scarcely more time than it took Roderick and his knights to heave a sigh, the tower burnt to the ground. Then, a great flock of birds flew up from the ashes and sped off to the four winds.

Museo Hospital de Tavera

Madrid

CALLE CARDENAL TAVERA

PZA. HONDA

Bus Station

AVENIDA DE CASTILLA-LA MANCHA

PZA. SOLAR ANTEQUERUELA

LA ALMOFARA

PUENTE DE AZARQUIEL

ALLE AZACAR

DIEZ DE ARCE

VENANCIO GONZÁLEZ

CALLE GERARDO LOBO

Train Station

Hospital de Santa Cruz

PASEO DE LA ROSA

DE LA ROSA

ILUSTRÍSIMA

LAS CABRIAS

SAN AGUSTÍN

CONCEPCIÓN

PLAZA DE ZOCODOVER

SANTA FE

CALLE CERVANTES

PUENTE DE ALCÁNTARA

Castillo de San Servando

PZA. MAGDALENA

CUESTA DE CARLOS V

ALFÉREZ PROVISIONAL

PZA. DE LA CONCEPCIÓN

Alcázar

GRAL. MOSCARDÓ

PUENTE DE ALCÁNTARA (NUEVA)

LA CANDELARIA

Río Tajo

CARRETERA DE CIRCUNVALACIÓN

Of course the invaders were the Moors; both Toledo and Roderick fell to them in the year 716. The beauty and strangeness of the old legend betray its Moorish origins, and Toledo, under its new masters, was about to embark on a career that itself would become the stuff of legends. Here, long before the Crusades, the Christian and Islamic worlds first met, in a city renowned throughout the Mediterranean world for learning. A school of translators grew up over the centuries in which Arab, Jewish and Christian scholars transmitted Greek and Arabic science, as well as Islamic and Jewish theology and mysticism, to the lands of the north. The first medieval troubadours most likely gained some inspiration from the Arab originals here. Toledo, conveniently close to the mercury mine at Almadén, became a centre for the study of alchemy. Schools of occult philosophy and mathematics proliferated, attracting students from all over Christian Europe. One was Sylvester II, the late 10th-century Pope, who was said to have stolen a famous book of magic while he was a student in Toledo, and was accused during his papacy of consulting with a prophetic magic 'head' of gold called a 'Baphomet' (the same charge that was later raised against the Templars).

The chroniclers claimed a population for Moorish Toledo of some 200,000 people, over three times as large as it is today. Even so, it was never a centre of political power, and to the sultans and emirs of Al-Andalus it meant little more than the central bastion of their defence line against the rapacious Christians of the north. In a moment of inattention they lost it to Alfonso VI and El Cid.

The conquest of the city in 1085 was never reversed, and tipped the balance of power irreparably against the Moors. For a long time, Toledo under Castilian rule continued its role as a city of tolerance and scholarship, and its Moorish and Jewish populations easily accommodated the Christian settlers introduced by the Castilian kings. Alfonso the Wise was born here, and he did much to make Toledo's learning and experience become Spain's in common. After the accession of Ferdinand and Isabel, however, disasters followed thick and fast. The church and the Inquisition were given a free hand, and soon succeeded in snuffing out Toledo's intellectual lights. The expulsion of the Jews, and later the Moors, put an end to the city's long-established culture, and the permanent establishment of the capital at Madrid ended for ever the political importance Toledo had enjoyed in medieval Castile. To make matters worse, Toledo had been a focal point of the Comunero revolt, and suffered greatly after its suppression. By the 18th century the city had become an impoverished backwater, and except for the famous siege of the Alcázar during the Civil War, little has happened there since. Long ago, Toledo made its living from silk and steel; the silk industry died off with the expulsion of the Moors, and the famous Toledo blades, tempered in cold water from the Tajo, are only a memory except for the cheap versions the tourists buy. The visitors keep this town going, though the Toledans despair when the convoys of tour buses from Madrid stuff themselves through the tiny streets throughout July and August. Do not be discouraged; relatively few people spend the night, and after museum hours the old town becomes surprisingly tranquil.

Getting There

By train: Toledo is off the main road and rail lines, and it's hard to get there from anywhere but Madrid. That, however, is easy enough; there are nine trains a day at one to two hourly intervals from Madrid-Atocha to Toledo's charming *mudéjar*-style station east of town (Regionales line 9 f, journey time 60–85mins).

Any city bus will take you from the station into the centre. RENFE information, Madrid: © 91 563 0202, Toledo © 925 22 3099.

By bus: There is also a convenient bus service run by Empresa Galiano Continental, © 91 527 2961, with departures every half hour from Estación Sur, C/Méndez Álvaro, Ⓜ Méndez Álvaro, © 91 468 4200.

Tourist Information

Just outside the Puerta de Bisagra (Bisagra Gate), © 925 22 0843, ✉ 925 25 2648, on the road from Madrid (stop on your way if you can, so you won't have to make the steep trip down again).

Around the Plaza de Zocodover

The name, like the *souk* of a Moroccan city, is from the Arabic for market, and this square—triangle, really—has always been the centre of Toledo. Despite bearing the brunt of Toledo's success as a tourist destination (a McDonald's now dominates one side), the square endures as a favourite place for residents to meet up and exchange gossip, and a traditional market is still held here on Tuesdays. On the long, eastern edge of the triangle, the stately building with the clock is the seat of the provincial government, rebuilt after it burned down during the Civil War. From the archway under the clock, stairs lead down to the Calle Cervantes and the enormous, fascinating museum contained within the 1544 **Hospital de Santa Cruz**, C/Cervantes 3 *(open Tues–Sat 10–6.30, Sun 10–2, closed Mon)*, a building by Enrique de Egas with a wildly decorated façade. A little bit of everything has been assembled here: archaeological finds from Toletum, paintings and tapestries, Toledo swords and daggers. The building itself is worth a visit, its long airy halls typical of hospitals of the period, with beautiful ceilings and staircases. Spanish medicine was quite advanced in the 16th century (most of the physicians were Jewish and exempt from the persecutions) and the surroundings were held to be an important part of the cure. Notable among the displays are Don Juan's huge standard from his flagship at the Battle of Lepanto, paintings by El Greco (*Santiago*, *Saint John*, an *Assumption*, and a *Crucifixion* with a view of Toledo in the background), some eccentric holy scenes by the 16th-century Maestro de Sigena, and a sculptural frieze from a pre-Roman Toledo house. A lovely 15th-century Flemish tapestry, the *Tapiz de los Astrolabios*, shows the northern constellations in a kind of celestial garden; other tapestries detail scenes from the life of Alexander the Great.

Just around the corner of Calle de la Concepción, the chapel of **San Jerónimo** is one of the best examples of Toledo's 16th-century *mudéjar* churches.

Gates of the Town

North from the Plaza de Zocodover, the Cuesta de las Armas is the old main road to Madrid. The street descends gradually, past the **Mirador**, to the **Puerta del Sol**, a pretty gate-house from the 12th century. In the 14th century, the Knights of St John rebuilt it and added the curious relief medallion, much commented on as a late example of Toledan mysticism; it shows the sun, moon, and a large triangle around a scene of San Ildefonso, patron and 4th-century bishop of Toledo, receiving a chasuble woven by angels from the hands of the Virgin. According to local legend, it was presented in return for a treatise the saint wrote on the meaning of the Immaculate Conception.

Further down, in the old quarter called the **Arrabal** outside the Moorish walls, is another fine *mudéjar* church, a joyous excess of pointed arches and towers done in brick, the 11th-century **Santiago del Arrabal**. In the 1480s, this was the church of San Vicente Ferrer, the anti-Semitic fire-eater whose sermons started regular riots and helped force the expulsion of the Jews.

Here the modern road curves around the **Nueva Puerta de Bisagra**, more like a palace than a gate with its pointed spires and courtyard. Charles V built it, strictly for decoration, and added his enormous coat of arms in stone after the Comunero wars, to remind the Toledans who was boss.

Just outside the gate, the city's tourist office is on the edge of a large park called the **Paseo de Merchán**, on the other side of which stands another 16th-century charitable institution converted into a museum, the **Museo Hospital de Tavera**, Avda. de los Duques de Lerma (*open daily, 10.30–1.30 and 3.30–6*), lovingly guarded by three old ladies. Cardinal Tavera was a member of the house of Mendoza, a grandee of Spain, and an adviser to Charles V. His collection, including his portrait among several works by El Greco, and the memorable *Bearded Woman* by Ribera, share space with objects and furnishings from the Cardinal's time.

The Alcázar

C/General Moscardó, open Tues–Sat 9.30–1.30 and 4–5.30, till 6.30 Fri, Sun 10–1.30 and 4–5.30, closed Mon.

Romans, Visigoths and Moors all had some sort of fortress on this spot, at the highest point of the city. The present plan of the big, square palace-fortress, the same that stands out so clearly in El Greco's famous *View of Toledo*, was constructed by Charles V, though rebuilt after destructions in the Napoleonic Wars and again in the Civil War. The second siege was a bitter one, and gave Toledo's Alcázar the curious fate of becoming the holy-of-holies for Spain's fascists and Francoists. Toledo declared for the Republic in July 1936, but a number of soldiers, civilians and Guardia Civil barred themselves inside with the idea that the coup would soon be over. Instead, what they got was a two-month ordeal, with Republican irregulars keeping them under constant fire. When the Nationalists began to exploit the brave defence for propaganda, the Republicans got serious, and finally Asturian miners succeeded in collapsing most of the fortress with dynamite charges. Still the defenders held out, under the leadership of Colonel José Moscardó, in the ruins and underground tunnels, until a relief column finally arrived in September. The courage shown by the men of the Alcázar was quite real, but Francoist Spain was never content to leave it at that. The climax of the visit here is Colonel Moscardó's office, where plaques in 19 languages record a telephone conversation in which the Republican commander threatened to kill Moscardó's son, whom he had captured, if the Alcázar did not surrender. With his son on the line, Moscardó intoned 'Shout *Viva España* and die like a hero!' The story is a blatant copy of that of Guzmán el Bueno in Tarifa. In this case, it's all a fake, and Moscardó's son was later found alive and well in Madrid.

The trip through the dungeons is interesting, with relics such as the old motorcycle that was hooked up to a mill to grind flour for the defenders, and the spot where two babies were born during the siege. The corridors are covered with plaques sent from overseas to honour the memory of the besieged soldiers, contributed by such groups as the Chilean army and an association of Croatian Nazis in exile.

Mezquita del Cristo de la Luz

From the Plaza de Zocodover, Calle Comercio leads off towards Toledo's great cathedral; on the way, you'll notice a big street sign proclaiming Calle de Toledo de Ohio, decorated with the Ohio state seal in *azulejos* (Toledans are proud of their little sister on Erie's shore, with its newspaper called the *Blade*; few of them have probably ever seen it). You may consider a detour here, up typically Toledan steep, narrow streets, to the church of **Cristo de la Luz**, in reality a mosque built around 980 and incorporating elements of an earlier Visigothic church. When Alfonso VI captured the city (the story goes), he and El Cid were making their triumphal entrance when the king's horse knelt down in front of the mosque and refused to move. Taking this as a portent, the king ordered the mosque searched, and a hidden niche was discovered, bricked up in the walls, with a crucifix and a lamp that had been miraculously burning since the days of the Visigoths. The tiny mosque, one of the oldest surviving Moorish buildings in Spain, is an exceptional example of their work.

The Cathedral

Open daily, 10.30–2 and 4–6.30; museum open Tues–Sat 10.30–1 and 3.30–6, Sun, 10.30–1, closed Mon.

This isn't a building that may be approached directly; most of its bulk is hidden behind walls and rows of old buildings, with corners peeking out where you least expect them. The best of its portals, the **Puerta del Reloj**, is tucked away in a small courtyard where few ever see it, at the end of Calle Chapinería. Circumnavigating the great building will take you all through the neighbourhood. On Calle Sixto Romano, behind the apse, you'll pass an old inn called the **Posada de la Hermandad**, seat of a permanent militia-police force called the 'Holy Brotherhood' that kept the peace in medieval Castile. Coming around Calle Hombre de Palo, past the cathedral cloister, you pass the entrance used today, the **Puerta del Mollete** (muffin) where bread was once distributed to the needy.

Finally, arriving at the Plaza Ayuntamiento (still often referred to as the Plaza del Generalísimo) you may enjoy the final revelation of the west front. It's a little disappointing. Too many cooks have been at work, and the great rose windows are hidden behind superfluous arches, over three big portals where the sculpture is indifferent but grandiose. Before too long, the interest fades; look across the square and you'll see one of Spain's most beautiful city halls, the 1618 **Ayuntamiento**, by El Greco's son, Jorge Theotocópoulos.

Don't give up on the cathedral yet; few Gothic churches in Spain can match its interior, unusually light and airy and with memorable works of art in every corner. Some 800 fine stained-glass windows from the 15th and 16th centuries dispel the gloom. Sculpture takes the place of honour before painting, unlike in most other cathedrals of Spain. Some of the best work is in the Old Testament scenes around the wall of the *coro*, at the centre of the Cathedral (note the interesting versions of the Creation and story of Adam and Eve). The *coro*'s stalls are famous, decorated with highly detailed scenes from the conquest of Granada, done just three years after the event by Rodrigo Alemán. Behind the *coro* is the freestanding **Chapel of the Descent**, dedicated to San Ildefonso; with its golden pinnacle it seems to be some giant monstrance left in the aisle. Another oddity is the 30ft-tall painting of St Christopher on the south wall.

The **Capilla Mayor**, around the main altar, contains some fine sculpture. A famous statue on the left-hand wall is that of Martín Alhaga, a mysterious shepherd who guided Alfonso VIII's army through the mountains before its victory at Las Navas de Tolosa, then disappeared; only the king saw his face, and he directed the sculptor at his work. On the right, another statue honours the memory of Alfaqui Abu Walid. When Alfonso VI conquered Toledo, he promised this Moorish *alcalde* that the great mosque, on the site of the cathedral, would be left in peace. While he was on a campaign, however, the bishop and the king's French wife Constance conspired to tear it down; upon his return the enraged Alfonso was only dissuaded from punishing them by the entreaties of the generous Moor. Behind the altar, the beautiful *retablo* reaches almost to the vaulting.

The Transparente

Even in a cathedral where so much is unusual, this takes the cake. Early in the 18th century, someone decided that Mass here would seem even more transcendent if somehow a shaft of light could be directed over the altar. To do this a hole was chopped in the wall of the Capilla Mayor, and another in the vaulting of the ambulatory. The difficult question of how to reconcile this intrusion was given to the sculptor Narciso Tomé and his four sons, and in several years' work, they transformed the ungainly openings into a Baroque spectacular, combining painting, sculpture and architecture into a cloud of saints, angels and men that grow magically out of the cathedral's stones—many of the figures are partly painted, partly sculpture fixed to the walls. The upper window becomes a kind of vortex, through which the Virgin at the top and all the rest appear in the process of being vacuumed up to heaven. Even those who usually find Baroque extravagance a bore will at least raise a smile for the Transparente, completed in 1732. Antoni Gaudí would have approved, and it's hard to believe he did not gain just a little of his inspiration from this eccentric masterpiece.

Near the Transparente, the ratty old bit of cloth hanging from the vaulting is a Cardinal's hat—cardinals in Spain have the privilege of hanging them wherever they like before they die. It is one of several in the cathedral. Toledo's arch-bishop is still the Primate of Spain, and of cardinals it has known quite a few.

The Mozarabic Chapel

After the Christian conquest of Toledo, a dispute arose immediately between the city's old Christians and the officious Castilian prelates over which form of the liturgy would be used in Masses: the ancient Mozarabic form descended from the time of the Visigoths, or the modern, Church-sanctioned style of the rest of Europe. Alfonso, as any good Crusader might have done, decided on a trial by combat to decide the issue. The Mozarabic champion won, but the Churchmen weren't satisfied, and demanded a trial by fire. So they ignited some prayer-books. The Roman version was blown from the flames by a sudden wind, the Mozarabic wouldn't burn, and Alfonso decreed that the two versions of the faith would co-exist on equal footing. Though the numbers of those faithful to the Mozarabic liturgy have dwindled, their Mass is still regularly celebrated in the large chapel in the southwest corner of the cathedral, built by Cardinal Cisneros, a friend and protector of the Mozarabs. You'll be lucky to see it; this chapel, the only home of the oldest surviving Christian ritual in Western Europe, is usually locked up tight. Other sections of the cathedral are open by separate admission, from the enormous souvenir stand inside the Puerta del Mollete. The **Treasury** has little of interest, though the 3m-high silver reliquary does not fail to impress. In the **Sala Capitular**, a richly decorated room with a gilt *artesanado* ceiling, you can see some unusual frescoes and portraits of all Toledo's archbishops. El Greco painted the frescoes and altarpiece of the **Sacristy**, and there are other works of his, as well as a Holy Family by Van Dyck, and a gloomy representation of the arrest of Christ by Goya that makes an interesting contrast to his famous *Los Fusilamientos de Moncloa* in the Prado.

West of the Cathedral

Here the streets become even narrower and more winding; it's surprising just how long you can stay lost in a town only 1 sq km in area. Just three intractable blocks northwest of the cathedral, the 13th-century church of San Román has been converted into the **Museo de los Concilios y de la Cultura Visigótica** (Museum of the Councils and Visigothic Culture), C/San Clemente (*open Tues–Sat 10–2 and 4–6.30, Sun 10–2, closed Mon*), the only one of its kind in Spain. 'Councils' refers to the several General Councils of the Western Church that were held in Toledo in the days of Visigothic rule, but the majority of the museum's exhibits are simple Visigothic relics, jewellery and religious-artworks. Some of the buckles, brooches and carved stones show an idiosyn-cratic talent, but the lesson here is that the artistic inspiration of Spain did not really change in the transition from Roman to Visigothic rule—only there was much less of it. The building itself is much more interesting, half-Christian and half-Moorish, with naive, original frescoes of the Last Judgement and the 12 Apostles in a garden. Painted angels and saints peer out from the ceilings and horseshoe arches.

The Judería

As long as the streets continue to slope downwards, you'll know you're going in the right direction. The **Judería**, Toledo's Jewish quarter before 1492, occupies a narrow strip of land overlooking the Tajo in the southwestern corner of the city. El Greco too lived here, and the back streets of the Judería hold a concentration of some of old Toledo's most intruiging and interesting monuments.

The church of **Santo Tomé**, on the street of the same name, is unremarkable in itself, but in a little chamber to the side, surrounded by souvenir stands, they'll show you El Greco's *El Entierro del Conde de Orgaz* (The Burial of the Count of Orgaz). The tourists come here in greater numbers than to any sight in Toledo, and more nonsense has been written about this work, perhaps, than any other Spanish painting. A miracle was recorded at this obscure count's burial in 1323. SS. Stephen and Augustine themselves came down from heaven to assist with the obsequies, and this is the scene El Greco portrays. A group of the Count's friends and descendants had petitioned Rome for his beatification, and it is perhaps in support of this that El Greco received the commission, over 200 years later. The portrayal of the burial has for a background a row of gravely serious men, each one a notable portrait in itself (the artist is said to have included himself, sixth from the right, and his son, the small boy in the fore-ground, and some commentators have claimed to find even Lope de Vega and Cervantes among the group of mourners). Above, the earthly scene is paralleled by the Count's reception into heaven.

This painting is perhaps the ultimate expression of the intense, and a little twisted, spirituality of 16th-century Castile. Its heaven, packed with grim, staring faces, seems more of an inferno. Nowhere in the work is there any sense of joy or release, or even wonder at the miraculous apparition of the saints. It is an exaltation of the mysteries of power and death, and the longer you look at it, the more disturbing it becomes.

The **Casa-Museo de El Greco**, not far away at C/Samuel Leví 3 (*open Tues–Sat 10–2 and 4–6, Sun 10–2, closed Mon*), is where the painter lodged for most of the years he lived in Toledo. The city itself, as seen from across the Tajo, was one of his favourite subjects (though his most famous *View of Toledo* is now in the Metropolitan Museum of Art, New York). The best parts of the restored house are the courtyard and tiled kitchen; only a few of El Greco's paintings here are of special merit—notably a portrait of *St Peter*, another favourite subject.

Greek Fire

Instead of making people pray, you make them admire.
Beauty inserts itself as an obstacle between our souls and God.

Grand Inquisitor Cardinal Guevara, to El Greco

Born in 1541 in Venetian-ruled Crete, Domenikos Theokotopoulos was trained as an icon painter, but had more talent than his native island could hold. By the time he was 25, he was in Titian's workshop in Venice, although it was the elongated, linear, mystical style of another Venetian, Tintoretto, that proved the greatest influence on the young painter. By 1570 he was in Rome, coming into contact with the works of Michelangelo and the great central Italian Mannerists (Pontormo, Rosso Fiorentino), whose strange, startling colours, unrealistic perspectives, and exaggerated, often tortured poses were to make their mark on his own art.

A true Cretan, El Greco had a proud and passionate nature. When Pius V was casting about for an artist to paint clothes on the figures of Michelangelo's *Last Judgement* in the Sistine Chapel, El Greco suggested that the Pope would be better off destroying the fresco all together, because he could paint a better one that was chaste to boot. 'Michelangelo was a good man, but he didn't know how to paint,' he said. The Romans were so astounded by his audacity that they ran him out of town.

Fortunately, he had a place to go. In Rome, the Greek had met Diego de Castilla, dean of canons of Toledo Cathedral, who gave him his first major commission: a triptych for the high altar of Toledo's Santo Domingo de Antiguo (central panel in Chicago and two panels in the Prado). It was with this great altarpiece that he perfected his unique, highly personal style of elongated spiritual forms, a nervous line, and figures that rise up like flames in his compositions, all perceptions heightened to a fervent rapture and honed to the spiritual essential of truth. Not everyone was ready for it. The poet Hortensio Paravicino told him: 'You make snow itself burst into flame. You have overstepped nature, and the soul remains undecided in its wonder which of the two, God's creatures or yours, deserves to live.'

El Greco never found favour with that otherwise discriminating art patron Philip II, who panicked at the sight of the *Martyrdom of San Maurizio* that the Cretan had painted for a chapel in the Escorial in 1587. The painter refused all hints that supplication or an offer to soften the colours might win him the king's approval, and in a huff he took his brushes off to Toledo, where he spent his last 37 years with his common-law wife, Jeromina de las Cuevas.

Incapable of doing anything halfway, he lived as extravagantly as a lord, buying a 24-room palace in the former Jewish quarter, and paying a lutanist and guitarist to accompany his every meal. Although he never lacked for commissions from the Church or for portraits (usually of clergymen), after his death all of his worldly possessions fitted into a single trunk. He had spent it all.

The **Taller del Moro** (Moor's Workshop), just around the corner from Santo Tomé church on C/Taller del Moro (*open Tues–Sat 10–2 and 4–6.30, Sun 10–2, closed Mon*), gets its name from the days it spent as a shop for the cathedral workmen. The building itself is an interesting work of *mudéjar* architecture; inside is a collection of the sort of things the craftsmen made. Next door is the 15th-century **Palacio de Fuensalida**, which has been restored and is now the private residence of the President of Toledo. (*Visits are possible in small private groups; contact the custodian at the palace.*)

The Synagogues

Not surprisingly, in a city where Jews played such a prominent and constructive role for so long, two of Toledo's best buildings are synagogues, saved only by good luck after centuries of neglect. **La Sinagoga de Santa María la Blanca** (*c*. 1180), Pza. de Barrionuevo (*open Sat–Thurs 10–2 and 3.30–6, Fri 10–2 and 3.30–7*), so called from its days as a church, is stunning and small, a glistening white confection of horseshoe arches, elaborately carved capitals and geometric medallions that is rightly considered one of the masterpieces of *mudéjar* architecture.

Just as good, though in an entirely different style, is the **Sinagoga del Tránsito**, Pso. del Tránsito (*open Tues–Sat 10–1.45 and 4–5.45, Sun, 10–1.45, closed Mon*), built by Samuel Leví, treasurer to King Pedro I (the Cruel) before that whimsical monarch had him executed. The synagogue is much later than Santa María la Blanca, and shows the influence of the Granada Moors—the interior could be a room in the Alhambra, with its ornate ceiling and carved arabesques, except that the calligraphic inscriptions are in Hebrew instead of Arabic, and the Star of David is interspersed with the arms of Castile and León. The building now houses the **Museo Sefardí** (Sephardic Museum), assembled out of a few surviving relics around the city. Elements of Jewish life and culture such as wedding costumes, a *torah* and a *shofar* are displayed with explanatory notes, to reacquaint Spaniards with a part of their heritage they have quite forgotten.

Monasterio de San Juan de los Reyes

Pza. de San Juan de los Reyes; open daily, in summer 10–1.45 and 3.30–7; in winter 10–1.45 and 3.30–6.

Before the conquest of Granada, Ferdinand and Isabel built a church here with the intention of making it their last resting-place. The architect was Juan Guas, working the perpendicular elegance of Isabelline Gothic to perfection in every detail. Los Reyes Católicos wanted no doubt as to whose monument this was; their F and Y monogram, coats-of-arms, and yoke-and-arrows symbols are everywhere, even on the stained glass.

There's little of the elaborate furnishings of Toledo's cathedral here, but one of the side chapels contains one of the most grotesque, emaciated carved Jesuses in Spain. The exterior of the church is famous, with its western wall covered with the chains of prisoners released from the Moors during the Granada campaigns. The **Cloister**, surrounding a peaceful courtyard where a lone orange tree keeps meditative company with a lone pine, is another of Toledo's architectural treasures, with elegant windows and vaultings on the lower level.

The same merry band of 1880s restorers who did Valladolid's San Gregorio were let loose here, and if you go up to the second floor and gaze up from the arches you will see the hilarious collection of **gargoyles** they added—all manner of monsters, a farting monk and a frog riding a fish; see if you can find the cat.

South of the City

The **Plaza de San Juan de los Reyes Católicos**, in the front of the church, has a wide prospect over the valley of the Tajo; from here you can see another of Toledo's fancy 16th-century gateways, the **Puerta del Cambrón**, and the fortified, medieval **Puente de San Martín**. If you would like to take the measure of this famous town from a little distance, on the other side of the Tajo there's a peripheral road called the **Carretera Circunvalación** that will give you more views of Toledo than El Greco ever did. On its way it passes a goodly number of country houses called *cigarrales*, the *parador*, and finally, the 14th-century **Castillo de San Servando**, rebuilt from an older Templar foundation. Beneath the castle, the old **Puente de Alcántara**, even better than the Puente de San Martín, will take you back across the Tajo in the neighbourhood of the Plaza de Zocodover.

Toledo's Countryside

It isn't pretty, and most of the attractions are castles—over 20 of them within a 48km radius of the city. **Guadamur** and **Barcience**, both west of Toledo, are two of the most interesting. Among the towns and villages, **Talavera de la Reina** is a famous pottery centre, and **Illescas** has five El Grecos on display in its **Hospital de la Caridad**. **Orgaz** and **Tembleque**, on the threshold of La Mancha, are suitably ancient and evocative; each has an interesting Plaza Mayor. At Melque, on a back road southwest of Toledo, is one of the oldest churches in Spain, the 9th-century **Santa María de Melque**.

Eating Out

Dining in Toledo is largely a matter of avoiding overpriced tourist troughs. You'll get your money's worth (over *3000 pts*, though) at the fine restaurant of the **Hostal del Cardenal** (*moderate—see* above). As elsewhere in Toledo, stuffed partridge is a speciality, well-hung and gamey the way the Spaniards like it.

Venta de Aires, C/Circo Romano 25, © 925 22 05 45 (*moderate*) also serves traditional Toledano fare.

You can eat kosher at the **Sinai**, on C/Reyes Católicos in the Judería (*moderate*), with a menu of Jewish and Moroccan specialities.

La Lumbre, C/Real del Arrabal 3, © 925 22 03 73 (*expensive*) mixes local cooking with French-inspired dishes; this is one place where vegetarians generally have plenty to choose from, such as onion tart, leek pie, and mushroom-stuffed artichokes.

The **Asador Adolfo**, C/Granada 6, © 925 22 73 21 (*expensive*) is considered to be Toledo's best restaurant and is the place to go for truly flamboyant dining.

Equally good is **El Ábside**, C/Marqués de Mendigorrín 1, © 925 21 32 02 (*expensive*) located in a 15th-century mansion, where the house specialities include fresh leeks with prawns.

Inexpensive restaurants are not as hard to find as you might think; there's a small colony of them along the C/Barrio Rey, just off the Plaza de Zocodover, including **Maravilla**, Pza. de Barrio Rey 5, © 925 222 33 00 (*cheap*), a reliable choice for good, basic cooking. **Hierbabuena**,

Cristo Luz 9, © 925 222 39 24 (*moderate*), offers light, imaginative cooking with a hint of vegetarian. **La Abadía**, on the corner of Nuñez de Arce and San Nicolás (*cheap*), can get a bit hectic, but that's part of the appeal.

One of the prettiest places in which to enjoy a drink is the tiny square off C/Santo Tomé; here the **Cafetería Nano** sets tables out under the trees. Lastly, you should try Toledo's old speciality, *mazapán*, made from almond paste and sugar.

Castellano, as Spanish is properly called, was the first modern language to have a grammar written for it. When a copy was presented to Queen Isabel in 1492, she understandably asked what it was for. 'Your majesty', replied a perceptive bishop, 'language is the perfect instrument of empire'. In the centuries to come, this concise, flexible and expressive language would prove just that: an instrument that would contribute more to Spanish unity than any laws or institutions, while spreading itself effortlessly over much of the New World.

Among other European languages, Spanish is closest to Portuguese and Italian—and of course, Catalan and Gallego. Spanish, however, may have the simplest grammar of any Romance language, and if you know a little of any one of these, you will find much of the vocabulary looks familiar. It's quite easy to pick up a working knowledge of Spanish; but Spaniards speak colloquially and fast, and in Andalucía they do it with a pronounced accent, leaving out half the consonants and adding some strange sounds all their own. Expressing yourself may prove a little easier than understanding the replies. Spaniards will appreciate your efforts, and when they correct you, they aren't being snooty; they simply feel it's their duty to help you learn. There are dozens of language books and tapes on the market; one particularly good one is Teach Yourself Spanish, by Juan Kattán-Ibarra (Hodder & Stoughton, 1984). If you already speak Spanish, note that the Spaniards increasingly use the familiar tú instead of usted when addressing even complete strangers.

Pronunciation

Pronunciation is phonetic but somewhat difficult for English speakers.

Vowels

a	short *a* as in 'pat'	**u**	silent after *q* and gue- and gui-; otherwise long *u* as in 'flute'
e	short *e* as in 'set'		
i	as *e* in 'be'	**ü**	*w* sound, as in 'dwell'

Language

o	between long *o* of 'note' and short *o* of 'hot'	**y**	at end of word or meaning *and*, as **i**

Dipthongs

ai, ay	as *i* in 'side'	**ei, ey**	as *ey* in 'they'
au	as *ou* in 'sound'	**oi, oy**	as *oy* of 'boy'

Consonants

c	before the vowels *i* and *e*, it's a *castellano* tradition to pronounce it as *th*; many Spaniards and all Latin Americans pronounce it in this case as an *s*
ch	like *ch* in 'church'
d	often becomes *th*, or is almost silent, at end of word
g	before *i* or *e*, pronounced as **j** (*see below*)
h	silent
j	the *ch* in loch—a guttural, throat-clearing *h*
ll	*y* or *ly* as in million
ñ	*ny* as in canyon (the ~ is called a tilde)
q	*k*
r	usually rolled, which takes practice
v	often pronounced as *b*
z	*th*, but *s* in parts of Andalucía

Stress is on the penultimate syllable if the word ends in a vowel, an *n* or an *s*, and on the last syllable if the word ends in any other consonant; exceptions are marked with an accent.

If all this seems difficult, consider that English pronunciation is even worse for Spaniards. Young people in Spain seem to be all madly learning English these days; if your Spanish friends giggle at your pronunciation, get them to say *squirrel*.

Practise on some of the place names:

Madrid	ma-DREED	**Trujillo**	troo-HEE-oh
León	lay-OHN	**Jerez**	her-ETH
Sevilla	se-BEE-ah	**Badajóz**	ba-da-HOTH
Cáceres	CAH-ther-es	**Málaga**	MAHL-ah-gah
Cuenca	KWAYN-ka	**Alcázar**	ahl-CATH-ar
Jaén	ha-AIN	**Valladolid**	ba-yah-dol-EED
Sigüenza	sig-WAYN-thah	**Arévalo**	ahr-EB-bah-lo

Driving

rent	*alquiler*	driver	*conductor, chófer*
car	*coche*	exit	*salida*
motorbike/moped	*moto/ciclomotor*	entrance	*entrada*
bicycle	*bicicleta*	danger	*peligro*
petrol	*gasolina*	dangerous	*peligroso*
This doesn't work	*Este no funciona*	no parking	*estacionamento prohibido*
road	*carretera*		
Is the road good?	*¿Es buena la carretera?*	give way/yield	*ceda el paso*
		road works	*obras*
breakdown	*avería*		
(international) driving licence	*carnet de conducir (internacional)*	Note: Most road signs will be in international pictographs

Transport

aeroplane	*avión*	platform	*andén*
airport	*aeropuerto*	port	*puerto*
bus/coach	*autobús/autocar*	seat	*asiento*
bus/railway station	*estación*	ship	*buque/barco/embarcadero*
bus stop	*parada*		
car/automobile	*coche*	ticket	*billete*
customs	*aduana*	train	*tren*

Directions

I want to go to...	*Deseo ir a...*	Have a good trip!	*¡Buen viaje!*
How can I get to...?	*¿Cómo puedo llegar a... ?*	here	*aquí*
		there	*allí*
Where is...?	*¿Dónde está... ?*	close	*cerca*
When is the next...?	*¿Cuándo sale el próximo... ?*	far	*lejos*
		left	*izquierda*
What time does it leave (arrive)?	*¿Parte (llega) a qué hora?*	right	*derecha*
		straight on	*todo recto*
From where does it leave?	*¿De dónde sale?*	forwards	*adelante*
		backwards	*hacia atrás*
Do you stop at ...?	*¿Para en... ?*	up	*arriba*
How long does the trip take?	*¿Cuánto tiempo dura el viaje?*	down	*abajo*
		corner	*esquina*
I want a (return) ticket to...	*Quiero un billete (de ida y vuelta) a*	square	*plaza*
		street	*calle*
How much is the fare?	*¿Cuánto cuesta el billete?*		

Time

What time is it?	*¿Qué hora es?*	morning	*mañana*
It is 2 o'clock	*Son las dos*	afternoon	*tarde*
... half past 2	*...las dos y media*	evening	*noche*
... a quarter past 2	*...las dos y cuarto*	today	*hoy*
... a quarter to 3	*...las tres menos cuarto*	yesterday	*ayer*
		soon	*pronto*
month	*mes*	tomorrow	*mañana*
week	*semana*	it is early	*está temprano*
day	*día*	it is late	*está tarde*

Days

Monday	*lunes*	Friday	*viernes*
Tuesday	*martes*	Saturday	*sábado*
Wednesday	*miércoles*	Sunday	*domingo*
Thursday	*jueves*		

Shopping and Sightseeing

I would like...	*Quisiera...*	pharmacy	*farmacía*
Where is/are...?	*¿Dónde está/ están...?*	post office	*correos*
		postage stamp	*sello*
How much is it?	*¿Cuánto vale eso?*	sea	*mar*
open	*abierto*	shop	*tienda*
closed	*cerrado*	Do you have any change?	*¿Tiene cambio?*
cheap/expensive	*barato/caro*		
bank	*banco*	telephone	*teléfono*
beach	*playa*	toilet/toilets	*servicios/aseos*
booking/box office	*taquilla*	men	*señores/ hombres/ caballeros*
church	*iglesia*		
museum	*museo*		
theatre	*teatro*	women	*señoras/damas*

Accommodation

Where is the hotel?	*¿Dónde está el hotel?*	... with 2 beds	*con dos camas*
Do you have a room?	*¿Tiene usted una habitación?*	... with double bed	*con una cama grande*
Can I look at the room?	*¿Podría ver la habitación?*	... with a shower/ bath	*con ducha/baño*
How much is the room per day/ week?	*¿Cuánto cuesta la habitación por día semana?*	... for one night/ one week	*una noche/ una semana*

Fish (*Pescados*)

acedías	small plaice	*langosta*	lobster
adobo	fish marinated in white wine	*langostinos*	giant prawns
		mariscos	shellfish
almejas	clams	*mejillones*	mussels
anchoas	anchovies	*merluza*	hake
anguilas	eels	*mero*	grouper
ástaco	crayfish	*navajas*	razor-shell clams
bacalao	codfish (usally dried)		
		ostras	oysters
bogavante	lobster	*percebes*	barnacles
calamares	squid	*pescadilla*	whiting
cangrejo	crab	*pez espada*	swordfish
chanquetes	whitebait	*platija*	plaice
chipirones	cuttlefish	*pulpo*	octopus
… en su tinta	…in its own ink	*rape*	anglerfish
dorado, lubina	sea bass,	*trucha*	trout
escabeche	pickled or marinated fish	*veneras*	scallops
gambas	prawns	*zarzuela*	fish stew

Meat and Fowl (*Carnes y Aves*)

albóndigas	meatballs	*pato*	duck
asado	roast	*pavo*	turkey
buey	ox	*perdiz*	partridge
callos	tripe	*pinchitos*	spicy mini kebabs
cerdo	pork		
chorizo	spiced sausage	*pollo*	chicken
chuletas	chops	*rabo/cola de toro*	bull's tail with onions and tomatoes
cochinillo	sucking pig		
conejo	rabbit		
corazón	heart	*salchicha*	sausage
cordero	lamb	*salchichón*	salami
faisán	pheasant	*sesos*	brains
fiambres	cold meats	*solomillo*	sirloin steak
hígado	liver	*ternera*	veal
jabalí	wild boar		
jamón de York	raw cured ham		
jamón serrano	baked ham		
lomo	pork loin		
morcilla	blood sausage		

Note: *potajes, cocidos, guisados, estofados, fabadas* and *cazuelas* are various kinds of stew.

Vegetables (*Verduras y Legumbres*)

alcachofas	artichokes	espinacas	spinach
apio	celery	garbanzos	chickpeas
arroz	rice	judías (verdes)	French beans
arroz marinera	rice with saffron and seafood	lechuga	lettuce
		lentejas	lentils
berenjena	aubergine (eggplant)	patatas (fritas/salteadas)	potatoes (fried/sautéed)
		(al horno)	(baked)
cebolla	onion	puerros	leeks
champiñones	mushrooms	remolachas	beetroots (beets)
col, repollo	cabbage	setas	Spanish mushrooms
coliflor	cauliflower		
endibias	endives		
espárragos	asparagus	zanahorias	carrots

Desserts (*Postres*)

arroz con leche	rice pudding	pajama	flan with ice cream
bizcocho/pastel/torta	cake		
blanco y negro	ice cream and coffee float	pasteles	pastries
		queso	cheese
flan	crème caramel	requesón	cottage cheese
galletas	biscuits (cookies)	tarta de frutas	fruit pie
helados	ice creams	turrón	nougat

Restaurant Vocabulary

menu	carta/menú	Can I see the menu, please?	Déme el menú, por favor
bill/check	cuenta		
change	cambio	Do you have a wine list?	¿Hay una lista de vinos?
set meal	menú del día		
waiter/waitress	camarero/a	Can I have the bill (check), please?	La cuenta, por favor
Do you have a table?	¿Tiene una mesa?		
... for one/two?	¿... para uno/dos?	Can I pay by credit card?	¿Puedo pagar con tarjeta de crédito?

412	Visigoths, allies of Rome, make Toledo their capital
713	Arabs under Tarik ibn Zivad defeat Roderick, last king of the Visigoths
718	Battle of Covadonga; Pelayo the Conqueror wins first battle against Arabs
860	Madrid founded on the order of Emir Mohammed I of Córdoba
1001–35	Sancho III the Great of Navarra rules most of north Spain as Rex Iberorum
1035	Sancho III's kingdom divided between Ramiro in Aragón and Ferdinand I of Castile
1085	Alfonso VI of Castile and El Cid capture Toledo and Madrid
1109	Madrid besieged by Moors
1202	Alfonso VIII gives Madrid its Statutes
1212	Battle of Las Navas de Tolosa; a united Christian army under Alfonso VII of Castile crushes the Moors in Spain
1309	Cortes held in Madrid for first time
1350–69	Reign of Pedro the Cruel of Castile and León; rebuilding of Madrid's Alcázar
1476	Union of the crowns of Castile and Aragón under the Catholic Kings, Ferdinand and Isabel
1492	Ferdinand and Isabel conquer Granada, banish the Jews from Spain, and send Columbus to find a shortcut to the East Indies
1495	Ferdinand and Isabel's daughter Juana weds Philip, son of Habsburg Emperor Maximilian
1516	The son of Juana and Philip becomes Carlos I of Spain
1519	Carlos I becomes Emperor Charles V, ruler of Spain, Italy, the Low Countries, Austria and the New World
1520	Comunero revolt against Charles in Castile
1547	Cervantes born in Alcalá de Henares
1556	Charles V abdicates; succeeded by son Philip II; Spain bankrupt
1560	Madrid made the capital of Spain
1563	Philip II begins El Escorial
1580	Philip II declares himself King of Portugal
1588	Philip sends the Invincible Armada against England
1599	Birth of Velázquez
1601–6	Cortes returned to Vallodolid
1609	Philip III expels the Moriscos, depriving Spain of farmers and wrecking the economy
1614	Death of El Greco
1630	Building of Buen Retiro Palace for Philip IV
1643	Defeat at Rocroi; end of Spanish ambitions in Europe

Chronology

1668	Portugal regains its independence

1700	Charles II dies without heir; Philip V crowned first Bourbon king of Spain
1714	War of Spanish Succession ends, Spain loses the Netherlands, Kingdom of Naples, Gibraltar
1746	Birth of Goya
1759–88	Reign of the 'Mayor King' Charles III: political and economic reforms
1777	Flagellation in religious processions is banned
1788–1808	Charles IV undoes all the good works of his father
1805	Nelson annihilates the Spanish fleet under French command at Trafalgar
1808	Charles IV abdicates; Napoleon installs Joseph Bonaparte as king; Madrid revolt of 2 May brutally suppressed by the French
1808–13	Peninsular War: Napoleon battles the Spaniards and their British allies
1812	Constitution of Cádiz
1820	Revolt against the reactionary Ferdinand VII suppressed by French and British
1833–40	First Carlist War: Liberals supporting Isabel II defeat pretender Don Carlo
1868	General Prim proclaims the First Republic, causing Second Carlist War
1876	Alfonso XII, son of Isabel II, restored to throne
1898	Spanish-American War; Spain loses Cuba, the Phillipines and Puerto Rico
1923	King Alfonso XIII recognizes General Primo de Rivera's coup d'etat
1930	Primo de Rivera resigns with the Depression
1931	Alfonso XIII abdicates when municipal elections vote overwhelmingly for a Republic
1931–36	Republic tainted by political violence. Antonio Primo de Rivera forms fascist Falange Española
1936	Left-wing Popular Front wins elections; military coup starts Civil War
1939	Republican government flees to Barcelona and Madrid falls in final Nationalist victory. Franco keeps Spain out of Second World War
1953	Military co-operation treaty signed with United States
1973	Resistance to Franco grows; Prime Minister Carrero Blanco blown up in Madrid bomb
1975	Death of Franco and coronation of Juan Carlos I
1978	Signing of a new social democratic constitution
1981	Officers' right-wing coup attempt defeated
1982	Spain joins NATO; Socialist Felipe González elected Prime Minister
1983	Spain divides into 17 autonomous communities
1986	Spain and Portugal join the European Community
1992	500th anniversary of Columbus's trip: World's Fair in Sevilla, Olympics in Barcelona, and Madrid is the Cultural Capital of Europe
1995	Partido Popular (PP) under José Maria Aznar defeats González's Socialists in general elections
1996	PP under José Maria Alvarez de Manzano takes control of Madrid

Almodóvar, Pedro, *The Patty Diphusa Stories and Other Writings* (Faber & Faber, 1992). Effervescent tales of the *Movida.*.

Brown, Jonathan, *Velázquez: Painter and Courtier* (Yale, 1988). Fine study of the master's art, life and times; also the highly acclaimed *Velázquez, The Technique of Genius* (Yale, 1998), which appraises his art.

Carr, Raymond, *Spain 1808–1975* (Oxford, Clarendon Press, 1982). A learned and monumental account of Spain from the end of the French occupation to the end of Franco.

Cela, Camilo José, *The Hive* (Sceptre, 1992). Biting novel about Madrid in the Franco years, centred on the do-nothing literati in the Café Gijon.

Elliott, J.H., *Imperial Spain 1469–1716* (Penguin, 1990). Wonderfully readable account of Spain's glory days. Also, *The Count-Duke of Olivares: The Statesman in an Age of Decline* (Yale, 1986) and with Jonathan Brown, *A Palace for a King: The Buen Retiro and the Court of Philip IV*, Yale 1980, an account of the splendours of the Habsbourg court in the Golden Age.

Fraser, Ronald, *Blood of Spain: The Experience of the Civil War 1936–39* (Pantheon, 1986). Compelling compilations of oral accounts of the Civil War, but hard to find.

Gibson, Ian, *Fire in the Blood: The New Spain* (Faber & Faber, 1992). A brave unravelling of modern Spain, by the maker of the BBC series.

Gilmour, David, *Cities of Spain* (Pimlico, 1994). Insightful account of Madrid, also interesting in the context of other Spanish cities.

Jacobs, Michael, *Madrid Observed* (Pallas Athene, 1992). Delightfully opinionated walking tours of Madrid, based on various themes.

Hooper, John, *The New Spaniards* (Penguin, 1995). Excellent in depth introduction to contemporary Spain.

Múnoz Molina, Antonio, *Prince of Shadows* (Quartet, 1994). A thriller set in modern Madrid, by one of the Spain's most popular writers.

Pérez Galdós, Benito, *Fortunata and Jacinta* (Penguin, 1988). Spain's greatest 19th century novelist tackles love and class amid the sound and fury of Madrid in the 1860s. A classic. Also, *That Bringas Woman* (translation of *La de Bringas*) (Everyman, 1996).

Further Reading

Preston, Paul, *Franco* (Harper Collins, 1993). Extensive and fascinating account of the Caudillo; also *A Concise History of the Spanish Civil War*, Fontana 1996, best short account.

Quevedo, Francisco de, *Two Spanish Picaresque Novels* (Viking, 1969). Written in 1626, Quevedo' classic *The Swindler* (El Buscón) is rife with atmosphere of Golden Age Spain and Madrid; the volume also includes the anonymous tale of *Lazarillo de Tormes*.

Thomas, Hugh, *Madrid: A Travellers' Companion* (Constable, 1988). A wonderful collection of 500 years' of writing about Madrid by a wide range of writers and visitors; also *The Spain Civil War,* Hamish Hamilton 1977 (3rd edition). The definitive history—monumental and compelling.

Thomlinson, Janis, *Francisco Goya y Lucientes 1746–1828* (Phaidon, 1999). Excellent account of his life and work.

Main page references are in **bold**. Page references to maps are in *italic*.

ABC Building 131
Academia Real de la Historía 89
Acciona-Museo Interactivo de la Ciencia 10
accommodation *see* where to stay
air pollution 41
airline addresses 2–3
airport 2
Al-Mansur 22
Alba, Dukes of 166
Alcalá de Henares 244, **245–6**, 247–8
Alfonso VI of Castile 22, 258
Alfonso the Wise 254
Alfonso XII 29
Alfonso XIII 30, 69
Allegory of Madrid (Goya) 160
Alvarez del Manzano, José María 34
América, Museo de **171**, 175
Angel Caído 112
Antigua Pastelería del Pozo 85
Antiqua Hervería 159
Antonio de Alarcón, Pedro 90
Antropología, Museo de **118**, 175
Aquasur 10
Arabs 22–3
Aranjuez 249–50
architecture **36–8**
    casas a la malicia 25
    Ciudad Lineal 44
Arco de los Cuchilleros 67
Arco de la Victoria 171
Argüelles 170

Armería Real 147
Army Museum **109**, 176
Arqueológico Nacional, Museo de **127–8**, 175
Arrabal (Toledo) 256
Art Deco 38
Art Nouveau 38
Artes Decorativas, Museo de **109–10**, 175
asadores 178
Atenio Científico y Literario de Madrid 86
Atocha station *3*, 6, 113
Ávila 238–44
    Basílica de San Vicente 239
    Cathedral 241
    Convento de la Encarnación 242
    Convento de las Madres 242
    Convento de Santa Teresa 241–2
    eating out 243–4
    getting there 238–9
    Los Verracos 240
    Museo Provincial 240
    Nuestra Señora de la Soterana 239
    Plaza de Santa Teresa 240
    Puerta de Alcázar 240
    San Pedro 240
    San Segundo 241
    tourist information 239
    walls 238, **240–1**
bail bonds 4
Bankinter 130
banks 16–17
    Bilbao-Vizcaya 155
    Central-Hispano 155
    de España 125

Español de Crédito 154–5
Europa 132
Hipotecario 126
Santander 130–1
Bankunión 132
Barajas airport 2
Barbara de Bragança 162
Barcience 265
Barrio de Salamanca *122–3*, 129–30
barrios bajos 72, 74
bars 203–4
    see also cafés, bars, restaurants
Basílica de Atocha 119
Basílica de San Francisco el Grande 70
Basílica de San Miguel 69
Basílica de San Vicente (Ávila) 239
basketball 206
Bautista de Toledo, Juan 222
bear symbol 40–1
beer 186
Bellver, Ricardo 112
Biblioteca Nacional 126–7
bicycles 207
blues music 205–6
Bolsa de Commercio 102
Bonaparte, Joseph 28
book shops 211
border formalities 4
Bosch, Hieronymous 96–7
Botín 67
Bourbons 27–8, 29
brandy 186
bullfighting 48–9, 206
    museum **126**, 176
buses 3–4, 6
Caballero, Largo 52, 133

Index

Café Barbieri 80
Café Gijón 126
café society 187–9
cafés, bars, restaurants
    177–90, 203–4
  asadores 178
  cafeterías 178
  Castellana 122, 179
  Chinese restaurants 178
  Chueca 152, 183–5
  comedores 178
  Embajadores 74
  Gran Vía 152, 183–5
  Italian restaurants 178
  La Latina 74
  language 271–2
  Lavapiés 74, 181–3
  Malasaña 152, 183–5
  marisqueras 178
  Old Madrid 65
  open-air eating 185
  Opera 183–5
  parklands 166
  Paseo del Arte 92
  Plaza Mayor 181–3
  Plaza Santa Ana 84
  Puerta del Sol 56
  Retiro 180
  Royal Madrid 140
  Salamanca 122, 179
  Santa Ana 181–3
  tapas bars 179
  vegetarian 185
  ventas 178
  see also cafés, bars,
    restaurants; drink
cafeterías 178
Calcografía Nacional 154
Calder, Alexander 116
calendar of events 13–15
California café 129
Calle de Alcalá 152
Calle Almirante 16
Calle del Arenal 140
Calle de Atocha 89

Calle de la Baja 67
Calle Cinema 157
Calle de los Cuchilleros 67
Calle Echegaray 87
Calle Hortaleza 161
Calle Mayor 67
Calle de la Paloma 76
Calle de Preciados 157
Calle de Ribera de
    Curtadores 77
Calle de Toledo 66
Campo del Moro 148
Candelas, Luis 75
Capilla del Cristo 142
Capilla del Cristo de los
    Dolores 70
Capilla del Osbispo 70
Capilla de San Isidro 70
Capitol 157
car hire 7
car travel 4
  language 269
Carlist Wars 28–9
Carretera Circunvalación
    (Toledo) 264
Carruajes, Museo de 147
Casa de América 125
Casa de Campo 169–70
Casa Ciriaco 69
Casa Cisernos 68–9
Casa de Correos 58–9
Casa Gallardo 167
Casa Mira 85
Casa Panadería 64
Casa Pérez Villamil 89
Casa de los Picos (Segovia)
    234
Casa de las Siete Chimeneas
    155
Casa de Vacas 111, 176
Casa de la Ville 68
Casa-Museo de El Greco
    (Toledo) 261–2
Casa-Museo de Lope de
    Vega **87**, 176

casas a la malicia 25
Casino de Madrid 154
Casón del Buen Retiro
    100–1, 174
Castellana 122–3, 130–6
  food and drink 124, 180
  where to stay 194–6
Castile 22–3
Castillo de San Servando
    (Toledo) 264
castizos 42–3
Cathedral (Ávila) 241
Cathedral de Santa María
    Real de la Almudena
    147
Cathedral (Segovia) 232–3
Cathedral (Toledo) 258–60
Centro de Arte Reína Sofía
    114–18, 174
Centro Cultural de la Ville
    128
Cera, Museo de 128
cercanías 6
Cerralbo **167**, 175
Cervezería Alemana 87
Chamartín station **3**, 6
changing of the guard 146
Charles II **26–7**, 64
Charles III 27
  statue 59
Charles IV 27
Charles Stuart, Prince of
    Wales 46
Charles V, Holy Roman
    Emperor 24
Chicote 156
children 10
Chillida, Eduardo 118
Chinese restaurants 178
Chocolatería San Ginés 142
Christ on the Cross
    (Velázquez) 158
Chueca 150–1, 159–61
  food and drink 152,
    183–5
  where to stay 192–4

church opening hours 17
Churrigueresque
    architecture 37
Ciencias Naturales, Museo
    de **133**, 176
Cine Doré 89
cinema 201–2
Círculo de Bellas Artes 155
Ciudad Lineal 44
Ciudad, Museo de **134**, 175
Civil War 31–2, 50–2, 257
classical music 200
climate 11
comedores 178
Comendadoras 167
Compañía Nacional
    Hispánica 132
Comunero Revolt 24
Concilios y de la Cultura
    Visigótica (Toledo)
    260–1
convents
    de las Carboneros 69
    de las Carmelitas
        Descalzas (Segovia) 236
    de las Descalzas Reales
        140–2, 174
    de la Encarnación
        143–4, 174
    de la Encarnación (Ávila)
        242
    Las Calatravas 155
    de las Madres (Ávila) 242
    de Santa Teresa (Ávila)
        241–2
    de las Trinitarias
        Descalzas 88
The Cortes 82, 85
credit cards 17
crime 17–18
Cristo de la Luz (Toledo)
    258
Cuartel del Conde Duque
    166–7
Cuesta de Claudio Moyano
    112

currency 16
Customs House 152
cybercafés 11
cycling 207
Dalí, Salvador 116–17
dance 200
day trips **220–66**, *220–1*
    Alcalá de Henares 244,
        245–6, 247–8
    Aranjuez 249–50
    Ávila 238–44
    El Escorial 222–8
    Guadalajara 244, **246**,
        248
    Segovia 229–38, *230–1*
    Sigüenza 244, **246–7**,
        248
    Toledo 251–66, *252–3*
    Valle de los Caídos
        228–9
disabled travellers 12
discos 203
Don Quixote 88, 90
Dos de Mayo revolution 28
drink 186
    beer 186
    brandy 186
    water 41
    wine 186
driving in Madrid 4
    car hire 7
    language 269
Dürer, Albrecht 97
E111 forms 15
Edificio España 166
Edificio Metropólis 155
Ejército, Museo del **109**,
    176
Ekseption 129–30
El Capricho de Osuna 136
El Cid 258
El Escorial 222–8
    Basilica 226–7
    Biblioteca 226
    Bourbon Apartments 224

Casita del Arriba 227
Casita del Príncipe 227
eating out 228
getting there 223–4
Hall of the Battles 224
New Museums 225
Palacio de Philip II 225
Panteón Real 226
Patio de los Reyes 226–7
Prudería 226
Sacristía 226
Salas Capitulares 226
Terreros 228
tourist information 224
El Estanque 110
El Greco (Domenicos
    Theokotopoulos) 98,
    261–3
El Mundo Fantastico 90
El Parral (Segovia) 236
El Rastro 77
El Viso 134
electricity 12
Embajadores *72–3*
    cafés, bars, restaurants 74
    Fábrica de Tabacos 78
    Instituto de Ensañanza
        Media Cervates 78
    La Corrala 78–9
    San Cayetano 78
    San Fernando 78
embassies 12–13
emergency services 15
entertainment and nightlife
    200–8
    bars 203–4
    blues music 205–6
    cinema 201–2
    classical music 200
    dance 200
    discos 203
    flamenco 202
    gay bars 204
    jazz music 205–6
    lesbian bars 205

entertainment and nightlife (cont'd)
  nightclubs 202–5
  rock music 205–6
  sports and activities 206–7
  theatre 207–8
  zarzuela 200
Ermita de San Antonio de la Florida 168–9
Ermita de San Isidro 77
Ermita de la Virgen del Puerto 148
Escuelas Aguirre 125
Escultura al Aire Libre 131
Eslava Club 142
Espartero, General, statue of 125
Estadio Santiago Bernabéu 135
Estadio Vicente Calderón 76
Fábrica de Tabacos 78
Farmacia 147
Farmacia de la Reina Madre 67
Faro de Madrid 172
fashion shops 210
Ferdinand of Aragon 23–4
Ferdinand VI 27
Ferdinand VII 28
Feria de Madrid 136
Ferroviario **120**, 176
festivals **13–15**, 42–3
Filmoteca Nacional 89
films 201–2
First Republic 29
First World War 30
flamenco 202
football 206
Fountain of Apollo 94
Fountain of Neptune 94
Franco, Francisco 31–2, 50–2
  statue 133–4
  tomb 229

French Institute 162
Fuente de la Alcachofa 113
Fuente Castellana 131–2
Fuente de la Fama 160
Fundación Arte y Tecnología de Telefónica **156**, 176
Fundación de la Casa de Alba 174
Fundación Juan March 130
Fundación Mapfre Vida 135
Galdiano, Lázaro 132
Galván, Enrique Tierno 33–4
gay bars 204
Glorieta Emilio Castelar 131
Godoy, Manuel 27–8
golf 207
González, Felipe 33
Gonzalo, Eloy 77
Gothic architecture 36
Goya y Lucientes, Francisco de **47–8**, 67, 100, 168–9
  Allegory of Madrid 160
  grave 169
  Madrid Fair 75
  Pantheon 168–9
Gran Vía *150–1*, **156–7**
  food and drink 152, 183–5
  where to stay 192–4
Grassy 156
Grimau, Julián 59
Guadalajara 244, **246**, 248
Guadamur 265
Guernica 114, 116
Habsburgs 25–7
health 15
Henry III 23
Henry IV 23
Herrera, Juan de 36, 222
hiring cars 7
history **22–34**
  Arabs 22–3

Bourbons 27–8, 29
Civil War 31–2, 50–2, 257
First Republic 29
Habsburgs 25–7
Second Republic 30–1
Hospital de Maudes 134
Hospital de Santa Cruz (Toledo) 255–6
Hospital de Tavera (Toledo) 256–7
Hotel Mónaco 161
Hotel Reina Victoria 87
hotels *see* where to stay
Ibárruri, Dolores 51
Iglesia de las Maravillas 159
Illescas 265
IMAX cinema 10, 120
Instituto de Ensañanza Media Cervates 78
Instituto Valencia de Don Juan 131
insurance
  health 15
  motor 4
International Brigades 31
international driver's licence 4
Isabel I 23–4
Isabel II 28–9
  statue 143
Isabella Farnese 67
Isabelline Gothic architecture 36
Italian restaurants 178
Jardines del Descubrimiento 128
Jardines Sabatini 144
jazz music 205–6
Jesús de Medinaceli 88
jogging 207
Juan Carlos I 33
Juan (St John of the Cross) 243
Juana of Austria 140

Judería (Toledo) 261
Juvarra, Filippo 145
Kilometro Cero 59
KIO Towers 135
La Casa del Abuelo 85
La Comunista 161
La Corrala 78–9
La Granja de San Ildefonso
   (Segovia) 236–7
La Latina 72–3, 75–7
   cafés, bars, restaurants 74
   Calle de la Paloma 76
   Calle de Ribera de
      Curtadores 77
   El Rastro 77
   Ermita de San Isidro 77
   Estadio Vicente Calderón
      76
   La Virgen de la Paloma 76
   Mercado Puerta de
      Toledo 75–6
   Plaza de Cascorro 77
   Plaza del La Cebeda 75
   Puente de Toledo 76–7
   Puerta de Toledo 75
   Puerta de Toledo
      complex 76
La Rosaleda 168
La Taberna de Antonio
   Sánchez 80
La Trinidad (Segovia) 234
La Vera Cruz (Segovia)
   235–6
La Villa del Oso y Madroño
   40–1
La Virgen de la Paloma 76
Laboratorio de
   Especialidades Juanse
   159
language 267–72
Las Calatravas 155
Las Delicias 120
Las Salesas 162
Lavapiés see Plaza de
   Lavapiés

Lázaro Galdiano, Museo
   132, 175
left luggage 4
Leon VI 23
Lerma, Duke of 26
lesbian bars 205
Lhardy, Emilio 82
Libro, Museo del 127
litter 41–2
living and working in
   Madrid 216–18
Lope De Vega 87, 176
Los Verracos (Ávila) 240
lost and found 16
Madrid Fair (Goya) 75
magazines 16
Malasaña 150–1, 157–9
   food and drink 152,
      183–5
   nightlife 204
   where to stay 192–4
Malasaña, Manuela 158–9
March, Juan 130
marisqueras 178
markets 213
media 16, 211
Melque 265
Mendizábel 29
Mercado Puerta de Toledo
   75–6
Mercado de San Miguel 67
Mérimée, Prosper 82
metro 5
Mezquita del Cristo de la
   Luz (Toledo) 258
Ministry of Agriculture 113
Ministry of Air 170–1
Mohammed I 22
Mola, Emiliano 31
Monasterio de San Juan de
   los Reyes (Toledo) 264
Moneo, Rafael 38
money 16–17
Monument to Columbus
   128

Mora, Juan Gómez de 36
Moriarty Gallery 162
Morral, Mateo 69
movida 45
mudéjars 22–3, 36
Municipal Museum
   159–60, 175
museums 174–6
   Acciona-Museo
      Interactivo de la
      Ciencia 10
   América 171, 175
   Antropología 118, 175
   Army Museum 109, 176
   Arqueológico Nacional
      127–8, 175
   Artes Decorativas
      109–10
   Bullfighting Museum
      126, 176
   Carruajes 147
   Casa de Vacas 176
   Casa-Museo de El Greco
      (Toledo) 261–2
   Casa-Museo de Lope de
      Vega 87, 176
   Casón del Buen Retiro
      100–1, 174
   Centro de Arte Reína
      Sofía 114–18, 174
   Cera 128
   Cerralbo 167, 175
   for children 10
   Ciencias Naturales 133,
      176
   de la Ciudad 134, 175
   Concilios y de la Cultura
      Visigótica (Toledo)
      260–1
   Convento de las
      Descalzes Reales
      140–2, 174
   Convento de la
      Encarnación 143–4,
      174
   Ejército 109, 176

museums (*cont'd*)
  Escultura al Aire Libre
    131
  Ferroviario **120**, 176
  Fundación Arte y
    Tecnología de
    Telefónica **156**, 176
  Fundación de la Casa de
    Alba 174
  Hospital de Tavera
    (Toledo) 256–7
  Instituto Valencia de Don
    Juan 131
  Lázaro Galdiano **132**,
    175
  Libro 127
  Lope De Vega **87**, 176
  Municipal **159–60**, 175
  Naval **109**, 175
  Observatorio
    Astronómico **112**, 176
  opening hours 17
  Palacio Real **145–7**, 175
  Panteón de Goya **168–9**,
    174
  Postal y de
    Telecomunicaciones
    125
  Prado **94–101**, 174
  Provincial (Ávila) 240
  Real Academia de Bellas
    Artes de San Fernando
    152–4, 174
  Real Fábrica de Tapices
    119–20, 175
  Reina Sofía **114–18**, 174
  des Reproducciones
    Artisticas 172
  Romántico **160–1**, 175
  Sefardí (Toledo) 264
  Sorolla **131**, 174
  Taurino **126**, 176
  Thyssen-Bornemisza
    102–8, 174
Naval Museum **109**, 176
neo-classical architecture 37

neo-mudéjar architecture 37
New Club 155
newspapers 16, 211
nightclubs 202–5
Nuestra Señora de la
  Soterana (Ávila) 239
Nuevos Ministerios 133
Observatorio Astronómico
  112, 176
Oíza, Francisco Saénz de 38
Old Madrid **62–70**, *62–3*
  Arco de los Cuchilleros
    67
  Basílica de San Francisco
    el Grande 70
  Basílica de San Miguel 69
  Botín 67
  cafés, bars, restaurants 65
  Calle de la Baja 67
  Calle de los Cuchilleros
    67
  Calle Mayor 67
  Calle de Toledo 66
  Capilla del Cristo de los
    Dolores 70
  Capilla del Osbispo 70
  Capilla de San Isidro 70
  Casa Ciriaco 69
  Casa Cisernos 68–9
  Casa Panadería 64
  Casa de la Ville 68
  Convento de las
    Carboneros 69
  Farmacia de la Reina
    Madre 67
  Mercado de San Miguel
    67
  Palacio de Santa Cruz 66
  Palacio de los Vargas 70
  Plaza Mayor 64
  Plaza de la Paja 69–70
  Plaza de la Puerta
    Cerrada 66–7
  Plaza de la Ville 67, 68
  Sala de Actos 68

San Andrés 70
San Isidro 66
San Nicolás de los
  Servitas 69
San Pedro el Viejo 69–70
statue of Philip III 64
Torre de los Lujanes 68
Olivares, Conde-Duque de
  26
open-air eating 185
opening hours 17
Opera
  food and drink 183–5
  where to stay 192–4
Oratorio del Cabellero de
  Gracia 157
Orgaz 265
Oso y Madroño 59
Osuna, Duchess of 136
Pacha 160
Pacheco, Juan, Marqués de
  Villena 236
Palace Hotel 85–6
palacio
  de Comunicaciones
    124–5
  de Cristal 112
  Episcopal (Segovia) 234
  de Fuensalida (Toledo)
    263
  de Gaviria 142
  de Linares 125
  de Liria 166
  de los Marqueses de
    Perales 80
  Municipal de Congresos
    135, 136
  de la Música 157
  de la Prensa 157
  Real 145–7
  Real de El Pardo 172
  de Santa Cruz 66
  de Santoña 89
  del Senado 144
  de los Vargas 70

de Velázquez 111–12
de la Zarzuela 172
Palacio, Antonio 38
Panteón de Goya **168–9**, 174
Panteón de Hombres Ilustres 119
parking 4
parklands **164–72**, *164–5*
  Arco de la Victoria 171
  Argüelles 170
  cafés, bars, restaurants 166
  Casa de Campo 169–70
  Casa Gallardo 167
  Comendadoras 167
  Cuartel del Conde Duque 166–7
  Edificio España 166
  Ermita de San Antonio de la Florida 168–9
  Faro de Madrid 172
  La Rosaleda 168
  Ministry of Air 170–1
  Museo de América 171
  Museo Cerralbo 167
  Museo des Reproducciones Artisticas 172
  Palacio de Liria 166
  Palacio Real de El Pardo 172
  Palacio de la Zarzuela 172
  Parque de Atracciones 10, 170
  Parque del Oeste 168
  Parque Zoológico 170
  Plaza de España 166
  Puerta de Hierro 172
  Santa Maria la Real de Monserrat 167
  teleférico 170
  Templo de Debod 168
  Torre de Madrid 166
  Universidad Complutense 171

Parque de Atracciones 10, 170
Parque Emir Mohammed I 147–8
Parque Juan Carlos I 136
Parque del Oeste 168
Parque del Retiro 10
Parque Tierno Galván 120
Parque Zoológico 170
Paseo del Arte **92–120**, *93*
  Atocha station 113
  cafés, bars, restaurants 92
  Casón del Buen Retiro **100–1**, 174
  Fountain of Apollo 94
  Fountain of Neptune 94
  Fuente de la Alcachofa 113
  Imax cinema 10, 120
  Las Delicias 120
  Ministry of Agriculture 113
  Museo de Artes Decorativas **109–10**, 175
  Museo Collección Thyssen-Bornemisza **102–8**, 174
  Museo del Ejército **109**, 176
  Museo Nacional de Antropología **118**, 175
  Museo Nacional Centro de Arte Reína Sofía **114–18**, 174
  Museo Nacional Ferroviario **120**, 176
  Museo Naval **109**, 176
  Museo del Prado **94–101**, 174
  Panteón de Hombres Ilustres 119
  Parque Tierno Galván 120
  Paseo del Prado 94
  Planetarium 120

Plaza Emperador Carlos V 113
Plaza de la Lealtad 102
Real Academia Española de la Lengua 108–9
Real Basílica de Atocha 119
Real Fábrica de Tapices 119–20
Retiro 110–12, *111*
San Jerónimo el Real 108
Paseo de Castellana *see* Castellana
Paseo del Prado 5, 94
Paseo de Recoletos 126–8
passports 4
Pedro the Cruel 23
Peninsular War 28
Philip II **24–5**, 64, 79, 169–70, 225
Philip III **26**, 64
  statue 64
Philip IV 26
  statue 145
Philip V 27, 145
Picasso, Pablo 114, 116
Planetarium 120
Plateresque 36
Plaza de Cascorro 77
Plaza Chueca 161
Plaza de la Cibeles 124
Plaza del Colón 128
Plaza de Dos de Mayo 158–9
Plaza Emperador Carlos V 113
Plaza de España 5, 166
Plaza del La Cebeda 75
Plaza de Lavapiés *72–3*
  Café Barbieri 80
  cafés, bars, restaurants 74, 181–3
  La Taberna de Antonio Sánchez 80
  Palacio de los Marqueses de Perales 80

Plaza de Lavapiés (*cont'd*)
Plaza Tirso de Molino 80
Teatro Olímpia 79–80
where to stay 196–8
Plaza de la Lealtad 102
Plaza del Marqués de
Salamanca 129
Plaza Mayor 5, 65
food and drink 180–2
where to stay 196–8
Plaza de Oriente 144
Plaza de la Paja 69–70
Plaza Picasso 135
Plaza de la Puerta Cerrada
66–7
Plaza del Puerta del Sol
see Puerta del Sol
Plaza de San Juan de la
Cruz 133
Plaza Santa Ana *83*, **86–7**
Academia Real de la
Historía 89
Antigua Pastelería del
Pozo 85
Atenio Científico y
Literario de Madrid 86
cafés, bars, restaurants 84
Calle de Atocha 89
Calle Echegaray 87
Casa Mira 85
Casa Museo de Lope de
Vega **87**, 176
Casa Pérez Villamil 89
Cervezería Alemana 87
Cine Doré 89
Convento de las
Trinitarias Descalzas 88
The Cortes 82
Cortes 85
Filmoteca Nacional 89
food and drink 181–3
Hotel Reina Victoria 87
Jesús de Medinaceli 88
La Casa del Abuelo 85
Lhardy 82, 85

Palace Hotel 85–6
Palacio de Santoña 89
San Sebastián 89
Teatro de la Comedia 87
Teatro Español 87
Teatro Monumental 89
Teatro de la Zarzuela 86
where to stay 196–8
Plaza Tirso de Molino 80
Plaza de Toros Monumental
de las Ventas 125–6
Plaza de la Ville 67, 68
police 17–18
pollution 41
post offices 18
Postal y de
Telecomunicaciones
125
practical A–Z **10–20**
Prado **94–101**, 174
Primo de Rivera, Miguel 30
tomb 229
Provincial Museums (Ávila)
240
public holidays 18–19
Puente de Segovia 148
Puente de Toledo 76–7
Puerta de Alcalá 125
Puerta de Europa 135
Puerta de Hierro 172
Puerta del Sol 5, **56–60**, *57*
cafés, bars, restaurants 56
Casa de Correos 58–9
Kilometro Cero 59
Oso y Madroño 59
statue of Charles III 59
Puerta de Toledo 75, 76
Purísima Concepción 129
railway stations 3, 6
rainfall 11
Real Academia de Bellas
Artes de San Fernando
152–4, 174
Real Academia Española de
la Lengua 108–9

Real Basílica de Atocha
119
Real Fábrica de Tapices
119–20, 175
Real Jardín Botánico 112
Real Madrid stadium 135
Recoletos 126–8
record shops 211
Reina Sofia **114–18**, 174
Reproducciones Artisticas
172
Residencia de Estudiantes
132–3
restaurants *see* cafés, bars,
restaurants
Retiro 110–12, *111*
food and drink 180
where to stay 194–6
Ribera, Pedro de 37
Riego, General Rafael de 75
Ritz Hotel 102
rock music 205–6
Roderick, King 251, 253
Rodríguez, Ventura 37
Romántico, Museo de
160–1, 175
Royal Madrid **138–48**,
138–9
Armería Real 147
cafés, bars, restaurants
140
Calle del Arenal 140
Campo del Moro 148
Capilla del Cristo 142
Catedral de Santa María
Real de la Almudena
147
changing of the guard 146
Chocolatería San Ginés
142
Convento de las
Descalzas Reales
140–2, 174
Convento de la
Encarnación **143–4**,
174

Ermita de la Virgen del Puerto 148
Eslava Club 142
Farmacia 147
Jardines Sabatini 144
Museo de Carruajes 147
Palacio de Gaviria 142
Palacio Real 145–7
Palacio del Senado 144
Parque Emir Mohammed I 147–8
Plaza de Oriente 144
Puente de Segovia 148
San Ginés 142
statue of Isabel II 143
statue of Philip IV 145
Teatro Real Opera 145
Sabatini, Francesco 37
Sacchetti, Giovanni Battista 145
Sala de Actos 68
Salamanca and the Castellana *122–3*, **124–36**
Barrio Salamanca 128–29
cafés, bars, restaurants 122, 179
where to stay 194–6
Salamanca, Marquis de 128
San Andrés 70
San Andrés (Segovia) 234
San Antón 161
San Antonio de los Alemanes 158
San Cayetano 78
San Esteban (Segovia) 234
San Fernando 78, **152–4**, 174
San Ginés 142
San Ildefonso 237
San Isidro 66
San Jerónimo el Real 108
San Jerónimo (Toledo) 256
San José 155
San Juan de los Caballeros (Segovia) 234

San Lorenzo de El Escorial 228
San Martín (Segovia) 234
San Millán (Segovia) 234
San Nicolás de los Servitas 69
San Pascual 126
San Pedro (Ávila) 240
San Pedro el Viejo 69–70
San Placido 157–8
San Sebastián 89
San Segundo (Ávila) 241
Sánchez, Antonio 80
Santa Maria la Real de Monserrat 167
Santiago del Arrabal (Toledo) 256
Santo Tomé (Toledo) 261
Sebastian of Portugal **79**, 141
Second Republic 30–1
Sefardí, Museo de (Toledo) 264
Segovia 229–38, *230–1*
Alcázar 233–4
Aqueduct 235
Casa de los Picos 234
Cathedral 232–3
Convento de las Carmelitas Descalzas 236
eating out 237–8
El Parral 236
getting there 232
history 229–31
La Granja de San Ildefonso 236–7
La Trinidad 234
La Vera Cruz 235–6
Moneda 236
Palacio Episcopal 234
Plaza Mayor 232
San Andrés 234
San Esteban 234
San Juan de los Caballeros 234

San Martín 234
San Millán 234
tourist information 232
sewers 41
shopping **210–14**
book shops 211
El Mundo Fantastico 90
fashion shops 210
language 270
markets 213
newspapers 211
opening hours 17
record shops 211
sweets and pastries 212, 213
Sigüenza 244, **246–7**, 248
soccer 206
Sociedad de Autores 161
Soria y Mata, Arturo 44
Sorolla, Museo de **131**, 174
Sota, Alejandro de la 38
Soto, Luis Gutíerez 38
Spanish-American War 29–30
sports and activities 206–7
statues
of Charles III 59
of General Espartero 125
of Isabel II 143
of Philip III 64
of Philip IV 145
strawberry tree symbol 40–1
Suárez, Adolfo 33
swimming 10, 206–7
Sylvester II, Pope 254
Talavera de la Reina 265
Taller del Moro (Toledo) 263
tapas bars 179
Taurino, Museo de **126**, 176
Taverna de Angel Sierra 161
taxis 6–7
Teatriz 130

Teatro de la Comedia 87
Teatro Español 87
Teatro Monumental 89
Teatro Olímpia 79–80
Teatro Real Opera 145
Teatro de la Zarzuela 86
Tejero, Colonel 85
teleférico 170
Telefónica **156**, 174
telephones 19
Téllez, Fray Gabriel 80
Tembleque 265
temperature chart 11
Templo de Debod 168
Teresa de Ávila, Saint 242–3
theatre 207–8
Thyssen-Bornemisza collection **102–8**, 174
Tienda de Vinos 161
Tiepolo, Giambattista 146
time 19, 270
tipping 20
Toledo 251–66, *252–3*
  Alcázar 257
  Arrabal 256
  Ayuntamiento 258
  Carretera Circunvalación 264
  Casa-Museo de El Greco 261–2
  Castillo de San Servando 264
  Cathedral 258–60
  Cristo de la Luz 258
  eating out 265–6
  getting there 255
  history 251, 254–5
  Hospital de Santa Cruz 255–6
  Judería 261
  Mezquita del Cristo de la Luz 258

Mirador 256
Monasterio de San Juan de los Reyes 264
Museo de los Concilios y de la Cultura Visigótica 260–1
Museo Hospital de Tavera 256–7
Museo Sefardí 264
Nueva Puerta de Bisagra 256
Palacio de Fuensalida 263
Paseo de Merchán 256
Plaza de San Juan de los Reyes Católicos 264
Plaza de Zocodover 255–6
Posada de la Hermandad 258
Puente de Alcántara 264–5
Puente de San Martín 264
Puerta del Cambrón 264
Puerta del Sol 256
San Jerónimo 256
Santiago del Arrabal 256
Santo Tomé 261
synagogues 263–4
Taller del Moro 263
tourist information 255
Tower of Hercules 251
Torre de Europa 135
Torre de los Lujanes 68
Torre de Madrid 166
Torre Picasso 135
Torres Heron 130
tour operators 7–8
tourist information 20
Tower of Hercules (Toledo) 251
trains 3, 6
travel **2–8**

border formalities 4
disabled travellers 12
getting around 5–7
getting there 2–4
insurance 15
language 269
tour operators 7–8
travellers' cheques 16
Trienio Liberal 28
Universidad Complutense 171
Urbanización AZCA 134–6
Valle de los Caídos 228–9
vegetarians 185
Velázquez, Diego de Silva y 99
  Christ on the Cross 158
ventas 178
Villanueva, Jerónimo 157–8
Villanueva, Juan de 37
visas 4
Visigoths 260–1
water, drinking 41
weather 11
when to go 11
where to stay **192–8**
  Castellana 194–6
  Chueca 192–4
  Gran Vía 192–4
  language 270
  Lavapiés 196–8
  living in Madrid 217
  Malasaña 192–4
  Opera 192–4
  Plaza Mayor 196–8
  Retiro 194–6
  Salamanca 194–6
  Santa Ana 196–8
wine 186
working in Madrid **216–18**
zarzuela 43, 200
zoo 10, 170